City of London Libraries

CITY
OF
LONDON

Please return on or before the latest date above.
You can renew online at
http://prism.talis.com/cityoflondon
(My Account) or by telephone 020 7638 0568

www.cityoflondon.gov.uk/libraries

JACK THE RIPPER

Scotland Yard Investigates

Stewart P. Evans
and Donald Rumbelow

SUTTON PUBLISHING

First published in 2006 by
Sutton Publishing Limited · Phoenix Mill
Thrupp · Stroud · Gloucestershire · GL5 2BU

British Library Cataloguing in Publication Data
A catalogue record for this book is available from the British Library.

ISBN 0-7509-4228-2

*To Rosie and Molly,
with love and thanks for the
gentle guidance*

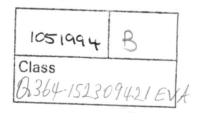

Typeset in 11/13pt Photina MT.
Typesetting and origination by
Sutton Publishing Limited.
Printed and bound in England by
J.H. Haynes & Co. Ltd, Sparkford.

Contents

Acknowledgements

WE gratefully acknowledge the following for the material and the assistance they have provided: Bishopsgate Institute, British Library Picture Library, Evans/Skinner Crime Archive, Guildhall Library and Art Gallery, Library and Museum of Freemasonry, London Library, London Metropolitan Archives, Metropolitan Police Archives Section, Metropolitan Police Commissioner's Library, the National Archives, Kew.

Both authors would like to thank the following individuals for their support: Maggie Bird, Bernard Brown, Martin Cherry, Rob Clack, Michael Conlon, Nicholas Connell, John Fisher, the late Melvin Harris, Jon Ogan, Roger J. Palmer, Stephen P. Ryder, Neal Shelden, the late Jim Swanson, Jeremy White, Richard Whittington-Egan, Sarah Wise.

All the images reproduced here belong to the authors' collections unless otherwise stated.

Preface

REVIEWING the literature on the subject of Jack the Ripper, both authors were struck that despite the plethora of books, nobody had approached the subject from the police viewpoint. Usually suspect theories dominate any account of the Whitechapel murders and the police, notably Commissioner Sir Charles Warren, come in for abuse, ridicule and charges of incompetence at best. We decided to look at the investigation as far as was possible from the police perspective, including only suspects known to the original police investigators and their contemporaries. This means that well-known theories, such as those involving the Duke of Clarence (Queen Victoria's grandson), the artist Walter Sickert, James Maybrick and many others have been excluded from this book. That they will not have to go through yet another reworking of these ideas will no doubt come as a great relief to the reader, just as it did to the authors.

The police documents that survive, including letters from the public, can be found in the National Archives at Kew and in the Corporation of the City of London Records now deposited (temporarily) in the London Municipal Archives. Stewart Evans spent more than five years transcribing the handwritten police documents to get as accurate a record of the case as was possible. His work was subsequently published, in collaboration with Keith Skinner, as *Jack the Ripper: The Ultimate Source Book*. This was our primary documentary source for the Scotland Yard investigation. What survives is only a fraction of the original documentation, however. Much was destroyed because of pressure on storage space. Some was borrowed or stolen by contemporaries and their successors, and worse, by the modern-day document thief still active in the National Archives. Contemporary newspapers covered the investigation in great detail and we were able to use them to expand upon the available material still further. Newspaper reporters dogged the heels of the detectives, making the investigations more difficult, but adding to the record extra detail that otherwise might have been lost.

To understand the investigation more completely, it is necessary to show how the two London police forces, the Metropolitan and the City, worked both at the investigative and the beat level. This has led us to include here explanations of force structures, organisation and methods of work. The authors' own experience gave them some insight because some of the work practices discussed were still continuing when, armed only with the Victorian truncheon and whistle, they pounded their beats in the swinging sixties.

It is necessary, too, to clear away some of the misconceptions about the Victorian chain of command. Popular belief greatly influenced by several movies which have him as their hero, is that Inspector Abberline was in charge of the case and the key investigator. While important, he was much further down the chain of command than is generally believed. The key players for the Metropolitan Police were Sir Charles Warren, the Commissioner; James Monro, who was his head of CID; and Dr Robert Anderson, who was to replace Monro when he resigned in the summer of 1888. To understand the relationship between these men and the politicians at the Home Office it is necessary to explore the background to their careers and to examine why there was such conflict within Scotland Yard at the time of the Whitechapel murders. Warren, it became clear, had to play the biggest role in this book and without understanding his past it is almost impossible to understand his behaviour during his period as commissioner. This made it necessary to go back to the time when he was a soldier-archaeologist, the Indiana Jones of his day, which is why the book begins with the early career of Captain Warren in Jerusalem. His subsequent treatment by Home Secretary Henry Matthews generally gets downplayed in examinations of the Ripper case, which is unfair to Warren, but it is instructive to note that Monro, when he succeeded Warren, was treated hardly more fairly. When he in turn resigned it must have constituted something of a record for a home secretary to lose two commissioners in under two years.

Warren's character and the effect he had on the investigation form the spine of this story. With the police angle in mind, we have concentrated on examining the ideas and suspect theories put forward by the leading officers in the case, especially Sir Robert Anderson, who claimed that the identity of the murderer was a definitely ascertained fact. If any sort of solution to this case does exist, it has to be found in the police sources. If it is not there, then it may be safely assumed not to exist at all.

Stewart P. Evans
Donald Rumbelow

Authors' note: Letters, reports and notes are reproduced here in their original form without the introduction of modern punctuation or spelling, which could, the authors feel, unintentionally alter the writer's original meaning.

A Gentleman of Angularities

THE underground passage through which the young army engineer and his sergeant had to travel was a mere 4 feet wide and had smooth, slippery sides. Worse still, it was filled with sewage 5 to 6 feet deep. Swimming was impossible and the planks they were planning to float on looked certain to sink under their weight. Casting about for an alternative, they managed to procure three old doors and, with candles in their mouths and measuring instruments in their pockets, they began to leap-frog their way through the tunnel, each man floating on a door and passing the increasingly slippery third one from the back to the front of the convoy. As they slowly moved deeper into the tunnel the constant sucking of the sewage and the increasing difficulty of passing the third door to the front set up violent tipping motions which constantly threatened to overturn them. Fortunately their luck held. Had it not done so, as Lieutenant Warren said, 'What honour would there have been in dying like a rat in a pool of sewage?'

Charles Warren, this subterranean archaeologist, was born in 1840. He was the second son of Major-General Sir Charles Warren, a professional soldier, who at 16 had served under Wellington as an ensign and was twice wounded while fighting in China, India and the Crimea. He and his elder son John were in the same regiment; both were wounded at the battle of the Alma in 1854. John died of his wounds. Charles's mother died when he was 6 years old and he determined quite early to follow his father and brother into the army. He was good at mathematics and had no difficulty in getting into the Royal Military Academy at Sandhurst and subsequently Woolwich Academy, where he enrolled in February 1856.

Two very noticeable traits remained with him from his school years. As a boy he was fond of poetry and enjoyed learning lessons by turning them into rhyming Latin or Greek. This facility stayed with him and was eventually noted in the press when a correspondent, recalling Warren's frequent 'uncontrollable urge to drop into poetry' while drafting police orders, gave this example:

> The Commissioner has observed there are signs of wear
> on the Landseer lions in Trafalgar Square.

Unauthorised persons are not to climb
on the Landseer lions at any time.

The other trait was the monocle he habitually fixed to his right eye. Like Churchill's hats, it became for cartoonists his most distinguishing feature. Without it, he reckoned he would never have got into the army at all.

He also had a streak of boyish enthusiasm which never left him. He would stand on his head, run on all fours and perform other tricks. Once, in Palestine, excited by a particular piece of news, he sought out a quiet terrace garden where cauliflowers were being grown and stood on his head. It was in this upside-down position that he saw the cauliflowers on a terrace wall begin to change into turbans and the green leaves into a row of open-mouthed heads. Men had followed him to ask for work. Seeing his strange behaviour, they assumed, Warren wrote, 'that I had been performing a religious ceremony, unlike the ordinary Christian forms, and not so different to their own, except that the Moslem stood on their feet facing Mecca, and the Frank stood on his head; whether it was a sign of madness, foolishness, or holiness, was to them an indifferent matter'.

Because of his talent for mathematics Warren was able to choose to join the Royal Engineers and was commissioned in December 1857. Two years later, and still under 20, he was initiated into the Royal Lodge of Friendship in Gibraltar to begin his Masonic career. From 1858 to 1865 he was stationed there, designing and building new gun batteries and making a trigonometrical survey of the Rock, which took him four years to complete. In 1864 he was married to Miss Fanny Haydon of Guildford.

Throughout his life people were always giving Warren nicknames – 'the Mole', 'Colonel Why' and 'Jerusalem' Warren. The latter was acquired in 1866 when a society called the Palestine Exploration Fund asked the War Office for the services of Warren and three Royal Engineer non-commissioned officers to form an expedition to make a reconnaissance of the Jordan Valley and Gilead and to carry out excavations in Jerusalem. In the Jordan Valley Warren sometimes travelled and was dependent upon Bedouin hospitality for his survival. Just how dangerous this could be became clear when once, alone and hopelessly trapped in a thorn thicket, he saw a Bedouin from another tribe approaching. Instead of offering help, it was clear that the man was intent on killing him. With difficulty Warren managed to reach his revolver and persuade his would-be killer to cut him free. Had he not succeeded in freeing his gun, Warren's throat would almost

THE TRAFALGAR SQUARE LIONS.

SIR CHARLES WARREN.   MR. HENRY MATTHEWS.

Moonshine, 25 February 1888, cartoons of Sir Charles Warren and Home Secretary Henry Matthews, depicted as the Trafalgar Square lions.

certainly have been cut. The brutality of the Bedouins' nomadic existence was brought home by the execution of a man for murdering a fellow Muslim:

> The executioner was a novice, the victim was unsteady. First, the blow swerved, and a cut was received across the shoulders; the unfortunate man exclaimed, 'You are hurting me!' Then blow after blow struck him wildly, hither and thither, until at the sixteenth cut he was yet not dead. Then this ruffian, the executioner, turned his victim on his back, and sawed away at his throat as though he were killing a sheep, and at last severed the head and part of the shoulder from off the trunk; they were left together during the day for the amusement of the multitude.

Warren's instructions from the Palestine Exploration Fund were to make discoveries in Jerusalem, particularly in and around the Haram Ash-Sharif, the Noble Sanctuary. This large, broad-based platform dominates Old Jerusalem and on it stands the Dome of the Rock. The site covers the area where the Temple once stood and part of the Temple Mount, the Sakhra, protrudes through the floor of the mosque itself. The main purpose of the excavations was to try to answer some of the questions that were troubling biblical scholars, particularly the exact location of Solomon's Temple and the true site of the crucifixion. One of Warren's chief objectives was to dig down to try to match biblical descriptions of the Temple to the physical terrain. Beneath the Sakhra lies a maze of tunnels and it was these that Warren was intent on exploring, but it was this site, sacred to Muslims, Jews and Christians alike, where the Turkish authorities explicitly forbade him to dig. The British consul warned him that the kind of excavation he planned was simply out of the question and that the Muslim faithful would certainly not allow it. Warren was to ignore all objections; throughout the next three years he constantly acted in opposition to the protests and pushed his way ahead in spite of efforts to restrain him.

Jerusalem he found to have filthy streets, narrow and crooked. The underground city was worse. It was a labyrinth of tunnels, caves and sewers. Unable to excavate by exposing different levels from the surface downwards, Warren was forced to sink shafts as much as 80 feet deep and then, with the help of torches and candles, to tunnel outwards into the passages, sewers and vaults that he found. His explorations were made with the use of mining trestles to stop the tunnels from falling in (there were never enough), ladders and hand-over-hand rope climbing. His discoveries confirmed that beneath the Temple Mount was a whole series of hidden caves and secret passages. It was unhealthy work. At different times his helpers – he began with three corporals from the Royal Engineers – were taken ill with inflammatory fever caused by the foul air in the shafts and working in sewage. One soldier died in the later stages of the excavations. Warren himself developed a chronic fever on his return to England.

His costume for the subterranean explorations provoked mirth in visitors who met him for the first time. He wore a Jerusalem-made Norfolk jacket, knickerbockers, stockings, Spanish shoes and a sun helmet. His costume, Warren would explain, was designed so that it would not catch on the sides of the holes and tunnels through which he would crawl.

To uncover the Temple foundations Warren had to dig through over 130 feet of rubbish to reach the massive walls which then extended to a further depth of 200 feet. Once his sergeant, another replacement, was buried for two hours under a fall of debris. Had they both been buried the natives would have left them there. On another occasion they crawled through a steadily flooding tunnel with candles in their mouths so that Warren could take his observations; there were only 4 inches of air above them.

Lieutenant Charles Warren, seated first left, at Jerusalem in 1868 during archaeological excavations.

Possibly his most dangerous moment came in the Dome of the Rock where he vaulted over a railing on to the Sakhra, his 'unhallowed feet' making contact with the rock which could only be touched by a mortal once a year when the Turkish pacha attended a great religious festival. On a previous early morning visit he had spotted a piece of flagging which was loose and jumped over the guard rail to feel underneath it. He found that the space beneath was hollow. This was a chance not to be lost: this opening might lead him to the mysterious and unexplored Well of Souls. He returned several days later, having set up a series of diversions to distract the guards. Concealed in his sleeve was a small iron bar. At the given moment Warren jumped over the railing and levered up the piece of loose flagging but he was unable to hold it and it fell into the hole below with a great crash, which echoed and reverberated throughout the building. Undeterred, Warren dived into the hole and took measurements of the blocked-up tunnel he found there. (He later came to think it was a gutter for carrying off the blood and refuse from the animals that were sacrificed on a Temple altar.) He then scrambled back without being discovered. Who replaced the stone Warren never knew. Although he never made claim to it, it has been suggested that Warren is the man who came closest to discovering the Israelites' long-lost Ark of the Covenant which some believe is hidden in a secret chamber such as this. Warren risked his life on a number of occasions but there is little doubt that had he been discovered when making his sacrilegious jump on to the Sakhra on which Abraham had sacrificed and from which Mohammed took flight up to Heaven, he would have been killed for his blasphemy.

His insensitivity to these religious feelings is clear from a speech he gave in 1885 to fellow Freemasons. In it he said that during the excavations he had opened 'a Lodge in a cavern which directly runs under the old Temple'. The occasion itself was unique and the first in that location since the Knights Templar were expelled from Jerusalem nearly seven centuries before. Such an event would have held a special significance for Warren: not only is modern Freemasonry said to originate with the building of Solomon's Temple but also in 1863 he was made a Knight Templar in Freemasonry. Subsequently Warren was to found the Quatuor Coronati Lodge, the first Masonic lodge of research into the history and traditions of the Craft. Warren was its first master and the lodge, after various delays, was consecrated in January 1886. Curiously, despite his passion for the Craft, Warren was to cease all Masonic activity after 1901 and was almost a stranger to his Masonic brethren for the last twenty-five years of his life. Several explanations have been given as to why he fell away from his Masonic brethren. The likeliest reason is that he was disillusioned by the lack of support that he received from some of the senior army command, who were brother Masons, following the disastrous Boer War battle of Spion Kop (1900), for which he shouldered much of the blame.

Warren still has a high reputation today among archaeologists for the work he did in underground Jerusalem, much of it at his own expense. When he returned to England in the spring of 1870 he was a sick man, ill with fever and fatigue. The former he did not shake off for another three years.

The bearded Lieutenant-Colonel Charles Warren and officers of the Diamond Fields Horse in South Africa in 1878. Warren is centre row, third from left, wearing a bandolier of ammunition.

A series of home-based military appointments followed over the next six years, during which time he wrote, published books and lectured, but gradually found himself drifting back to civilian life. In 1876 he was asked by the Colonial Office to go to South Africa to act as a special commissioner to settle a boundary dispute between Griqualand West and the Orange Free State over the Diamond Fields. In temperatures at times over 100°F, with the air frequently punctuated by giant electrical storms and constantly plagued by mosquitoes and flies, the work was eventually concluded in 1877 to the satisfaction of both sides. On the way back home, crossing through the Transvaal to Delgoa Bay, he was stopped by the British High Commissioner at Cape Town, Sir Bartle Frere, who appointed him a special commissioner and sent him back for six months to investigate and settle land disputes in appeal before the High Court of Griqualand West. Allegedly the only people disappointed by his subsequent judgments were the lawyers who were denied the benefits of prolonged litigation.

The land disputes settled, Captain Warren thought once more that he could return home but a Kafir rising threatening the Cape Colony led to his being placed in command of a volunteer regiment called the Diamond Fields Horse. Initially this was a body of about 120 men. Their uniform comprised brown moleskin coats, cord trousers and brown felt hats with bandoliers of bullets slung across their chests. Few of the men knew anything about horses or military warfare. The 38-year-old soldier had to drill and train his irregulars from scratch. Though small in number, they took part in many engagements. At Debe Nek Warren attacked and repulsed a force of 1,600 Kafirs with just 75 men. In the hand-to-hand fighting he lost only one trooper who died from assegai wounds. Warren was wounded twice in the campaign. Once he was crushed by the bough of a tree that had been partly cut through and toppled over by the enemy. The attack left him with serious internal injuries which eventually necessitated his being invalided home nearly a year later. His conspicuous bravery led to his being mentioned three times in dispatches. In 1878 he was promoted to major and the following year given the brevet rank of lieutenant-colonel.

Early in May 1878 the whole native population of Griqualand West who lived west of the Vaal river rose in rebellion and, joined by their former enemies, began making depredations to the west of Hopetown. Warren was telegraphed to bring the Diamond Fields Horse to the Kimberley government's assistance and on arrival was given command of the northern column of the force that was to put down the rebellion. In the skirmishing that followed Warren successfully stormed strongholds, completely routing the enemy. At Takoon, which was described as the Gibraltar of South Africa, Warren tried to persuade the rebels to surrender but when his efforts failed he led his mounted troops to the base of the fortress and then stormed the position on foot. In the hand-to-hand fighting that followed about 200 of the enemy were killed but the volunteers lost only 3 men. Although the first rising had been quelled, hostilities quickly resumed and within a month of Warren's return to Kimberley orders were given for a second campaign.

Warren was now instructed to secure the north-west border of the province and to get the rebels to surrender, by peaceful means if possible. Small bands frequently attacked the Diamond Fields Horse but were repeatedly driven off until they finally concentrated themselves in strongholds in the Lange Berge Range. A battle fought over three days brought about the surrender of some of the rebels and the dispersal of the rest, who broke up into small bands of marauders living in the mountains. By November 1878 Warren had successfully secured the submission of all the tribes. Much of his success is attributed to the amnesty he offered and the humane way in which he treated the wives and children the rebels had abandoned in the mountains and desert to die of starvation and thirst.

The women now refused to accept their liberty and return to their men folk, preferring to stay under the white man's protection.

In January 1879 came news of the great British defeat at Isandhlwana by the Zulu army. Warren offered to go to support the British Army with 500 men but was turned down. A further outbreak of fighting followed which Warren brought to an end in August by capturing the rebel leaders. Warren was still suffering from the effects of injuries received over a year before and in October 1879 he was invalided home. On his return he received the thanks of Parliament. Such was the impression that he made in Africa, the town of Warrenton, 50 miles north of Kimberley, was named after him. Local Freemasons honoured him by forming the Charles Warren Masonic Lodge. Other medals and honours were also bestowed on this soldier-archaeologist.

From 1880 to 1882 he was posted as Inspector of Surveying at the School of Military Engineering but his time there was interrupted when he was selected by the government to go to Egypt to head a search party for a Professor Palmer and Captain Gill who, with others, had gone to Syria to win over the Bedouin tribes to the cause of Britain undertaking military operations in the area and had disappeared, believed murdered. Warren's task was to locate them or, if the rumours proved true, to bring the murderers to justice. He found the Bedouin uncooperative but eventually learned that the men had been murdered and led a search party into the desert. There he discovered the remains of the five men in the gully where they had been killed. Their scattered bones were placed in a specially prepared case and taken back to England for burial in the crypt of St Paul's Cathedral. Warren painstakingly gathered evidence against the men involved by reconstructing the murder scene. He crossed and re-crossed the Sinai Desert, making archaeological observations as a diversion on the way, until he had the evidence and names that he wanted. His efforts led to five Bedouin tribesmen being executed for the murders and eight others sentenced to imprisonment. For his services as leader of the Palmer Search Expedition Warren was created a KCMG (Knight Commander of the Order of St Michael and St George) in Queen Victoria's birthday honours list of 1883.

In 1884 Sir Charles Warren was sent out again to South Africa, this time to Bechuanaland, which lies to the north of Griqualand West. It was six years since Warren had commanded the Diamonds Field Horse to stop the Bechuanans invading Cape Colony. Now he was going to their defence. Two republics had been set up in Bechuanaland by Boer settlers, one called Stellaland and the other Goshenland. The native tribes were being 'eaten-up' by the Boer settlers. They were not merely being exploited but were stripped of much of their land. In 1884 Bechuanaland was proclaimed to be under the protection of the Boer republic. All attempts to arrange a settlement with President Paul Kruger, the Boer leader, had failed; the British government, fearing the expansion of the Boer republic across the continent to German South-West Africa and the continuation of Boer attacks, reluctantly decided to use force to settle the dispute. Having been so deeply involved just six years before, Colonel Sir Charles Warren was the obvious choice for command of this military expedition of 5,000 men. His orders were to remove the Boer filibusters from Bechuanaland, to restore order in the territory and to reinstate the natives in their lands. Warren moved with speed. In a bloodless campaign he broke up the illegal republics and brought the Transvaal government, which was unwilling to fight, to the negotiation table. In 1886 Bechuanaland (now Botswana) was taken under British protection. Warren returned to England to receive the thanks of Parliament for a second time.

Seeing no prospect of any further military employment at this time Warren, now on half-pay, had no hesitation in accepting an offer to stand as Liberal candidate in the Hallam

Moonshine, 17 October 1885, cartoons of Sir Charles Warren depicting aspects of the man and his actions.

division of Sheffield. However, he insisted on standing as an Independent Liberal and refused to avail himself of party funds for his election expenses. In his election manifesto he stressed that the prosperity of the nation depended on the moral tone of the people continuing at a high standard; he emphasised the religious education of children and campaigned for free education for all children in elementary schools; he promoted reforms regarding land tenure, the House of Lords and House of Commons, favoured self-government as far as was practicable for Ireland, and supported the establishment of county councils.

Just as his campaign got under way, he was sent for by Lord Wolseley, the model for the modern Major-General in Gilbert and Sullivan's *Pirates of Penzance*, who requested that he give up his candidature on the grounds that an officer on half-pay was not entitled to take other employment. Warren refused, saying that he had already pledged his word to the electorate and could not let them down. Wolseley told him to think again and threatened that if he did not comply he would never get another military appointment. Still Warren refused. Wolseley threatened again but Warren was adamant: he could not in honour back down and the two men parted. It seemed that Warren had thrown away his army career and any chance of further military promotion. It seemed too that his gesture had been a futile one. He had come late into the campaign and lost the election to his Conservative opponent by just over 600 votes. Rejected by the army and by the voters, Charles Warren faced prospects that looked bleak indeed.

—— **TWO** ——

Policing the Metropolis

LONDON had in 1888, and still has today, two police forces: the City of London Police and the Metropolitan Police. Metropolitan Police headquarters, at the time of the force's formation in 1829, was at 4 Whitehall Place.[1] Its business entrance backed on to Scotland Yard, a legacy, in name only, of part of the Palace of Whitehall which had been destroyed in 1692. Scotland Yard soon became the public name for the police office and, with time, the public name for the force itself.

In 1888 the Metropolitan Police boundary extended over a radius of 15 miles from Charing Cross, excluding the City of London – an area of 688.31 square miles. It was policed by an establishment of 12,025 constables, 1,369 sergeants, 837 inspectors and 30 superintendents.

In 1839 a police force of 500 men under the command of a commissioner was appointed for the one square mile of the City of London. The Metropolitan Police had no jurisdiction within this area. Incredibly, it was not until 1844, 15 years after its formation, that the Metropolitan Police force was given jurisdiction over Trafalgar Square. This right had been refused until then because the area was Crown Property. An equivalent anomaly existed within the City with regard to the Temple in Fleet Street, which was home to two Inns of Court, the Inner and Middle Temple. Jurisdiction there was not granted until the Police Act 1964, and it was the personal experience of many City policemen to be ordered out of the Temple for trespassing even beyond that date by barristers wishing to demonstrate their authority.

There had been tremendous resistance to the formation of a metropolitan police force in 1829. It was widely believed that it would be modelled on the French system of spies and *agents provocateurs*. Among the many insults hurled at the men was that they were 'Jenny Darbies' (a corruption of the French *gens d'armes*, suggesting that they were spying not only on the streets but on the people). Other nicknames included 'Raw Lobsters', 'Blue Devils', 'crushers' (because of the way they hustled people), 'Peel's Bloody Gang' and the more familiar 'Bobby'.[2] It would be several years before the public attitude towards them changed: they were not a well-liked body of men. Patrolling constables were sometimes beaten up,

The entrance to Old Scotland Yard.

26 Old Jewry, headquarters of the City of London Police at the time of the murders. This ancient entranceway can still be seen, virtually unchanged, although the City Police headquarters have moved.

spiked on railings, blinded and on occasion held down on the road while a coach was driven over them. In 1831 an unarmed police constable was stabbed to death in a riot. Not only did the Coroner's Inquest bring in a verdict of 'justifiable homicide', but an annual banquet was held every year to commemorate and celebrate the event. Unsurprisingly, four years later in 1833 only 562 men were left out of the 3,389 who had joined in 1829. Charles Dickens, a much quoted admirer of the police, was not so well disposed towards them in the early years after the force's formation. His attitude, as reflected in his novel *Martin Chuzzlewit*, was probably a true reflection of public opinion in 1841. Old Martin Chuzzlewit's nephew, Chevy Slime, after years of debts and debauchery, has purposely become a policeman to shame the family. His class has given him the rank of inspector. By joining he hopes that his uncle may feel some of the disgrace visited on the family by his being employed in such a way. For a working man joining the police force at this date seems to have been on a par with joining the army. Both were disgraceful professions. Public hostility is more understandable when it is appreciated that the recruits for both came from the same source of otherwise largely unemployable manpower.

'Men, dwarfs in height, and old in years, of divers bodily deformity, mentally weak, and with little or no character, had no hesitation to apply', wrote the City Police Commissioner in 1861. His advertisement in 1861 attracted 570 applications for 43 vacancies; only 38 places could be filled, one of the main reasons for rejection being the poor physical condition of the majority of applicants. This was a problem that faced both London forces. In the first eight years of the Metropolitan Police 8,000 men were dismissed or forced to resign; the force's average annual strength on paper, was 3,000. Contrary to popular myth, replacements were not chiefly from the army. In 1832 the two Metropolitan commissioners gave a breakdown of the former professions of those employed in order to rebut accusations that the police were nothing more than a disguised military force. These statistics make it clear that the police force was overwhelmingly working class. There were butchers, bakers, shoemakers, tailors, servants, blacksmiths, sailors, weavers, stonemasons and men from other trades. Over a third of the force comprised former labourers and the number of ex-soldiers was in the proportion of one to eight. The statistics also suggest that a high number had been unemployed when recruited. There were 20 Englishmen to every 10 Irishmen and 2 Scotsmen.

'Curious looking policemen we were,' said Thomas Arnold, who joined in 1855 and was superintendent of the Whitechapel Division in 1888, when reminiscing about the early days. The constable's basic uniform was a blue swallow-tail coat with a high stand-up collar bearing his divisional letter and number, a tall chimney-pot hat, sometimes with a glazed leather top to aid identification when it was knocked off, a rattle and a 17-inch truncheon in the swallow-tail pocket. This was the same uniform issued to a 20-year-old clocksmith, Frederick George Abberline, when he joined the Metropolitan Police force in 1863. Only a year later his swallow-tail coat was changed to a frock tunic and the top hat swapped for a combed Britannia helmet. His wooden rattle was only to be sprung in emergencies. In 1884 the rattle was replaced by a whistle. The whistle and truncheon remained the beat policeman's only aids until the 1960s.

To avoid the accusation of spy and *agent provocateur*, the London policemen had to wear their uniform both on and off duty. An armband showed whether a constable or sergeant was on or off duty. Constables and sergeants wore the duty armbands on their tunic wrists, for constables on the left wrist and for sergeants on the right. Metropolitan Police sergeants came to wear the band on the left wrist with the introduction of numerals on their collars which ran from 1 to 16. The Metropolitan Police's armbands bore blue and white stripes,

An interesting 'montaged' group photograph showing, centre row, left to right: Henry Smith (City Police), Edward Bradford (Metropolitan Police), Bolton Monsell (Metropolitan Police); and at front right, Superintendent Thomas Arnold (Metropolitan Police). (*S.P. Evans/Metropolitan Police*)

the City's red and white. When washed the white stripes of the latter would, before the use of nylon, turn a delicate shade of pink, which the liberal use of chalk before a parade could never quite conceal. 'Idling and gossiping' was frowned upon and to avoid being caught City policemen would signal the sergeant's approach by rubbing the right wrist in an exaggerated manner or the inspector's approach by rubbing the tunic buttons up and down. In 1870 the uniform regulations were relaxed and for the first time in forty years policemen were allowed to wear their own clothes when at home or off duty.

Initially the recruiting age was between 19 and 45. A candidate had to be able 'to read and write generally', as contemporary advertisements put it. Physical strength was needed for the long hours of work and frequent changes of shift, which made recruitment from the working or labouring classes inevitable. Promotion could only be achieved rung by rung, upwards through the hierarchy. Officers were recruited from the sergeant-major class.

On appointment each man was issued with a training manual setting out his duties. The first policemen had no training school to teach them the basics and were literally pushed out on the street to learn the job for themselves. Some had to be stopped from carrying umbrellas! They were, however, under strict discipline, as there were fears for several decades that there would be no break with the past and that bribery and corruption would continue as they had done under the old watch and constable system. Discipline was imposed by drill and because this was carried out in public places it inevitably fuelled accusations that the police were a military organisation providing a bodyguard for the government. When he became Commissioner, Warren was frequently and unfairly criticised for militarising the police by excessive drilling. Part of the drill consisted of training in the use of cutlasses, a rack of which was normally kept in the inspector's office for use in emergencies. That a policeman should use such a weapon is too bizarre to contemplate – the 1819 Peterloo massacre where the yeomanry cut down large numbers of peaceful demonstrators should have been warning enough. The one recorded instance of cutlasses being issued was in the Tottenham Outrage of 1909. Had the policemen involved tried to use them it would have been a somewhat unequal contest as the two gunmen were using Mausers.

Drilling, in fact, was necessary to ensure large numbers of men could get to an emergency in a hurry. It was equally important as a means of establishing that at the beginning of each shift men could be marched from the station and dropped off at their point or beat, and the beat man they had relieved could be marched back. Beats in the 1880s were worked at a regulation speed of 2½ miles per hour. The average length of a beat was 7½ miles for day duty and for night duty 2 miles. In densely populated areas this could be shorter still. In the City on the night of the Eddowes murder, it took PC Watkins just 15 minutes to patrol his beat. In the suburbs a beat normally took 4 hours. By day a policeman kept to the kerb side of the pavement; at night he took the inside to make him slightly less visible and to allow him to check doors and locks more easily. Inevitably complaints were made that officers could never be found when wanted and so, after 1870, fixed points were introduced where the public could find them and from which they were

Victorian Metropolitan police officers filing out on patrol from Bow Street police station. Shifts left the stations and walked to their allocated beats in file, like this, both night and day.

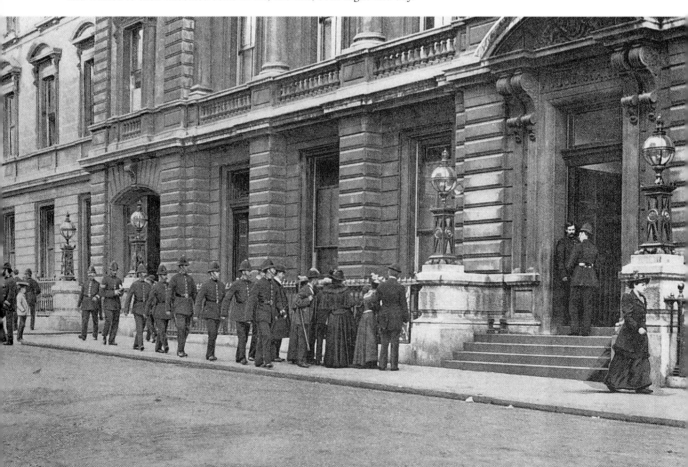

ordered not to move. The monetary fines that could be imposed meant such orders were rigidly obeyed and led to the ludicrous example of the Spitalfields constable who, when told of the Annie Chapman murder, refused to leave his post until relieved. By 1889 there were 500 fixed points where constables could be found between the hours of 9 a.m. and 1 a.m.

Police officers were timed over their beats so that it was possible for the patrolling inspector or sergeant to go to a particular point knowing that the constable would be there too. This rigidity of practice meant, as noted by a City police officer writing anonymously to the *Daily Telegraph* in 1865, that a man could miss the chance of an arrest to guarantee that he kept the point with the patrolling inspector. A non-arrest would lead to the assumption that the constable was malingering or not correctly patrolling his beat, resulting in a fine which the ill-paid constable could not afford. Beat books were issued to City Police probationers until the 1960s. Each book contained a street map of every beat with the boundaries highlighted, together with a list of vulnerable properties on each beat. A constable was expected to check every building on the beats that he had been assigned and try the door-handles to make sure that the building was secure. A door found open on the next shift necessitated an explanation in writing by the first patrolling constable to the divisional superintendent. A later variation (no date has been found for its implementation) was for a constable to patrol his beats so many minutes one way and then walk a similar amount of time in the opposite direction. No break period was allowed during a shift and the unofficial practice, sanctioned by decades of use, was for the patrolling constable to take his refreshment at the back door of a convenient pub. At night, the practice was to take a tin flask of tea, shin up a lamppost on the beat and place it by the gas flare to keep warm so that a hot drink was available throughout the night. On high-value beats, night-duty constables were given bags of whalebone clips to insert in doors as wedges which would spring out if opened, giving warning of a possible illegal entry. Cotton marks were another way of seeing if illegal entry had been gained. The practice was still continuing in 1963 when Rumbelow was a probationer on 'C' Bishopsgate Division. As night-duty cyclist he had to check cotton marks throughout the division. That the practice was not taken seriously by the constables themselves was obvious: when Rumbelow went to his first building to cotton mark the protecting grille, which could not have opened in years, he found it so laced with threads that it would have been possible to use them as a ladder and climb in through the window. A City constable of an earlier generation recalled how when he went into Mitre Square, site of the Eddowes murder, to check his cotton mark, he found that one of his night-duty colleagues had pegged paper dolls along the thread.

By 1889 the policemen were being given one day's leave every fortnight. There was no annual leave. One month's day duty was followed by two months' night duty. The day shift of 16 hours was split into four reliefs of 4 hours on and 4 hours off, beginning at 6 a.m. and finishing at 10 p.m. This engaged 40 per cent of the force. Night duty was 10 p.m. until 6 a.m. and 60 per cent of the force was available for this shift.

A policeman's powers were limited to the area within his force's jurisdiction, in other words, the police boundary. Outside that boundary, and within another force's area, the only powers a policeman had were the ordinary rights of a citizen. As such, if he were sued, it would be as an ordinary citizen and not as a police officer. This did not change until the Police Act 1964 when jurisdiction was extended to the whole of England and Wales.

The most senior posts came under the patronage of the home secretary. According to historian David Ascoli, writing in 1979, 'The six top posts in the Metropolitan Police are Crown appointments made on the advice of the Home Secretary, who is under no statutory obligation to consult the Commissioner. It is a potentially dangerous form of patronage, for there is absolutely nothing – other than the certainty of public retribution – to stop a Secretary of State from appointing three bus-conductors and three Methodist ministers of whatever impeccable virtue.'[3] The dangers of such patronage were clearly evident when Howard Vincent was appointed Director of Criminal Investigations in 1878. His only superior at Scotland Yard was the chief commissioner but unofficially the home secretary told him that in his separate and independent department he could come and see him any time he liked. He should report direct to the Home Office and 'not pay too much attention to what was said of him either by the chief commissioner, or anyone else at Scotland Yard'. This was a dangerous precedent; James Monro followed it in defying Commissioner Sir Charles Warren in 1888, an act that proved to be a major factor in the quarrel between the two men.

In 1867, while Warren was excavating in Jerusalem, outbreaks of Fenian disturbances disrupted the British mainland. The Fenians, the name derives from the old Irish *fianna* and means soldiers, were Irish nationalists; their chief aim was to force British withdrawal from Ireland. They had been organised in 1858 as the Irish Republican Brotherhood and in 1867 in America as the Clan na Gael. During the mainland disturbances, a police sergeant was killed when he was caught up in a Fenian rescue of two members from a prison van in Manchester in 1867. One of those heavily involved in the manhunt that followed was plain-clothes sergeant Fred Abberline, then based at Caledonian Road in north London. According

to his own reminiscences, he discovered in the capital one of the men who made the attack upon the prison van; this man, a coachmaker, was sentenced to death but had his sentence commuted to penal servitude for life. Three other Fenians were hanged for the murder of the police sergeant. To the Irish community they became the 'Manchester martyrs', victims of British injustice. In November 1867 two more Fenians were arrested, one of whom had planned and organised the prison van rescue. Both men were committed to the Clerkenwell House of Detention, where a plot was made to rescue them. A hole was to be blown in the prison yard wall when the men were

Chief Constable Adolphus ('Dolly') Williamson, aged 58 and ailing at the time of the murders, was probably the wisest and most experienced senior police officer in the Metropolitan Police force of the day. Anderson relied on him for advice. He died on 9 December 1889 and was replaced by Macnaghten. Williamson was the first career police officer to achieve this high rank and did so through merit.

taken out for exercise. News of the planned escape was leaked to the authorities but security remained lax. On the day, a barrel containing 200 pounds of gunpowder was placed against the prison wall and several attempts were made to light the fuse, which proved to be damp and would not ignite. The first attempt was aborted by the approach of a passing policeman who watched without interest as the conspirators wheeled the barrel away. They returned the next day with a bigger barrel and nearly three times (548 pounds) as much gunpowder, which not only demolished a 60-foot section of the prison wall but also severely damaged the working-class houses on the opposite side of the street. Chief Inspector Adolphus 'Dolly' Williamson said that with their front walls gone they looked like so many 'dolls' houses with the kettles still singing on the hobs'. In the event, the rescue operation failed because the prisoners had been moved deeper into the gaol. Some 12 people were killed or died indirectly as a result of the explosion and a further 120 were injured, some seriously. In May 1868 Michael Barrett, one of six Fenians tried for this crime, became the last person to be hanged in public in England. It is possible that Abberline, involved in the case and based close by, witnessed this execution. The official explanation for the police failure to foil the plot was that although they had been told that a prison break was imminent, they were looking for signs of tunnelling because their information was that the wall was to be *blown up*; they were unprepared for it to be *blown down*!

A warning of the planned break-out had been forwarded to the police by a young Irish barrister named Dr Robert Anderson who has been said by some to have drifted into secret service work. Anderson's father was the Crown solicitor for Dublin and his brother had charge of all state prosecutions. These family connections led to his being asked to sift and

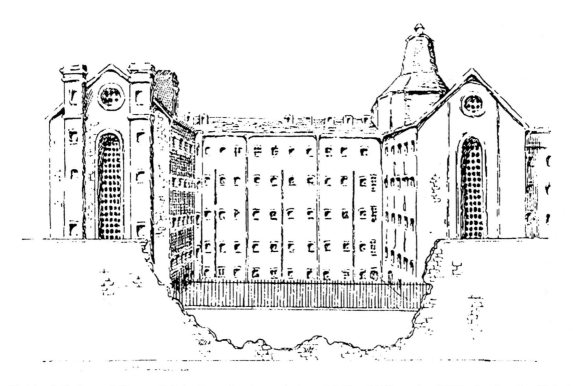

Sketch of Clerkenwell House of Detention after the explosion of Friday 13 December 1867, showing the 60-foot section of wall demolished in the failed bid to liberate two Fenian prisoners. Twelve people died and one of the Fenians tried for this crime, Michael Barrett, was the last man to be hanged in public in the United Kingdom.

sort a mass of foreign dispatches and reports, most supposed to be extremely secret, which were stored, unindexed and unregistered, in the chief secretary's office. That was when, Anderson said, he took the queen's shilling. The 24-year-old was entrusted with making a précis of the documents. His services were requisitioned again by the attorney-general when there was a Fenian uprising in 1867. Some 200 to 300 prisoners were marched into Dublin Castle and committed for trial on the charge of high treason. The problem the authorities now faced, nicely expressed, was that having caught so many hares, how would they cook them? Anderson was asked to look into each case and advise the Crown on which cases to prosecute. This gave him a rare insight into the workings and conspiracies of the Fenian brotherhood. His investigations allowed him to give London an early warning of the bombing campaign that was about to start but his warning was ignored.

In the panic that followed the Clerkenwell explosion, a police Secret Service organisation was formed and Anderson was summoned to England to take charge of it. The planned unit proved to be just a temporary expedient, lasting a mere three months, and Anderson was on the point of returning to Ireland to resume practice at the Bar when he was asked to take charge of Irish affairs at the Home Office. He was not only to advise on matters relating to political crime but was also given certain powers of investigation. Although his main work was to be centred on Fenianism and political crime, Anderson was given other tasks too. He became secretary to royal and departmental commissions, including the Prison Commission in 1877 and afterwards the Loss of Life at Sea Commission. In his spare time he dabbled in journalism, writing on 'Criminals and Crime' and 'Morality by Act of Parliament' as well as a number of religious books including *The Bible and Modern Criticism*, *The Coming Prince: the Last Great Monarch of Christendom* and *A Doubter's Doubts*, which attracted the attention of Gladstone himself.

The death of Richard 'King' Mayne on Boxing Day 1868 brought to an end a 39-year reign. He was joint commissioner with Colonel Sir Charles Rowan when the Metropolitan Police force was created in 1829 and had ruled alone since Rowan's death in 1852. Rowan was a soldier and Mayne a lawyer. The decision that had to be made now was whether the new commissioner should be a soldier or a civilian: in the event, a professional soldier with civilian experience was chosen. Lieutenant-Colonel Sir Edmund Henderson was a professional soldier by training, a Royal Engineers officer like Warren, but he also had a practical knowledge of the criminal classes acquired over thirteen years as

This nice contemporary artist's study of Dr Robert Anderson, the Assistant Commissioner, shows him at the time of the Whitechapel murders with his arm resting on his desk in his study at home.

The year 1877 was a bad one for the Metropolitan Police. The scandal of corruption in the Detective Department resulted in the infamous 'Trial of the Detectives'. *Punch* ran this satirical cartoon, 'Honesty the Best Polic(e)y', in October, showing Commissioner Henderson speaking with John Bull about honesty and the extra price that should be paid for it.

PUNCH, OR THE LONDON CHARIVARI.—NOVEMBER 24, 1877.

HONESTY THE BEST POLIC(E)Y.

COLONEL H-ND-RS-N. "WHAT ARE YOU DOING THERE, SIR?"
DIOGENES (MR. BULL). "WELL, YOU SEE, COLONEL, TILL NOW IT SEEMS WE'VE SET A *THIEF* TO CATCH A THIEF. I'M LOOKING FOR AN HONEST MAN!!"
COLONEL H. "ALL RIGHT! ONLY, WHEN YOU'VE FOUND HIM, YOU'LL HAVE TO *PAY FOR HIM!*"
DIOGENES. "AND CHEAP AT THE MONEY!"

comptroller of a convict settlement in Western Australia, followed by six years as director and surveyor-general of prisons at the Home Office. Described as a man of great personal charm he was able during his seventeen years as commissioner to work well with a succession of home secretaries. His early decision to allow policemen to wear beards and moustaches, so long as they did not cover the divisional numbers on their tunic collars, provoked a certain amount of public mirth. More importantly, under his regime men were allowed to wear plain clothes when off duty, although the blue-and-white duty armband continued to be an anachronistic piece of equipment until the 1970s.

Inadequate pay for the lower ranks, however, was a major grievance and in 1872 a small number of policemen went on strike, holding meetings and public demonstrations to air their complaints. Initially Henderson said that he did not have the funds to pay for increases but when money was found it simply fuelled the men's grievances about pensions and the lack of any sort of trade union to negotiate on their behalf, something the government refused to allow. Other improvements were made in living and working conditions. The size of the Detective Department was increased from 15 to nearly 200 men, eventually rising to nearly 260, which allowed detectives to be put into every division. There was still a great deal of public suspicion about plain clothes policemen, and, as Henderson recognised, a plain clothes detective was something 'entirely foreign to the habits and feelings of the Nation'. In charge was Chief Inspector Adolphus Frederick Williamson, who had joined in 1852, and was eventually promoted to superintendent. Williamson was a second-generation policeman. When he joined in 1850 his father was the superintendent of the T or Hammersmith Division. He had a dry sense of humour, he was ambitious, and he spent his evenings learning French. His detective's plain clothes were anything but plain: he normally wore a broad floppy hat and sported a large rosette in his buttonhole.

In 1877 public suspicions about detectives seemed to be justified when a scandal of epic proportions hit the headlines. It was corruption at the heart of the Detective Department. In the 'Trial of the Detectives' held at the Old Bailey three high-ranking men were shown to have been deeply involved with a gang of swindlers in turf betting frauds. The detectives had initially been able to protect their accomplices when investigations got too close, but eventually they over-reached themselves, were brought to trial and were given heavy prison sentences. One of the arresting officers was Detective Sergeant John Littlechild. He had been sworn to secrecy by Williamson himself who had begun to suspect his officers, one of whom was his immediate deputy. The sergeant found himself in the unpleasant situation of having to arrest three of his superior officers. 'Dolly' Williamson's integrity was never in doubt. From their knowledge of the man it had been clear to the conspirators that he was someone who could not be bought but for a long time afterwards he, like others, was tainted by suspicion of corruption. Before the trial ended, a Home Office commission into the working of the Detective Department had already begun. Clearly there had to be a thorough overhaul of the department and it was necessary to bring someone in from the outside to head it. Even before the commission's report was published it was widely assumed that the head of the reorganised department would have to be not just an assistant commissioner but someone who was also 'an astute and experienced lawyer'. The successful applicant was a young barrister, Howard Vincent, who, seeing an impending opportunity, had gone to Paris and studied the French detective system. He then submitted a report, which he is said to have redrafted eighteen times, to the departmental committee investigating the scandal. Its members were persuaded by his arguments and accepted some of his recommendations. Vincent, however, was appointed not as a policeman but as a lawyer, ranking not as an assistant commissioner but as director, which made him responsible not to the commissioner but to the home secretary. Worse, he had no statutory or disciplinary powers over his department, although he could reform and reorganise it. Over the next six years he increased the size of the department to about 800 men.

Vincent's assistant was Williamson, now promoted to chief superintendent. Vincent increased the detectives' pay, improved the standard of training, compiled a police code and law manual which, with regular updates, became the policeman's bible for another eighty years. More controversially, he brought in outsiders with special qualifications or skills, used *agents provocateurs* and courted press publicity. One reason for bringing in outsiders was that Vincent found the old divisional detectives, instituted by Henderson, to be mostly illiterate men, 'many of whom had been put into plain clothes to screen personal defects which marred their smart appearance in uniform'. They were inefficient and did very little, living 'a life unprofitable to themselves, discreditable to the service, useless to the public'. To emphasise the break with the past the old title of Detective Department was abandoned. The new name was the Criminal Investigation Department, or CID.

Between 1881 and 1885 there was a resurgence of 'Fenian Fire'. A bombing campaign was carried out on mainland Britain with London the chief target. On 6 May 1882 the new Chief Secretary for Ireland, Lord Frederick Cavendish, and the Permanent Under-Secretary, Thomas Burke, were stabbed to death in Phoenix Park, Dublin, by four men. The weapons used were surgical knives. Similar knives were to be linked with the Jack the Ripper murders. In response to this 'Fenian Fire' (the term was used in Home Office circulars after the Clerkenwell explosion and is a reference to the incendiary Greek fire of classical times), Howard Vincent formed the Special Irish Branch (the 'Irish' was dropped in 1888) to combat this terrorism and the social unrest that was leading to large-scale demonstrations. Robert Anderson was one of those who advised on its creation. Anderson, who had remained in London after the Clerkenwell explosion to liaise between Dublin Castle and the Home Office, was still retained by the Irish government to look after its interests in London and to maintain contact with a network of informants on Irish and Irish-American

Dynamiting London Bridge.

conspiracies on both sides of the Atlantic. His role was now to liaise with 'Dolly' Williamson on a daily basis and brief him on intelligence matters.

Initially the Special Irish Branch was a squad of four detectives and eight uniformed officers. Nominally in charge was Williamson but as he had command of the entire CID, day-to-day running was placed in the hands of John Littlechild, who had gone undercover for five months in Dublin after the Phoenix Park murders but was now promoted to inspector. In religion, Littlechild was a staunch Protestant and almost certainly anti-Catholic. His will would stipulate that no person professing or following any other than the Protestant religion would be entitled to reap any benefit under his will.

Special Branch headquarters was in a small two-storeyed building in the centre of Great Scotland Yard. An anonymous letter sent to Scotland Yard late in 1883 threatened 'to blow Superintendent Williamson off his stool and dynamite all the public buildings in London on 30 May 1884'. Shortly after 9 p.m. on that date a bomb placed in the public urinal let into the ground floor of the building for the use of customers of the Rising Sun pub opposite blew away a corner of the Special Branch premises to a height of 30 feet, completely destroying Williamson's office and extensively damaging the Rising Sun. Littlechild's office was in the same building. He normally worked late but that evening a friend had given him two tickets for the opera and, as a musical man, he could not resist the temptation to use them. When he next saw his office it was in ruins, a large brick sitting on his desk chair. Other bombs were exploded that same night in central London. One unexploded device was found the next day at the foot of Nelson's column.

An unexpected consequence of this resurgent bombing campaign was the resignation of Howard Vincent as head of the CID. He had been anxious to retire for the past year but the home secretary had insisted on retaining him, much against his wishes. The bombing of the Special Irish Branch offices allowed him to break free, to enter politics as the Tory Member of Parliament for Central Sheffield. A successor was quickly found in the person of 50-year-old James Monro, who was home on leave from Bengal when the bomb destroyed the Special Branch offices. He was inspector-general of police in India. The home secretary was anxious to know whether his police experience in India had given him any practical experience in dealing with political crime. Monro was easily able to reassure him on that point. In 1864–5

Moonshine, 25 February 1888, cartoons of Chief Inspector Littlechild of the Special Branch.

he had been deeply involved in the detection and punishment of the Wahabi conspirators at Patna and was used to dealing with secret societies.

The Police Act 1856 had authorised the appointment of two assistant commissioners and in 1884 James Monro was appointed third Assistant Commissioner (Crime) to take over Howard Vincent's role as Director of Criminal Intelligence, a rank that was now abolished and replaced by Assistant Commissioner (Crime). This new rank brought the appointee into the police hierarchy; he was a subordinate officer answerable direct to the commissioner. With his new position came the office of magistrate. Monro was sworn in as an executive justice of the peace which meant that he could swear in and command constables, and issue warrants and summonses. He could not, however, try criminal cases. Monro's appointment regularised this situation but raised a more important issue: although as Assistant

Just after 9 p.m. on 30 May 1884 Old Scotland Yard was rocked by a Fenian dynamite explosion which severely damaged the north-east corner of the central building (which housed the Special Branch offices) and the Rising Sun pub opposite. There were five minor casualties, including the duty policeman, but Littlechild and Williamson were not in their offices.

The entrance to Old Scotland Yard, another view.

James Monro, Assistant Commissioner (Crime), 1884–8.

Commissioner (Crime) and Director of the Special Irish Branch (Section B) he was responsible to the commissioner, as head of Special Branch (Section D), which was imperially funded and not paid for out of Metropolitan Police funds, he was answerable only to the home secretary. This meant that the commissioner had no control over a subordinate officer, who, when acting as head of Special Branch (Section D), could draw on police manpower without giving any explanation as to how or why it was being used. This would have been an intolerable position under any circumstances.

Monro was a Scotsman, born in Edinburgh in 1839, and educated at Edinburgh and Berlin universities. As a 19-year-old, he joined the Indian Civil Service (Legal Branch) in what his obituary notice describes as 'one of the early batches of "competition-wallahs"' in 1858. He was sent to Lower Bengal and after various district and secretarial posts was appointed inspector-general of police in 1877, a position he held until 1883, the year prior to his posting to the Metropolitan Police. According to *The Times* obituary of 30 January 1920, he had a tenacious memory for facts and faces, names and details of cases, which made him the terror of the criminal classes of Bengal and subsequently of London. The story was later told of an old Punjab Brahman who had been making a nuisance of himself and was brought to Scotland Yard and shown into a large office. Confronting him was a sun-tanned, military-looking man with grey hair and a moustache, who said sharply, 'What do you mean, you shameless one, by coming into a sahib's room with your shoes on?' Hearing Hindustani, the man hurriedly shuffled off his shoes as he began his explanations to Monro whom he saluted throughout their brief conversation as 'Protector of the Poor' and 'Incarnation of Justice'. He was cautioned by the Assistant Commissioner as to his future behaviour and led out.

On his appointment Monro learned that there was a kind of central bureau of intelligence collecting information on the Fenian dynamiters and acting as a clearing house for this material which was gathered chiefly from America and then circulated to police forces. Head of this department was Edward Jenkinson who was unofficially dubbed 'spymaster-general'. He was Harrow educated and, like Monro, had been an Indian civil servant. After the Phoenix Park murders of 6 May 1882 he had been appointed assistant under-secretary for police and crime at Dublin Castle. Threats from abroad to blow up the London bridges and to explode a little dynamite near to the queen led to Jenkinson's secondment from Dublin Castle to the Home Office in London in 1884. This gave him direct access to the home secretary and Anderson, and to Williamson at Scotland Yard. Jenkinson, originally in Dublin, and Anderson in London had begun their almost three-year working association in the autumn of 1882 and their relationship continued, it is said, on the basis of 'mutual distrust and jealousy'. Both men protected the names of their informants from each other – Anderson went so far as to refuse to tell the home secretary when asked for informants' names.

Jenkinson's move to London, to the Home Office, on 7 March 1884 meant that Anderson was now working for both him and Vincent. At his insistence Great Britain and Ireland were to be treated as one. Not only was Jenkinson to be the one pair of hands through which all information gathered at home and abroad would pass. He could issue emergency orders without consulting the minister (something that Anderson had never claimed nor tried to do), only informing him afterwards of what action he had taken, and he could spend secret service money at his own discretion. The centre of his web at the Home Office was room 56. He had a low opinion of Anderson's abilities and lack of informants, about which he regularly made criticism to the home secretary. Within three months of Jenkinson's move to London, Anderson was stopped from liaising with Williamson and retained only on the understanding that he would increase his number of informants. The evidence suggests that he had only one. When this did not happen, the home secretary gave him a brutal dressing down, which should have precipitated his resignation but Anderson said he could not do without the money. A way out of this impasse was found by compensating him with a gift of £2,000 and relieving him of all his duties relating to Fenianism in London. He was then consigned to the bureaucratic wilderness as secretary to the Prison Commissioners.

Monro was initially prepared to work with Jenkinson until he discovered that Jenkinson was going far beyond his brief to collect intelligence. Although he was not a policeman and

Left: This enlarged detail of the Leman Street police station group photograph shows the bowler-hatted, mutton-chopped detective with a stick that Donald Rumbelow feels fits the sketches and descriptions of Inspector Abberline, of whom no photograph has been found thus far.

Below: A Victorian group photograph of police officers of H Division at the rear of Leman Street police station. This photograph would appear to pre-date January 1887, when truncheon cases were abolished (one is visible in the photograph), therefore Abberline would still have been at Leman Street.

had no police authority, he had his own private force of Irish policemen stationed in London, acting under his directions and without any reference to the London forces. Jenkinson's abuse of his position, even before Monro took up his post, was already causing friction between the two and Monro's irritation soon became evident when he realised that while he was expected to give Jenkinson all the information that came into his possession, the arrangement was not reciprocal.

The frustrations under which Monro was labouring peaked in 1885. On 2 January an underground train was bombed at Gower Street. On 24 January Monro was at Scotland Yard when he was told that a bomb had exploded in the chamber of the House of Commons and another at the Tower of London. Grabbing hold of Williamson he asked him to put out an all-ports alert and then go to Westminster while he, Monro, went to the Tower. The explosion there had been in a room below the armoury and the blaze had already been extinguished by the time of Monro's arrival. Immediately after the bomb went off the Tower gates had been shut, and tourists and visitors had been held for security checks. Already on the scene was Inspector Abberline – the Tower was H Division's responsibility – and he was questioning an Irish-American suspect. Dissatisfied with the man's replies, he took him to Monro for further questioning. While the interview was taking place a succession of telegrams, three in all, arrived for Monro from an increasingly irate Home Secretary, Sir William Harcourt, who demanded the assistant commissioner's immediate return to the Home Office. Monro ignored them until their increasingly hysterical tone forced him to comply. He hurried back to the Home Office only to discover that in his absence the home secretary had personally gone to Scotland Yard and sent fourteen of Monro's detectives to the ports to watch for suspicious persons. In the assistant commissioner's private opinion the man simply went 'off his head' whenever there was any talk of explosions. In Cabinet his violence of expression on one occasion led to the suggestion by a fellow minister that he seemed to want to expel all Americans including his wife. His hysteria was such that he had fifteen men front and back of his house to protect him as well as two plain clothes policemen.

Between them, Sir William Harcourt and Jenkinson drove Monro nearly frantic with their interference. Jenkinson was scathing of both Monro and Williamson, the former he thought had too little originality and the latter was 'very slow and old fashioned'. At one point, in a sweeping denunciation of the Scotland Yard detectives, he even alleged corruption and the wholesale taking of bribes. He withheld, or would not exchange, information with Monro until eventually the home secretary had to threaten him with disobeying orders unless he told Monro what he knew. In 1888 Jenkinson's role was ultimately reduced to a passive one and his Irish detectives sent home. The clash had been between two styles of policing: Monro and Williamson favoured the old Peelite style of preventive policing, similar to the role of the uniform police, where it was better to nip a scheme in the bud than allow it to become fully developed; Jenkinson favoured the spy system, which was the Irish method, allowing plans to become fully developed before closing in on them. At times the latter could be dangerously close to a system of *agents provocateurs*. Frequent changes of minister had allowed Jenkinson to continue his unjustifiable interference – they were never in office long enough to see how pernicious his system was.

More worrying was the continuing hostility of the press towards police generally. Criticism was not limited to the controversies of the police strike or the trial of the detectives but was part of a sustained campaign of general vilification. The policeman was pilloried 'as a nincompoop, a figure of fun, or a downright brute. If he made a mistake it was reported at length, and probably made the subject of a leading article; if he did a good piece of work that was not news in those days.'[4] Unfavourable comparisons were regularly drawn between Commissioner Henderson and his predecessor Sir Richard Mayne, who himself had been the target of a great deal of hostile criticism but who was now found to have virtues that had not always been recognised in his lifetime, and it was inevitable that sooner or later Henderson would be forced out of office. The campaign to oust him began on 8 February 1886 when small-scale rioting broke out in the West End of London. There were demonstrations in Trafalgar Square. A small mob broke away from the main meeting and marched through Pall Mall and St James's (London's clubland) to Oxford Street, hurling stones and breaking windows on the way. Henderson had been out in the square all day but the press reaction to his response was still hostile. A *Punch* cartoon showing a somnolent commissioner reclining in his office was labelled 'The Great Unemployed'. The newly appointed Home Secretary, Hugh Childers, had no need for excuses to make Henderson the scapegoat for the riots on that 'Black Monday'. Henderson knew it was inevitable that he would be 'thrown over by the government' and resigned before he could be dismissed.

A new commissioner was required. London was threatened from within and without by large-scale, working-class demonstrations and a continuing bombing campaign. A strong hand was needed to get a grip on the situation. Inevitably the choice was a military one.

When the Metropolitan Police was formed in 1829, it was to be a police force for the whole of London with the glaring exception of the City of London. The square mile around St Paul's Cathedral had been excluded as part of a political deal because of concerns about its ancient rights and privileges and fear of control passing from a democratically elected council, the most powerful in the country, to a minister of an unreformed Parliament. The consequences of this ill-judged separation, so it was said, would be that 'Thieves would assemble in London as an asylum. When they threw a dog into the water, the fleas all got into the head to avoid drowning, and in the same way all the thieves would get into the City to avoid hanging.' Not until 1839, ten years later, was the City to form its own police force of 500 men under the command of a commissioner with headquarters at 26 Old Jewry, close to the ancient Guildhall.

In 1863 Daniel Whittle Harvey, the City of London Police Commissioner, died. He had been the first commissioner and a controversial one. He was a Liberal Member of Parliament at the time of his appointment and had only taken up the position to relieve his debts. He was a powerful speaker and

'The Great Unemployed' – Sir Edmund Henderson, Metropolitan Police Commissioner, is shown in this *Punch* cartoon of 20 February 1886 reclining in his chair on 8 February 1886, the first day of the rioting.

had expected to continue as an MP even after his appointment. It was too much for the government to have a police commissioner sitting in opposition and a clause was inserted into the City of London Police Act debarring the commissioner from having a seat in Parliament. Harvey was outraged but too far committed to withdraw and always said that he would never have applied to be commissioner had he known that such a rule would be passed. His time as commissioner was one of constant conflict with the City fathers and only relief was expressed when he died. His successor was a Scotsman, James Fraser, who had joined an English regiment at the age of 16, eventually rising to command it. He then exchanged to another regiment but seeing no prospect of active service had retired as colonel of the 72nd Foot less than a year before the Crimean War broke out in 1854. According to Henry Smith, who would eventually succeed Fraser as chief commissioner, he bitterly repented what he had done, for his decision was an irrevocable one, and he was unemployed for some months. In desperation, as the work was distasteful to him, he became governor of a female reformatory before successfully applying to be the chief constable of Berkshire where he spent some years before being appointed as Harvey's successor as commissioner of the City of London Police. He was created a Companion of the Bath in 1869 and promoted to a Knight Commander in 1886.

One of the enduring myths of police history is the supposed conflict between the two London forces and especially between the two commissioners. The explanation given for the alleged friction by Henry Smith, who became Fraser's deputy and then succeeded him as commissioner, was that on the death of Sir Richard Mayne, Sir George Grey sent for Fraser, who was then Chief Constable of Berkshire, and appointed him to the commissionership of the Metropolitan Police. Smith said Fraser returned to the congratulations of the county and was on his way to take up the appointment when he received a letter from the Home Office saying that there had been a change of mind and that Grey was appointing Colonel Henderson to the vacancy. Smith added that Fraser felt the injustice of his treatment very strongly but then within a few months gained the City appointment, which in some ways

was a more desirable one. This account has often been put forward as a reason for Fraser to feel hostile towards the Metropolitan Police and as an explanation for why in a later incident, again told by Smith, he was prepared to turn back mounted Metropolitan policemen by force from the City boundary. The problem with the first part of the story is that Mayne died in 1868, five years after Fraser was appointed Commissioner of the City of London Police: Fraser could simply not have been appointed Commissioner of the Metropolitan Police. As for the second part of the story, the idea that Fraser could have ordered Smith to the boundary with 200 City policemen to 'stop by force, if necessary' a Metropolitan-police-escorted

Colonel Sir James Fraser, the 74-year-old City of London Police Commissioner, at the time of the murders. He had been in office since 1863 and retired in 1890, making way for Henry Smith.

Major Henry Smith, Acting Commissioner of the City of London Police at the time of the murders, was later promoted to commissioner. When the Mitre Square murder was committed Smith was 'tossing about in his bed at Cloak Lane Station'; he was roused to join the hunt for the Ripper.

procession from entering the City, with the possibility of a 'free fight between the two police forces', is too ludicrous even to consider.

Henry Smith was born in 1835 and was 53 years old at the time of the Ripper murders. He had been educated at Edinburgh Academy and University and worked as a book-keeper until the death of his father. In 1869 he was com-missioned in the Suffolk Artillery Militia but he was very much a social butterfly, first in London and then in Northumberland. London did not agree with his mother, which prompted a move in 1872 to Alnmouth on the coast of Northumberland. His mother died the following year but Smith kept the house on and stayed there for the next twelve years. His only employment during this time seems to have been the management of the local lifeboat. When he was not so engaged, his life seems to have been a social whirl of hunting, shooting and staying at friends' houses for weeks at a time. One of his hunting friends, a former chief constable of Northumberland, asked this butterfly if he would like the job of chief constable because it was shortly to become vacant. Nothing would suit him better, Smith replied. Surprisingly (to him), he was not appointed to the post but his thoughts now turned to police work and he decided to prepare himself for another vacancy should one occur. A three-month stay with a Scottish chief constable (little work was involved) earned him a testimonial. This was followed by a month's police work in Newcastle and with powerful backing he applied unsuccessfully for the post of detective superintendent in Liverpool. Somewhat crestfallen, Smith returned to Alnmouth where he received a letter from Major Bowman, Chief Superintendent, City of London Police, inviting him to the capital. At this time the chief superintendent was in effect the assistant commissioner of the force. Bowman told Smith that he was planning to retire and Smith would seem to be the sort of man that would suit the post. That was in 1879. In fact it was another six years before Bowman retired and Sir James Fraser made Smith his number two. Owing to his age, this was the only police appointment in Great Britain for which Smith was eligible. Those six years of waiting, said Smith, had been weary ones. He hunted, shot and played golf, but whenever he was summoned to the City to see Bowman he was ready to go. Quite shamelessly he called his autobiography *From Constable to Commissioner*.

About the same time as Smith's appointment, Charles Warren was just recovering from his election defeat. For a half-pay officer, with no party backing, the costs would have been a heavy burden but the local Liberal Party was so delighted with his efforts that, knowing he had refused party funds to fight his campaign, raised a subscription on his behalf to pay off his election expenses.

Still unemployed, Warren now had more time for his Masonic interests.[5] In January 1886 he was installed as first master of the Quatuor Coronati Lodge devoted to Masonic research. Shortly before the consecration of the lodge, Warren was astonished, in view of Wolseley's threats, to receive a communication from the War Office telling him that he had been appointed to the Army Staff in Egypt with the local rank of major-general. He was amazed to be told that he had been recommended for the post by Wolseley. There were rumours that he was becoming something of a thorn in the side to Wolseley, but how it is not clear. The most obvious explanation for his appointment is that, although Warren was a failed Liberal candidate, the machinery of the party in government had swung behind him and quietly overruled Wolseley's determination that Warren should never again be given a military appointment.

At Suakin, in early February, he found a garrison of mixed nationalities, British, Indian and Egyptian, which he swiftly reorganised. With the help of local Arabs they cleared a safety zone around the city and drove back inland the enemy Arabs who had been firing into Suakin every night. At Government House, Warren found that the servants and batmen were convicts, some murderers, on parole. Warren chose a well-known poisoner to make the coffee to serve to visitors and since, as host, he always had to drink the first cup, he made sure that he was preceded by the poisoner who had to taste the first brew.

However, within two months of taking up this appointment, Sir Charles was on his way back to England. The post of Metropolitan Police commissioner was vacant and there were over 400 applicants for the post. This list had been reduced to three officers and three civilians. Curiously Warren's name seems to have been put forward without his being aware of it. Possibly his Liberal politics may have had some bearing upon his appointment as he and Home Secretary Hugh Childers were both staunch supporters of Gladstone and shared other interests in common besides politics. On 13 March 1886 he received a telegram from Childers offering him the vacancy. To his even greater astonishment, it seems that Wolseley had once again intervened on his behalf by recommending the 46-year-old soldier in preference to the other applicants. If this was Wolseley's way of permanently removing Warren from the army, then Sir Charles must have been more of a thorn in the side than is generally supposed. The *Pall Mall Gazette* described his appointment as 'the succession of King Stork to the throne of King Log'.

One of the more curious anecdotes Warren told of his time excavating in Palestine is about a recurring nightmare that might be interpreted as a warning of things to come in his future appointment as head of the Metropolitan Police. Not surprisingly it generally followed a late heavy supper:

> I have now and then been visited by the unwelcome intruder, which usually, on these occasions, took the form of my being surrounded in a defile and attacked hand to hand: invariably it was attended with the same result; my revolver never missed fire, my cudgel never swerved from the head of my victims, one after another they were shot down or laid low, until, flushed with victory, I would awake, pleased to have done my duty towards my fellow-men, and in a healthy glow settle to sleep again, feeling all the better for my supper and at peace with the world. It was not only when well-guarded that my dreams took such a pleasant course, it was just the same when among thievish villages with no other companion than the cook, the muleteers having gone to a more secure place; and again it was the same when in a tent on a lonely spot the west of Jerusalem, the reputed haunt of thieves there, where even my servant left me and my little dog disappeared, I tucked my clothes under the mattress to prevent their being stolen,

buckled my revolver round my night-shirt and slept as pleasantly as though I had been in the most secure position. The insecurity of this spot was so well known that I was urgently advised to come into the hotel: I had no sooner done so than all my combats were reversed in their results. The revolver would not go off, my club hung in mid-air, I was cudgelled by my assailants and slain over and over again. It was ever the same with me, I slept miserably in thick-walled houses but happily in a tent.[6]

Looking back to his postings as a colonial administrator, to Griqualand and Bechuanaland, the Sinai Peninsular and Suakin, postings where he could act independently, and because of the distances involved, unchecked by the hand of authority, and where his on-the-spot decisions and actions could go unchallenged, it would seem clear that any job that limited this freedom and independence of action might provoke a violent reaction. The contrast in his dream between the country and the city could hardly be clearer. By 1886 he had been untrammelled by authority for nearly two decades. That he would be determined to have his own way in anything he did is clear from his autobiographical *Underground in Jerusalem*. His instructions from the Palestine Exploration Fund were that he was to excavate around the Temple Mount but a vizierial letter forbade such work: 'yet in the teeth of this letter, in direct opposition of the Pacha's order, and contrary to the advice of the Consul' and entirely contrary to the wishes of the local Muslims he persisted. A native said his words were like pebbles, smooth and hard. Warren's attitude to officialdom can best be witnessed in his relations with Nazif Pacha, the Governor of Jerusalem; Warren admitted that he was 'constantly under the necessity of acting in opposition to his wishes and

pushing my way in spite of efforts to restrain me'. Warren's object was never 'simple opposition, it was pressure continued until my adversary began to yield, and then when he felt he must give way, endeavour to make arrangements by which he should have the appearance of bestowing gracefully, and this before he should feel bitterly disposed by the prospect of the exposure of his failure'.

Such insistence on having his own way was bound to cause resentment and provoke controversy. It is a pattern of behaviour which reappeared again and again throughout his career – in Jerusalem in 1869, with Lord Wolseley in 1885, with the home secretary in 1888, and with Sir Redvers Buller in the Boer War. When he was made Metropolitan Police commissioner, controversy seemed inevitable from the beginning. In the cockpit of Whitehall and Whitechapel, Warren's quarrels with his political masters and troublesome subordinates might have been foreseen.

Sir Charles Warren, Chief Commissioner of the Metropolitan Police at the time of the murders in 1888. Many of the letters were addressed personally to him.

King Stork Takes Command

THE *Pall Mall Gazette*'s warning on 6 December 1887 that Henderson's replacement by Colonel Sir Charles Warren would be like King Stork succeeding King Log was quickly proved correct. An editorial said:

> I am not surprised, but somewhat amused, at the indignation which you have expressed. After all, was it not you that killed the old Dodo, and you have largely yourself to blame for the fidgety ferocity that reigns at Scotland Yard. Sir Charles Warren may overdo it, but you must remember that he was appointed because his predecessor was said to underdo it.

It would have been small consolation to the *Gazette*'s readers to know that the 46-year-old colonel saw his appointment as a short-term one and that he fully intended to return to his military career.

Warren understood that the major reason for his appointment was the need for the organisation or reorganisation of the police. This was subsequently denied and then half-admitted by Childers in a parliamentary debate on Warren's appointment but it is evident that Warren believed this to be part of his brief. He was confirmed in this belief by the fact that a committee was appointed after the February 1886 riots to inquire not only into the disturbance itself but also into the conduct of the Metropolitan Police. The committee reported that the duties and responsibilities of the force were not well distributed, that the senior officers who had risen from the ranks were performing badly and there was a shortage of men coming up through the ranks to replace them, and that there was a lack of communication between different branches. A unanimous recommendation was made that the administration and organisation of the police should be the subject of a further inquiry. A second committee of four civilians and Warren, newly appointed as commissioner, then met. Their final report was the civilians', not Warren's, as Childers was to admit. The report pointed out that for local purposes the force was practically without superior officers; beyond the district superintendents there were none to implement the commissioner's orders or to make inquiries; there was no independent and effective inspection of the stations. The want of superior officers led to undue centralisation in Scotland Yard with recommendations for promotion coming from those who had just recently risen from the ranks. For these and other reasons, the committee proposed that another rank should be introduced between the commissioner and the divisional superintendents. A similar recommendation had been made in 1879 but had only been partially carried out. The persons to be appointed to this new rank of chief constable[1] should be gentlemen of good social standing from the army or navy and it was further recommended that they should be exclusively from these classes. In thirty years the only exception to this rule was Williamson and then only after he had threatened to resign. In 1886 four chief constables were appointed.

In a parliamentary debate two years later a friend gave a character sketch of Warren.

> There were some men who did take an extraordinarily rigid and high view of the duty they had to perform. As soon as they believed they understood their duties they would not, for any consideration, neglect or overstep what they believed to be the bounds of those duties, and in them they would not allow any other person to interfere. . . . They might like or dislike such a character, and undoubtedly a character such as that did present some angularities and difficulties that did not exist in more pliant men. . . . He would ask the House to consider the view such a man would take when a person invaded a province in which he believed that person had no right to interfere.

Warren was subsequently to say that he would not have accepted the post of commissioner if he believed someone outside might interfere with his duty. He was clear in his own mind what he had to do, and that was to reorganise the police and make them more efficient. Implementing the committee's recommendation, in which he had had only a minority role, would inevitably lead to charges of militarism and militarisation of the police force. Conflict was inevitable with a man of such 'angularities and difficulties'.

By the autumn of 1886 Warren was in a full-scale departmental war with the Receiver, A. Richard Pennefather. One outraged official subsequently complained that the manner in which the commissioner carried on the interdepartmental negotiations and correspondence made it practically useless to make concessions to him as these only had the effect of making him more aggressive. Unless the receiver was prepared to surrender every vestige of control, it was absolutely necessary to make a decided stand, even at the risk of causing open war between the two sides. Warren, it was said, 'carried on in a tone and spirit unlike anything whatsoever has been seen before in official correspondence'.

The receiver is a Crown appointment. His original function, prior to the formation of the Metropolitan Police force in 1829, was to collect the monies raised on the rates for the maintenance of the old parish constables and watchmen. As receiver for the Metropolitan Police district every item of police property or equipment, from police stations to whistles, from boots to stabling, was bought and disposed of in his name. All contracts, for which he was legally liable, had to be signed by him, all purchases made through his office. In practice, this insulated the commissioner from personal involvement in purchasing and possible accusations that certain contractors had been given preferential treatment. The downside of the arrangement was that the commissioner had to indent for every item, down to doormats and inkwells. This wasted a great deal of time and required a lot of unnecessary form-filling and bureaucracy. It seems explanations and justifications as to why items were being indented for were demanded of everyone, including the commissioner. Warren went into a rage when, having indented for seven inkwells, he was asked to explain their necessity. As the crisis deepened between the commissioner and the receiver, Warren famously started indenting for single sheets of paper. The commissioner, it was said, did many things to aggravate his relationship with the receiver, some of them trivial but each performed in an annoying way and without any respect for the official etiquette so essential in all departments, especially in a small outfit like the police office. When Warren was refused permission to mark the policemen's lamps with their divisional letters and numbers, he went ahead anyway. He refused to give explanations as to why items were wanted from the stores. He would not sign a requisition for a doormat at Wanstead station until he had been given the estimated cost. When he found a large quantity of the receiver's waste paper lying in a basement he ordered Williamson to have it thrown into the street unless it was removed that afternoon. Warren's predecessors had been involved in similar conflicts but none had been prepared to quarrel in such a spectacular fashion.

Warren accused the receiver of disposing of truncheons in an improper manner, brought charges against him with regard to the purchase of police lamps and resented what the receiver considered legitimate financial criticisms of an extension of the telegraph system. Warren then began briefing on financial matters himself and in many other ways made it almost impossible for the receiver to carry out the duties of his office. He justified his interference by arguing that he was more interested in economy than the receiver because every £100 saved put an extra man on the street. More damning was his argument about the purchase of police stations: leases which would not expire for thirty or forty years were being converted into freeholds when the force did not know whether it would need those sites for police stations at all that far in the future. A truce was engineered between the two sides but this proved short-lived. In fact Warren, it was alleged, did not desire peace and made every trivial matter an excuse to override the receiver. In some cases he was right, but the manner in which he made his suggestions and the tone of his letters eventually made it necessary for the Home Secretary, Henry Matthews, to intervene.

The irony is that Receiver Pennefather agreed with Warren that the posts of commissioner and receiver could not and should not coexist in their current form. Unknown to the commissioner, on 15 January 1885 Pennefather had written to the previous Home Secretary Sir William Harcourt, taking the opportunity of the introduction of a new Police Bill to say that his experience of seventeen months in post led him to suggest that the relative position of the commissioner and receiver was unsatisfactory. There were two distinct offices, each with an expensive staff of clerks. In theory, the receiver was there to check any extravagances of the commissioner and generally to administer the finance. Instead, Pennefather told Harcourt, he thought the commissioner should be responsible for everything, finance and the stations, as well as the discipline and administration of the force. He suggested that the commissioner and assistant commissioner should become a corporation (the receiver was a corporation sole, nothing could be done without his approval), that the receiver as an independent officer should be abolished and that in his place an assistant commissioner for finance should be appointed. He had discussed this with Henderson and the assistant commissioner and they were all agreed. He concluded,

> That the present dual government is inconvenient, it leads to friction, causes delay in the transaction of business, is expensive in that it needs two separate staffs of clerks, and is to a great extent inefficient, seeing that the Receiver, who is supposed to have all financial matters under his control, has practically nothing to do with a considerable portion of the financial administration.

Henry Matthews, 1st Viscount Llandaff, a barrister, was home secretary at the time of the murders. The first Roman Catholic to serve in the post since the reign of James II, he was as unpopular with the radical press as Warren.

Home Secretary Harcourt dismissed his suggestion in a minute sent eight days later: 'My dear Pennefather, I cannot say either of these proposals "smile upon me", as at present informed. W.V.H.' Nothing of this exchange could have been known to Warren and, while the situation worsened between the two men, it seems possible that Pennefather had second thoughts about the wisdom of his suggestion and did not make it again. Not until July 1888 was a committee formed to gather evidence from both the commissioner's and the receiver's sides and it was still sitting when the last Ripper murder took place. As postscript, it was not until 1968 that the independence of the receiver's department was ended and the commissioner made head of the whole Metropolitan Police force.

The more serious side to the problem was the home secretary's reluctance to involve himself not only in this but in other police matters. Warren never knew from day to day whether Matthews was going to back him or not. A *Punch* cartoon carried the legend 'Now then, Matt, move on! Don't interfere with the Police in the execution of their Duty.' Normally he didn't. Matthews was generally content to ignore Warren's views and left matters to subordinates who would issue instructions in Matthews' name but without any direct orders from him. This inevitably created a three-fold friction between Warren, Matthews and Pennefather which grew steadily worse. Matthews' private secretary, Sir Evelyn Ruggles-Brise, summed up the problem many years later.

> Pennefather was a very able man, but disagreeable to deal with; he rubbed everybody up the wrong way. Warren was the finest man we had in Whitehall, but probably the worst appointment, because he *must* be independent, and the Commissioner of Police is held in very tight bonds by the Home Office. Matthews, aged 62 years in 1888, was an exceedingly able lawyer, but quite incapable of dealing with men: he was a regular Gallio [a byword for indifference] in his attitude to Warren's complaints. Later on he quarrelled with Bradford, and if you couldn't get on with Bradford you could get on with nobody.

Warren tried to make Matthews understand the effect that this backstairs treatment had on the performance of his duties. He wrote asking for the following points to be observed:

The Home Office building in Whitehall, Matthews' base for his protracted battles with Commissioner Warren.

- that he should have the opportunity to see all minutes made on his letters by the receiver, the Home Office clerks or the permanent under-secretary and that he should be given the chance to correct any erroneous impressions which might be laid before him
- that he should see the home secretary on all matters connected with his office before adverse decisions were made on proposals which he considered necessary for police efficiency
- that if he were to be censured, or censure implied, it should be done only on the direct instructions of the home secretary
- that decisions against the commissioner should be made by the secretary of state, and not by the under-secretary in the name of the home secretary
- that suggestions made by the receiver or other official and then forwarded by the home secretary should not be represented as being the home secretary's opinion – the commissioner would naturally view a matter very differently if he knew that the suggestion had not come from the secretary of state.

Apart from a formal acknowledgement, this, like almost all Warren's other communications on this subject, was simply ignored.

The pattern of the 8 February 1886 riots, which had forced Henderson's resignation, was to be repeated again and again during the next three years and was marked by ever-increasing violence between police and demonstrators. Unemployment, hunger, and revolutionary socialism brought the homeless and dispossessed of London's East End out on to the streets.

As Queen Victoria's golden jubilee approached in 1887 the streets were regularly filled with demonstrators carrying red and black flags and singing the 'Marseillaise'. To them the East End was not part of the grandeur of Victoria's global empire but was rather 'The Empire of Hunger'. Nearly two-thirds of its population lived below the poverty line, while 13 per cent faced daily starvation.

The early 1880s had seen sensation-seeking journalists and others who wanted to explore this 'City of Dreadful Night' 'slumming' in the East End, hoping to experience horrors and dangers which they could share with their readers. W.T. Stead and George R. Sims were among those who sometimes went in disguise in search of copy. The writer, in this case the novelist Margaret Harkness writing under the pseudonym 'John Law', might turn into the Whitechapel Road to walk

> past the flaming gaslights of the costermongers, the public houses and the street hawkers. An old woman offered him pigs' feet; a newspaper man shouted the last ghastly details of a murder, tipsy men and women rolled past him singing East End songs set to Salvation music. He caught sight of the slum lassies in a public house. . . . Turning away he stumbled over two half-naked children who were waiting for their drunken parents. A woman with a sickly infant on her breast asked him for money to fund a night's lodging. A small boy tried to trip him up, and ran to join some gutter children.[2]

Such observations often had a sexual side, barely disguised in some writings: men were made to strip naked, washed in the dirty, oatmeal-coloured water used by a dozen others, and then forced to huddle in a bed shared with two, three or four other naked men. Sleeping accommodation was cheap. An iron bedstead and a blanket in an overcrowded dormitory could be had for *4d* for a single or *8d* for a double. For *2d* a casual could try to sleep leaning on a rope stretched across the room. Both sexes were willing to share with a partner of either sex if they had not got the money to pay for a bed. Beds and sex were cheap. The age of consent was 13 years. In 1902 women who could be had for *3d, 2d* or a loaf of stale bread were pointed out to Jack London.[3] Half a pound of cheese cost 4½*d*.

The area that was to become Jack the Ripper's killing ground was centred on the old Flower and Dean Street rookery, a tightly packed maze of courts and alleys considered by many to be the foulest and most dangerous part of London. The construction of Commercial Street in the early 1870s destroyed part of the rookery by separating it from Petticoat Lane but Thrawl Street and Fashion Street survived. The neighbourhood sheltered the most violent of criminals and its warren of streets and alleys made escape easy from the pursuing police. Policemen had to patrol in pairs or risk a beating, possibly with an iron bar. Prostitution and crime were inseparably linked. Women could be as violent as men, deploying fists, teeth, feet or, more lethal still, a hatpin or a knife.

There were further part-demolitions of the rookery. By 1883 about a third of the population had been displaced and policing had become a little easier but overcrowding was still endemic. Outside the East End the average number of people per acre was 50; in Whitechapel the figure was generally 176, but in the Bell Lane district of Spitalfields it rose to 600. Dorset Street in the Bell Lane area, was shelter every night to some 1,500 people, including three of the Ripper's victims. The number of people sheltering in a lodging house generally averaged about thirty a night. The construction of nearby Spitalfields' fruit and vegetable market in 1887 became another in the list of nuisances in addition to prostitution and drinking. Christ Church Spitalfields dominated both rookery and market and the rumble of the horses and carts below.

From 1882 onwards, Jewish refugees escaping the pogroms in Tsarist Russia and eastern Europe added to the overcrowding and aggravated the worsening work and housing conditions. In 1884 London's Jewish community, led by Baron Rothschild, came together to provide housing for the Jewish poor. It was believed housing could be built to be let out at cheap rents which the poor could afford to pay and still reward investors with a return of 4 per cent. In 1887 Rothschild buildings were opened. The two six-storey blocks containing 198 flats faced Flower and Dean Street and Thrawl Street. In the smoke-polluted atmosphere their fresh yellow bricks were soon covered with grime.

In nearby Hanbury Street strike meetings were regularly held in Christ Church Hall. A near neighbour was a Masonic lodge of instruction. A Yiddish theatre was not far away at 3 Princelet Street: during a performance on 18 January 1887 a false fire alarm prompted the audience of 500 to stampede and 17 were killed in the panic. In Berner Street, a shabby lane off Commercial Road, there was an International Workers' Educational Club, an old two-storey building that could hold about 200 people. Czechs, Poles and Russians were just part of the international crowd who gathered there at weekends when plays were performed, mostly in Russian, and speeches given by leading socialists like William Morris. It was from Berner Street that some demonstrators began their march into the City and West End. A contemporary described one such demonstration in 1889 as 'headed by a German brass band and a repulsive looking black and white banner bearing the words "JEWISH UNEMPLOYED AND SWEATERS VICTIMS". . . . A more abject and miserable set of men it would have been impossible to have seen anywhere. Ill-clad, dirty, unwashed, haggard and ragged, they looked in the bright sunlight, a picture of abject misery.' Inside the City they were blocked by Superintendent Foster and fifty policemen and, having been refused permission to hold a meeting in nearby Mitre Square, turned back.

Between 1886 and 1889 demonstrations by the hungry and unemployed were a permanent feature of London policing. For much of the nineteenth century, Clerkenwell Green on the north edge of the City had been the traditional location for protests but as the marches got bigger, Trafalgar Square and Hyde Park became the new battlegrounds. The 'Black Monday' riots on 8 February 1886 and a clash two weeks later between 50,000 demonstrators and the police had brought Henderson down. Warren, however, as the *Pall Mall Gazette* warned, was a man with very firm and authoritarian ideas.

Warren's first six months passed peacefully enough but the impending lord mayor's day in November brought warnings of possible disturbances. City Police detectives, directed by Inspector James McWilliam, tailed the socialist leaders – John Burns, H.M. Hyndman, H.H. Champion and Jack Williams – to locate their private addresses and to listen to what they had to say about plans for action on lord mayor's day. In a speech to demonstrators Burns said that they, the people, did not care about the City Police commissioner or lord mayor and would it not be a fine thing to kidnap the lord mayor? He provoked a deal of laughter by adding, just fancy, a lord mayor's show without the lord mayor. Hyndman, at least, was aware that they were being shadowed. At one point he rounded on the detective following him and told him that he would have him locked up if he kept so close to their heels.

The unemployed were now regularly camping out in Trafalgar Square – among them, it was said, was the first of the Ripper's victims, Polly Nichols – and demonstrations happened constantly. Prior to a march of about 2,000 unemployed through the City on 17 October 1887 a small deputation made its way to the Mansion House to ask for help in getting work. The lord mayor, they were told, was away attending a great Masonic celebration at Northampton. With a police escort of Major Henry Smith and Superintendent Alfred Foster, they were taken before the sitting alderman who told them that indiscriminate charity was the greatest curse on society: respectable men never got the aid, it was the cadger and loafer who obtained the benefit, he said. The bulk of people in the processions – he had seen them – were the cadgers, blackguards and loafers who were to be found in every city. And, he added, it was an unscrupulous calumny to allege that £4,000 was wasted on the lord mayor's show when double or treble that sum was spent in wages in preparation for that event. The deputation reported back to Trafalgar Square and as the procession headed away towards the City, with the familiar black and red flags fluttering at their head, the mounted police feared that the February riots might be repeated.

'The Police and the Mob' became a familiar headline in *The Times* for several weeks. Deciding how to handle the constant round of protests, violence and the threat of looting that accompanied them was Warren's major headache. Worse still, he did not know from day to day whether Home Secretary Matthews would back his decisions. He did not anticipate too many problems from the socialists and other political groups who were determined to take possession of Trafalgar Square; the threat lay with criminals and looters who always attached themselves to the demonstrations. So far the police had managed to stop large outbreaks of looting but could this continue? Warren began by breaking up the processions as they marched towards Trafalgar Square and when this did not seem to prevent the crowds massing, he banned all public meetings in the square. No demonstrators were to gather there nor speeches be delivered. The ultimatum was delivered shortly before Sunday 13 November when yet another huge demonstration was planned. His proclamation was greeted by howls of protest from the opposition in Parliament and some sympathetic sections of the press. It was, they said, an attack on the common law right of public assembly, a ruling made with no legal backing whatsoever. Opponents of the decision argued political meetings had always taken place in the square: it was a democratic right. The official view put forward by Matthews' under-secretary, and not by Matthews himself, was that these were not political meetings but meetings of the unemployed 'which were growing into a system of propagating by disturbance opinions which could not find their way to the public ear by argument'. Whether Matthews himself actually approved of Warren's actions is not clear. It was assumed that he did, but the home secretary's approval did not make Warren's action legal. Clearly there had to be a trial of strength between the two sides. The outcome was 'Bloody Sunday'.

When demonstrators broke through to Trafalgar Square on 13 November, Warren was there, on horseback, wearing his full dress commissioner's uniform but without the old-fashioned chimney pot hat he had worn at an earlier demonstration much to the amusement of the press. There would be no poking fun this time. After 'Bloody Sunday' simply the mention of his name would bring a shrill storm of whistling and shouts of abuse.

Months of having their leave cancelled so that they could handle increasingly violent confrontations meant that the policemen on duty that day were high-handed and brutal in their treatment of the demonstrators. For some time now, any procession, whatever police guarantees were given before it took place, had been liable to find itself charged by baton-wielding constables or mounted policemen whose brutalities were commemorated on trade union banners still carried on marches eighty years later. 'Bloody Sunday' was the most violent demonstration of all. Crowds 70,000 to 100,000 strong advanced in defiance of Warren's orders. The commissioner had deployed 2,500 constables to break them up before they reached the square where he had some 1,500 men in position. Mounted police, later joined by 300 Life Guards, patrolled the perimeter. In reserve were 300 Grenadiers who, late in the afternoon, lined the front of the National Gallery with fixed bayonets. Police had been placed at strategic points about a quarter of a mile from the square. It was a net into which the demonstrators marched and they could not escape.

'The Riot in Trafalgar Square', *Graphic*,
19 November 1887. This fight took place at the
bottom of Parliament Street between the police
and mob from South London and Battersea.

'The Riot in Trafalgar Square', *Graphic*,
19 November 1887. A fight in St Martin's Lane
between the police and the mob contingents from
Clerkenwell Green.

'The Riot in Trafalgar Square', *Graphic*,
19 November 1887.

'The Riot in Trafalgar Square', *Graphic*,
19 November 1887. 'Here They Come!' – the
procession from South London advancing over
Westminster Bridge.

Protesters came armed with a variety of weapons including metal bars, pokers and sticks. The *Pall Mall Gazette* of 14 November reported:

> Borne by members of the procession were about fifteen banners, with devices of various kinds, and for these the police made, as they seemed the rallying points for the crowd. The police batons were drawn, and headed by their mounted companions, the men divided the ringleaders, and drove the body of the procession in all directions. During the mêlée the police freely used their weapons where any stand was made against their authority. Sticks were in the hands of almost all the crowd, and for the short period in which the people came into collision with the police blows were freely given upon both sides.

The fighting was violent on all approaches to the square. Casualties were high: 150 people had to be taken to hospital. Some 300 demonstrators were arrested. Throughout it all, Warren was in the thick of things, on horseback, surrounded by his staff, calmly giving orders. *The Times* congratulated him on his success and sympathised with the policemen who had been assaulted.

Warren did genuinely care about the plight of the unemployed and in the aftermath of 'Bloody Sunday' offered to keep a register at each police station of those without work, showing their names and addresses and the particulars of the employment needed. The intention was that local businesses would use the register to find people to fill vacancies. The scheme could not guarantee work but might assist in bringing the two classes together. The gesture was well-meaning but naïve. The *Pall Mall Gazette* acidly commented that having asked for bread and been given only the baton, the unemployed were about as likely to register themselves at a police station as at the North Pole.

The year before, 1886, there had been a rabies scare. By seizing stray dogs and enforcing the laws on muzzling Warren had suppressed a potential epidemic in the capital in four months – the disease was still raging in the countryside outside London. One cartoon, among many, showed policemen using lassoes and muzzles to capture stray dogs. Even more apt would have been a cartoon of some years before which showed a kennel marked 'Scotland Yard' with a chained dog in front wearing a helmet and tunic. The caption read 'The Curs(e) of Scotland Yard'. A postcard, one of many addressed to Warren as 'the Dog Muzzler in Chief', told him to muzzle himself because the rabies was in him and not in the dogs. After 'Bloody Sunday', and throughout the demonstrations that took place into 1888

WANTED—A STRONG MASTER
(DEDICATED TO THE CURSE OF LONDON)

'The Curs(e) of London', the *Tomahawk*, 9 January 1869.

and beyond, Warren became a figure of even greater hate and a target for the liberal press. Demonstrations generally ended with loud renditions of the 'Marseillaise' and 'Rule Britannia'. A new line was added to another song sung even more heartily: 'We'll hang old Warren on a crab apple tree.'

In spite of the tremendous volley of hostility from some newspapers, and a number of anonymous personal threats, there was generally widespread support for Warren's high-handed decisions in November 1887. On the day after the riot *The Times* said that by his actions he had earned the thanks and congratulations of the country

> for his complete and effectual vindication of that law which is the sole bulwark of public liberty. Thanks to his masterly arrangements and to the ability and devotion with which they were carried out by the force under his control, the determined effort made yesterday to place the metropolis at the mercy of a ruffianly mob was totally and signally defeated.

Leaders of the demonstration now threatened to come better armed to take possession of the square the following Sunday. Warren swiftly enrolled a large number of special constables from the public at large and by the next weekend was able to reinforce the regulars there with 1,500 specials. Some minor rioting took place on the approaches to the square and in one of these incidents a man was trampled by a horse and died of his injuries. The socialist press subsequently became even more abusive towards Warren and capitalised on the incident by hailing the dead man a victim of police brutality, lauding him as 'The Martyr of Trafalgar Square'.

Warren's actions were soon vindicated: the threat of further disturbances and rioting died away. Orderly meetings continued to be held, not in Trafalgar Square but, with police permission, in Hyde Park. In the New Year honours list for 1888, official recognition and approval of Warren's action came with the conferring of a Knight Commandership of the Bath. In addition to his regimental rank of lieutenant-colonel he was now both GCMG and KCB. In March 1888, he was elected to the Athenaeum, the most intellectually elite of all the London clubs.

At the time of Warren's appointment, concern had been expressed at whether the force had enough senior police officers with the necessary education, experience and rank to fill the higher command posts. As a result of two committees of inquiry, five additional higher command posts were created, all filled by army officers – two were appointed chief constables and three assistant chief constables. Discipline was strengthened by the appointment of more inspectors and sergeants.

From the outset Warren had never considered his tenure as commissioner to be anything other than short term and in March 1888 offered his resignation. He felt that he had achieved all he wanted. He had restored discipline within the force and because of his handling of the demonstrations, in his own words, 'almost for the first time during this century the mob failed in its ascendancy over London and in coercing the government'. Warren was persuaded not to resign although he repeated his request again some months later. There were now other problems to concentrate on, in particular the CID and Warren's worsening relations with its head, Assistant Commissioner James Monro.

At the time of Warren's appointment in 1886, the relationship between Jenkinson at the Home Office, employing his own network of secret agents answerable to him personally, and Monro as Assistant Commissioner CID could not have been worse. The former was constantly thwarting Metropolitan Police actions. The problem was compounded by the fact that in just two years, 1885 and 1886, there had been a total of four home secretaries. Monro complained that ministers were never in office long enough to know just how bad the situation was and Jenkinson took advantage of the situation to continue his interference in the work of the police. By the autumn of 1886 Monro had had enough of the lies and meddling. He began to look for lodgings in Edinburgh with the intention of leaving the police. Faced with this threat, Home Secretary Matthews shook off his lethargy at last. He had a three-hour interview with Monro who told him bluntly that he could no longer work with Jenkinson and declined to have any further dealings with him. The upshot was that in December 1886 Jenkinson was forced to resign and in January 1887 Monro, under protest, replaced him as Head of the Secret Department, now known as Section D, while still retaining his position as Assistant Commissioner CID.

In 1886 the detectives migrated from the building in the centre of the square at Scotland Yard to nos 21 and 22 Whitehall Place, where the Special Branch office was established in the corner building facing Whitehall. The assistant commissioner, the superintendent and their subordinates took possession of the adjoining house.[4] On the ground floor of the house, in a large front room on the right, were the first-class inspectors, with Superintendent Shore in his office behind and the clerks in a little 'den' close by. In the basement were the sergeants. The first floor was occupied by the assistant commissioner at the back and Chief Superintendent Williamson at the front, both rooms communicating. Above them, on the second floor, were the inspectors and accommodation had to be found for the Corresponding Department, under Chief Inspector Butcher, who had several sergeants to assist him as clerks.

Queen Victoria's golden jubilee year, 1887, was threatened by disruption from a Fenian bombing campaign. Monro had specific information that an attempt would be made to bring off a dynamite bombing in jubilee week. He had always tackled dynamite cases on the assumption that prevention was better than cure and, with the help of Littlechild and Williamson, worked hard to disrupt the bombers' plans. His most terrifying moment came on 21 June, at the height of the ceremonies: as the royal procession was making its way to Westminster Abbey for a service of thanksgiving, Monro was told that dynamiters had managed to get explosives into the abbey's vaults. With the procession already on its way and the abbey packed with royalty and dignitaries, the easy way out of the dilemma would have been for Monro to pass the intelligence on to Warren and get him to make the decision about how to proceed. Instead, Monro took responsibility himself. His reasoning was that he thought Warren 'was just the man to have injudiciously, in some way or other, caused the very panic which' Monro was anxious to avoid. In the circumstances, all Monro could do was pray and being a religious man, that is exactly what he did. He was never again to feel such relief as when the ceremony was over and Queen Victoria safely returned to her palace.

Monro's appointment as head of Section D was always bound to cause problems with Warren who was working to centralise control. As head of Section D, Monro answered directly to the home secretary, completely bypassing the commissioner. As assistant commissioner CID, the reverse was true: Monro was directly answerable to Warren. Quite justifiably, Warren objected to the fact that when acting in his capacity as head of Section D, Monro did not have to inform him of his plans and could use police manpower in ways of which the commissioner might not approve. For example, Warren never knew how many policemen were guarding public buildings or ministers' houses, and when he tried to reduce their numbers on the grounds of cost, he was either thwarted by Monro or overruled by the Home Office. This happened in December 1887 when Monro successfully resisted the commissioner's plans to reduce the number of policemen guarding public buildings from 320 to 150. Warren argued that the men could be redeployed because the threat of a Fenian bombing campaign had abated; Monro disagreed. In April 1888 Warren again failed to reduce Monro's manpower levels and this may have prompted him to complain the same month to the home secretary. He said the special relationship he had with his assistant commissioner 'was eating into the heart of the Police Force, having a system under which the Assistant Commissioner can go direct to the Secretary of State without reference to the Commissioner'. He suggested they revert to the arrangement as it had been in Jenkinson's time when the two responsibilities were shared. A telling point in favour of this suggestion was Monro's complaint that he was being overworked, and yet at the same time he was unwilling to risk any dilution of control over the CID or Section D by sharing them.

The year's events had taken their toll on Monro and Williamson. The latter broke under the strain, 'suffering from debility and fainting attacks', and was given three months' sick leave from February 1888. In Williamson's absence Warren agreed that an assistant chief constable should be temporarily appointed to assist Monro with the duties of the CID. Monro already had a nominee in mind, Melville Leslie Macnaghten, aged 35, an old India man like Monro himself. The two men had met when Monro was Inspector-General of Bengal Police and Macnaghten was manager of his father's tea plantations. As Monro explained to Warren, he had been impressed by the way Macnaghten handled the natives. The fact that Macnaghten had neither police nor military experience (a similar case to Henry Smith) seems to have been a complete irrelevance to Monro but it was hardly reassuring to Warren who wanted to appoint someone with more skills. Nor did Monro's candidate comply with the 1886 committee's recommendation that a rank at the level of assistant chief constable should be filled by someone from the army or navy. So confident had Monro been, however, that Macnaghten would get the post, he had virtually guaranteed it to him. To Monro's fury, Warren found out and revealed to the Home Office that Macnaghten had provoked an incident in India in which he had been attacked and worsted by the natives; he said he thought the appointment unwise. For once the Home Office agreed with him and Macnaghten's instatement was duly cancelled.

The squabble between Warren and Monro now became more bitter. Warren claimed that Monro's divided duties were endangering the capital's safety, and Monro that Warren's constant interference reduced the efficiency of the CID. Monro, because of his previous detective experience, had a champion in the *Pall Mall Gazette* under its crusading editor W.T. Stead. Initially Stead had welcomed Warren's appointment but now, after his handling of demonstrations, the editor saw him only as a 'soldier in jackboots', trampling on the rights and liberties of the people of London. Warren was put on the defensive by the *Gazette*'s attacks. Senior officers were regularly branded by the *Gazette* as 'dodos' and as 'an assortment of living antiquities'. Later, in an article he wrote for *Murray's Magazine* (November 1888), he rebutted the charges that by his policies policemen were being turned into soldiers; as far as drilling was concerned, he said, this amounted to only 6 hours per annum and in 1886 and 1887 had been almost entirely given up. Stirred up by the daily journals, the public mood, Warren complained in the same article, had 'oscillated violently from period to period, and there seems no inclination for it to settle down to "set fair"'. Beneath all this turmoil, two things remained abundantly clear: Warren resented Monro's independence and his access to the Home Secretary; and Monro resented the commissioner's frequent interference in CID/Section D matters. Someone had to give way and in the end, it was Monro. *The Link*, the newspaper of the Law and Liberty League, would subsequently comment:

> Mr. Monro could think of nothing but dynamite and Invincibles. Sir Charles Warren dreams of the threatened Revolution, and sends his horsemen to smash up political meetings. In the meanwhile the thief and the burglar flourish, and a series of horrid murders are perpetrated with impunity and under the very noses of the police.

Tired of the restrictions Warren was attempting to impose on him, Monro wrote to the home secretary on 11 June 1888 disclaiming all responsibility 'for any unfavourable results to which the system now initiated will lead'. As Bernard Porter points out, 'That let him off the hook for the Whitechapel murders, which started just three months later.'[5] Before then, Monro had resigned as Assistant Commissioner CID and gone instead to the Home Office, still as head of Section D and, with the home secretary's acquiescence, under the title 'Head of Detectives'. Nothing could have been more of a slight to the commissioner's authority. The home secretary was actively encouraging detectives to go behind Warren's back.

Monro no longer had any responsibility for criminal investigations and had become just a bystander in the unfolding drama. However, the killings that were to become collectively known at Scotland Yard as 'The Whitechapel Murders' had already begun some weeks earlier.

FOUR

First Blood

UP to 1887, 6,000 prostitutes a year were arrested in the Metropolitan Police district but then the Miss Cass scandal occurred. Miss Cass had been arrested for disorderly conduct on jubilee night in the area of Oxford Street by PC Bowden Endacott who believed she was soliciting. Miss Cass protested her innocence and a great scandal resulted when it emerged that PC Endacott had been mistaken. The case against her was dismissed, providing more fodder for the anti-police press and resulting in a drop in the number of prostitutes arrested.

The series of crimes that were later to be collectively filed in police records as 'The Whitechapel Murders' began in April 1888 with an attack on a prostitute, Emma Elizabeth Smith, aged 45, in Osborn Street, Whitechapel. Smith was a poverty-stricken, poorly clothed example of the destitute women that wandered the streets of the East End. The only details we have of the attack are those the victim herself gave. In a report dated 16 April 1888 Inspector Reid noted that Emma Elizabeth Smith was a 'common prostitute of low type' living at 18 George Street, Spitalfields. She was 'a supposed widow' with a son and daughter living somewhere in the neighbourhood of Finsbury Park and she had been heard to say that they ought to do something for her. She had lodged at George Street for eighteen months and was in the habit of leaving at 6 or 7 p.m. and returning 'all hours, sometimes very drunk – acted like a mad woman when in that state'. It was common to see her with a black eye and suffering other injuries, which she would explain by saying she had been in a fight or had fallen down.

Smith had been seen at 12.15 a.m. on the 3rd talking to a man with dark clothes and a white scarf in Farrance Street, Limehouse. Between 4 and 5 a.m. she walked into the lodging house in George Street and told the deputy that she had been assaulted and robbed in Osborn Street at its junction with Brick Lane and that her 'private parts had been injured'. Against her will she was made to go to the London Hospital for treatment. They walked her there, a distance of about a half a mile, and did not inform the police. She died at 9 a.m. on the 4th and the police were not informed until the 6th when the coroner's officer notified them that an inquest was to be held the next day.

Osborn Street, Whitechapel. It was in this street that Emma Smith, the first victim in the 'Whitechapel murders' series, was attacked, with fatal results, on 3 April 1888.

The murder was investigated by 42-year-old Edmund Reid, the Local Inspector[1] of H Division. He was the shortest man in the Metropolitan Police force at only 5 feet 6 inches instead of the regulation minimum of 5 feet 8 inches. The chief inspector who interviewed him when he applied to join the force considered that because he came from the boats – he had been a ship's steward on the packet boats from London to Margate – he was healthy and strong and so he waved him through. Reid's hobby was ballooning. He once made a parachute jump from a balloon at 1,000 feet and in 1883 he had been presented with a gold medal for making a record ascent in the *Queen of the Meadow*. He featured in a series of detective novels by the Scottish author Charles Gibbon as Detective Sergeant Dier (Reid's name in reverse). Reid was not always in favour. A cartoon showing 'this clever East End detective' mounted upon a donkey which 'is the noisy, asinine system of Scotland Yard by which more criminals are lost than captured' can hardly have endeared him to his superiors. He was promoted to inspector in 1885 and two years later was transferred from the newly formed J (Bethnal Green) Division to the neighbouring H (Whitechapel) Division. He replaced the highly experienced Local Inspector Frederick George Abberline who was being transferred to the Central Office at Scotland Yard with a view, he said, to bettering his prospects as he was getting on in years.

Of Smith's injuries, Reid noted that the 'partition between front & back passage' had been 'broken not cut', and that the surgeon could not suggest any weapon that might have been used. There was no blood found in Osborn Street but Reid felt this could be explained by 'exam [of her] clothing woollen wrapper saturated in blood took off her shoulders & placed between her legs & soaked in blood'. Reid also noted: 'Clothing in such dirty ragged condition that it was impossible to tell if any part of it had been fresh torn.' The scene of the attack was about 300 yards from 18 George Street. Reid finally noted that on arrival at the lodgings, 'She was sober face bleeding & head cut (fallen down). Helped by another lodger.'

There is little doubt that Smith was the victim of a gang of street hooligans, probably a random attack to steal any money she might have on her as a result of soliciting. Some modern writers have stated that Smith was raped, but there is no evidence to support this contention. It is based on the assumption that 'outrage' was synonymous with 'rape'. Although the word was sometimes used as a euphemism for rape, it was also generally used to describe gross, wanton or violent offences, in this case the thrusting of a blunt object, possibly a stick, into the woman's vagina.

The vicious assault had been presaged by a similar attack in the same location four months earlier. On 8 December 1887 Margaret Hames, a friend of Smith, had received

London Hospital, Whitechapel Road, 1899. (*Guildhall Library, Corporation of London*)

injuries to her face and chest that necessitated an extended stay in the Whitechapel Infirmary. She was not released until 28 December. There is little doubt that the attack on Margaret Hames was the main ingredient for the later press invention of a 'Christmas 1887' Whitechapel murder victim. It is clear from the evidence that the perpetrator of these early attacks was not the villain of the coming autumn – 'Jack the Ripper'.

The murder of Emma Smith did not go unnoticed in the newspapers. *Lloyd's Weekly News* of Sunday 18 April 1888 reported on her inquest:

HORRIBLE MURDER IN WHITECHAPEL

Mr. Wynne Baxter held an inquiry yesterday morning at the London Hospital into the terrible circumstances attending the death of an unfortunate, named Emma E. Smith, who was assaulted in the most brutal manner on Tuesday morning last in the neighbourhood of Osborn-street, Whitechapel, by several men. The first witness, Mary Russell, the deputy-keeper of a lodging-house in George-street, Spitalfields, deposed to the statement made by the deceased on the way to the London Hospital, to which she was taken between four and five o'clock on Tuesday morning. The deceased told her she had been shockingly maltreated by a number of men and robbed of all the money she had. Her face was bleeding, and her ear was cut. She did not describe the men, but said one was a young man of about 19. She also pointed out where the outrage occurred, as they passed the spot, which was near the cocoa factory (Taylor's). The house-surgeon on duty, Dr. Hellier, described the internal injuries which had been caused, and which must have been inflicted by a blunt instrument. It had even penetrated the peritoneum, producing peritonitis, which was undoubtedly the cause of death, in his opinion. The woman appeared to know what she was about, but she had probably had some drink. Her statement to the surgeon as to the circumstances was similar to that already given in evidence. He had made a post-mortem examination, and described the organs as generally normal. He had no doubt that death was caused by the injuries to the perineum, the abdomen and the peritoneum. Great force must have been used. The injuries had set up peritonitis, which resulted in death on the following day after admission. Another woman gave evidence that she had last seen Emma Smith between 12 and one on Tuesday morning, talking to a man in black dress, wearing a white neckerchief. It was near Farrant-street, Burdett-road. She was hurrying away from the neighbourhood as she had herself been struck in the mouth a few minutes before by some young men. She did not believe that the man talking to Smith was one of them. The quarter was a fearfully rough one. Just before Christmas last she had been injured by men under circumstances of a similar nature, and was a fortnight in the infirmary. – Mr. Chief-inspector West, H division, said he had made inquiries of all the constables on duty on the night of the 2nd and 3rd April in the Whitechapel-road, the place indicated. – The jury returned a verdict of 'Wilful murder against some person or persons unknown.'

The only suspects were the unidentified men that Smith mentioned to Mary Russell. Although this murder, early in the year of 1888, was patently unrelated to those that occurred later in the year, it did influence perception of the later crimes and the way in which the early suspect theories were considered. Smith's murder had been truly brutal and rather pointless in view of the fact that she could have had little money in her possession. The forcing of a blunt object into her vagina, however, does indicate that the attack had a sadistic sexual aspect. The incident also serves to illustrate the terrible risks that women ran merely by being on the streets at night, despite the greatly increased number of police on

Martha Tabram, murdered on 7 August 1888 in George Yard
Buildings, Whitechapel. Stabbed 39 times, she lacked the
'trademark' signs of a Ripper killing although many theorists
feel that she was the first Ripper murder victim.

duty and theoretically giving greater
protection. In 1888 about 5,000 officers
were on duty from 10 p.m. to 6 a.m,
alternating in two 4-hour shifts. This
was nearly four times the number on
ordinary beat duty during the day.

The next prostitute murder in Whitechapel attracted little more comment
than the killing of Emma Smith and is
the second included in the police files on
the series. Although there is no consensus of opinion among authorities on
the case, it is probable that this was not a
Ripper killing either. The body of Martha
Tabram (or Turner) was found at 4.50 a.m.
on Tuesday 7 August 1888, on the first-floor
landing of George Yard Buildings, Whitechapel, by John Saunders Reeves, a 23-year-old
waterside labourer of 37 George Yard Buildings. He
discovered Tabram as he was leaving home to seek
work; she was lying on her back in a pool of blood. Reeves
immediately informed the patrolling beat police officer, PC 226H Thomas Barrett, who sent
for a doctor. Another witness, Alfred George Crow, a 24-year-old cab driver of 35 George
Yard Buildings, said he had returned home at 3.30 a.m. and had seen something on the
first-floor landing as he passed but had taken no notice of it because he was accustomed to
seeing vagrants lying about there. It was usual for tramps and others to sleep on common
stairs in the East End but the police believed that he had seen the body. On the day of the
murder Inspector Reid took statements from the residents of George Yard Buildings.
Suspicion attached to none of them and none knew the deceased woman. At 2 a.m.
25-year-old Elizabeth Mahoney and her husband Joseph had passed the spot where the body
was afterwards found but they did not see it.

Dr Timothy Robert Killeen of 68 Brick Lane attended at about 5.30 a.m. and found the
dead woman had received thirty-nine stab wounds to her body. He estimated she had been
dead some 3 hours. The body was well nourished. She was lying on her back, her hands by
her sides and tightly clenched, and her legs apart. Her clothing was turned up as far as the
centre of her body, leaving the lower part of her exposed, which gave PC Barrett the
impression that she was lying in a position for sexual intercourse. Dr Killeen, however, saw
no reason to believe that intercourse had recently taken place. There was a deal of blood
between the legs. At a later post-mortem examination the doctor found that the left lung
had been penetrated in five places and the right lung in two. The heart had been penetrated
in one place, a wound sufficient to cause death. The liver was penetrated in five places, the
spleen in two and the stomach in six. The lower portion of the body was penetrated in one

place, the wound being 3 inches long and 1 inch deep. The doctor felt that not all the wounds had been inflicted with the same weapon. Many might have been made with an ordinary knife but one went through the chest bone and was probably caused by some sort of dagger. Tabram was not immediately identified but she was described as aged about 37, 5 feet 3 inches in height with dark hair and complexion. She was dressed in a green skirt, brown petticoat, long black jacket, brown stockings, side-spring boots and a black bonnet, all of them old.

About 2 o'clock on the morning of the murder PC Barrett was patrolling George Yard and spoke to a private of the Guards at the north end where the street joined Wentworth Street. The soldier told Barrett that he was waiting for his mate who had 'gone away with a girl'. Barrett felt that he would recognise this man if he saw him again and described him as a Grenadier Guard, aged 22 to 26 years, 5 feet 9 or 10 inches in height. The man had a fair complexion, dark hair and a small dark brown moustache turned up at the ends. He wore one good conduct badge but no medals. Barrett's encounter with the soldier took place only 50 yards or so from the scene of the murder and within 30 minutes of the estimated time of Tabram's death, which was about 2.30 a.m. Little wonder that subsequent police inquiries were to focus upon a soldier as the prime suspect.

This view was reinforced on 9 August when a friend of Tabram's, Mary Ann Connelly (alias 'Pearly Poll'), another prostitute, presented herself at Commercial Street police station to volunteer her story. She said that she and Tabram were with two soldiers, one a corporal

Whitechapel High Street, looking east, in the days of Queen Victoria, then as now a busy thoroughfare and at the heart of Jack the Ripper's area of operations. In the background is St Mary's Matfelon church which was bombed by the Luftwaffe in 1940 and finally demolished in 1952.

and the other a private in the Guards, from 10 p.m. until 11.45 p.m. on Monday 6 August, less than 3 hours before the estimated time of the murder. The two couples had been walking about Whitechapel, drinking at several public houses. Tabram's sister-in-law, Ann Morris, stated that she had seen her outside the White Swan in Whitechapel Road at 11 p.m. The couples separated at 11.45, Connelly going off with the corporal and Tabram with the private, 'for immoral purposes'. Connelly and her partner walked up Angel Court while Tabram and her 'client' went off up George Yard. Connelly's was the last sighting of Tabram alive. The evidence from Connelly and Barrett must weigh heavily in favour of the argument for the murderer being a soldier/client, whether it was Tabram's earlier companion or another soldier she had picked up in the interim.

Detective Inspector Edmund Reid took charge of the investigation. On Monday 14 August 1888 the body was formally identified by the woman's estranged husband, Henry Samuel Tabram of 6 River Terrace, East Greenwich. He was a foreman packer at a furniture warehouse. The couple had parted some thirteen years previously. She was, he said, 39 years old and a prostitute. Tabram was also known as Martha Turner because she had been living, on and off, for about twelve years with a carpenter named Henry Turner. She had a history of drunkenness which had led to periods of separation from him. In 1888 Turner was out of regular work and the two of them had been eking a living by hawking small items. Prostitution brought in supplementary earnings for Martha. For the past four months or so they had been lodging at 4 Star Place, Commercial Road, with a Mrs Mary Bousfield who stated that Tabram had left that address, in debt, about six weeks previously. Henry and Martha had separated about three weeks before her murder.

Reid's inquiries began with an attempt to identify the Guardsman seen by PC Barrett. Later on the morning of 7 August Reid went with Barrett to the Tower of London and saw the sergeant major. The constable was conducted to the guardroom where he saw several prisoners but was unable to identify his man because, he said, they were not dressed. Reid arranged for a parade of all privates and corporals who were on leave on the night of the murder and this was conducted on 8 August. Reid told Barrett to be careful because many were watching him and it was important to pick out the correct man and no other. Barrett waited in the sergeants' mess while the parade was formed. When the men were ready, he was brought out and directed by Reid to walk along the line. He was to touch the man he had seen in George Yard if he was present.

George Yard Buildings.

Reid and the officers walked away. Barrett passed along the rank from left to right, stopped in the middle, stepped up to a private who was wearing medals and touched him. Reid told Barrett to be certain he had the right man, so Barrett returned to the rank and passed along it again. To Reid's consternation Barrett then picked out a different man, about six or seven away from the first. Reid asked Barrett to account for his actions and the officer replied that the man he had seen in George Yard had no medals while the first one picked out had. One can only assume that in all other respects this soldier fitted Barrett's rather detailed description of the man he saw in George Yard. Reid directed him to stand away.

The two men picked out by the constable were taken to the orderly room and the rest were dismissed. Barrett said he had made a mistake in pointing out the man with medals and the soldier was allowed to go without leaving his name. The second gave his name as John Leary. Leary was asked by Reid to account for his movements on the night of the murder and the soldier stated that he and Private Law had gone to Brixton that night and stayed there until the pubs closed. At that point he missed Law and looked for him. Unable to find him, he made off to Battersea, Chelsea and then along Charing Cross and into the Strand, where he met Law about 4.30 a.m. They walked together to Billingsgate where they had a drink before returning to barracks at 6 a.m. Private Law, who was not allowed to communicate with Leary, was sent for and was also questioned about his movements. He made a statement that agreed, in every particular, with Leary's. However, if there had been anything untoward in their actions on the night of the murder they could easily have already agreed on the story they were going to tell. Both were unable to give the name of anyone who could confirm their version of events. Reid felt certain that PC Barrett had 'made a great mistake' and the two soldiers were allowed to leave the room. It is a little surprising that Leary and Law were peremptorily dismissed on the strength of their own uncorroborated story, although Barrett's uncertainty would certainly account for this.

On 9 August Reid was at the Tower when a Corporal Benjiman, to whom suspicion had attached because he had been absent without leave since the 6th, returned. Reid took charge of Benjimin's clothing and bayonet and asked him to account for his time. He stated that he had been staying with his father who was the landlord of the Canbury Hotel at Kingston upon Thames. Enquiries confirmed the man's story and no marks of blood were found on his clothing and bayonet.

At 11 a.m. on 11 August a parade of soldiers was arranged at the Tower for Mary Ann Connelly to see if she could identify the two soldiers she and Tabram had been with, but Connelly could not be found. She was finally traced by Sergeant Caunter on the 12th and the identification parade was rearranged for the next day. Scanning the line-up the woman said, 'They are not here, they had white bands round their caps.' This embellishment indicated that the men were members of the Coldstream Guards and not the Scots Guards. A parade of Coldstream Guards was then arranged at Wellington Barracks and Connelly selected two privates as the men she and Tabram had been with. She was 'quite positive' that they were the men, one named George, whom she had been with, and the other, Skipper, was Tabram's partner. Both men 'proved an alibi and the identification failed'.

The final sitting of the inquest on Tabram's death was held at the Working Lads' Institute, Whitechapel Road, at about 1.30 p.m. on Thursday 23 August before the Deputy Coroner, George Collier. Obviously unhappy with Connelly's evidence, Inspector Reid asked that she might be cautioned. The coroner explained to Connelly that she need not answer any question but that what she did say would be taken down and could be used in evidence against her on a future occasion. She then stated that she had left the corporal at the corner of George Yard about 5 or 10 minutes past 12 and then went off along Commercial Street

Working Lads' Institute,
Whitechapel Road, the scene of
inquests held by Coroner Wynne
Baxter, 1890. (*Guildhall Library,
Corporation of London*)

towards Whitechapel. She had heard no screams and was first informed of the murder on the Tuesday.

Reid then asked her, 'Did you threaten to drown yourself since this occurrence.' She replied, 'Yes, but only in a lark. I went to my cousin's and stayed there for two days. My cousin lives in Fuller's Court, Drury Lane.' Reid felt that after learning of Tabram's murder Connelly had 'kept out of the way purposely' and it was only by searching that the police found her.

In his closing remarks, Reid informed the court that many people had come forward and made statements which, 'when threshed out, ended unsatisfactorily, and up to the present the police have been unable to secure the guilty party or parties.' The matter of identification, with regard to both PC Barrett and Connelly, was very unsatisfactory and unresolved. The expected verdict of wilful murder by person or persons unknown was returned. Reid ended his report by informing the court that 'careful inquiries are still being made with a view to obtain information regarding the case'. The shakiness of PC Barrett's evidence and Connelly's apparent prevarication had both played their part in frustrating Reid's progress. The murder of Martha Tabram, like that of Emma Smith, remained unsolved.

— FIVE —

Ghastly Crimes Committed by a Maniac?

AT about 3.40 a.m. on Friday 31 August 1888 a carman (horse-cart driver) named Charles Cross of 22 Doveton Street, Cambridge Heath Road, Bethnal Green, was walking to work in a westerly direction along Buck's Row, Whitechapel. This section of the street was narrow and ill-lit. Not far from a board school situated at a point where Buck's Row widened out, Cross saw something lying on the opposite, south, side of the street. It lay at a stable entrance at the end of a row of terraced houses. At first Cross thought it was a tarpaulin but he went to investigate. By the time he reached the middle of the road he could

see that it was the body of a woman. At this moment he was aware of someone approaching from the same direction he had walked. It was another carman, Robert Paul, of 30 Foster Street, Bethnal Green. Cross touched him on the shoulder and said, 'Come and look over here, there's a woman lying on the pavement.'

The woman was on her back with her skirts raised almost to her abdomen. Cross felt her hands, which were cold and limp. 'I believe she's dead,' he said. Paul was not so sure: he also found her face and hands to be cold and initially he could not detect breathing, but he thought there was slight movement when he touched her breast. He said that he believed she was breathing, although barely, and suggested propping her up. Cross demurred. In the gloom, both failed to

Buck's Row, Whitechapel, scene of the murder of Mary Ann Nichols on 31 August 1888.

Buck's Row, Whitechapel. Scene of murder of Mary Ann Nichols on 31 August 1888. The body was lying on the footpath at the stable, now the garage-entrance.

notice that the woman's throat had been cut. The men were keen to get to work and Paul said he would tell a policeman what they had found. They pulled the woman's skirt down and left the scene.

At this time PC 55H Jonas Mizen was engaged in 'knocking-up'[1] in the area of Hanbury Street at its junction with Baker's Row. Cross and Paul appeared from the direction of Buck's Row and told Mizen about the woman's body. Cross remarked, 'She looks to me to be either dead or drunk, but for my part I think she is dead.'

Meanwhile, beat officer PC 97J John Neil (aged 38, with thirteen years' police service) had found the woman. At 3.45 a.m. he had been patrolling Buck's Row in an easterly direction. There was a street lamp shining at the end of the row but it was otherwise in darkness. The woman was lying along the line of the footpath outside the gates with her head towards the east and her left hand touching the gate. With the aid of his lamp Neil saw that there was blood oozing from a wound in the woman's throat. Her arm was warm above the joint and her eyes were wide open. Her bonnet was off her head and lying by her side, close to her left hand. Neil heard a fellow officer, PC 96J Thain, in Brady Street, at the eastern end of Buck's Row, and flashed his bull's-eye lantern at him. Thain hurried to join him. Thain was later to state that he passed that end of Buck's Row every 30 minutes and that he had noticed nothing there at 3.15 a.m. Thain went off to inform a doctor, Rees Ralph Llewellyn, and PC Mizen approached from Baker's Row direction. Neil sent him for an ambulance. On the opposite side of the road to the body was Essex Wharf where Neil raised the manager,

THE WHITECHAPEL MYSTERY.

The front page of the *Penny Illustrated Paper* of 8 September 1888 featured the Nichols murder in Buck's Row.

Walter Purkis. He and his wife had seen and heard nothing. Mrs Green who lived at New Cottage, the house immediately to the eastern side of the gateway where the body was found, had noticed nothing either.

Dr Llewellyn attended, saw the wounds to the throat and pronounced death. He found that although her lower arms and hands were cold, the woman's body and legs were still warm. He thought that she had not been dead for more than 30 minutes. Three horse slaughterers from a nearby slaughterhouse, Harrison, Barber & Co., in Winthrop Street had arrived at the scene along with other early-morning passers-by. The three slaughterers, Henry Tomkins, James Mumford and Charles Britton, had been working overnight until 4.20 a.m. and went to see the body after PC Thain told them about it when he called at their premises to collect the cape he had left there.[2] Another night-worker employed nearby was Patrick Mulshaw, the Board of Works' nightwatchman at the sewage works in Winthrop Street, at the rear of the Working Lads' Institute. He, too, went to view the body. He had neither seen nor heard anything suspicious. The doctor instructed the police to remove the body to the mortuary. Initially there was only a small pool of blood visible where the woman was lying, about half a pint, but when the body was moved the officers noted a patch of congealed blood about 6 inches in diameter. More had run towards the gutter, apparently from the throat wounds. PC Thain was at the scene when the blood was washed away and stated that there was a large 'mass of congealed blood' where she had been lying. The woman's clothing had absorbed quite a lot more blood at the back, thus creating the initial appearance of minimal blood loss. This led to some unfounded speculation that the woman was killed elsewhere and deposited at that spot. There was no evidence to support such an idea.

The duty inspector from Bethnal Green station, John Spratling, aged 48, arrived and was shown the spot by PC Thain. The inspector then went to the mortuary. This was a shed or 'deadhouse' in the Pavilion Yard, off Old Montague Street, and belonged to the workhouse – Whitechapel's only mortuary had been demolished. The deadhouse was locked up but the body was on a hand-pushed ambulance in the yard. Spratling took notes about the woman and between 5 and 5.20 a.m. the mortuary-keeper, Robert Mann, arrived. He unlocked the premises and the body was wheeled in. Spratling made a further examination of the body and lifted the woman's clothing. He then discovered that her abdomen had been crudely 'ripped' open to the sternum and the intestines were exposed. Dr Llewellyn was called to

Brady Street, Whitechapel, off the end of Buck's Row, a dreary Victorian scene of smoky terraced dwellings. (*Guildhall Library, Corporation of London*)

In Victorian times bodies were often wheeled to the mortuary, if it was nearby, on hand-guided carriages such as this, which were referred to as ambulances.

Dr. Llewellyn.

Dr Rees Ralph Llewellyn, the local doctor who pronounced death at the scene of the Nichols murder.

attend and made a fuller examination of the body. *Reynolds' Newspaper*, playing up the sensational nature of the case, quoted the doctor as saying, 'She was ripped open just as you see a dead calf at the butcher's.'

Local Inspector Joseph Helson, aged 43, took initial charge of the inquiry. He was informed of the murder at 6.45 a.m. and went to the mortuary where he saw the body which was still dressed. He witnessed the removal of the clothing, noting there was no bruising on the arms to indicate that a struggle had taken place. The abdominal wounds were visible with the woman's stays still on. A search of nearby railway property was carried out by PC Thain, and later by Inspector Spratling with Detective Sergeant George Godley.[3]

The doctor's final examination of the body revealed that the woman's throat had been slashed from left to right in two distinct cuts and the windpipe, gullet and spinal cord were severed. There was a small bruise, possibly caused by a thumb, on the right lower jaw, and another, circular, one on the left cheek, possibly caused by the pressure of fingers. The abdomen had been cut open from the centre of the bottom of the ribs along the right side and under the pelvis to the left of the stomach, where the wound was jagged and the omentum, or coating of the stomach, was cut in several places. There were two small stabs on her private parts. The doctor's early speculation that the wounds had been inflicted by a 'left-handed person' led to a widespread, but probably mistaken, belief that this was a fact, despite Llewellyn's later statement that he now doubted this was the case. Death would have been almost instantaneous.

The doctor performed a full autopsy on the morning of Saturday 1 September but his report has not survived. All we are left with is the material that appeared in police reports and in newspaper coverage of the inquest testimony. Of the two throat wounds, one was about 4 inches long, beginning at the left side of the neck immediately below the ear and running about 1 inch below the jaw. The second was about 8 inches long and ran right around the throat from the left side, about 1 inch in front of the first. It followed a line about 1 inch below the other wound and ended about 3 inches below the right jaw. The cut had severed both carotid arteries and all the tissues down to the vertebrae. The knife, the doctor thought, must have been 'strong-bladed . . . moderately sharp' and was 'used with great violence'. Of the cuts to the lower abdomen, 2 or 3 inches from the left side was a long, very deep and jagged wound which had cut through the tissues. Several incisions ran across the abdomen and on the right side were three or four similar cuts running

Mary Ann Nichols, murdered in Buck's Row,
Whitechapel, on 31 August 1888, is generally regarded
as the first definitive Ripper victim.

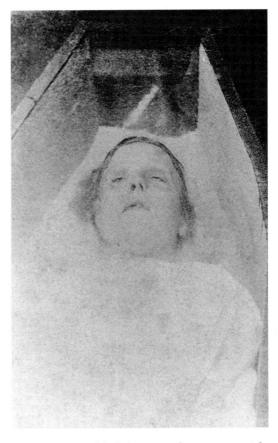

downwards. There were also two small stabs
on the private parts. The doctor felt the
abdominal wounds had been inflicted with a
knife used violently and downwards. All the
injuries appeared to have been delivered with
the same weapon. When questioned at the
inquest Llewellyn felt that the murderer 'must
have had some rough anatomical knowledge,
for he had attacked all the vital parts'. The
murder, in his opinion, could have been
executed in just 4 or 5 minutes.

The woman, sill unidentified at the time of
the doctor's examination, had a small scar on
her forehead and three missing teeth, one on
the front upper and two on the left lower jaw.
She was not more than 5 feet 2 or 3 inches
tall, middle-aged, with dark brown hair that
was turning grey and a dark complexion. Her
face was bruised and much discoloured. Her
possessions amounted to a comb, a piece of
mirror and a white handkerchief. She was wearing a worn, reddish-brown ulster coat with
seven large brass buttons, an apparently new brown linsey frock, a white chest flannel (the
brassiere of the day), two petticoats (one of grey wool the other flannel), a pair of brown
stays, a pair of black ribbed woollen stockings, a pair of men's side-spring (elasticated) boots
cut on the uppers and with steel tips on the heels, and a black straw bonnet trimmed with
black velvet. She was quickly identified as the news of the murder gained circulation. She
had been living in a common lodging house at 18 Thrawl Street and a friend from there,
Ellen Holland, identified the body as that of 'Polly'. Proper identification ensued when the
mark of Lambeth Workhouse, Prince's Road, was found on her petticoats. Inquiries there
located a Mary Ann Monk who attended the mortuary and gave the victim's name as Mary
Ann Nichols. Soon her estranged husband, William Nichols, a printer's machinist, and her
father, Edward Walker, were found. They identified the body on Saturday 1 September. She
had been murdered only five days after her forty-third birthday.

Mary Ann Nichols was another typical example of the casual prostitute who frequented
the streets of the East End. Like so many of her kind, her sad condition could be largely
attributed to the 'demon' drink. She was the daughter of Edward Walker, a locksmith, and
his wife Caroline, and was born in Dean Street, off Fetter Lane, on 26 August 1845. On
16 January 1864 she married William Nichols. The couple had five children born between
1866 and 1879 but the marriage ended with some acrimony in 1880. William Nichols and
Edward Walker did not get along. Walker stated at the inquest that the breakdown of the
marriage was a result of William Nichols having an affair with the nurse who attended his
wife in her last confinement. Nichols denied this and said that Polly had deserted him
several times, leaving him with the children. There seems to be little doubt that too much

From a series of sketches of a common lodging house in Spitalfields, *Illustrated London News*, 22 September 1888. This image shows a professional beggar.

drink and a predilection for raising money by prostitution largely contributed to her downfall. She had been living in workhouses, common lodging houses and on the streets since her fall from grace.

On the afternoon of Saturday 1 September, Coroner Wynne E. Baxter, a 44-year-old solicitor, opened his inquiry at the Working Lads' Institute, Whitechapel Road. According to the *Observer* he was a striking figure in 'a pair of white-and-black checked trousers, a dazzling white waist-coat, a crimson scarf, and a dark coat'. Nichol's husband looked 'very gentlemanly' in a black coat and tall silk hat, while her father was 'an old grey-bearded and grey-headed man . . . with head lowered and hands behind his back'. Detective Inspector Abberline and other officers watched the proceedings on behalf of the police, just as they were to do in subsequent inquests.

Unsolved murder cases, especially when there is no apparent suspect, quickly become the object of speculation and theory. The *East London Advertiser* of Saturday 8 September 1888 reported the funeral of Mary Ann Nichols before news of the discovery of the body of Annie Chapman, that same morning, had broken. The article contained the inevitable speculation about the identity of Nichols' murderer:

Of course, there are many rumours as to the action of the police. It is stated, though not authoritatively, that the detectives are carefully watching a number of persons in the vicinity, but that no arrests will be made until there is further substantial evidence, unless the suspected persons attempt to leave the district. Inquiries have also been made, but apparently without result, amongst the employees of a slaughterhouse close at hand. Nothing, however, seems to have come of it. A mysterious individual in the character of a seaman has also been dragged into the affair, but with what foundation in fact has not yet transpired. All that can safely be said is that the public may rest assured that everything is being done by the police that can possibly be done to clear up this alarming incident.

The idea that the killer might be a slaughterman or a seaman had quickly entered the public arena. However, the early speculation that this was a gang murder also continued:

One point of satisfaction is to notice the energetic way in which the coroner, Mr. Wynne E. Baxter, has thrown himself into the inquiry, and until the adjourned inquest is held it will be impossible to say exactly what steps the police have taken to unravel the mystery.

The officers engaged in the investigation are Inspector Abberline, Inspector Helson, Inspector Spratling, Detective Sergeant Enright, and numerous other minor officials. It has been asserted that a clue has been obtained, but in what direction the officers are not permitted to make the slightest allusion, as justice might be frustrated. There is a strong belief current that there is more than one person concerned in the outrage, and this opinion is strengthened by the report of another attempted outrage, which is alleged to have occurred on Saturday night last.

A woman, it is stated, was leaving the Foresters' Music Hall, Cambridge-road, where she had been spending the evening with a sea-captain, when she was accosted by a well-dressed man, who requested her to walk a short distance with him, as he wanted to meet a friend. They had reached a point near the scene of the murder of the woman Nicholls [sic], when the man violently seized her by the throat and dragged her down a court. He was immediately joined by a gang of bullies, who stripped the unfortunate woman of necklace, ear-rings, and brooch. Her purse was also taken, and she was brutally assaulted. Upon her attempting to shout for aid one of the gang laid a large knife across her throat, remarking, 'We will serve you as we did the others.' She was, however, eventually released. The police have been informed, and are prosecuting inquiries into the matter, it being regarded as a probable clue to the previous tragedies. There is, however, a belief that this last sensational story has been exaggerated, though it is not altogether denied that something of the kind did take place.

This story, whatever its degree of accuracy, clearly shows the prevalent belief that gangs were at work. As we have seen, this was the case in the murder of Emma Smith some four months previously.

Police activity was being monitored by the press and suggestions on how to investigate the murders were not lacking. The *East London Advertiser*'s piece concluded:

Some of the jurymen engaged on the case announce their intention of impressing upon the Scotland-yard authorities the necessity of further precautions being taken at the common lodging houses in the metropolis, for the purpose of ascertaining the names and, if possible, addresses of every lodger (male and female) who enters, together with the time of entry. This plan, it is thought, will greatly help the police in their work of tracing and detecting crime. In the meantime, the authorities are extremely reticent and guarded in all the information they tender, and most of the particulars and information has to be obtained from other sources.

Upon inquiring at Bethnal Green Police Station, just before going to press, our representative was informed that up to the present no arrests have been made, and also that the investigation of the matter has been now transferred entirely to the detective force. The uniform constables therefore now have nothing to do with the solution of the mystery.

The inquest jury returned the expected verdict of wilful murder against person or persons unknown. The 'autumn of terror' had begun on the same day that James Monro, following his resignation six days before and taking advantage of Warren's absence on holiday, officially left his post as head of the CID. His replacement was Robert Anderson whom Monro had apparently groomed for the position. Anderson now emerged from the wings, where he had been confined as secretary to the Prison Commissioners. Rumours had been circulating in the CID about who was to succeed Monro. For some reason, the matter was kept secret and Anderson was told not to make his appointment known until the official date of Monro's resignation, 31 August. Anderson had been in the habit of frequenting Monro's rooms because they were working together on political crime matters; but when he did so now, Warren, who had similarly been sworn to secrecy, took advantage of his visits to see him. Anderson's relationship with Warren, as he said in his autobiography, was always 'easy and pleasant'. CID officers immediately assumed from Warren's visits that the Commissioner was spying on Anderson because he was Monro's friend. According to Anderson, 'the indignation felt by the officers was great, and I had some difficulty in preventing Chief Superintendent Williamson from sending in his resignation'.

Monro had resigned on 25 August, his last official day in post was the 31st, but the name of his successor had to be kept secret, possibly until it had been ratified by the Home Secretary, and all sorts of rumours were in circulation as to his replacement. Warren was away and could do nothing to quell the speculation. Anderson succeeded Monro on

Sir Robert Anderson.

1 September but was already in contact with Warren, who was in France, complaining about his bad health. Warren wrote to him on 28 August saying that he would be back in London about 7 September and he saw no reason why Anderson should not go away on leave a day or two after, for a month if necessary, if that would put his throat right. Warren's major concern, as his letter[4] makes clear, was the possibility of a recurrence of the 1887 demonstrations. The seasonal lay-offs took place in October and Warren felt the police could expect a good deal of trouble that winter. Other key figures were also away at this time; Superintendent Charles Cutbush of the Executive Branch CO was granted 29 days leave of absence from 25 August, Superintendent Arnold was absent from 2 to 30 September, putting Acting Superintendent West in charge of his Whitechapel Division. Anderson went on sick leave to Switzerland on Friday 7 September and did not return to England until 6 October. It must be emphasised that Anderson was not even in the country when the next three murders generally recognised as having been committed by the Ripper took place. However, on his return he was not only tasked with taking control of the investigation, but also had everyday CID matters to consider and a new job to settle into.

Another problem troubling Anderson at this time was the pending Parnell Commission hearings and the subsequent action against *The Times* newspaper, which had published letters allegedly written by the Irish MP Charles Stewart Parnell, and reputedly proving his involvement in Fenian activities. However, the correspondence had been forged by a disreputable Irish journalist and enemy of Parnell, Richard Piggott. Anderson's trusted Fenian informant Henri Le Caron (real name Thomas Billis Beach) had stated his intention to come to England and 'blow his cover' to give evidence at the inquiry, an idea that horrified Anderson. Anderson was uncomfortably aware that he himself would be called to give evidence. He had acted less than properly in anonymously writing a series of three articles in *The Times* in May and June 1887 called 'Parnellism and Crime: Behind the Scenes in America'. He had also, in his official capacity, personally retained letters from Le Caron and these he later returned to the spy, who gave evidence to support *The Times*' cause. In the event, the possibility that Anderson might appear before the Special Commission was discussed but he was never called. In giving his evidence Le Caron used correspondence returned to him by Anderson, at Anderson's home address, with 'hundreds' of other documents. Anderson did this without telling his superiors and caused great consternation and embarrassment for Home Secretary Matthews. Sir William Harcourt was particularly outspoken about it in the House of Commons, saying that Matthews had no control over his subordinates who were 'slapping him in the face'. Harcourt left no doubt that had he still been home secretary, Anderson would have been looking for a new job. In a speech at a Liberal meeting on 19 March 1889 Harcourt said, 'I confess, if there was anything wanting to convince people where the charge of the police ought to be it is such a miscarriage of the police under the conduct of the Crown. Why, who is ever to trust them? They have not been very successful in their criminal investigations in Whitechapel and elsewhere. How can you trust people who act in this manner?' Anderson, smarting under the criticism, wrote a letter to *The Times* excusing his actions and stating he was merely handing Le Caron's own correspondence back to him. This resulted in further comment in the House and Matthews was asked if Anderson had permission to write this letter to *The Times*, which, of course, he didn't.

—— **SIX** ——

Horror upon Horror

REGARDED by many researchers as the second 'Jack the Ripper' killing, the murder of Annie Chapman took place in the backyard of 29 Hanbury Street, Spitalfields, on the morning of Saturday 8 September 1888. Chapman was another casual prostitute who was always struggling to raise cash. Her situation was made worse by ill-health. Her nickname was 'Dark Annie' and her alias was shown in police records as Annie Siffey, or Sivvey, because she lived with a sieve-maker for a time. She was 47 years of age and 5 feet tall with a fair complexion, dark brown wavy hair and a large thick nose. Her body was clothed in a black figured jacket, brown bodice, black skirt and lace boots, all of them old and dirty. She was seriously, probably terminally, ill with lung disease and had recently been given some pills for her condition.

She married John Chapman, a coachman, on 1 May 1869, and after living at various addresses in London the couple had moved to Windsor by 1881. They had three children born between 1870 and 1881. Annie led a sad and unlucky life: her son was a cripple and a daughter died of meningitis when she was only 12. She and her husband were both alcoholics and the couple separated in about 1880 as a result of the drink and her 'immoral ways'. In 1886 Annie was lodging at 30 Dorset Street with the man who made sieves. The same year her estranged husband died at Windsor as a result of his heavy drinking; he was only 44 years old. The weekly allowance of 10 shillings that Annie had been receiving from him thus ended, plunging her into a financial crisis. By 1888 her relationship with the sieve-maker was over. She had a man-friend named Ted Stanley, known as 'the pensioner', whom she saw occasionally. He gave evidence at the inquest but denied any close relationship with her.

On the night of her murder Annie was again on the streets, desperately trying to raise a few pennies to pay for a bed. She had been in the kitchen of her common lodging house, Crossingham's, at 35 Dorset Street in the early hours. The deputy, Timothy Donovan, said she was a quiet woman who gave no trouble. That night she had no money. The nightwatchman, John Evans, saw her leave about 1.45 a.m. after he asked if she could pay for a bed. She said she would not be long before she got it and went off in the direction of

Annie Chapman and her husband John, a photograph taken around the time of their wedding. (© Neal Shelden)

Annie Chapman, murdered at the rear of 29 Hanbury Street, Spitalfields, on 8 September 1888, is generally regarded as the second Ripper victim.

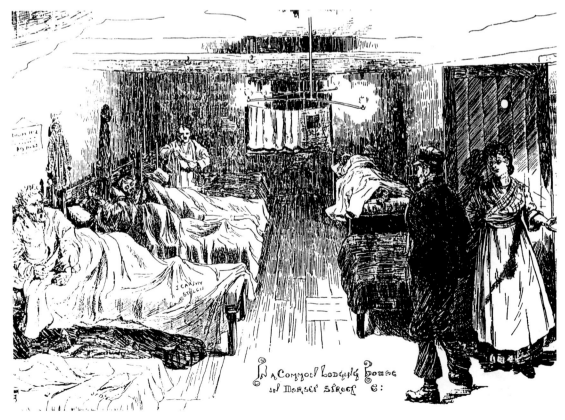

A typical scene in a common lodging house in Dorset Street at the time of the murders.

Brushfield Street. He reported that she had been eating baked potatoes and was 'the worse for drink'. There are no known further sightings of her until around the time of her murder. Her movements remain a mystery but she may merely have been sleeping rough somewhere.

The Victorian press did not spare the feelings of its readers when describing the horrific scene of the murder:

The thrill of mingled indigestion and terror which passed over the whole of the metropolis at the terrible details attending the murder of the woman Nicholls [*sic*] in Buck's-row had scarcely had time to shape, when last Saturday morning – just about a week after the Buck's-row occurrence – the whole of London was again sent almost crazy by the news of still another tragedy having been enacted, this time in Hanbury-street. The particulars of the murder as they became public were far more horrible even than those connected with the murder of Polly Nicholls. John Davis, who lives at 29, Hanbury-street – a house of three floors, the front room on the ground floor of which is used as a cat's meat shop,[1] while a notice board above the doorway which leads into the yard, tells in straggling white letters that Mrs. A Richardson, a rough packing-case maker, lives there – happened at about six o'clock in the morning to go into the back yard. The yard is reached by three stone steps leading from the passage, the steps having on their left the fence separating the yard from the next, and this fence the door – which opens outwardly shutting off the passage from the back yard – nearly touches when open. So soon as he had arrived at the top of the first step, Davis saw lying between the steps and the fence – a space of some three feet [*sic*] a sight which froze his blood with horror.

A woman lay there with her clothes so disarranged as to expose her knees drawn up as if in agony, together with the lower portion of the abdomen, which had been mutilated in a frightful manner, the intestines, with the viscera and the heart [*sic*], having been literally torn out of the mangled body and laid by her side. The head of the woman was turned back, revealing an enormous gash, so broad and so deep as almost to have severed the connection with the body. The face – that of a woman of about forty – was deadly white, and the hair, which was wavy brown, was slightly disarranged. Portions of the flesh on the lower part of the body hung in shreds, the dress was

+ WHERE THE BODY
LAY

: THE SCENE OF
THE MURDER

This excellent contemporary sketch from *Pictorial News*, Saturday 15 September 1888, of the backyard of 29 Hanbury Street gives a good idea of the layout. The open lean-to of the cellar access door and the dividing fence between nos 29 and 27 can easily be seen.

The murder scene at the rear of 29 Hanbury Street.

bespattered with blood – as, indeed, was a portion of the fencing, as if it had received a spurt from a severed artery – beside the woman two pools of blood had formed, and upon her shoulders were slashes of blood and some of the viscera. Her head was lying towards the house, and her feet towards the end of the yard.[2]

Little wonder that the news of each murder resulted in great public fear, morbid interest and speculation.

The first police officer on the scene was 38-year-old Divisional Inspector Joseph Luniss Chandler,[3] H Division, 'a tall, dark man', who was informed of the murder in Commercial Street at 6.10 a.m. and went straight to the scene. Two rings, a wedding ring and a keeper, both of cheap brass, appeared to have been pulled from Chapman's hand and were never found, despite inquiries at pawnbrokers and other establishments. Much has been made of items found near the feet of the body, which included a small piece of coarse muslin, a small, toothed comb, and a pocket comb in a paper case. These, the doctor felt, had been 'placed there in order – that is to say arranged there'. The press later added farthings to the list but they do not appear in any of the police reports. Two pills were also found with the body. They were in a piece of envelope bearing the handwritten letter 'M' and lower down 'Sp', as well as the figure '2'. The envelope had the stamp of the Sussex Regiment. Initially it was treated as a clue and investigated but William Stevens of 35 Dorset Street (Chapman's lodgings) later confirmed that Annie had picked it up from the kitchen floor near the fireplace after her pill box fell to pieces. A leather apron discovered near a tap in the yard was found to belong to John Richardson, who worked there for his mother. She had washed it and left it there. Talk of this object initially fuelled stories in the press of a suspect nicknamed 'Leather Apron'.

Chief Inspector Donald Sutherland Swanson,[4] who had overall charge of the investigation and of collating documentation, recorded a timetable for the murder of Annie Chapman on which the following summary is based. His report is dated 19 October 1888.

REMOVING THE BODY

Police removing the body of Annie Chapman from 29 Hanbury Street. (Pictorial News, *Saturday 15 September 1888*)

- At 2 a.m. Chapman was last seen alive by Donovan, the deputy of the lodging house at 35 Dorset Street. She was under the influence of drink and could not pay for a bed. She left the house in order to earn money.
- At 4.45 a.m. John Richardson of 2 John Street, Spitalfields, son of Amelia Richardson who also lived in the house, went to sit on the steps leading to the backyard to cut a piece of leather off his boot, but he did not see the body of the woman.
- At 5.25 a.m. Albert Cadosch of 27 Hanbury Street, next door on the west side, went into the yard at the rear of that address. This area was separated from the yard at no. 29 by a wooden fence about 5 feet high. Cadosch heard people talking, apparently in the yard of no. 29, but the only word he could make out was 'No'. He went back into the house.
- At 5.28 a.m. Cadosch went outside again and heard a noise 'as of something falling against the fence' at no. 29. However, he took no notice.
- At 5.30 a.m. Mrs Elizabeth Long[5] saw a man and a woman talking near to 29 Hanbury Street. She heard the man say, 'Will you?' and the woman replied, 'Yes.' Mrs Long walked on. She saw only the back of the man and would not recognise

him again, she said. He was 'apparently over 40 years of age'. He appeared to be a little taller than the woman and, in Mrs Long's opinion, looked like a foreigner, although she did not see his face. She thought he was wearing a dark coat.

- At 6 a.m. Chapman's body was discovered in the backyard of no. 29 by John Davis, a resident of that address.
- At 6.30 a.m. Dr Bagster Phillips arrived at the scene and gave his opinion that death had occurred two or three hours earlier.

When he examined the body Dr Phillips found that the throat had been cut deeply with a jagged incision. A flap of the wall of the belly, the whole of the small intestines and other tissues had been removed from the body and placed above the right shoulder but they were still attached. Two other portions of belly wall and the pubes were found above the left shoulder in a large quantity of blood. There was an abrasion at the top of the first phalanx of the ring finger and distinct marks of a ring or rings (probably the latter) on the proximal phalanx of the same finger. Part of the belly wall (including the navel), the womb, the upper part of the vagina and the greater part of the bladder were missing.

When the coroner asked the doctor to estimate 'the quantity of matter taken from the abdomen' Phillips replied, 'It would all go into a breakfast cup.' In his opinion the murderer 'was possessed of anatomical knowledge from the manner of the removal of viscera' and he

Police guarding the front door of 29 Hanbury Street on the Saturday morning of the murder. Contemporary illustrations show the premises to have had only one front door in 1888. A second front door, to a shop, was added many years later. (Pictorial News, *Saturday 15 September 1888*)

HANBURY ST
ON SUNDAY MORNING

This animated scene in Hanbury Street on the Sunday morning after the killing, and depicted in *Pictorial News*, Saturday 15 September 1888, shows how great crowds gathered outside the murder locations in the days following the crimes.

believed that no ordinary knife was used but one 'such as a small amputating knife, or a well-ground slaughterman's knife, narrow and thin, sharp, and blade of six to eight inches in length.' According to *The Lancet*, 'Obviously the work was that of an expert – or of one, at least, who had such knowledge of anatomical or pathological examinations as to be enabled to secure the pelvic organs with one sweep of a knife.'

Chapman also had bruising on her right temple and upper chest but this had been sustained a week previously in a fight with an Eliza Cooper in the lodging house kitchen. There were more recent marks on her face and around the sides of her jaw, and two fresh bruises on the right side of her head and neck, one on the cheek and the other at a point that corresponded with scratches on the left side. Phillips deduced that she had been seized by the chin before her throat was cut from left to right. In addition, the tongue had thickened and he thought that she had been partially strangled.

It is clear that Dr Phillips' estimate of the time of death does not tie in with the evidence of the three independent witnesses, Richardson, Cadosch and Long. However, Cadosch apparently heard the presumed killer and victim in the rear yard of no. 29 about 5 minutes before Mrs Long saw them in front of the property. Mrs Long was certain of the time because she heard the brewer's clock strike the half-hour as she passed. These apparent discrepancies have prompted much speculation about the actual time of the murder and the validity of the witnesses' evidence. The problem was acknowledged by Swanson in his 19 October report:

If the evidence of Dr. Phillips is correct as to time of death, it is difficult to understand how it was that Richardson did not see the body when he went into the yard at 4.45 a.m. but as his clothes were examined, the house searched and his statement taken in which there was not a shred of evidence, suspicion could not rest upon him, although police specially directed their attention to him. Richardson is a market porter. Again if the evidence of Mrs. Long is correct that she saw the deceased at 5.30 a.m. then the evidence of Dr. Phillips as to probable time of death is incorrect. He was called and saw the body at 6.20 a.m.[6] and he then gives it as his opinion that death occurred about two hours earlier, viz: 4.20 a.m.[7] hence the evidence of Mrs. Long which appeared to be so important to the Coroner, must be looked upon with some amount of doubt, which is to be regretted.

Doctors often disagreed when calculating time of death. After the Kelly case on 9 November estimates made by Dr Thomas Bond (aged 47), and Dr George Bagster Phillips (aged 54), both police surgeons, were 3 to 4 hours apart, which does nothing to instil confidence in their accuracy. It is necessary to assess the three indicators of time of death considered by Dr Phillips and his contemporaries in the light of modern knowledge on the subject.[8]

Loss of body heat   After death the body loses heat until it becomes the same temperature as its surroundings. Body temperature should be taken in the rectum with a thermometer. 'The environmental temperature should be taken at the same time if the body temperature is to have any meaning.' Dr Phillips did neither.

Rigor mortis   This is caused by changes in chemicals within the muscles after death and can be slowed by cold ambient conditions. As a general rule, rigor mortis begins between 2 and 4 hours after death and is first noticed in the jaws and neck. (It actually commences at the same time throughout the body but is noticeable at the head first.) It is complete after 8 to 12 hours. Modern science says, 'This factor is the poorest of the gauges used in estimating time of death because of the many variables involved. The various theories on rigor mortis are loaded with contradiction and misinterpretation . . . a fight or body shock usually accelerates it; no two bodies even under similar circumstances develop it at the same time.' The phenomenon of cadaveric spasm, where the stiffening of the hands or arms occurs immediately at the time of death, adds to the problems of using rigor mortis to calculate time of death.

Dr Bagster Phillips, the H Division Police Surgeon, who featured in many of the Whitechapel murder cases.

Digestion of Food   Different foods remain in the stomach for different periods of time and speed of digestion is affected by the nature and size of the meal. 'It has been determined through extensive research that under ordinary circumstances the stomach empties its contents four to six hours after a meal.'

By modern standards, therefore, the methods Dr Phillips used in his time-of-death estimate were questionable. His conclusions are certainly not reliable enough to warrant dismissing the witness evidence. Dr Phillips took no temperatures, merely relying on touch, and did not detail the location and extent of the stiffness that was 'commencing'. These points may have been covered in his post-mortem report but it has not survived. Even if it had, it would merely supply more detail on how his conclusions were reached rather than improving their accuracy. At the inquest Dr Phillips' observations on the temperature of the body were qualified: he said 'that the deceased had been dead at least two hours, and probably more, when he first saw her; but it was right to mention that it was a fairly cool morning, and that the body would be more apt to cool rapidly from its having lost a great quantity of blood'.[9] He also stated that 'The body was cold, except that there was a certain remaining heat, under the intestines, in the body. Stiffness of the limbs was not marked, but it was commencing.'[10] Of food in the stomach, Phillips stated it 'contained a little food'.

Coroner Baxter appears to have been impressed with the lay witnesses and in his summing up he said:

Coroner Wynne Baxter presiding over the inquest into the death of Annie Chapman at the Working Lads' Institute, Whitechapel Road. (Pictorial News, *Saturday 15 September 1888*)

It was true that Dr. Phillips thought that, when he saw the body at 6.30, the deceased had been dead at least two hours, but he admitted that the coldness of the morning and the great loss of blood might affect his opinion, and if the evidence of the other witnesses was correct, Dr. Phillips had miscalculated the effect of those forces.[11]

Indeed, it is unlikely that the three independent witnesses were seriously mistaken or lying. Most witness statements do contain small errors, discrepancies and inconsistencies, and it would be most unusual to find that they all agreed in every respect.

'Richardson's appearance [at the inquest] and his hoarse voice were not altogether prepossessing', reported the *East London Observer*, but he had no apparent reason to lie or be mistaken in his timing. His statement actually put him into the frame as a suspect, albeit fleetingly. Dawn was at 4.51 a.m., the sun rose at 5.25 a.m. and it was bright with only 30 per cent cloud cover on the morning of Chapman's murder. Richardson observed that it was not yet light when he first went outside, but he could still see 'all over the place'. He could not have failed to notice the deceased had she been in the yard at that time. The surviving photograph and contemporary sketches confirm that the backyard at 29 Hanbury Street was remarkably small. Chapman was lying on her back to the left of the steps, i.e. nearer to the fence, with her head about 6 inches in front of the bottom step and her feet towards a shed at the end of the yard. She would have been clearly visible to anyone on the steps and even the opened door would not have obscured the view. A strong smell is usually present with a freshly disembowelled body and Richardson would probably have noticed that too. He had been informed at the market of the murder and immediately returned to Hanbury Street, where he saw the body from the house next door just before the doctor arrived. He went into the hall passage of no. 29 at about 6.45 a.m. and saw Inspector Chandler. He told the policeman he had gone into the yard at about 4.45 a.m. and reported that the body was not there at that time. Chandler noted Richardson's details and the porter returned to work at the market.

The police later interviewed Richardson, by then entertaining some suspicions about him, which Swanson noted in the report dated 19 October. Initially, it would appear, Chandler entertained no suspicions with regard to Richardson. However, as soon as the detectives, under Abberline, started their inquiries he was investigated and subsequently cleared.

Those who espouse the idea of the murder taking place at the time suggested by Dr Phillips usually quote the contradictions in timing between Mrs Long and Albert Cadosch. This may be a fair argument, but the reason for the discrepancy is probably that one or both of them were mistaken as to the exact time. The difference appears to be a mere 5 minutes or so, and this is entirely understandable given the state of timekeeping in those days. Most of the labouring class had no personal timepiece and relied on public clock chimes. Other variables should be considered alongside this potential uncertainty. Were honest mistakes made by those trying to remember facts at a later date? Were the clocks heard striking showing the correct time? Was the witness certain that he or she had heard the half-hour rather than the quarter-hour strike? There is no way of finding out. We must rely on what we do know from the surviving records and decide the most probable, or likely, answer to our questions.

Is there any evidence that either Cadosch or Long was mistaken about the time? Certainly, if Mrs Long thought the clock was striking 5.30 a.m. and in fact it was striking 5.15, her evidence ties in perfectly with Cadosch's. If Mrs Long believed that she had passed the house at 5.30 a.m., then by extrapolation she would estimate her time of arrival at the market as 'a few minutes after half-past five'. More importantly, there is evidence to support the

THE SCENE OF THE MURDER.

This contemporary drawing of the rear door of 29 Hanbury Street and the spot where Chapman's body was found shows that the witness, John Richardson, could hardly have failed to see the body had it been there when he sat on the steps at about 4.50 a.m. on the day of the murder.

suggestion that Mrs Long's sighting took place earlier than she estimated. After giving her main evidence at the inquest she was questioned further by the coroner. Her address is given as 32 Church Street in the police report but newspaper inquest reports give it variously as 'Church Row', '3 Church Row' and '198 Church Row'. In his summing up, the coroner said Church Street. The address has never been positively identified. Church Street was, at one time, an extension of Hanbury Street running eastwards from the junction with Deal Street, but by 1888 it no longer took that name. The two most likely locations for Mrs Long's address are Church Street and Church Row (today's St Matthew's Row), in the parish of St Matthew's, Bethnal Green. These were off the north end of Brick Lane and would have brought Mrs Long to Hanbury Street via Brick Lane, where she heard the brewery clock. The 1891 census reveals that Church Street was numbered 9–95 (odds) and 24–60 (evens), while Church Row was numbered 1–61 (odds) and 4–30 (evens). Mrs Long (or Durrell/Darrell) does not appear in these lists. However, there is a William Long (aged 75 years, a bricklayer) and his wife Mary, aged 62, listed at 31 Church Row. It has not been possible to establish the facts but it is feasible that Mrs Long was related to William Long and living at the address in 1888. Perhaps her married name was Durrell but, for some reason, she used her maiden name.

At the inquest she was asked, 'What time did you leave home?' and she replied, 'I got out about five o'clock, and I reached the Spitalfields Market a few minutes after half-past five.' A walk from Church Street/Row, Bethnal Green, to 29 Hanbury Street should not take a full 30 minutes, so there is a reason to think that Mrs Long's belief that the time was 5.30 was indeed wrong. Thus, when all the evidence is considered, it seems Elizabeth Long made one of the most likely, and possibly the most reliable, suspect sightings reported during the murders. This not least because the sighting was made in daylight, at very close quarters, and she identified Chapman as the woman involved. The time was more or less right,

Nos 25 and 27 Hanbury Street, Spitalfields. No. 27, on the right, is where the witness for the Chapman murder, Albert Cadosch, lived. The front door of no. 29 is just visible at the far right. (*London Metropolitan Archives*)

Hanbury Street looking east from Commercial Street, *c.* 1918, still very much as it was at the time of the murder of Annie Chapman. (*London Metropolitan Archives*)

assuming that Cadosch heard the murder taking place. Mrs Long's evidence was given, under oath, at the Chapman inquest and was reported in the *Suffolk Chronicle* of Saturday 22 September. The newspaper's account includes details not in the police version:

> Elizabeth Long, a married woman living at 3, Church-row, said on the morning of the murder she was going along Hanbury-street on her way to Spitalfields Market. A neighbouring clock had just struck half-past five. She saw a man come to a woman and stand and talk with her near No. 29. The witness saw the woman's face. She had never seen her before, but she recognized the deceased when she saw her in the mortuary as the same person. She did not see the man's face and she could not recognize him again. He was, however, dark complexioned, and was wearing a brown deerstalker hat. She thought he was wearing a dark coat, but could not be sure. She heard him say 'Will you?' and she said 'Yes.' She left them standing and went to her work.

At 7 a.m. on the day of the murder a rough-looking man went into the Prince Albert pub on the corner of Brushfield Street and Steward Street and asked for a half-pint of ale. The establishment was run by a Mrs Fiddymont who later gave evidence to the police. She was worried by the man's appearance and asked a customer, Mrs Mary Chappell, to stay with her. The man's shirt was badly torn and there were marks of blood under his right ear and

IDENTIFYING THE BODY

A contemporary sketch from *Pictorial News*, Saturday 15 September 1888, of a witness (believed to be Mrs Long) identifying the body of Annie Chapman to the police at the mortuary.

29 Hanbury Street, Spitalfields, seen here in the 1960s just a few years before its demolition and as remembered by both authors.

on the back of his right hand. He wore a 'startling and terrifying' look which was topped by a stiff brown hat drawn down over his eyes. He was of medium height, middle-aged, with short sandy hair and a ginger moustache, slightly curled at the ends. He had faint hollows under his cheekbones. He quickly downed his drink and left. He was then followed by another witness, Joseph Taylor, a builder, as far as Half Moon Street, Bishopsgate. Taylor described the man's dress as 'shabby-genteel', with pepper-and-salt trousers and a dark coat. His manner was nervous and frightened and he seemed disoriented, walking rapidly with a peculiar, springy stride. In all, he seemed a very strange character. As the Prince Albert was not too far from Hanbury Street, the obvious conclusion was reached – this was a possible sighting of the murderer. This suspect was subsequently believed to be the 'mad pork butcher' of Holloway, Jacob Isenschmidt.

On the day of the Chapman murder several officers of H Division were put on plain clothes duty, including Inspector Chandler, Sergeant 4 Lee, and PCs 109 Cooke, 125 Barrett, 155 White, 195 Hussey, 205 Sziemanowicz and 243 Schmelzer. Their deployment was undoubtedly to facilitate the many avenues of inquiry then pursued by the police. Chandler, for example, was later sent by Abberline to Farnborough to follow up inquiries with the 1st Battalion, Sussex Regiment regarding the piece of envelope found near Chapman's body. The police also interviewed all the inhabitants of 29 Hanbury Street and the adjoining houses; made detailed inquiries at all common lodging houses to ascertain if anyone had entered that morning with blood on them or in suspicious circumstances; visited all pawn-brokers, jewellers and dealers in an effort to trace the rings missing from Chapman's finger; delved into the history of the victim; investigated several people who were detained pending inquiry into their movements on 7 and 31 August and 8 September; circulated details of other suspicious persons who could not be immediately found; traced suspects whose addresses or particulars had been supplied to the police in correspondence; attempted to trace three insane medical students who had attended London Hospital (two were traced but one was found to have gone abroad); and made other various inquiries at public houses and among women 'of the same class' as the deceased. All this failed to supply the police with the slightest clue as to the identity of the murderer. Chief Inspector Swanson reported that:

The only indication of the direction to find the murderer lay in the evidence of Dr. Phillips, which was in substance that the individual possessed some skill and anatomical knowledge, and that the instrument with which the injuries were inflicted was probably a small amputating knife, or a well-ground butchers knife, narrow and thin, sharp with a blade from six to eight inches long.[12]

There was a further mention of the three insane medical students by William Byrne of the Home Office in a note of 27 October to his colleague Charles Murdoch. He wrote, 'Shall the Police be asked at the same time for report as to what has become of the 3rd Insane Medical Student from the London Hosp? about whom (under the name of Dr ——[)] there is a good deal of gossip in circulation.' This third student was John Sanders of 20 Abercorn Place, Maida Vale, whom the police were told by neighbours that he had gone abroad. In a reply dated 1 November Warren told Byrne, 'With regard to the latter portion of your letter I have to state that searching enquiries were made by an officer in Aberdeen [*sic*] Place, St John's Wood, the last known address of the insane medical student named "John Sanders", but the only information that could be obtained was that a lady named Sanders did reside with her son at No. 20, but left that address to go abroad about two years ago.' In fact, Sanders was in a private asylum at West Malling Place in Kent. He died, aged 39, in Heavitree Asylum, Exeter, in 1901. The dearth of information on this man and other suspects is accounted for by the loss of the police investigative paperwork over the years.

The most widely publicised suspect to emerge during the investigation into the Chapman murder was a character nicknamed 'Leather Apron'. The *Star*, in its Wednesday 5 September 1888 edition, introduced this memorable name to the public – it was the stuff of penny dreadfuls. The paper's headlines proclaimed: '"**LEATHER APRON.**" THE ONLY NAME LINKED WITH THE WHITECHAPEL MURDERS. A NOISELESS MIDNIGHT TERROR. **The Strange Character who Prowls About Whitechapel After Midnight – Universal Fear Among the Women – Slippered Feet and a Sharp Leather-knife**'. It described the mystery character as:

> quite an unpleasant character . . . he is a more ghoulish and devilish brute than can be found in all the pages of shocking fiction. He has ranged Whitechapel for a long time. He exercises over the unfortunates who ply their trade after twelve o'clock at night, a sway that is BASED ON UNIVERSAL TERROR. He has kicked, injured, bruised, and terrified a hundred of them who are ready to testify to the outrages. He has made a certain threat, his favourite threat, to any number of them, and each of the three dead bodies represents that threat carried out. He carries a razor-like knife, and two weeks ago drew it on a woman called 'Widow Annie' as she was crossing the square near London Hospital, threatening at the same time, with his ugly grin and his malignant eyes, to 'rip her up'. He is a character so much like the invention of a story writer that the accounts of him given by all the street-walkers of the Whitechapel district seem like romances. The remarkable thing is, however, that they all agree in every particular. They told of how the name had been universally cried as the perpetrator of the crimes 'women have been shaking their heads and saying that "Leather Apron" did it'. And, 'he is five feet four or five inches in height and wears a dark close-fitting cap. He is thickset, and has an unusually thick neck. His hair is black, and closely clipped, his age being about 38 or 40. He has a small, black moustache. The distinguishing feature of his costume is a leather apron, which he always wears, and from which HE GETS HIS NICKNAME.

The newspaper demanded his arrest by the police. The report also told of a Mrs Colwell and bloodstains found in Brady Street but police reports on the Chapman murder and the

Detective Sergeant William Thick of H Division CID who was accused by a member of the public in a letter of being the Whitechapel murderer. On the right, seated next to Thick, is Detective Inspector Edmund Reid. (*S.P. Evans/Metropolitan Police*)

published details of the inquest fail to reveal any evidence of the bloodstains mentioned, neither did Mrs Colwell of Brady Street give evidence. The *Star* appears to have compiled its 'Leather Apron' sensation from uncorroborated stories told to reporters. Unfortunately, it is impossible say how much is factual. 'Leather Apron' quickly became the popular name for the murderer and as a result of depiction of this Jewish suspect in the press, many Jews came under public suspicion.

John Piser (or Pizer), aged 38, was arrested on Monday 10 September by 43-year-old Detective Sergeant William Thick. Otherwise known as 'Johnny Upright', this officer had twenty years' service under his belt. Thick was described by the *East London Observer* as 'a fresh-coloured, youngish looking man, with dark hair and a heavy, drooping, brown moustache'. When he gave evidence he was 'flashily' dressed in a suit of loud checks. The reason for the swift arrest, within 48 hours of the murder, was that the detective had known Piser for many years and when neighbours

A contemporary illustration from *Pictorial News*, Saturday 15 September 1888, of an 'arrest on suspicion', thought to show the arrest of 'Jack' Piser.

spoke of 'Leather Apron' he knew exactly whom they meant. The two men lived just streets away from each other. Piser, giving evidence at the inquest two days later, described himself a bootmaker and confirmed that he was known by the nickname 'Leather Apron'. He gave an alibi to the court, it was confirmed by the police, which 'cleared his character' and led to his immediate release. A witness, vagrant Emmanuel Delbast Violena, who claimed to have seen Piser arguing with a woman in Hanbury Street on the morning of the murder was discredited and Piser also had an alibi for the time of the Nichols murder. After Piser was cleared of any connection with the crimes, the sobriquet 'Leather Apron' quickly lost its popularity as a name for the murderer.

Now the newspapers constantly threw up new suspects. And worse, from the police point of view, since the murders were so localised, reporters followed detectives as they pursued clues and then interviewed potential witnesses of whom the inquiries had been made. (Warren called the reporters 'touts' in a letter of complaint to the Home Office.) Rumours and counter-rumours, backed by few hard facts, kept the murders on front pages and the

GHASTLY
MURDER
IN THE EAST-END.
DREADFUL MUTILATION OF A WOMAN.

Capture : Leather Apron

Another murder of a character even more diabolical than that perpetrated in Buck's Row, on Friday week, was discovered in the same neighbourhood, on Saturday morning. At about six o'clock a woman was found lying in a back yard at the foot of a passage leading to a lodging-house in a Old Brown's Lane, Spitalfields. The house is occupied by a Mrs. Richardson, who lets it out to lodgers, and the door which admits to this passage, at the foot of which lies the yard where the body was found, is always open for the convenience of lodgers. A lodger named Davis was going down to work at the time mentioned and found the woman lying on her back close to the flight of steps leading into the yard. Her throat was cut in a fearful manner. The woman's body had been completely ripped open, and the heart and other organs laying about the place, and portions of the entrails round the victim's neck An excited crowd gathered in front of Mrs. Richardson's house and also round the mortuary in old Montague Street, whither the body was quickly conveyed. As the body lies in the rough coffin in which it has been placed in the mortuary —the same coffin in which the unfortunate Mrs. Nicholls was first placed—it presents a fearful sight. The body is that of a woman about 45 years of age. The height is exactly five feet. The complexion is fair, with wavy dark brown hair; the eyes are blue, and two lower teeth have been knocked out. The nose is rather large and prominent.

Broadsheet announcing the capture of John Piser, known as 'Leather Apron'.

Brick Lane was at the heart of Ripper territory and was traversed by Hanbury Street. Here it is seen on a busy market day crowded with Victorian shoppers.

public interest stimulated. Warren had to admit that although a large number of men were being employed in the investigation, nothing definite so far had been found.[13]

By noon on Monday 10 September 1888 seven suspects were under detention. One was William Henry Piggott, aged 53, a ship's cook who was arrested by Inspector Abberline at Gravesend on the Sunday night. Piggott had been loudly denouncing women in the Pope's Head Tavern and inquiries revealed he had left a paper parcel containing clothing at a local fish shop – it contained a bloodstained shirt. Piggott explained that his hand had been bitten by a woman; he had been walking down Brick Lane in Whitechapel about 4.30 a.m. on the Saturday morning when a woman had fallen in a fit. He had stopped to help her up and she had bitten him. He responded by hitting her and then ran away when he saw two policemen approaching. There were some blood spots on two shirts he was carrying in a bundle and his strange behaviour convinced the police to detain him. The police doctor opined that blood had been wiped from off his boots. After being cautioned, he allegedly stated that the woman who bit him was at the back of a lodging house at the time. He also stated that on the Thursday night he slept at a lodging house in Osborn Street, Whitechapel, but on the Friday night was walking around the area all night. He had travelled from London to Gravesend by road on the Sunday. He was detained pending the arrival of witnesses. In the afternoon he was put in a line-up and confronted by Mrs Fiddymont and other witnesses. She did not think that he was the man she had seen in the pub on the morning of the murder. Piggott was taken to the Whitechapel Union Infirmary the same day and treated for delirium tremens. He was detained until 9 October and was absolved of any connection with the murders.

The police themselves were sometimes guilty of being heavy-handed. On 13 September after the arrest of a suspect, Friedrich Schumacher, at Leman Street police station, the circumstances of which are not clear, a woman was assaulted and the clothing she was carrying destroyed. This led to Inspector Charles Pinhorn being severely reprimanded and Detective Sergeant New reduced in rank and transferred to another division.[14]

On 14 September Inspector Abberline reported that an itinerant pedlar named Edward McKenna had been detained at Commercial Street police station for identification because he fitted the description of a man seen at Heath Street and other places with a knife. The identification failed and he was released because there was no evidence to incriminate him.

The pressure was on the police to make a quick arrest, not just from the press and public, but from the Home Office itself. A 22 September memo from Home Secretary Matthews to his Private Secretary, Ruggles-Brise, said: 'Stimulate the Police about Whitechapel murders. *Absente* Anderson, Monro might be willing to give a hint to the C.I.D. people if needful.' The request would almost certainly have been ignored by the former head of CID because before his resignation he had disclaimed all responsibility for any irregularities in the investigative system now initiated and would have been unlikely to want to help out. Monro subsequently vetoed Anderson from putting difficult investigations to him, telling him plainly 'that he was not going to do my work for me', although Monro softened the blow by saying that if Anderson came to him as a friend to talk over difficult cases, he would be better pleased. Nominally in charge of investigations were the ailing and overworked Chief Constable Williamson and his deputy, Superintendent John Shore. The *Pall Mall Gazette* was scathing about the situation:

> Two years ago Mr. Williamson was described in these columns as 'one of the veterans of the service, under whose grey hairs are stowed the fruits of nearly half a century of experience. Faithful, diligent, and unsparing, Mr. Williamson was on the track of crime before the majority of Londoners of the present generation were born.' . . . The exact date when he joined the force is lost in the mists of antiquity. . . . He . . . may probably claim with justice to be the grandfather of the force. His second in command, Mr. Shore, a rough diamond from Gloucestershire, would have been a useful inspector where rough work is required to be by a vigorous instrument. . . . But these two men, one superannuated and both practically handcuffed by jealousy and red tape, have at this juncture to fulfil the duties of a Vidocq [a notorious French criminal turned policeman and detective] in a capital containing five million inhabitants.

In effect, in the early stages there was no obvious Scotland Yard chief with direct responsibility and overall control of the Whitechapel murders investigation. The press was commenting on the fact that the head of the CID was away and that the detectives were thus leaderless, a situation of which the Home Office was uncomfortably aware. Perhaps as a result of this, on 15 September Warren sent an instruction to the Acting Assistant Commissioner CID, Alexander Carmichael Bruce, who appeared to be handling the paperwork side of Anderson's affairs in his absence. Warren, in retrospect very foolishly, said:

> I am convinced that the Whitechapel Murder case is one which can be successfully grappled with if it is systematically taken in hand. *I go so far as to say that I could myself in a few days unravel the mystery provided I could spare the time & give individual attention to it.* I feel therefore the utmost importance to be attached to putting the whole Central Office work in this case in the hands of one man who will have nothing else to concern

Warren's instruction of
15 September 1888 putting
Chief Inspector Swanson in
charge.

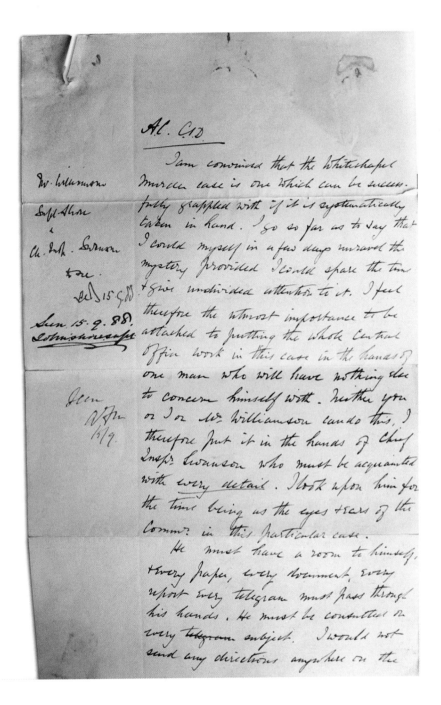

himself with. Neither you or I or Mr. Williamson can do this. I therefore put it in the
hands of Chief Inspr. Swanson who must be acquainted with every detail. I look upon
him for the time being as the eyes & ears of the Commr. in this particular case.

He must have a room to himself, & every paper, every document, every report[,] every
telegram must pass through his hands. He must be consulted on every subject. I would
not send any directions anywhere on the subject of the murder without consulting him.
I give him the whole responsibility. On the other hand he should consult Mr. Williamson,
you, or myself on every important particular before any action unless there is some
extreme urgency. [*Authors' italic*]

Superintendent Donald Swanson, centre rear, who was the CID officer delegated by Warren on 15 September 1888 to take charge of all the inquiries into the Whitechapel murders. (*S.P. Evans/Metropolitan Police*)

Warren went on to emphasise the instruction and state that all paperwork and plans relative to the case should be kept in Swanson's office. The instruction passed down through the chain of command from Warren to Bruce, then via Williamson and Shore to Swanson, who retained it.[15]

Another suspect in the Chapman murder was Charles Ludwig, aged 40, a respectably dressed German hairdresser. On Tuesday 18 September he was charged at Thames police court with being drunk and several times attempting to stab a man at a coffee stall in Whitechapel. He had earlier accosted a prostitute, Elizabeth Burns, which didn't help his cause. He was arrested and was finally discharged from custody on Tuesday 2 October 1888, having satisfactorily accounted for his whereabouts at the time of the murder and having been in custody for two weeks.

Meanwhile, in a letter dated 19 September 1888 Sir Charles Warren reported to Ruggles-Brise, at the Home Office, that:

> No progress has as yet been made in obtaining any definite clue to the Whitechapel murderers. A great number of clues have been examined & exhausted without finding any thing suspicious.
>
> A large staff of men are employed and every point is being examined which seems to offer any prospect of a discovery.
>
> There are at present three cases of suspicion.
>
> 1. The lunatic Isensmith [*sic*], a Swiss arrested at Holloway – who is now in an Asylum at Bow & arrangements are being made to ascertain whether he is the man who was seen on the morning of the murder in a public house by Mrs. Fiddymont.
>
> 2. A man called Puckeridge was released from an asylum on 4 August. He was educated as a Surgeon – has threatened to rip people up with a long knife. He is being looked for but cannot be found as yet.
>
> 3. A Brothel Keeper who will not give her address or name writes to say that a man living in her house was seen with blood on him on morning of murder. She described his appearance & said where he might be seen – when the detectives came near him he bolted, got away & there is no clue as to the writer of the letter.

All these three cases are being followed up & no doubt will be exhausted in a few days – the first seems a very suspicious case, but the man is at present a violent lunatic.

I will say tomorrow if anything turns up about him.

Moreover the reporters for the press are following our detectives about everywhere in search of news & cross examine all parties interviewed so that they impede police action greatly – they do not however as yet know of the cases 2 & 3.

C.W.

The first man referred to by Warren was Jacob (the police reports refer to him as Joseph) Isenschmidt, a pork butcher whose business had failed. He was detained at Holloway and placed in an infirmary as a 'dangerous lunatic'. At this stage he was the prime suspect and much time was spent investigating him. He was actually brought to the notice of the police by two Holloway doctors, Cowan and Crabb, who called at Holloway police station on 11 September.

The *East Anglian Daily Times* of 19 September gave an update to the story of Isenschmidt, colourfully described as 'The Holloway lunatic'. He was a Swiss who had kept a pork-butcher's shop in Elthorne Road, Holloway, some time previously. He was what was known in the trade as a 'cutter-up'. Some years earlier he had suffered sunstroke and since then he had been subject to yearly fits of madness. These attacks had usually come on in the latter part of the summer, and on several occasions his conduct had been so alarming that he had been carried off to Colney Hatch asylum. He had last been released just before Christmas. One of his delusions was that everything belonged to him and he had called himself 'the King of Elthorne Road'. On several occasions he had threatened to put certain people's 'lights out', and more than once the landlord of the shop had been warned not to approach

Colney Hatch inmate Jacob Isenschmidt, photographed in 1895 and 1896. 'The Mad Pork Butcher' was one of the earliest serious suspects for the Whitechapel murders. (*London Metropolitan Archives*)

his tenant. When he was having an attack, Isenschmidt had an alarming habit of continually sharpening a long knife. His disappearance from home for a few days was not unusual. He had 'gone mad' some weeks before the murder and his frightened wife had obtained an order for his detention in a lunatic asylum but Isenschmidt could not be found and the police spent some time looking for him. His house had been watched. He was finally arrested at home on 12 September; he had been living at 97 Duncombe Road and 60 Mitford Road, Holloway. He was handed over to the parochial authorities as a lunatic.

Isenschmidt very closely answered the description of the man with bloodstains on his hands who was seen at the Prince Albert public house on the morning of the murder. He was about 38 years of age, approximately 5 feet 7 inches tall, of rather stout build, and had ginger hair on his head and face. Detective Sergeant Thick was able to examine Isenschmidt's clothes for blood but found none. The medical superintendent at the Infirmary Asylum, Fairfield Road, Bow, reported that Isenschmidt said that the girls at Holloway had called him 'Leather Apron' and he had joked to them 'I am Leather Apron.' He had had 'a few words with his wife' and left her. When the police found him he was earning a living by making early morning visits to the market where he bought sheep's heads, feet and kidneys which he dressed and then sold. Abberline confirmed it was believed that Isenschmidt, by his description, was the man seen by Mrs Fiddymont and her customers at the Prince Albert. The medical superintendent would not, however, allow his patient to take part in an identification process as he was concerned for Isenschmidt's safety. Isenschmidt was said at times to be very violent. Abberline went so far as to state, 'Although at present we are unable to procure any evidence to connect him with the murders he appears to be the most likely person to have committed the crimes, and every effort will be made to account for his movements on the dates in question.' However, he was later dismissed as a Ripper suspect because he was still confined in the asylum at the time of the next murders.

The second of Warren's named suspects was Oswald Puckridge, a chemist and a mental patient aged 50 years, who eventually died in Holborn workhouse in 1900. We may only assume that his mental condition and date of release, three days before the Tabram murder, led to the suspicion against him because no hard evidence existed to connect him with the murders. The third suspect was not traced, and the brothel-keeper was not identified.

The many stories of suspicious incidents and characters that appeared in the newspapers at this time confused the issue in 1888 and continue to do so today. Perhaps the most sensational and influential suspect story to emerge in September 1888 was the 'American Doctor theory'. This was an important development because it was the coroner who proposed a major suspect theory and introduced an American angle to proceedings. The story was described by Wynne Baxter in his summing up on the final day of the Chapman inquest, Wednesday 26 September 1888. Baxter engaged in his own brand of deductive reasoning and his conclusions were reported in all the major newspapers. The coroner observed that there were two items missing from Chapman's body: her rings had been wrenched from her fingers and had not been found, and the uterus had been taken away. Baxter then went on to make his tremendously influential statement regarding the murders and the possible identity of the murderer. He said that although the body had not been dissected, the injuries appeared to have been made by someone

who had considerable anatomical knowledge and skill. There are no meaningless cuts. The organ has been taken away by one who knew where to find it, what difficulties he would have to contend against, and how he should use his knife so as to abstract the organ without injury to it. No unskilled person could know where to find it, or have recognised it when it was found. For instance, no mere slaughterer of animals could have carried out these operations. It must have been someone accustomed to the post-mortem room. The conclusion that the murderer's desire was to possess the missing organ seems overwhelming. If the object were robbery, injuries to the viscera were meaningless, for death had previously resulted from the loss of blood at the neck.

The difficulty in believing that the purpose of the murderer was the possession of the uterus is natural; it is abhorrent to our feelings to conclude that a life should be taken for so slight an object, but, when rightly considered, the reasons for most murders are altogether out of proportion to the guilt. It has been suggested that the criminal is a lunatic with morbid feelings. This may or may not be the case, but the object of the murderer appears palpably shown by the facts, and it is not necessary to assume lunacy, for it is clear that there is a market for the missing organ. To show you this, I must mention a fact which at the same time proves the assistance which publicity and the newspaper press afford in the detection of crime.

Within a few hours of the issue of the morning papers containing the report of the medical evidence given at the last sitting of the Court, I received a communication from an officer of one of our great medical schools, that they had information which might or might not have a distinct bearing upon our inquiry. I attended at the first opportunity, and was informed by the sub-curator of the Pathological Museum that some months ago an American had called on him, and asked him to procure a number of specimens of the organ that was missing in the deceased. He stated his willingness to give £20 for each specimen, and said his object was to issue an actual specimen with each copy of a publication on which he was then engaged. He was told that his request was impossible to be complied with, but he still urged it, saying he wished them preserved, not in spirits of wine, the usual medium, but in glycerine, in order to preserve them in a flaccid condition, and he wished them sent to America direct. It is known that this request was repeated to another institution of a similar character.

Now, is it not possible that the knowledge of this demand incited some abandoned wretch to possess himself of specimens. Our criminal annals prove that every crime is possible. I at once communicated my information to Scotland Yard. I do not know what use has been made of it, but I believe that publicity may further elucidate this fact, and therefore I have not withheld from you the information. By means of the press, some further explanation may be forthcoming from America, if not from here.

Such a public airing of a theory that reflected upon the medical community and, indeed, even suggested that the killer may be a medical man, was sure to be met with disdain by doctors. *The Lancet* of Saturday 29 September 1888 made the following cautionary observations:

In the face of these facts, the statement made by Mr. Wynne Baxter presents great *prima facie* probability, but we must deprecate strongly any tendency to jump at a conclusion in a matter which may admit of another interpretation. [Baxter's theory is then repeated in full.] Although this statement seems to afford a satisfactory explanation for the motive for the deed and mutilation of the corpse, it is impossible to read it without being struck with certain improbabilities and absurdities that go far to upset the theory altogether. We do not for a moment question the possibility of an application being made to museum curators for specimens of uteri. This is not an unnatural or unreasonable request to be preferred by a medical man engaged in the study of disease of that organ. But does it not exceed the bounds of credibility to imagine that he would pay the sum of £20 for every specimen? – whilst the statement that he wished for a large number, because '*his object was to issue an actual specimen with each copy of a publication on which he was engaged*', is too grotesque and horrible to be for a moment entertained. Nor, indeed, can we imagine that an author of a medical work to be published in America should need to have uteri specially procured for him in England and sent across the Atlantic.

The whole tale is almost past belief; and if, as we think, it can be shown to have grown in transmission, it will not only shatter the theory that cupidity was the motive of the crime, but will bring into question the discretion of the officer of the law who could accept such a statement and give it such wide publicity. The plea that the interests of justice will be furthered thereby is one that cannot be sustained. Such information as was given to the coroner would have been far more appropriately placed at the disposal of the Home Office and the police; for the clue, if there is one, was for them to follow up.

In our opinion a grave error in judgment was made by the coroner's informant in this respect. The public mind – ever too ready to cast mud at legitimate research – will hardly fail to be excited to a pitch of animosity against anatomists and curators, which may take a long while to subside. And, what is equally deplorable, the revelation thus made by the coroner, which so dramatically startled the public last Wednesday evening, may probably lead to a diversion from the real track of the murderer, and thus defeat rather than serve the ends of justice. We believe the story to be highly improbable, although it may have a small basis of fact, which will require the exercise of much common sense to separate from the sensational fiction that surrounds it.

Wynne Baxter was a lawyer and not a medical man. The aggressive manner in which he conducted his inquests and his open disputes with some expert witnesses, in this case with Dr Bagster Phillips over how much of the medical evidence should be publicly disclosed, had now come to a head. It seems probable that two medical schools had been approached for specimens but the accuracy of the rest of Baxter's story is open to question. Wynne Baxter was almost certainly spoken to for his alarmist public theorising – it seems he did not openly espouse the theory again in Britain. In addition, inquiries were made to trace the source for his information and someone was undoubtedly severely reprimanded.

So what are we to make of all this? The *Daily Telegraph* followed the story closely and an illuminating report appeared in the Saturday 29 September 1888 edition:

THE WHITECHAPEL MURDERS.
WAS THE ASSASSIN AN ANATOMIST?

Assurances have been given by responsible officers of the medical schools attached to all the great London hospitals, with two exceptions, that no such extraordinary application was ever made to them of the nature described by Mr. Wynne Baxter, the coroner, in his recent summing up. At the schools of the University College Hospital and of the Middlesex Hospital the authorities, for some inscrutable reason, decline to give any information as to whether the 'American student' did prefer his singular request to them or not. From certain admissions of the gentlemen concerned there does not appear to be reason to doubt that to one or other of these two institutions belongs the distinction of having given certain information to the coroner, which he subsequently communicated to the Scotland-yard detectives, and upon which he based the theory which has caused such consternation.

He assumed that some abandoned wretch had been incited by the knowledge that a demand existed, and that the criminal must have been some one accustomed to the post-mortem room, and possessed of sufficient knowledge of anatomy to enable him to perform an unusual operation under harassing conditions. After Mr. Baxter had insisted that Mr. Phillips, the police divisional surgeon, should no longer withhold the most important part of his evidence respecting his post-mortem examination of the body of Annie Chapman, and when the report was published, it is clear that on the next day the coroner received a communication from an official connected with a leading London hospital, and that in consequence he attended at the pathological museum belonging to the institution, where some one – not the 'sub-curator', for the post that gentleman holds is otherwise described – made him acquainted with the outlines of a rumour which had circulated in the dissecting-rooms during the past summer, and to which not the slightest importance was attached until the murder in Hanbury-street occurred, and the startling medical evidence was published. The rumour, at most, appears to have been an idle one, and in respect of the sum mentioned to the coroner – viz., £20 – as the price offered, and the object of the American, as stated by him, the story is discredited.

At the Middlesex Hospital the official who, on other points, refused to elucidate the matter, characterised the tale, as far as the above details are concerned, as a silly story. Furthermore, at University College, where pains were taken to return an unqualified answer of 'no information', it was hinted that the story as it has been made public had, in some way, become mixed with error, and that it was very certain that it provided no explanation of the motive of the crime. Under these circumstances, when the true facts are deliberately withheld by the persons who are responsible for the allegations which have created general alarm, the public have a right to know what is the origin of the story, and upon what foundation this piece of sensationalism rests. The coroner surely could not have imagined the particulars of the incident, or was he misled, intentionally or purposely, by any responsible authority? Those gentlemen who assert that they have 'no information', somewhat indignantly repudiate the suggestion that it was a hoax, or that the matter has no importance. In fact, they talk somewhat mysteriously about the 'interests of justice' being imperilled by disclosure.

Whether the real object is to prolong public excitement, or for some other reasons the persons who could set the whole affair at rest are making a sham mystery of it, it is seriously discreditable to the authorities who indulge in want of candour, and it is opposed to the interests of the public and of the police. It is difficult to understand why they should give the coroner information, who considered that it should be made public in order to detect the criminal, and then refrain, possibly for some reason of pique, from telling the public the truth. There is nothing in the matter which reflects upon the character of the management of medical schools; the only discredit falls upon people who create, or at any rate sustain, apparently false alarms.

In general, skilled anatomists agree that the incident, as at present narrated, is ridiculous, and not worthy of serious consideration. It is admitted that, if the published details be correct, the murderer must have been a more or less practised anatomist, but it is pointed out that this idea depends entirely upon the fact whether great skill was displayed. The evidence at the inquest was to that effect, but professional men and eminent demonstrators in medical schools are now saying that they would be much more satisfied on that head had there been a second medical opinion at the inquest to confirm Mr. Phillips' evidence. Had that precaution been taken, it could never have been questioned whether the operation was so successful as has been alleged. Why did the police neglect this simple measure, when they had the resources of the Government at their disposal?

It was assumed, until recent years, that Wynne Baxter made no further mention of this intriguing story. However, examination of American sources by researcher Michael Conlon revealed a story in the *Chicago Tribune* that had thus far been missed by Ripper students. It was in the edition of Monday 1 October 1888 among coverage of the Stride and Eddowes murders. It would appear that, because of the American interest, the *Tribune* had secured an exclusive interview with Baxter:

> All the prominent doctors in town are ridiculing Coroner Baxter's suggestion that the murders are instigated by the American who offered large sums for specimens of the missing organs of the murdered bodies. I talked with the Coroner about it today as he was examining the body of Hippy Lip Annie [*sic* – Stride] and asked him why he thought the matter of sufficient importance to mention to the jury.
>
> 'I did not say the American committed the murders,' he answered, 'but thought the large sums of money he was offering for specimens sufficient provocation to tempt a depraved person to commit them. Besides, the persons to whom the American applied at the museums were convinced by the man's manner that he did not want the specimens for the purpose he represented. If the police sift thoroughly all the information I gave them you will hear more of that mysterious American.'

The *British Medical Journal* entered the fray on Saturday 6 October 1888 with the following comments:

> It is true that enquiries were made at one or two medical schools early last year by a foreign physician, who was spending some time in London, as to the possibility of securing certain parts of the body for the purpose of scientific investigation. No large sum, however, was offered. The person in question was a physician of the highest reputability and exceedingly well accredited to this country by the best authorities in his own, and he left London fully eighteen months ago. There was never any real foundation for the hypothesis, and the information communicated, which was not at all of the nature the public has been led to believe, was due to the erroneous interpretation by a minor official of a question which he had overheard and to which a negative reply was given. This theory may be dismissed, and is, we believe, no longer entertained by its author.

Sorting fact from fiction in Wynne Baxter's 'American theory' seems impossible at this remove in time. However, certain definite facts are apparent.

1. After the press published the medical evidence of the missing organ given at the inquest on Annie Chapman, the coroner was contacted the same day by some 'official' at either the University College Hospital or the Middlesex Hospital. And that 'official' worked in some capacity or other in the pathological department.
2. That hospital, and almost certainly the other one too, had been approached in 1887 (probably around March) with a request to obtain certain organs, probably uteri.
3. That request had been refused, but had become the subject of 'gossip' in pathological circles at the hospital, gossip which almost certainly persisted into the summer of 1888. (Obviously the 'gossip' would not have been based on any connection with murders, merely upon the unusual nature of the request.)
4. The person making the request was an American physician with apparently immaculate references.

From this starting-point we can make further deductions in relation to Baxter's theory. Baxter was, of course, not suggesting the American physician was the suspect for the murders. He thought the killer was rather 'some abandoned wretch' (presumably a mortuary attendant or someone in a similar menial position at the hospital) who was prepared to obtain the specimens for the American by killing women and extracting the required organ. This became commonly referred to as the 'Burke and Hare' theory. In the repetition, and no doubt embellishment, of this story, the following 'facts' were added:

1. The American was prepared to pay a large amount of money, i.e. £20 each, for the required organs.
2. He required them for issuing as actual specimens with each copy of a publication he was involved in.
3. The requests had been received only 'some months ago', rather than the true eighteen months previously.

Author and historian Philip Sugden has suggested[16] that the 'American physician' at the root of this story might be Irish-American Dr Francis Tumblety, whose emergence as a suspect will be seen later. This does not, of course, mean that Sugden believes Tumblety was the murderer, but merely that he may have been involved in the strange request made to the hospitals in 1887. Indeed, Tumblety's known frequent visits to London, his collection of dubious certificates of medical qualification and testimonials, an alleged collection of uteri, his known interest in gynaecology, and the fact that within a few weeks he was, indeed, a suspect for the murders give credence to this opinion.

Page 13 of the *Chicago Tribune* of Sunday 7 October 1888 contributed further interesting comments about an American suspect:

I learned today from a Scotland Yard man working on the case that the mysterious American who was here a few months ago offering money for specimens of the parts taken from the bodies of the victims has been discovered. He is a reputable physician in Philadelphia with a large practice, who was over here preparing a medical work on specific diseases. He went to King's College and Middlesex Hospitals and asked for specimens, and merely said he was willing to pay well if he could not get them otherwise. The statement that he offered £20 each or named any other large sum seems to be a delusion of the Coroner. These facts were given the police by an eminent London physician, who saw a great deal of the Philadelphian when he was here, but would only divulge the information on a written guarantee from Sir Charles Warren that neither his name nor the name of the physician in question should be given to the public. He said the doctor had gone back to America, and his mission here was purely legitimate.

An American who used to live in New York keeps a herb shop now in the Whitechapel district. A detective called at his place this week and asked him if he had sold any unusual compound of herbs to a customer since August. Similar inquiries were made at other shops in the neighborhood. The basis of this investigation has a startling Shakespearean flavor. An eminent engineer in London suggests to the police the theory that the murderer was a medical maniac trying to find the elixir of life and was looking for the essential ingredient in the parts taken from the murdered bodies; that, like the witches in 'Macbeth', he spent the time over a bubbling caldron of the hellbroth made from the gory ingredients looking for the charm.

The fact that the police are spending time looking up wild theories like this only shows the utter absence of anything like a clew. The wildest rumors are credited to the exclusion of sound ideas. The Whitechapel district is swarming with detectives, some disguised as laborers, talking with loose women and endeavoring to find out from them something to give the police a tangible basis to work on. Some private detective agencies, tempted by the $8,000 reward, have got decoy women in the street, but all avails nothing. Innumerable arrests have been made, but no one is now in custody.

The reference to an 'American who used to live in New York' and who 'keeps a herb shop now in the Whitechapel district' is fascinating. This description fits Tumblety, a herbal remedy doctor, who is recorded as having business premises in London. It is a pity that the stories lack further detail. However, it does appear that the police may have given some credence to the idea that another individual attempted to procure female organs for Tumblety. Several later American press reports spoke of his supposed 'complicity in' or 'involvement with' the Whitechapel murders.

'Military Drill *v.* Police'. A cartoon in *Funny Folks* of Saturday 15 September 1888 shows a hooded 'death' figure with bloodied knife listing the undiscovered murders in Osborn Street, George Yard, Buck's Row and Hanbury Street while the police practise drill in the background.

Another suspect description was added to the mix when the press reported that the following official telegram was dispatched at 8.20 on the evening of 9 September to every police station throughout the metropolis and suburbs:

> Description of man wanted who entered a passage of a house at which the murder was committed. Aged 37, height 5 feet 7 inches, rather dark beard and moustache; dress short dark jacket, dark vest and trousers, and black felt hat; spoke with a foreign accent.

In the lull following the Chapman murder the newspapers, not content just to recycle stories and speculate on the killer's identity, highlighted the hideous slum conditions of the East End. They also reported the supposed lack of police protection that made Whitechapel, in particular, such a dangerous place. Warren and Matthews were alternately praised or blamed for what was happening. Both were targets for the *Star* and the *Pall Mall Gazette* which had political axes to grind. Warren had never been forgiven, particularly by the *Star*, for his handling of the 'Bloody Sunday' riots and was accused, *inter alia*, of leaving London prey to the criminal classes. This is nonsense. After the Chapman murder a small number of uniformed men had been transferred to plain clothes duties to help the CID but the 'double event' on 30 September prompted a big increase in manpower. In total 161 constables and sergeants were drafted in to Whitechapel from other divisions to help the hard-pressed detectives. The difficulties of the investigation were recognised by the fact that these were six-month postings from 1 October 1888 to 31 March 1889.

The *Star*, the *Pall Mall Gazette* and other journals sought the resignation of Warren or Matthews. The unfairness of their accusations prompted the *East London Observer* to mount a vigorous defence of the police. In its opinion the East End had never been better protected and the new policing tactics had made the district as safe as anywhere in the country. As for Fleet Street's portrayal of Whitechapel as 'a plague spot on our civilization', that was simply 'rubbish'.

The 56-year-old MP for Whitechapel, Samuel Montagu, wrote to the commissioner of police offering a reward of £100 for information leading to the capture of the murderer. This prompted a lengthy exchange between Warren and the Home Office about the protocol regarding rewards and whether they should be offered in such a case. Based on past experience, such a course was deemed inadvisable and Home Secretary Matthews ruled against such a move. However, the reward debate rumbled on into October. In contrast, the City authorities were to offer a reward at the beginning of October when a murder was committed in the Square Mile. Whitechapel people were against Matthews' decision: they too wanted a reward to be offered. Their response to another refusal was to form the Whitechapel Vigilance Committee.

—— SEVEN ——

The London Terror

THE night of Saturday 29 September 1888 was an important turning point in the story of the Whitechapel murders. Over the weekend they became an international sensation and the grim name 'Jack the Ripper' entered the public domain. Two killings were committed in the early hours of Sunday 30 September 1888, the first at around 1 a.m. and the second at about 1.40 a.m. The first victim was Elizabeth Stride, aged 44 years, in Dutfield's Yard, Berner Street, St George's-in-the-East, and the second, Catherine Eddowes, aged 46 years, in Mitre Square, Aldgate, in the City of London. The City crime brought a second police force into the reckoning, the City of London Police.

Elizabeth Stride was a casual prostitute who had led a varied career and had long ago taken to the streets to earn a living. She was a Swedish woman but spoke almost flawless English as well as Yiddish, which was useful because she often worked as a char for Jews in the area. She was born Elisabeth Gustafsdotter, the daughter of Gustaf Ericsson, a farmer, and his wife Beata Carlsdotter, on 27 November 1843 in the parish of Torslanda, north of Gothenburg. In late 1860 she moved to Gothenburg to work as a domestic servant. In March 1865 the police in the city registered her as a prostitute – she was only 21 years old. The same year she was treated twice at a special hospital, Kurhuset, for venereal disease, and also gave birth to a stillborn child. On 7 February 1866 she took out a certificate of altered residence for the Swedish parish in London. She carried out domestic work in England and on 10 July 1866 was registered as an unmarried woman at the Swedish Church in Prince's Square, St George's-in-the East.

On 7 March 1869 she married John Thomas Stride, a carpenter, at St Giles-in-the-Fields. She later claimed that she bore nine children but this is not corroborated and she did not have a reputation for veracity. Shortly after the marriage the couple were living in East India Dock Road, Poplar, and Stride was the keeper of a coffee room in Upper North Street, Poplar. From 1872 to 1875 Stride ran the business from 178 Poplar High Street. The marriage broke down and by March 1877 Elizabeth Stride was an inmate of Poplar workhouse. From 1882 she lodged on and off at the common lodging house at 32 Flower and Dean Street where she was known as 'Long Liz'.[1] The clerk of the Swedish Church, Sven Olsson, later

The 'Double Event', as portrayed by the *Illustrated Police News*.

No. 32 Flower and Dean Street, Spitalfields, the last address of Elizabeth Stride.

stated that Stride had told him her husband drowned in the *Princess Alice* disaster on the Thames. (She was accepting charity while telling this lie.) She repeated this story to others, including her partner Michael Kidney, her lodging house deputy Elizabeth Tanner, the lodging house watchman Thomas Bates and fellow lodger Charles Preston. In fact, her estranged husband died of heart disease at the sick asylum at Bromley on 24 October 1884.

For the last three years of her life Stride set up home with Michael Kidney, a waterside labourer. The couple lived in Devonshire Street, close to where Kidney worked on the river. On Thursday 27 September 1888 she turned up at 32 Flower and Dean Street saying that she had had words with the man she lived with.[2]

Kidney said he had last seen her on the Tuesday and that they were still on friendly terms. He had expected to see her when he got in from work. She had returned home and gone out again. In his absence, she returned once the next day to collect some belongings. His account says she left apparently for no reason. This may be the result of his fear of raising suspicion after her death and it is far more likely that there had been a dispute, as Stride herself indicated. Kidney told police he had known Stride for about three years.

Dr Thomas Barnardo wrote a letter to *The Times* on 6 October in which he said he had visited 32 Flower and Dean Street on Wednesday 26 September and had seen Stride there. He later identified her body at the mortuary. Stride spent Thursday and Friday nights at the lodging house, according to the deputy Mrs Tanner, who last saw Stride alive when she had a drink with her at the Queen's Head, Commercial Street. The two walked back to the lodging house about 6.30 on Saturday evening. Stride went into the kitchen and the next time Mrs Tanner saw her was to identify the body at the mortuary.

Stride was found inside the gateway of 40 Berner Street, which was the International Working Men's Educational Club. It was a socialist institution with an international membership of between 75 and 80. On the ground floor, facing the street, were a window and a door. At the rear was a kitchen, while the first floor consisted of a large room used for meetings and entertainment. At the side of the club was a passage leading into the yard, and at the narrow entrance (approximately 9ft wide) to the passage

Elizabeth Stride's man friend Michael Kidney – he denied a bitter separation just before her murder.

were two wooden gates that opened inwards, the right-hand one containing a small wicket-door. To the left of the club was a house divided into three occupied tenements. At the end of Dutfield's Yard was a store owned by Hindley & Co., sack manufacturers. The club premises and a printing office[3] occupied the entire length of the right side of the yard. Most of the members had left by midnight and the remainder, between twenty and thirty people, remained, talking and singing Russian songs. There was no lamp in the yard and the only light came from the windows in the club room and the tenements. Two first-floor windows in the tenements were lit.

The body was found by the club steward, Louis Diemschutz, who lived on the premises and returned home at an hour after midnight on Sunday 30 September. As he drove his

Berner Street, west side, showing (right to left) nos 38–46. No. 40, the International Working Men's Educational Club, is the building at the right of the entrance to Dutfield's Yard. The nearest house, no. 44, is Matthew Packer's and the front room window from which he sold his grapes is clearly visible but shuttered. (*London Metropolitan Archives*)

An illustration of the witness Louis Diemschutz giving evidence before Coroner Wynne Baxter about finding the body of Elizabeth Stride. (Pictorial News, *Saturday 6 October 1888*)

OPENING OF THE INQUEST AT THE VESTRY HALL, ST. GEORGE'S-IN-THE-EAST.

HORRIBLE MURDER OF TWO WOMEN IN EAST LONDON. (*See page 3.*)

pony and costermonger's barrow into the yard, the pony shied away from a bundle inside the gateway. Without dismounting, Diemschutz felt the bundle with his whip. Then he got down and struck a match which gave him just enough light to see that the bundle was a woman's body. The alarm was raised and he was soon joined by other club members including Isaac Kozebrodski.

Witness, William Wess, gave evidence at the inquest. He was a printer living at no. 40 and gave details of the layout of the premises and was in the club at the time of the murder. Joseph Lave, a printer and photographer, was visiting England from the USA and was staying at the club. He had gone into the yard at about 12.30 a.m. for fresh air and walked into the street, but he saw no one before he went back inside 10 minutes later. Witness Morris Eagle, a member of the club, chaired the meeting that night. He had taken his young lady home at 11.45 p.m., leaving by the front door, and returned at 12.35 a.m. By this time the front door was locked and he entered by the back door, via the gateway and yard. He noticed nothing at that time. He had been back in the club 20 minutes, and was joining in some singing, when a member named Gilleman came in and told the assembled company that the body of a woman had been found in the yard. Eagle went down and struck a match to look at the body. The woman was lying by the side of the club wall in a pool of blood. Her feet were about 6 or 7 feet inside the gateway. Eagle ran off for the police.

PC 252H Henry Lamb was quickly on the scene – PC 12HR Albert Collins and other officers arrived during the following 30 minutes. Twenty-eight members of the International Working Men's Educational Club were searched, their clothes examined and statements taken. Some may not have spoken English or spoke it very badly and there were suggestions of rough handling by the police.[4]

Stride was clutching a packet of cachous in her left hand. Diemschutz, Kozebrodski and Fanny Mortimer were all later reported in the *Daily News*[5] as alleging that Stride was clutching a packet of sweetmeats (the cachous) in one hand and a bunch of grapes in the other. Thus was born the legend of the grapes. They did not actually exist, as may be seen from the inquest evidence.

Detective Inspector Reid went to the mortuary to get an accurate description of the woman. He guessed her age at 42 and, lifting an eyelid, found that her eyes were light grey. Parting her lips, he saw that she had lost her front upper teeth. She was wearing an old black skirt and an old black jacket trimmed with fur.

Details of the death of Elizabeth Stride emerged at the inquest hearings over subsequent days. The first medical man to arrive at the scene was Edward Johnston, assistant to Dr Frederick William Blackwell of 100 Commercial Road. Johnston checked Stride and found that the wound appeared to have stopped bleeding but the body was still warm apart from the hands. The blood that had streamed down to the gutter was clotted. Three or four minutes later Dr Blackwell arrived, closely followed by Divisional Inspector Pinhorn from Leman Street. Chief Inspector West and Detective Inspector Reid also attended. Dr Bagster Phillips was called at 1.20 a.m. and first went to Leman Street police station, then to the scene, where the body was still lying.

On Tuesday 2 October 1888 Dr Blackwell gave his evidence before Coroner Wynne Baxter at the inquest hearing held at the Vestry Hall in Cable Street. A detailed summary appeared in *Lloyd's Weekly London Newspaper* of 7 October. Blackwell stated that he was called by a police officer at 1.10 on the Sunday morning and arrived a very short time later at the scene to find the double doors of the yard gate closed. Stride was lying on her left side obliquely across the passage with her face looking towards the right wall (i.e. the wall of the working men's club). Her legs were drawn up and her feet were close against the wall, he

Elizabeth Stride, murdered in Dutfield's Yard, Berner Street, St George's-in-the-East on 30 September 1888. Although she is generally regarded as the third Ripper victim, some believe that she may have been the victim of another killer.

said. Her head was resting beyond the carriage-wheel rut in the passageway and her neck was lying over the rut. Her feet were 3 yards from the gateway entrance. Blackwell found that her neck and chest were quite warm, as were her legs. Her face was slightly warm but her hands were cold. The right hand was open, resting on the chest and was smeared with blood. The left hand, which was lying on the ground, was partially closed and contained a packet of cachous wrapped in tissue paper. There were no rings nor marks of rings on her hands. The face was placid and the mouth was slightly open. Around her neck she had a check silk scarf, the bow of which was turned to the left and pulled very tight. There was a long incision in the neck that exactly corresponded with the lower edge of the scarf. The fabric was slightly frayed, as if by a sharp knife. The incision on the neck began on the left side, 2½ inches below the angle of the jaw and ran almost in a direct line with it, nearly severing the vessels on that side and cutting the windpipe completely in two. It terminated on the opposite side of the neck 1½ inches below the angle of the right jaw, but without severing the vessels on that side.

Blackwell said he could not ascertain whether the bloody hand had been moved. The blood was running down the gutter and into the drain 'in an opposite direction to the feet'. He said there was about a pound of clotted blood close to the body and a stream all the way from there to the back door of the club. Asked by the coroner if there were any spots of blood about, Blackwell replied, 'No, only some marks of blood which had been trodden in.' There was no blood on the soles of Stride's boots. Wynne Baxter asked if there was any splashing of blood on the wall and Blackwell replied, 'No; it was very dark, and what I saw was with the aid of a policeman's lantern. I have not examined the place since.'

Blackwell examined Stride's clothes but found no blood on them. This, surely, was an indicator that she was lying down when her throat was cut. Her bonnet was on the ground a few inches from her head. Her dress was unbuttoned at the top. Blackwell was asked how long she had been dead and he estimated between 20 and 30 minutes. The clothes were not wet with rain. In Blackwell's opinion, Stride bled to death comparatively slowly because vessels had been cut only on one side of the neck and the artery had not been completely severed. He also stated there was no possibility that she could have uttered any sort of cry after her neck was cut.

Questioned by a juror as to when the throat was cut, before or after the woman fell to the ground, Blackwell replied, 'I formed the opinion that the murderer probably caught hold of the silk scarf, which was tight and knotted, and pulled the deceased backwards, cutting the throat in that way. The throat might have been cut as she was falling, or when she was on the ground. The blood would have spurted about if the act had been committed while she was standing up.'

Wynne Baxter then asked, 'Was the silk scarf tight enough to prevent her calling out?' Blackwell replied, 'I could not say that.' 'A hand might have been placed on her nose and mouth?' 'Yes, and the cut on the throat was probably instantaneous.'

The police surgeon, Dr Bagster Phillips, arrived at the scene 20–30 minutes after Blackwell. When Phillips later examined the body at the mortuary he discovered a bluish discolouration on the chest and both shoulders, especially under the right collar bone. The authors feel this means there can be little doubt that Stride was thrown to the ground and held down by pressure on her chest while her throat was cut.

Dr Phillips' evidence from the post-mortem examination provided further details of Stride's injuries. He conducted the examination on the Sunday afternoon with Dr Blackwell, who made the dissection while Phillips took notes. The body was fairly well nourished. The left-to-right incision on the neck was a clean cut, 6 inches in length. The men made other observations. The lower fifth of the bones in Stride's right leg was deformed; the limb bowed forward and there was a thickening above the left ankle, although the bones there were straighter. The only recent external injury was the one to the neck. The soles of Stride's feet were scaling, probably through lack of cleaning. The body was then washed and Phillips observed six, more or less scabbed, sores on the forehead. The lower lobe of the left ear was torn as if it had been forcibly removed, or worn through by an earring, but this wound was fully healed. The right ear was pierced but was not injured; Stride was wearing no earring. The brain was fairly normal. The left lung had old adhesions and both lungs were unusually pale. There was no fluid in the pericardium – the heart was small with the left ventricle firmly contracted and empty and the right slightly so. There was no clot in the pulmonary

This artist's impression from *Pictorial News*, Saturday 6 October 1888, of the body of Elizabeth Stride lying in the mortuary shows a peaceful face, not as harrowing as the photograph of her.

artery but the right ventricle was full of dark clot. The stomach was large and the mucous membrane only congested. It contained partly digested food consisting of cheese, potato and farinaceous powder. Phillips stated that the cause of death was undoubtedly the loss of blood from the left carotid artery and the division of the windpipe.

In the pocket of Stride's underskirt were found a key (possibly a padlock key), a small piece of lead pencil, a pocket comb, a broken piece of comb, a metal spoon, some buttons and a hook. There was a small amount of mud on the right side of her jacket while the left side was well plastered. No doubt as she had been found lying on that side.

Police inquiries resulted in the identification of several witnesses who claimed to have seen Stride with a man before the murder. Edward Spooner of 26 Fairclough Street stated that between 12.30 and 1 a.m. he was talking with a young woman outside the Bee Hive public house on the corner of Christian Street and Fairclough Street when, after about 25 minutes, two Jews came running up shouting 'Murder' and 'Police'. He went to the yard and saw the body. There were about fifteen people in the yard and he saw one strike a match. Spooner lifted Stride's chin and saw blood flowing from the throat. He could see that she had a piece of paper folded in her right hand and was wearing a red and white flower on her jacket. As an indication of how witnesses could be mistaken in their timing, Spooner stated that it was about 12.35 a.m. when he went to yard when, in fact, it was about 1 a.m. He had made his estimate based on the pub's closing time.

William Marshall, a labourer of 64 Berner Street, claimed to have seen Stride talking to and kissing a man at about 11.45 p.m. on the footpath opposite 68 Berner Street, between Christian Street and Boyd Street. The man was about 5 feet 6 inches tall and stout. He seemed to be middle-aged and was wearing a small black cutaway coat, dark trousers and a round cap with a small peak, something such as a sailor would wear, but overall, he had the appearance of a clerk. He heard the man say to the woman, 'You would say anything but your prayers.' He was mild-speaking and appeared educated.

James Brown of 35 Fairclough Street said he had seen Stride at about 12.45 a.m. when he went to the chandler's shop at the corner of Berner Street and Fairclough Street to get some supper. She was standing with a man against a wall by the board school in Fairclough Street. As Brown passed them he heard the woman say, 'No, not tonight, some other night.' He was certain that it was Stride, although it was at this very time that another witness, Schwartz, claimed to have seen her attacked at the murder scene. It is probable that Brown's timing is incorrect. He described the man as about 5 feet 7 inches tall and stoutish. It is probable that the people seen by Brown were not Stride and a suspect at all. Another witness at the inquest was Mrs Mary Malcolm who caused much confusion because she mistakenly identified Stride as her sister Elizabeth Watts. Mrs Malcolm's sister, Elizabeth Stokes (alias Elizabeth Watts), actually appeared at the inquest to put the lie to her story.

An unrelated incident reported at the time was the discovery of a knife in Whitechapel Road by a man named Thomas Coram at about 12.30 a.m. on the Monday morning, almost 24 hours after the murder. He pointed out the weapon to PC 282H Drage and both gave evidence at the Stride inquest. Their contribution served only to confuse matters because the knife had no connection to the murder.

Another witness, an immigrant Hungarian Jew named Israel Schwartz, did not appear at the inquest.[6] He had observed an attack on a woman he identified as Stride at 12.45 a.m. at the entrance to Dutfield's Yard. He was deemed important enough to be closely questioned by Inspector Abberline. At the time he gave his statement, Schwartz stated that he had seen a man stop and speak to a woman who was standing in the gateway to

Dutfield's Yard. The man tried to pull the woman into the street, turned her round and threw her down on the footway. She screamed three times but not very loudly. Schwartz, presumably to avoid getting too close to the confrontation, crossed the street and saw a second man lighting a pipe. The woman's attacker called out 'Lipski', apparently to the man with the pipe. Schwartz walked away but was followed by the second man. He ran as far as the railway arch but his follower did not stay with him. Schwartz was unable to say if the two men were together or if they knew each other. The man with the pipe was described as aged 35, 5 feet 11 inches tall with a fresh complexion and light brown hair. He was dressed in a dark overcoat, and an old, black, hard felt hat with a wide brim. He carried a clay pipe. It has been suggested that the man with the pipe was eventually traced. However, a reading of the surviving official reports clearly shows that he was not.

The *Star* of 1 October 1888 printed an interview with Schwartz, whom its man found in Backchurch Lane. The witness's English was imperfect so the reporter used an interpreter:

. . . the man's story was retold just as he had given it to the police. It is, in fact, to the effect that he

SAW THE WHOLE THING.

It seems that he had gone out for the day, and his wife had expected to move, during his absence, from their lodgings in Berner-street to others in Backchurch-lane. When he came homewards about a quarter before one he first walked down Berner-street to see if his wife had moved. As he turned the corner from Commercial-road he noticed some distance in front of him a man walking as if partially intoxicated. He walked on behind him, and presently he noticed a woman standing in the entrance to the alley way where the body was afterwards found. The half-tipsy man halted and spoke to her. The Hungarian saw him put his hand on her shoulder and push her back into the passage, but, feeling rather timid of getting mixed up in quarrels, he crossed to the other side of the street. Before he had gone many yards, however, he heard the sound of a quarrel, and turned back to learn what was the matter, but just as he stepped from the kerb

A SECOND MAN CAME OUT

of the doorway of the public-house a few doors off, and shouting out some sort of warning to the man who was with the woman, rushed forward as if to attack the intruder. The Hungarian states positively that he saw a knife in this second man's hand, but he waited to see no more. He fled incontinently, to his new lodgings. He described

THE MAN WITH THE WOMAN

as about 30 years of age, rather stoutly built, and wearing a brown moustache. He was dressed respectably in dark clothes and felt hat. The man who came at him with a knife he also describes, but not in detail. He says he was taller than the other, but not so stout, and that his moustaches were red. Both men seem to belong to the same grade of society. The police have arrested one man answering the description the Hungarian furnishes. This prisoner has not been charged, but is held for inquiries to be made. The truth of the man's statement is not wholly accepted.

Description of a Suspect.

Another man was, however, seen in the company of a woman by someone only a short time before the commission of the crime, and this is the description which the police have of him: – Aged about 28, and in height 5ft. 8in. or thereabouts; complexion dark, and wearing a black diagonal coat and hard felt hat, collar and tie. He was of respectable appearance, and was carrying a newspaper parcel.

It will be seen that Schwartz's newspaper statement differs somewhat from the one recorded by the police. The newspaper piece states that Schwartz had followed the man, who appeared 'partially intoxicated', from Commercial Road to Dutfield's Yard. The 'half-tipsy man' had pushed the woman back into the passage, then the second man had come out of 'the doorway of the public-house a few doors off' and had shouted a warning to the man with the woman. It says that Schwartz stated 'positively' that the second man came at him with a knife (as opposed to a pipe), had a red moustache and was carrying a newspaper parcel. Of course, the police version should be accepted as the more accurate: sensationalism and interpretation problems may have crept into the press version. The name Lipski referred to Israel Lipski, a Jewish murderer hanged in August 1887 for the killing of a woman lodger at 16 Batty Street. His motive appeared to have been sexual and the name 'Lipski' had been used since as a term of abuse to Jews. It was probably directed at Schwartz whose appearance was 'very Jewish'. Schwartz was, in fact, the most important witness if his statement was honest and accurate. His version of events also indicated the possibility that two men were involved in the murder of Stride. However, a further report in the *Star* the following day claimed that 'the Leman-street police have reason to doubt the truth of the story'.

A witness who caused the police some vexation at the time was Matthew Packer, a 58-year-old greengrocer who traded from his front window at 44 Berner Street, hard by the murder scene. Police house-to-house inquiries were instituted in the vicinity on Sunday, the day of the murder, and one of the officers involved was Sergeant Stephen White. He carried a special notebook issued to record the results of these investigations and at 9 a.m. he called on Packer and questioned him. Packer stated that he had closed his shop at 12.30 a.m. because of the rain and said he had seen no one and witnessed nothing of a suspicious nature. White also spoke to two other residents at no. 44, also with negative result. Then, on Tuesday 2 October Packer was seen by two private detectives, Le Grand and Batchelor of 238 The Strand, who had been employed by the Whitechapel Vigilance Committee to make their own investigations. (A man named James Hall was employed by Le Grand as a clerk in his private inquiry agency from September 1888 until June 1889 and he saw Le Grand 'writing almost daily during that period'.)

Packer informed the private detectives that at about 11.45 on the night of the murder he had sold grapes to a man who was with a woman fitting Stride's description. In addition, two sisters stated that they had seen a bloodstained grape stalk in Dutfield's Yard near where the body had lain. The two detectives visited the yard and claimed that they discovered a grape stalk. The *Evening News* picked up the story and saw an opportunity to find fault with the police for not discovering this important witness. On the Wednesday evening, 3 October, an *Evening News* reporter called to see Packer. Packer told the pressman that at some time between 11.30 and midnight a man and a woman had approached from the direction of Ellen Street and had stopped outside his window. The man had bought some black grapes. He described the man and detailed the conversation he had with him. The resulting *Evening News* article ended with criticism of the police: the reporter had extracted from Packer the statement that officers had not asked him if he saw anything but had only checked his backyard. This, as evidenced by White, was obviously a lie. But it was serious for the police because it amounted to an allegation of neglect of duty, a serious disciplinary offence. Packer lived only a couple of doors away from the murder scene and there was absolutely no doubt that he should have been questioned.

When the article appeared in Thursday's paper, Detective Inspector Henry Moore immediately started an internal disciplinary inquiry. The two private detectives took Packer to the mortuary that day to see if he could identify Stride's body, which he did. Packer was met by Sergeant White when he returned and this time he stated he had seen Stride about midnight on the night of the murder. White spoke with the two detectives who went off with Packer. Later the same day White again spoke with Packer at his shop. This time the two detectives arrived in a hansom cab and said they were taking Packer to Scotland Yard to see Sir Charles Warren.

It seems the three did go to Scotland Yard but they would not have been seen by the chief commissioner, who does not deal with members of the public at that level. It is likely that Packer saw a detective inspector, probably Moore, and a signed witness statement would have been obtained from him. The statement has not survived. However, a handwritten summary of what Packer had to say is in the official records. It was compiled by the senior Assistant Commissioner, Alexander Carmichael Bruce, who initialled it 'ACB' and dated it '4.10.88'. It noted:

Matthew Packer
  Keeps a small shop in Berner Str—— has a few grapes in window. Black & white
  On Sat night about 11 p.m. a young man from 25–30 – about 5.7. with long black coat buttoned up – soft felt hat. kind of yankee hat rather broad shoulders – rather quick in speaking rough voice. I sold him ½ pound black grapes 3d. A woman came up with him from Back Church end (the lower end of street) she was dressed in black frock & jacket, fur round bottom of jacket a black crape bonnet, she was playing with a flower like a geranium white outside & red inside. I identify the woman at the St George's mortuary as the one I saw that night –

  They passed by as though they were going up Comm—— Road, but instead of going up they crossed to the other side of the road to the Board School, & were there for about ½ an hour till I shd. say 11.30. talking to one another. I then shut up my shutters. Before they passed over opposite to my shop, they went near to the Club for a few minutes apparently listening to the music. I saw no more of them after I shut up my shutters.

  I put the man down as a young clerk. He had a frock coat on – no gloves He was about 1½ inches or 2 or 3 inches – a little bit higher than she was.
ACB
4.10.88.

Mr (later Sir) Alexander Carmichael Bruce, the senior Assistant Commissioner who covered part of Anderson's duties during September and early October 1888 while the latter was away on sick leave. Many of the official police reports on the Whitechapel murders are minuted or initialled by Bruce, who made notes of Packer's statement.

Some researchers have said that Packer was seen by Warren and that Warren took this 'statement'. This cannot be true. However, Assistant Commissioner A.C. Bruce, who was covering for Anderson as a supervisor, made this summary, no doubt composed from Packer's full statement, and his involvement indicates the seriousness attached to the allegation of police negligence.

Packer's change of mind was no doubt influenced by a reward being offered by the Whitechapel Vigilance Committee, and the changes he made to his story were no doubt made in the hope of collecting this reward. The two private detectives employed by the Whitechapel Vigilance Committee had found, with an accompanying press reporter, a grape stalk in the rubbish swept up by the police after their search of the yard and which seemed to confirm Packer's story. He had gone with them to the mortuary and identified Stride's body. The fact was that the police had not known about the grape story. Packer's original statement made no mention of the selling of grapes or of seeing the possible murderer. In his original statement he told police that he had seen no suspicious person about. The post-mortem on Stride showed that she had not eaten any grapes but the story of a missing clue and a missed witness, Packer, until discovered by the press, was too good a story with which not to beat the police and allege yet again the charge of police imcompetence. Packer's new evidence quickly unravelled but it had been enough to prompt the beginnings of a disciplinary inquiry and a waste of valuable police time disproving his fictions. So discredited did his evidence eventually become that he was not called as a witness at the Stride inquest.

If further doubt needed to be cast on the whole Packer episode, we need look no further than one of the two private detectives involved. Le Grand had a long criminal record stretching back to July 1877 when he was convicted of larceny (theft) and sentenced at Middlesex Sessions to eight years' penal servitude and seven years' supervision. He went by various aliases, including 'Charles Grant', 'Christian Nelson' alias 'Briscony' and 'Neilson'. After his release he failed to keep reporting to the police and was on the wanted list in 1884. He was described by the police as a German[7] 'who professes to be a waiter, obtains money and goods from young women in good situations, on pretence of marrying them'. In 1888 he was aged 38,[8] had light brown hair, scars on his nose and centre forehead and hands, and 'hair down centre of chest to bottom of stomach'. He was of above average height at 6 feet.

In May 1889, under the name Charles Grandy or Grand, he appeared at Marlborough Street police court, together with Amelia Pourquoi, alias Amelia Demay, both of York Place, Baker Street, charged with conspiring to defraud and injure a surgeon named Malcolm Alexander Morris of Harley Street. It was stated in court that Grand was also known as 'the French colonel' and had a previous conviction for assaulting a prostitute. The pair pleaded not guilty but were bailed for the sum of £300 each to await trial at the Central Criminal Court on 25 June 1889. *The Times* reported that Le Grand was sentenced to five years' imprisonment but he served only two. Amelia Pourquoi was sentenced to eighteen months' in gaol. 'Charles Grant', this time of 83 Kennington Road, was in trouble again soon after his release. He appeared at Westminster police court charged on warrant with 'feloniously and with menaces demanding £500 of Mrs. Baldock of 8 Grosvenor Place S.W.' He had been arrested the previous Saturday night at Maldon in Surrey with an eight-chambered revolver and a knuckleduster in his possession. He was tried at the Central Criminal Court on 20 November as 'Charles Grande' and was identified as being Christian Nelson, who had been convicted in 1877. On 25 November Grande received a shock when the judge, Mr Justice Hawkins, said that as the accused had tried to push the arresting officer, Sergeant James, under an incoming train, he was a man 'prepared to commit any act of violence' in

'Le Grand of the Strand', aka Christian Nelson, alias Briscony and Neilson. He was a convicted thief who posed as a private investigator in 1888 and was hired by the Whitechapel Vigilance Committee. He and his colleague 'Batchelor' were responsible for tracing the dubious witness fruiterer Matthew Packer. (*Metropolitan Police*)

self-preservation and perhaps a life sentence should be awarded. Grande 'fell back apparently in a fit'. The judge then sentenced him to twenty years for sending the threatening letter to Mrs Baldock and to seven years (concurrent) for being in possession of a forged bill of exchange. In his summary report of 19 October 1888 Swanson concluded, 'any statement he [Packer] made would be rendered almost valueless as evidence'.

With numerous reports of suspicious men and odd incidents, it can be imagined how busy the police were in the wake of the Stride murder. The *Star* of 2 October noted that the police had 'no clue whatever':

> the threads that had been taken up on the possible chance of their leading to something tangible have been laid down again. It is but fair to say that the police have clutched eagerly at every straw that promised to help them out, but there is nothing left to work on. People have come forward by scores to furnish the description of a man they had seen with some woman near the scene, and not a great while before the commission of one or the other of
>
> SUNDAY MORNING'S CRIMES,
>
> but no two of the descriptions are alike, and none of the accompanying information has thus far been able to bear investigation. In the matter of the Hungarian [Schwartz] who said he saw a struggle between a man and a woman in the passage where the Stride body was afterwards found, the Leman-street police have reason to doubt the truth of the story. They arrested one man on the description thus obtained, and a second on that furnished from another source, but they are not likely to act further on the same information without additional facts. If every man should be arrested who was known to have been seen in company with an abandoned woman in that locality on last Saturday night, the police-stations would not hold them. There are many people in that district who volunteer information to the police on the principle of securing lenient treatment for their own offences, and there are others who turn in descriptions on the chance of coming near enough the mark to claim a portion of the reward if the man should be caught, just as one buys a ticket in a lottery. Even where such information is given in good faith, it can rarely be looked upon in the light of a clue.

The paper reported there had been other scares too. The alarm was raised in Barnsbury at 1.30 that morning by a woman in Cloudesley Road. She shrieked that a man had threatened her with a knife. One of the men who ran to the spot blew a whistle, which brought several policemen on the scene. This was lucky for the suspected murderer, who was seriously threatened by a mob of people. He was taken to the Caledonian Road police station where the 'knife' was found to be a piece of harmless steel.

A black bag was repeatedly mentioned in the press in connection with the Whitechapel murders. Mrs Fanny Mortimer, aged 48, of 36 Berner Street, said that on the night of the murder, 'The only man I had seen pass through Berner-street previously was a young man who carried a black shiny bag. He walked very fast down the street from the Commercial-road. He looked up at the club, and then went round the corner by the Board school.' Her story was widely reported. Leon Goldstein of 22 Christian Street, a member of the club, presented himself at Leman Street police station as the man seen by Mrs Mortimer. He was able to clear himself, having left a coffee house in Spectacle Alley just before she saw him. His bag contained nothing more offensive than empty cigarette boxes.

Another story of a man with a black bag was told by Albert Bachert of 13 Newnham Street, Whitechapel. Bachert stated that on the Saturday night at about 7 minutes to 12 o'clock he entered the Three Nuns Hotel (also reported as the Three Tuns), Aldgate, where a stranger had asked him questions about local prostitutes, particularly about the age of 'the women outside'. It was noted that 'it has been singular that none of the victims were young women, all of them having been over 40 years of age'. The stranger was carrying a shiny black bag.

The Metropolitan police inquiry into the Stride murder was intensive and the findings are summed up in Chief Inspector Swanson's long report of 19 October. Swanson noted that

The west side of Berner Street showing (left to right) nos 36–28. The nearest house is no. 36, home of Mrs Fanny Mortimer, who stood at this door and saw 'a man with a shiny black bag' hurrying along the street on the night of the murder. This suspect was cleared when he was found to be a member of the club at no. 40, Leon Goldstein. (*London Metropolitan Archives*)

The scene outside the International Working Men's Educational Club at 40 Berner Street on the Sunday morning after the murder as police mingle with curious onlookers.

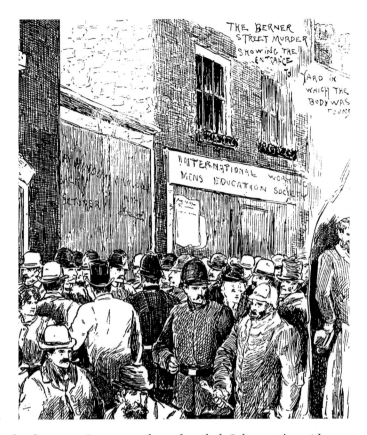

PC 452H William Smith[9] saw a man and woman, later identified as Stride, together in Berner Street at 12.35 a.m. and gave a description of the man as aged about 28, 5 feet 7 inches tall, with a dark complexion and a small dark moustache. He was wearing a black diagonal coat, white collar and tie, and a hard felt hat. In his inquest evidence PC Smith also stated that the man was carrying a newspaper parcel measuring about 18 inches in length and 6 or 8 inches wide. Stride and the man were on the opposite side of Berner Street to the club and a bit further up. Swanson then detailed Schwartz's evidence and recorded his description of the man's attack on a woman, apparently Stride, at 12.45 a.m. Schwartz described his man as aged about 30, 5 feet 5 inches tall and of fair complexion. He had dark hair, a small brown moustache and a full face, was broad-shouldered and wore a dark jacket and trousers and a black cap with peak. He had nothing in his hands. Although the physical attributes of the men described are tolerably similar, Swanson felt that the 'serious differences in description of dress' rendered it 'doubtful whether they are describing the same man'. This made it more probable that Schwartz, rather than Smith, saw the murderer. However, Swanson felt it necessary to point out that although Stride's body was found about 15 minutes after Schwartz's sighting, account should be taken of the fact that only her throat had been cut which left sufficient time for her to meet another man – the 'murderous action' would have taken only 5 to 10 minutes. Swanson said it was 'not clearly proved that the man that Schwartz saw is the murderer'. This is an important observation to bear in mind: it has been suggested that Schwartz was the witness Anderson had in mind as being able to identify the murderer, especially as Swanson is cited by theorists in support of Anderson's contention. A marginal Home Office note stated:

> But I understand the Inspector to suggest that Schwartz' man need not have been the murderer. True only 15 minutes elapsed between 12.45 when Schwartz saw the man & 1.0 when the woman was found murdered on the same spot. But the suggestion is that Schwartz' man may have left her, she being a prostitute then accosted or was accosted by another man, & there was time enough for this to take place & for this other man to murder her before 1.0.

POLICE NOTICE.

TO THE OCCUPIER.

On the mornings of Friday, 31st August, Saturday 8th, and Sunday, 30th September, 1888, Women were murdered in or near Whitechapel, supposed by some one residing in the immediate neighbourhood. Should you know of any person to whom suspicion is attached, you are earnestly requested to communicate at once with the nearest Police Station.

Metropolitan Police Office,
30th September, 1888.

Printed by McCorquodale & Co. Limited, " The Armoury," Southwark.

Police notice of 30 September 1888.

It could not be clearer that Swanson was well aware Schwartz's evidence alone could not prove that the man he saw was the actual murderer.

Swanson also gave the description of a man seen (by a witness, Joseph Lawende) with a woman at Church Passage, close to Mitre Square in the City, at 1.35 the same morning, just before the discovery of another victim, Catherine Eddowes. The man was aged 30, stood 5 feet 7 or 8 inches tall, had a fair complexion and fair moustache. He was of medium build and was dressed in a pepper-and-salt coloured loose jacket, a grey cloth cap with a peak of same colour and a reddish handkerchief tied in a knot round his neck. He had the appearance of a sailor. Swanson also noted that the woman in this instance had been identified as the victim, Eddowes, only by her clothing, 'which is a serious drawback to the value of the description of the man'. However, as the body was found in Mitre Square only 10 minutes later, Swanson felt it 'reasonable to believe that the man he saw was the murderer, but for the purposes of comparison, this description is much nearer to that given by Schwartz than to that given by the P.C.' Again, from this we can see Swanson clearly understood that the description given by the City witness, Lawende, did not amount to proof of the identity of the murderer. However, he did appear to think it more likely that Lawende, rather than Schwartz, had seen the actual murderer. This should be considered in relation to later claims that a witness's testimony was sufficient to identify the murderer.

Swanson's report also casts light upon the way general police inquiries were carried out in connection with the murder. After arriving at Berner Street, officers immediately searched the yard for a weapon. They also searched members of the socialist club, examining their clothing and taking statements. Extensive house-to-house inquiries were made in Berner Street to ascertain whether anyone had been seen with the victim. Subsequently, 80,000 leaflets were printed and distributed in H Division's area asking people to inform the police of anyone suspicious who might be lodging with them. The numerous statements were followed up and many of the people mentioned in them were 'required to account for their presence at the time of the murders'. Swanson said 'every care' was taken to verify each statement as far as was possible. As a result of responses to the leaflet campaign, further house-to-house inquiries were made. This involved:

a search by police & with a few exceptions – but not such as to convey suspicion – covered the area bounded by the City Police boundary on the one hand, Lamb St. Commercial St. Great Eastern Railway & Buxton St. then by Albert St. Dunk St. Chicksand St. & Great Garden St to Whitechapel Rd. and then to the City boundary, under this head also Common Lodging Houses were visited & over 2000 lodgers were examined.

There has been speculation about the search area described in Swanson's report. It is unthinkable that the area south of Whitechapel Road was excluded when that was the very location of Berner Street. Other reports make it abundantly clear that Berner Street was subjected to careful house-to-house inquiries immediately after the murder and these, undoubtedly, took in the adjoining streets. The area of the Buck's Row murder had also been covered at the beginning of the month. As they had already been covered in the investigation, they were excluded from the area prescribed in the later part of the inquiry.

The Thames Police also made inquiries regarding sailors on board ships in dock or on the river and tracked down 'asiatics' present in London homes and opium dens. About eighty suspects were detained at Metropolitan police stations. Their statements were taken and verified. More than 300 people about whom the police had received information were also investigated. Some 76 butchers and slaughterers were visited and the characters of the men they employed looked into; this included all those who had been taken on within the last six months. Inquiries were also made into the alleged presence of Greek gypsies but it was found that they had not been in the capital at the time of the previous murders. Three 'cowboys' who belonged to the 'American Exhibition' ('Buffalo' Bill's Wild West Show which had been touring in 1887) were traced and satisfactorily accounted for themselves. By the time of Swanson's report, 994 dockets[10] had been started in addition to the police reports. It is not surprising that Inspector Abberline said the police nearly broke under the strain.

Yet the second murder that night, within an hour of Stride's killing, was an even more horrific affair, and brought the City of London Police fully into the investigation for the first time.

——— EIGHT ———

A Thirst for Blood

THE second victim of 30 September 1888 was Catherine Eddowes of 55 Flower and Dean Street, another common lodging house. She also used the names Kelly (her current man-friend was John Kelly) and Conway (her ex-common-law husband was Thomas Conway). Catherine was a native of Wolverhampton and was born to George Eddowes, a tinplate worker, and his wife Catherine (née Evans) on 14 April 1842. She was one of eleven children. John Kelly was described as 'a peculiar looking man . . . of perhaps 40 years, with a fresh coloured face, bronzed by a recent hop-picking excursion, a head of thick black hair, a somewhat low forehead, and moustache and imperial. He wore the fustian clothes of a market labourer with a deep blue scarf round his neck, and spoke with a clear, deep, sonorous voice.'[1]

John Kelly and Eddowes had been hop picking in Kent up until Thursday 27 September. They both slept in the casual ward at Shoe Lane that night.[2] On Friday she found a bed in the casual ward at Mile End, while Kelly slept at 55 Flower and Dean Street. Kelly saw Eddowes next at 8 o'clock on Saturday morning. They had some tea and coffee, bought after he pawned the boots he stood in. Kelly last saw Eddowes alive at 2 p.m. that day in Houndsditch. They had no money to pay for their lodgings and she told him that she was going over to Bermondsey to see her daughter Annie (whose father was Conway) with a view to getting some money. She said she would be back by 4 p.m. but did not return. Kelly was later told by two women that Eddowes had been locked up in Bishopsgate for 'a little drop of drink'. He checked that she would be out on Sunday morning. In his statement to the police Kelly admitted that she was 'occasionally in the habit of slightly drinking to excess' but he made a point of saying that he 'never suffered her to go out for immoral purposes' – 'She has never brought money to me that she has earned at night.' This seems to indicate that he was anxious to avoid accusations that he was a pimp. However, when giving his evidence at the inquest on 4 October, Kelly stated that Eddowes was trying to borrow money so that 'she need not walk the streets'. Mr Crawford, the City solicitor, pointed out that Kelly had said that she did not walk the streets. Kelly then admitted that they were short of money at that time, virtually implying that she was indeed 'walking the streets', i.e., engaging in casual prostitution; see *The Times*, 5 October 1888.

A contemporary likeness of Catherine Eddowes that
appeared in the *Penny Illustrated Paper* of 13 October 1888.

Frederick William Wilkinson, the deputy of
their lodging house at 55 Flower and Dean
Street, told police that the pair lived as man and
wife. He said he had known them for the past 7
or 8 years and added that she had made a living
by hawking 'about the streets' and cleaning for
Jews. They had paid their rent pretty regularly.
Eddowes did not drink often, he said, and she
was a 'very jolly woman'. Wilkinson last saw her
alive, with Kelly, between 10 and 11 a.m. on
Saturday 29 September. He made a point of
saying, 'I did not know her to walk the street. I
never knew or heard of her being intimate with
any one but Kelly. She used to say she was
married to Conway and her name was bought
and paid for.' Wilkinson said that Kelly had returned to the lodging house between 7.30 and
8 p.m. and he had asked him 'Where's Kate?' to which Kelly had replied, 'I have heard she's
been locked up.' The records show Eddowes was not arrested until 8.30 p.m., so Wilkinson's
timing was incorrect – Kelly must have returned after 8.30. Kelly took a single bed for 4*d*,
half the price of a double. It had been four or five weeks since Kelly or Eddowes had slept at
Wilkinson's because they had been away hopping. Wilkinson told police he was positive
Kelly did not go out again that night.

At 8.30 p.m. on Saturday 29 September PC
931 Louis Robinson of the City Police was on
patrol in Aldgate High Street when he saw a
crowd of people outside no. 29. He went to
investigate and found a woman, later identified as
Eddowes, lying on the footway, drunk. He asked if
anyone knew her or where she lived but received
no reply. Robinson picked her up and carried her
to the side of the path near the shutters. She fell
sideways so he sought help from another officer
to deal with her. She was taken to Bishopsgate
Street police station, arriving at 8.45 p.m. They
were seen by the Station Sergeant, James Byfield.
At this time Eddowes was supported by the two
constables. She was asked for her name and
replied, 'Nothing.' She smelt very strongly of
drink.

John Kelly, who had lived with Catherine Eddowes as her
common law husband for seven years. She often adopted his
surname, as well as that of her ex-partner Tom Conway.

Bishopsgate police station, *c.* 1910.

Prisoners brought into the station for drunkenness were not searched but a handkerchief or anything else they could use to injure themselves was taken from them. This is in stark contrast to modern practice where all prisoners admitted, whatever the offence, are thoroughly searched and their property taken from them and noted down. From a list of the property later found on Eddowes' body, we know she was carrying a handkerchief, a table knife and needles and pins (among other things) but we don't know whether these were taken from her at the police station. She was placed in a cell. Robinson last saw her in the cell at 8.50 p.m. and noted that she was wearing an apron.

PC 968 George Henry Hutt came on duty as gaoler at 9.45 p.m. He saw Eddowes who was then asleep. Hutt visited her about every 30 minutes from 9.55 p.m. At 12.15 a.m. she was awake and singing to herself. At 12.30 she asked Hutt when she was going to be let out. He replied, 'When you are capable of taking care of yourself.' She said that she was then quite up to taking care of herself. At 12.55 a.m. Hutt decided she was sober. She was then taken from the cell and asked Hutt what time it was. Hutt said, 'Too late for you to get any more drink.' She replied, 'Well what time is it?' He said, 'Just on one.' She said, 'I shall get a damned fine hiding when I get home.' Hutt replied, 'And serve you right, you have no right to get drunk.'

They then went to the office where, at 1 a.m., Byfield agreed she was sober. (It was usually left to the discretion of the inspector, or acting inspector to decide when a drunk was in a fit condition to be discharged.) She gave her name and address as Mary Ann Kelly, 6 Fashion Street, Spitalfields, and said that she had been hopping. Byfield discharged her. Hutt pushed open the swing door leading to the passage and said, 'This way, Missus.'

She passed along the passage and to the outer door. Hutt asked her to pull it after her. She said, 'All right. Good night, old cock.' She went out, pulling the door to within 6 inches of closed and turned left in the direction of Houndsditch.

Like Robinson, Hutt noticed that she was wearing an apron. At the inquest he estimated that it would have taken her about 8 minutes, walking at an ordinary speed, to get to Mitre Square.

Since August 1888 the City commissioner had put out extra night patrols in plain clothes to police the eastern area of the City, hoping to prevent further murders and to keep close observation on all prostitutes frequenting public houses and walking the streets. At 1.30 a.m. PC 881 Edward Watkins, a seventeen-year veteran of the City Police, passed through Mitre Square, Aldgate, on his beat; all was quiet and in order. He returned 14 minutes later, entering the square from Mitre Street. Turning right into the gloomiest corner of the square, the south one, Watkins shone his bull's-eye lantern and instantly saw a woman lying on her back, her feet towards him. It was Catherine Eddowes, so recently released from police custody in Bishopsgate Street.

Her throat was deeply cut, her clothing shredded and thrown open, exposing her abdomen which had been opened up from the pubic area to the sternum. Her head was turned to her left, towards the wall of a house, and she was lying in a pool of liquid blood. Her arms were by her sides, spread out slightly away from her body, palms upward and fingers slightly bent. A 2-foot piece of intestines had been detached and was lying on the ground between her body and her left arm, apparently deliberately placed there. More intestines, smeared with feculent matter, were draped up from the abdominal cavity and over the right shoulder. There were also various cuts on her face. The lobe and auricle of the right ear were cut obliquely through. She presented a ghastly spectacle that shocked

55 Flower and Dean Street, where Catherine Eddowes lodged with John Kelly. If she had returned here on her release from Bishopsgate police station she would not have met the Ripper that night.

Nº 55 FLOWER & DEAN Sᵗ.

PC 881 Edward Watkins of the City of London Police. He discovered the body of Catherine Eddowes in Mitre Square.

PC. E.WATKIN
THE FIRST
TO DISCOVER
THE BODY
IN MITRE SQUARE

A contemporary drawing of the scene of the Eddowes murder.

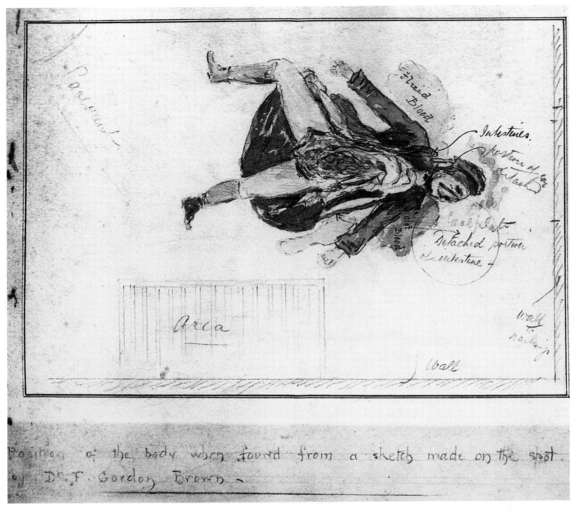

A contemporary drawing of the victim's body at the murder scene.

Mitre Square. The door at the far right (open at the time of the murder) led into Kealey & Tonge's warehouse where the warehouseman, George Morris, was sweeping the floor.

An enlargement of a detail from a City of London Police group photograph shows PC 964 James Harvey (middle of second row of three from top). He was almost certainly the police officer who came closest to catching the Ripper red-handed, in Mitre Square at 1.40 a.m. on Sunday 30 September 1888.

Mitre Square, Aldgate, looking west towards the corner where Eddowes' body was discovered. Mitre Street can be seen through the gap in the buildings. This photograph was taken from a spot just in front of where PC Harvey must have turned at the bottom of Church Passage while the Ripper was undoubtedly in the square with his victim.

Watkins. He immediately ran to the east side of the square where the door to Kearley & Tonge's warehouse stood slightly ajar. The nightwatchman, 54-year-old George James Morris, an ex-Metropolitan Police officer, was inside, sweeping the steps down to the door. It had been ajar only 2 or 3 minutes, according to Morris, when Watkins pushed it open.

Watkins said, 'For God's sake, mate, come to my assistance.' Watkins was so agitated that Morris thought he might be ill. Morris asked what was the matter and Watkins said, 'There is another woman cut to pieces.' She had been ripped up like 'a pig in a market', he said, and her entrails 'flung in a heap about her neck'. Morris took his lamp and looked at the body, then ran up Mitre Street towards the main road blowing his whistle for assistance. He was soon joined by two police constables whom he sent to Mitre Square. One of them was PC 964 James Harvey. Morris followed and returned to the warehouse. He said he had neither heard nor seen anything prior to Watkins' arrival.

PC Harvey said he had been down the narrow Church Passage as far as Mitre Square at about 1.40 a.m. and had seen and heard nothing untoward. He returned up the passage and back into Duke Street. There is no reason to suppose that Harvey shone his lamp into Mitre Square nor even took much notice of it because the area was PC Watkins' responsibility. However, when Harvey's account is combined with evidence from three Jewish witnesses located by later house-to-house inquiries, it seems the murder was committed after 1.35 a.m. (when the Jewish men passed by) and before 1.45. The murderer and his victim were probably already in the square as PC Harvey turned at the bottom of Church Passage and retraced his steps. He had been within yards of catching the killer literally red-handed. It was very shortly after 1.45 that Harvey responded to Morris's whistle in Aldgate.

Detective Constables Daniel Halse and Edward Mariott, and Detective Sergeant Robert Outram, had been engaged in the immediate neighbourhood, searching the passages of houses where doors were left open all night. After hearing of the murder at about 1.55 a.m. they set off in various directions to search for suspects. Halse went towards Whitechapel via

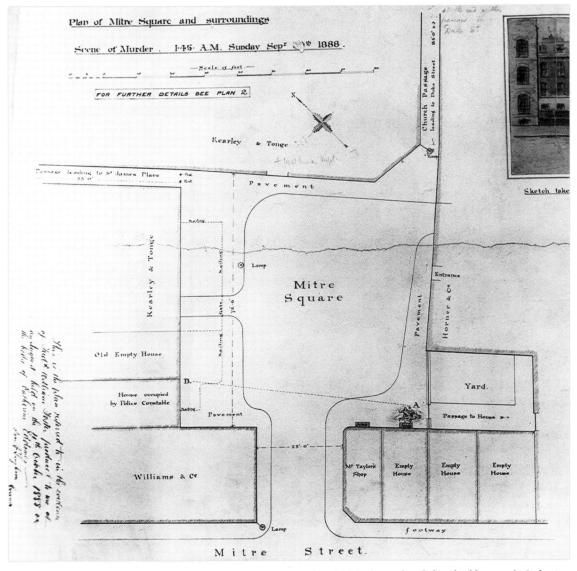

Sketch plan of the murder site in Mitre Square on 30 September 1888, the night of the 'double event'. Catherine Eddowes' body is in the southern corner marked 'A'. The sketch was prepared by Frederick W. Foster, the City Surveyor.

Middlesex Street and then into Wentworth Street where he checked two men. He then passed through Goulston Street at about 2.20 a.m., saw nothing and returned to Mitre Square.

A few private houses in Mitre Street backed on to the square's south corner. One of them, no. 3, was occupied by a City of London Police Constable, PC 922 Richard Pearce, who had retired to bed at 12.30 a.m. He heard nothing until he was called by a fellow officer at 2.20 a.m. and informed of the murder. The murder site was visible from his window. No. 5 Mitre Street was occupied by George Clapp who was caretaker of the premises. He and his wife had gone to bed at 11 p.m. and their bedroom, on the second floor, also overlooked the murder site. They heard nothing of the attack until between 5 and 6 a.m. At 3 a.m. the police checked the lodging house at 55 Flower and Dean Street.

The three Jewish witnesses already mentioned had been at the Imperial Club, 16–17 Duke Street, Aldgate, that night. They were Joseph Lawende, a 41-year-old commercial traveller in cigarettes of 45 Norfolk Road, Dalston; Joseph Hyam Levy, a 47-year-old butcher of 1 Hutchinson Street, Aldgate; and Harry (Henry) Harris, a furniture dealer of Castle Street, Whitechapel. At 1.30 a.m. they decided to leave the Imperial Club and actually departed the building at 1.35. It was raining. Lawende walked a little distance from the others. He noticed a man and a woman apparently conversing quietly on the opposite side of the road. They were about 30 feet away at the corner of Church Passage, 30 yards or so from Mitre Square. The spot was badly lit. The woman, who appeared to be about 5 feet tall, had her back to Lawende and he did not see her face, although he did notice that she was wearing a black jacket and a black bonnet. Her hand was on the man's chest. Lawende also said that, despite the description he gave, he doubted whether he would know the man again. The police also noted that the identification of the woman as Eddowes was by her clothes only, which Lawende later saw at the mortuary, and this was a 'serious drawback to the value of the description of the man'. However, as the body of Eddowes was found in Mitre Square 10 minutes later, the police thought it 'reasonable to believe that the man he saw was the murderer'. Lawende passed by on the opposite pavement without looking back.

Levy thought he and his friends had left the club about 1.33 or 1.34 a.m. and he too saw the man and woman standing at the corner of Church Passage. He said to Harris, 'Look there, I don't like going home by myself when I see those characters about.' Later, in answer to a question from the coroner, Levy said there was nothing about the man and woman which caused him to fear them and added he had not said he feared for his safety. He took no further notice of them, thinking that 'persons standing at that time in the morning in a dark passage were not up to much good'. He thought the man was about 3 inches taller than the woman but noticed nothing else. He walked on along Duke Street and into Aldgate, reaching home by 1.40 a.m. Levy was not used to being out so late at night – he said he was usually home by 11 p.m. – and it must have been fairly apparent that the two were prostitute and client, which probably explains his concern. Although Harris also saw the couple the police did not deem it necessary for him to give evidence at the inquest, so we must assume that he noted less than his companions.

The City night duty inspector, Edward Collard, was in charge of the division. He was at Bishopsgate Street police station when he received news of the Mitre Square murder at 1.55 a.m. He telegraphed the information to headquarters at 26 Old Jewry and sent a constable for the City Police surgeon, Dr Frederick Gordon Brown of 17 Finsbury Circus. Collard then made his way to Mitre Square, estimating that he arrived at 2 or 3 minutes past 2 a.m. Several police officers were there along with Dr George William Sequeira. The body was not touched until Dr Brown arrived at about 2.18 a.m. There was no sign of a

Dr Gordon Brown, City of London Police surgeon and the doctor who examined Catherine Eddowes and the 'Lusk kidney'.

struggle at the scene. Sergeant Jones picked up three small black buttons of the kind used on women's boots, a small metal button, a metal thimble and a small mustard tin containing two pawn tickets. He found these objects at the left side of the body and handed them to Collard. The body was examined. It was quite warm and there was no rigor mortis. The doctor found no bruising, no secretion of any kind on the thighs, and no spurting of blood on the bricks or surrounding pavement. There was no blood on the front of the clothes and no traces of recent sexual intercourse.

Eddowes was wearing a loosely tied black straw bonnet trimmed with green and black velvet. It had partially fallen from the back of her head and was lying in a pool of blood that had run from her neck. She had a black cloth jacket with imitation fur round the collar and sleeves and two outside pockets trimmed with black silk braid and imitation fur. A large quantity of blood was found inside the jacket, which was very dirty and bloody on the back. Eddowes also wore a chintz skirt with three flounces and a brown button on the waistband. This had a jagged 6½-inch cut from the left side of the front of the waistband. The edges of the cut were slightly bloodstained and there was blood on the bottom, front and back of the skirt. She had a brown linsey dress bodice with a black velvet collar and brown metal buttons down the front; there was blood inside and outside the back of the neck and shoulders and a clean 5-inch cut at the bottom of the left side, running from right to left. She wore a grey stuff petticoat with a white waistband which bore a 1½-inch cut with bloodstained edges in front. There were bloodstains on the front of the petticoat at the bottom. Eddowes also had a very old green alpaca skirt with a 10½-inch jagged cut made downwards through the front of the waistband. The garment was bloodstained inside under the cut. In addition, Eddowes had a very old, ragged blue skirt with a red flounce and a light twill lining. It had a 10½-inch jagged cut downward through the waistband and was bloodstained inside and out on the front and back. She had a white calico chemise which was bloodstained all over and cut in a zig-zag in the middle at the front. She also wore a man's white vest with buttons down the front and two outside pockets. It was torn at the back and there were blood and other stains on the front. She was wearing no drawers or stays. She had men's lace-up boots with mohair laces; the right one had been repaired with red thread and bore six blood marks. On her neck was a piece of red gauze silk which had various cuts in it. She also had a bloodstained white handkerchief; two unbleached calico pockets with tape strings which had been cut through – the top left-hand corner had been removed from one; one bloodstained, blue-striped, bed-ticking pocket with the waistband and strings cut; a white cotton pocket handkerchief with a red-and-white bird's-eye border; a pair of brown ribbed stockings, the

Inspector James McWilliam, head of the City of London Police Detective Department. He led the investigation into the Mitre Square murder.

feet mended with white thread; twelve pieces of white rag, some bloodstained; a piece of coarse white linen; a three-cornered piece of blue-and-white shirting; two small blue bed-ticking bags; two short black clay pipes; two tin boxes, one containing tea and the other sugar; a piece of flannel and six pieces of soap; a small-tooth comb; a white-handled table knife; a metal teaspoon; a red leather cigarette case with white metal fittings; an empty tin matchbox; a piece of red flannel containing pins and needles; a ball of hemp and a piece of old white apron.

An ambulance arrived to take the body to Golden Lane mortuary. Collard ordered the neighbourhood searched. Detective Inspector James McWilliam, head of the City detectives, arrived shortly afterwards with a number of men who were detailed to search streets and lodging houses. Several people were stopped and searched but without result. Later, many people flocked to Mitre Square to satisfy their morbid curiosity. Inspector Izzard, and Sergeants Phillips and Dudman were there to keep the crowds in order.

At the mortuary the body was carefully stripped and the property listed. A piece of Eddowes' ear dropped from the clothing. There was a portion of the apron which was cut through and the woman had apparently been wearing it on the outside of her dress. Dr Brown performed the post-mortem examination at 2.30 p.m. on Sunday 30 September in the presence of Dr Sequeira, Dr William Sedgwick Saunders (the City Public Analyst) and Dr Phillips. Brown recorded that rigor mortis was 'well marked' but the body was not quite cold. There was a green discolouration over the abdomen. When he washed the victim's left hand Brown found a recent red bruise the size of a sixpence on the back between the thumb and first finger. There were old bruises on the right shin. The hands and arms were bronzed by the sun. There was a ¼-inch cut through the lower left eyelid, dividing the structures completely. On the upper left eyelid there was a scratch through the skin near to the angle of the nose. The right eyelid was cut through to about ½ inch. There was a deep cut over the bridge of the nose, extending from the left border of the nasal bone down across the right cheek to near the angle of the right jaw. This cut was so deep that it went into the bone and divided all the structures of the cheek except the mucous membrane of the mouth. The tip of the nose was detached by an oblique cut from the bottom of the nasal bone to where the wings of the nose joined the face.[3] This incision also divided the upper lip and cut through the gum over the right upper incisor. There was a cut on the right angle of the mouth which appeared to be made by the point of a knife and extended 1½ inches parallel with the lower lip. Cuts on each cheek peeled up the skin and formed a triangular flap of about 1½ inches. On the left cheek there were two abrasions to the epithelium (the outer layer of skin). There was a little mud on the left cheek and two slight abrasions to the thin tissue under the ear. There was a 6- or 7-inch wound across the throat. A superficial cut began about 1½ inches below the left earlobe and about 2½ inches behind it, running across the throat to about 3 inches below the right ear. The big muscle across the throat was divided on the left and the large vessels on that side of the neck were severed. The larynx was cut below the vocal chords and all the deep structures were severed to the bone – the knife had marked the intervertebral cartilage. The sheath of the vessels on the right side was just opened and the carotid artery was pierced by a fine hole. The internal jugular vein was opened 1½ inches but was not divided. The vessels contained clotted blood. All the injuries, it was reported at the inquest, had been 'performed by a sharp instrument, like a knife, and pointed'. The cause of death was haemorrhage from the left common carotid artery. Death was immediate and the mutilations were inflicted afterwards. Brown believed the wounds on the face were made to disfigure the corpse.

The abdomen had been ripped open with a jagged cut from the pubes to the breast bone. The cut began opposite the ensiform cartilage (the pointed base of the sternum) and went upwards; it divided the cartilage but did not penetrate the skin over the sternum. The knife must then have cut obliquely at the expense of the front surface of the cartilage. Behind it the liver had been stabbed, apparently by the point of a knife. There was another incision in the liver measuring 2½ inches and below this the left lobe of the organ was slit by a vertical cut. Two cuts were indicated by a jagging of the skin on the left side. The abdominal walls were divided in the middle line to within ¼ inch of the navel. The cut then took a horizontal course for 2½ inches towards the right side. Next it passed round the left side of the navel and made a horizontal incision parallel to the previous one, leaving the navel on a 'tongue' of skin. Attached to the left side of the navel were 2½ inches of the lower part of the rectus muscle. The incision then ran obliquely to the right and down the right side of the vagina and rectum, ending ½ inch behind the rectum. A stab wound on the left groin measured about 1 inch. It had been made by a pointed instrument. Below it was a cut of approximately 3 inches through all the tissues: this wound had damaged the peritoneum to

Catherine Eddowes.

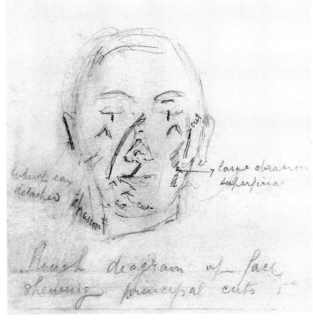

Catherine Eddowes.

THE MITRE SQUARE VICTIM

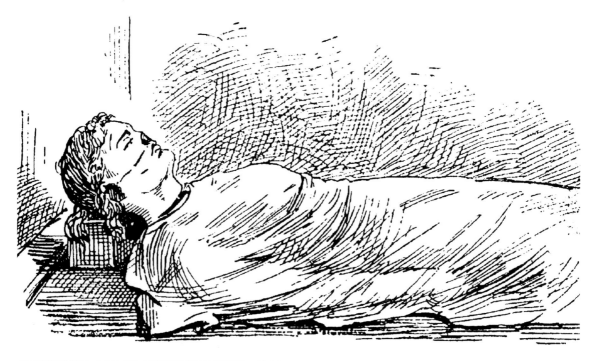

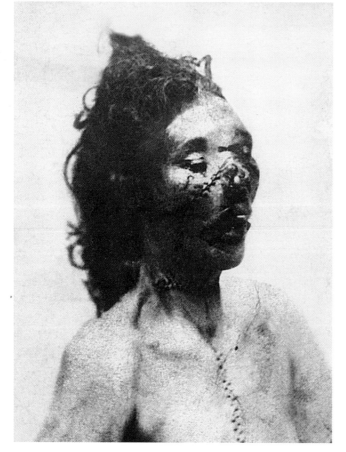

An artist's impression from the *Pictorial News*, Saturday 6 October 1888, of the body of Catherine Eddowes lying in the mortuary. It shows the nose was severed as well as the throat cut.

Catherine Eddowes, a police photograph.

Mortuary photograph of the body of Catherine
Eddowes discovered by Donald Rumbelow in 'the filthy
attic room' at Snow Hill police station in the 1960s.
This was one of a set taken of the body for the City
Police.

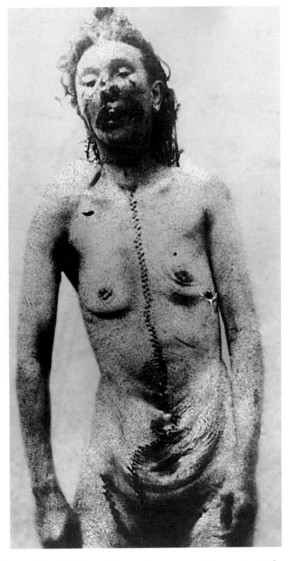

about the same extent. An inch below the
crease of the thigh, a cut extended from the
front spine of the pelvic bone obliquely
down the inner side of the left thigh. It
separated the left labia and formed a flap of
skin up to the groin. The left rectus muscle
was not detached. A flap of skin was formed
from the right thigh and the right labia; this
extended up to the spine of the pelvic bone.
The muscles that meet the poupart's
ligament on the right were cut through. The
skin was retracted through the whole of the
cut in the abdomen but the vessels were not
clotted, nor had there been any appreciable
bleeding.

Brown removed the contents of the
stomach and placed them in a jar for
further examination. There seemed to be
very little food or fluid in the stomach, but
some partly digested farinaceous food
escaped from the cut end. To a large extent
the intestines had been detached from the
mesentery (the tissue that attached them to
the wall of the abdomen). About 2 feet of
the colon was cut away. The curved end
of the S-shaped part of the large intestine, where it leads into the rectum, was invaginated,
or folded back on itself, very tightly into the rectum. The right kidney was pale and bloodless
and there was slight congestion of the base of the pyramids (part of the internal structure
of the kidney). There was one cut from the upper part of the slit on the under surface of the
liver to the left side and another at right angles to this; both incisions were about 1½ inches
deep and 2½ inches long. The liver was healthy and the gall bladder contained bile. The
pancreas was cut, but not right through, on the left side of the spinal column. A piece of
the lower edge of the spleen measuring 3½ inches by ½ inch was attached only to the
peritoneum. The peritoneal lining was cut through on the left side and the left kidney had
been carefully taken out, the left renal artery being severed. Dr Brown felt that someone
who knew the position of the kidney must have done this. The membrane over the uterus
was cut through and the womb was divided horizontally, leaving a ¾-inch stump. The rest of
the womb had been taken away with some of the ligaments. The vagina and cervix were
uninjured. The bladder was healthy and uninjured; it contained 3 or 4 ounces of water.
There was a tongue-like cut through the front wall of the abdominal aorta. The other
organs were healthy. There were no indications of sexual intercourse.

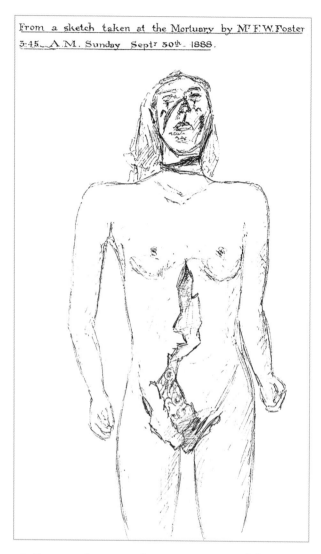

From a sketch taken at the Mortuary by Mr F.W.Foster 3.45. A.M. Sunday Sept 30th 1888.

Sketch of the body of Catherine Eddowes, drawn by Frederick W. Foster, the City Surveyor, for the inquest.

Dr Brown believed that the first wound was to the throat and that Eddowes must have been lying on the ground when it was inflicted. The injuries to the face and abdomen were inflicted with a sharp, pointed knife, the abdominal wounds indicating that it must have been 6 inches long. Brown also felt that the perpetrator must have had 'considerable knowledge of the position of the organs in the abdominal cavity and the way of removing them'. It required a great deal of knowledge to know where the kidney was located and how to remove it. Such knowledge might be possessed by someone in the habit of cutting up animals, he said. The fact that the lower eyelids had been nicked indicated to Dr Brown that the killer had time to carry out the attack and that the whole act took about 5 minutes. He was certain there had been no struggle and that only one offender had been involved. The throat had been so instantly severed that the victim can have made no noise. He did not think that the perpetrator would have much blood on him. Dr Brown concluded that the abdominal cut had been made after death and that there would not have been much blood on the murderer. He said that when the murderer made the cut he was kneeling on the victim's right side (that is on the side away from the house wall) and below the middle of the body.

Brown's attention was drawn to a piece of apron – a corner of the garment with a string attached and bearing blood spots of recent origin. It was impossible to say whether the blood was human.[4] Brown had seen another portion of apron, produced by Dr Phillips, that was found in Goulston Street and was marked with blood and what seemed to be faecal matter. He fitted the two together and their seams corresponded; the pieces also matched at a repair where a new section of material had been sewn in.

Dr George William Sequeira agreed with the evidence given by Dr Brown at the inquest.[5] He added that he knew the locality and although the corner of Mitre Square in question was its darkest, there would have been sufficient light for the perpetrator to commit the deed. When questioned by the coroner, he said he did not think that the murderer had any design on any particular organ or that he was possessed of any great anatomical skill. He did not think that the offender would necessarily have been spattered with blood.

Dr William Sedgwick Saunders of 13 Queen Street, Cheapside, the Public Analyst for the City of London, examined the stomach contents. He was especially looking for narcotic poisons but the results were negative. Like Dr Sequeira, he said he believed the murderer had no significant anatomical skill and was not looking for a specific organ. It seems odd that both Sequeira and Saunders should come to this conclusion when the left kidney and part of the womb were taken away by the murderer. Some excellent crime scene drawings and plans of the Mitre Square murder were prepared for the inquest by the City Surveyor, Frederick Foster. These are preserved at the Royal London Hospital.

Eddowes' daughter, Annie Phillips, aged 23, of 12 Dilstone Grove, Southwark Park Road, gave evidence to the inquest. She said she had not seen her father Thomas Conway for '15 or 18 months'. She described him as a teetotaller and reported that he had been on bad terms with Eddowes because she drank so much and had left her on account of this some 7 or 8 years previously. She had seen her mother frequently and Eddowes was in the habit of asking her for money. She said Conway was aware that Eddowes was living with Kelly.

The police felt that the three Jewish witnesses had probably seen the murderer. Lawende was required to treat his evidence as confidential until he appeared at the inquest. The same would have been true of Levy but Harris was not called, so he was probably not under the same restriction. That the police believed Lawende had seen the most, and could probably describe the murderer, is clear from the fact that the force paid all his expenses. According to the *Evening News* of 9 October:

> one if not two detectives are taking him about. . . . Mr. Joseph Levy is absolutely obstinate and refuses to give the slightest information. He leaves one to infer that he knows something but that he is afraid to be called on the inquest. Hence he assumes a knowing air. The fact remains, however, that the police, in imposing their idiotic secrecy, have allowed a certain time to elapse before making the partial description these three witnesses have been able to give public, and thus prevent others from acting upon the information in the event of the murderer coming under their notice.

Because it was proving difficult to obtain information from Lawende and Levy, the keen representatives of the *Evening News* approached Harris and found him more communicative. However, he was merely of the opinion that neither Lawende nor Levy saw anything more than he did, 'and that was only the back of the man'.

Some researchers and writers have read a great deal into police treatment of the three witnesses and have suggested that one of them, probably Levy, was able to recognise the man, or even knew him.[6] There is little reason to believe they knew or saw anything more than their statements indicate. The secrecy and 'knowing air' the frustrated press encountered in Levy was probably little more than self-importance.

Lawende gave his testimony on 5 October and Mr Henry Crawford, the solicitor for the City Police, asked that the details he gave of the suspect's description be withheld. However, the police had already issued a brief description of the man which appeared in *The Times* of 2 October: 'He was described as of shabby appearance, about 30 years of age and 5ft 9ins. in height, of fair complexion, having a small fair moustache and a cap with a peak.'

Perhaps one of the most controversial aspects of the Eddowes murder was the subsequent discovery of the freshly soiled section of her apron and some chalked writing at the entrance to a tenement building in Goulston Street. PC 254A Alfred Long had been seconded from Whitehall to supplement H Division, so he was patrolling an unfamiliar beat. He stated:

I was on duty in Goulston Street on the morning of 30th September at about 2.55 a.m. I found a portion of an apron covered in blood lying in the passage of the door-way leading to nos. 108 to 119 Model Dwellings in Goulston Street.

Above it on the wall was written in chalk 'The Juews are the men that will not be blamed for nothing.' I at once called the PC on the adjoining beat and then searched the stair-cases, but found no traces of any person or marks. I at once proceeded to the station, telling the PC to see that no one entered or left the building in my absence. I arrived at the station about 5 or 10 minutes past 3, and reported to the Inspector on duty finding the apron and the writing.

The Inspector at once proceeded to Goulston Street and inspected the writing.

From there we proceeded to Leman Street, and the apron was handed by the Inspector to a gentleman whom I have since learnt is Dr. Phillips.

I then returned back on duty in Goulston Street about 5.

It was here that the controversy began. There can be no doubt that Warren's decision to erase the writing caused much consternation and provoked much criticism, but what did the message mean? Had it in fact been written by the murderer – this could never be satisfactorily proved – or was it just a piece of fresh street graffiti.

Initial controversy was sparked by the question of why Warren, who attended the scene, did not wait for the message to be photographed but instead approved Superintendent Arnold's suggestion that it be erased immediately. Arnold, on his first day back after a month's leave, mentioned it in his own report:

my attention was called to some writing on the wall of the entrance to some dwellings No. 108 Goulston Street Whitechapel which consisted of the following words 'The Juews are the men that will not be blamed for nothing.' and knowing that in consequence of a suspicion having fallen upon a Jew named 'John Pizer' alias 'Leather Apron' having committed a murder in Hanbury Street a short time previously a strong feeling existed against the Jews generally and as the Building upon which the writing was found was situated in the midst of a locality inhabited principally by that Sect I was apprehensive that if the writing were left it would be the means of causing a riot and therefore considered it desirable that it should be removed. having in view the fact that it was in such a position that it would have been rubbed by the shoulders of persons passing in & out of the Building.

One of the most enduring and elaborate of the Ripper fantasy theories involves a royal/Masonic conspiracy. A royal connection with the crimes was suggested in the 1960s and developed in the 1970s to involve Freemasons too. The popularity of this tale was greatly increased by the fact that Warren was a high-ranking Freemason and he was responsible for erasing the message. This led some to interpret the writing as a 'Masonic message' incorporating ritual and legend.

According to author Stephen Knight and others, there was a Masonic conspiracy behind the murders. They say there was a plot to protect the Crown from the consequences of a supposed marriage between Prince Albert Victor (later the Duke of Clarence), second-in-line to the throne, and a Roman Catholic commoner named Annie Crook. Their theory has it that the word 'Juwes' was the collective name for Jubelo, Jubela and Jubelum, the mythical murderers of the equally mythical Hiram Abiff, master-mason of Solomon's Temple. Supposedly, the three men were caught and killed by having their throats cut and their bodies mutilated in a manner imitated by the killer of Annie Chapman and Catherine Eddowes. Unfortunately for this idea, the word 'Juwes' is not a Masonic one and the three murderers are referred to collectively in the third degree Masonic ritual as 'ruffians'. The names Jubelo, Jubela and Jubelum were used in the late eighteenth century but were dropped during a major revision of the ritual in 1814–16. In the USA the three are still named but, as in England, they are collectively referred to as 'ruffians' and the word 'Juwes' is not known. An explanation is given by the Grand Lodge:

> the three ceremonies of Craft Freemasonry are based on the Biblical story of the building of King Solomon's Temple. They do not claim to be historical truth but are allegories to present in a dramatic form the principles a Freemason is expected to practice. In the ritual Hiram Abiff represents the principle of fidelity to a promise. He was attacked and killed by three Fellowcrafts who demanded of him the 'secrets' of Master which he refused to divulge.

The killing of Hiram Abiff is still central to the third degree but his body was not mutilated by his attackers as Knight and others have suggested. The mutilations of the Ripper's victims do not parallel the symbolic physical penalties that are formally part of the obligations taken by a Freemason.

Part of Knight's theory depends upon his belief that all the key players were Freemasons, bound by oaths to protect one another. The reality is that the only Freemasons involved in Knight's story were the Prince of Wales, Sir Charles Warren and a man that he missed, George Akin Lusk, President of the Whitechapel Vigilance Committee. (Neither did Knight notice the Lodge of Instruction in Hanbury Street.) It is also necessary to point out that Freemasons do not swear to protect one another regardless of the circumstances. The opposite is true. In the third degree ritual the candidate swears: 'that my breast shall be the sacred repository of his secrets when entrusted to my care – murder, felony, and all other offences contrary to the laws of God and the ordinances of the realm being at all times most especially excepted'.

Warren founded the Quatuor Coronati Lodge, the first in the world devoted to Masonic history and research, and it might be assumed that he had a great knowledge of the subject. It might also be thought that he read something into the Goulston Street message which others missed and this would explain why he ordered it to be erased. However, it seems Warren did not have deep antiquarian knowledge of the Craft; at a lodge meeting he said he was only a novice in such matters. On other occasions he regularly confessed that he had not 'as yet studied the medieval legends' of Freemasonry, and knew 'very little of modern Masonry'.

If there is no Masonic connection, Warren must have had another motive for rubbing out the message and it seems he feared anti-Jewish riots. He explained his actions in a letter to the Home Office on 6 November 1888:

> The most pressing question at that moment was some writing on the wall in Goulston Street evidently written with the intention of inflaming the public mind against the Jews, and which Mr. Arnold with a view to prevent serious disorder proposed to obliterate, and had sent down an Inspector with a sponge for that purpose telling him to await his arrival.–
>
> I considered it desirable that I should decide this matter myself, as it was one involving so great a responsibility whether any action was taken or not. I accordingly went down

The doorway of the New Model Dwellings at 108–19 Goulston Street, Whitechapel, as it appeared, virtually unchanged, in the 1970s. It was here that a bloodstained piece of Eddowes' apron and the mysterious wall writing was discovered after the Mitre Square murder on 30 September 1888. (*Richard Whittington-Egan*)

to Goulston Street at once before going to the scene of the murder: it was just getting light, the public would be in the streets in a few minutes, in a neighbourhood very much crowded on Sunday mornings by Jewish vendors and Christian purchasers from all parts of London. – There were several Police around the spot when I arrived, both Metropolitan and City. – The writing was on the jamb of the open archway or doorway visible to anybody in the street and could not be covered up without danger of the covering being torn off at once. – A discussion took place whether the writing could be left or covered up or otherwise or whether any portion of it could be left for an hour until it could be photographed, but after taking into consideration the excited state of the population in London generally at the time the strong feeling which had been excited against the Jews, and the fact that in a short time there would be a large concourse of the people in the streets and having before me the Report that if it was left there the house was likely to be wrecked (in which from my own observation I entirely concurred) I considered it desirable to obliterate the writing at once, having taken a copy of which I enclose a duplicate.

As we have seen, PC Long said he found the piece of apron 'lying in the passage of the door-way . . . above it on the wall written in chalk "The Juews are the men that will not be blamed for nothing."' After a hasty search, if it can be called such, Long hurried away to the police station. All this happened in less than 15 minutes. In his report Superintendent Arnold said the writing 'was on the wall of the entrance' at shoulder height and could have been rubbed by people passing in and out of the building. City of London Detective Daniel Halse corroborated Long, adding that the message was on the black fascia of the wall; at the Eddowes inquest he said: 'The writing was in the passage of the building itself, and was on the black dado of the wall.'[7] Halse returned to Goulston Street and sent a message by a colleague to Inspector McWilliam to have the writing photographed. Directions were given for this to be done but the writing was rubbed out by the Metropolitan Police before it could be carried out. Halse claimed that he protested at what was being done and wished the wording kept until it could be seen by Major Smith, at this time Acting Commissioner. This series of events is one of the puzzles of the night. And where, indeed, was Major Smith? According to his own account:

The night of Saturday, September 29, found me tossing about in my bed at Cloak Lane Station, close to the river and adjoining Southwark Bridge. There was a railway goods depot in front, and a furrier's premises behind my rooms; the lane was causewayed, heavy vans were constantly going in and out, and the sickening smell from the furrier's skins was always present. You could not open the windows and sleep was an impossibility.

Suddenly the bell by his head rang violently and putting his ear to the tube, he was told there had been another murder. Inspector Collard at Bishopsgate police station was told at 1.55 a.m. and telegraphed headquarters immediately. Smith, according to his own account, jumped out of bed and ran into the street a couple of minutes later. Then he was in a hansom cab – designed for two, but with a 15-stone superintendent beside him and three detectives hanging on behind. They hurried to Mitre Square with the cab rolling like a 'seventy-four' in a gale. From there Smith went with Inspector Collard and Detective Halse to the mortuary before returning with Halse to Mitre Square. There they were told that a piece of apron had been found in Goulston Street. Later, he claimed, he went to Dorset Street where he saw bloodstained water in a street sink; he believed the murderer had washed his hands there but no indication of this survives in police reports. Even if it were the case, there were so many slaughter-houses in Whitechapel, the discovery of a bloody sink might be expected. Smith ends his report by saying that he wandered around the station houses hoping that someone might be brought in and 'finally got to bed at 6 a.m., after a very harassing night, completely defeated'.

The astonishing feature of this account is that Smith makes no mention of going to Goulston Street where one of his own detectives was waiting and had made arrangements with Inspector McWilliam for the writing to be photographed. Nor was Halse on his own – Warren himself said that when he arrived at the scene there were several police officers around, both Metropolitan and City. And it was less than ¾ mile from Mitre Square to Goulston Street – even less from Dorset Street. The writing was not rubbed out until 5.30 a.m. and Smith had at least two hours in which to be told of and view the message before its obliteration. He had already been in bed for about an hour when Warren, accompanied by Superintendent Arnold, went to the City

The City of London's Cloak Lane police station, where Major Henry Smith 'tossed about in his bed' on the night of the Mitre Square murder. It still stands, although it is no longer a police station. (*Donald Rumbelow*)

A City of London Police constable guards the entrance arch to the City of London Police headquarters at 26 Old Jewry. Note the duty armband worn on the left sleeve. Sergeants wore them on the right sleeve.

Police headquarters to liaise with Inspector McWilliam. According to Smith, McWilliam told Warren that rubbing out the message was a 'fatal mistake'.

Warren's statement that 'the house was likely to be wrecked' by people rising up against the Jews if the message was not removed is certainly misleading. The building, still standing, is not a house but a five-storey apartment block. There is, of course, always the possibility that the wall writing was simply a piece of graffiti totally unrelated to the murders. It is likely that both Long[8] and Halse had initially missed the piece of apron discarded by the murderer as he fled from Mitre Square around 1.50 a.m.

What is clear from statements made by Warren and others is that a genuine fear of disturbances, possibly developing into riots, prompted the erasing of the wall writing. If Smith is accurate in his assertion that Inspector McWilliam told Warren that by the rubbing out he had made a 'fatal mistake' then there may have come the belated realisation that by not photographing the message he had given the press yet another stick with which to beat him. Nor would he have been wrong. The news that Warren had destroyed what seemed to be the first genuine clue left by the murderer was eagerly pounced upon and he was seriously criticised for what he had done. The *Pall Mall Gazette*, malicious as ever, hoped that he would be censured by the coroner.

The City Police fared little better than the Met in the press. Superintendent Foster told a *Star* reporter on the morning of 2 October that he believed they were dealing with a man who was far too clever to go about boasting of what he was going to do. Every drunken man was likely to seek temporary notoriety by proclaiming himself the Whitechapel murderer, he said. Many reports of men claiming to be the killer were taken up by the detectives immediately, not so much because they expected to get a clue out of them but rather because it might be unsafe to 'neglect anything of that character'. When the *Star*'s man made his rounds of the police stations that morning 'the detectives had come to a standstill'. A man with a strong Birmingham accent was arrested in the City late on Monday 1 October and was detained at the police office in Old Jewry. He had been seen 'behaving in a mysterious manner' in the streets and when he was stopped by the police he refused to give an account of himself. He gave 'unintelligent answers' to their questions and as a result was thought to be insane. He was examined by two doctors. At 1.45 a.m. on Tuesday 2nd the attention of police on duty near Holborn Circus was attracted by screams and cries of 'Murder'. They found a woman who was apparently in great distress and arrested a man whom she said had tried to induce her to go up a neighbouring court. He had threatened to kill her if she did not comply with his demands. The man was a portly German with a heavy moustache who gave his name as Augustus Nochild, a tailor, of 86 Christian Street, Whitechapel. Sergeant Parry took him to Snow Hill police station. No knife was found on him.

After the sensation of two East End murders in one night, the newspapers were full of reports on the events in Whitechapel and its environs. Needless to say there were further stories of suspects. The *Star* boasted the 'largest circulation of any evening paper in the kingdom' and on Monday 1 October 1888 its coverage of the murders was extensive. Of the 24 columns in its 4 pages, more than 8 were devoted to the murders. The *Star* was critical of the authorities and not short of suggestions about what should be done. Needless to say, the newspaper considered many theories and suggested its own. The journalists were quick to dismiss the theory recently put forward by coroner Wynne Baxter:

> And, first, let us examine the facts, and the light they throw on any previous theories. To begin with it is clear that the BURKE and HARE theory is all but destroyed. There is no suggestion of surgical neatness, or of the removal of any organ, about the Mitre-square murder [*sic* – in fact, the uterus and left kidney had been taken]. It is a ghastly butchery – done with insane ruthlessness and violence. The gang theory is also weakened, and the story of a man who is said to have seen the Berner-street tragedy, and declares that one man butchered and another man watched, is, we think, *a priori* incredible. The theory of madness is on the other hand enormously strengthened. Crafty blood-thirst is written on every line of Sunday morning's doings. The rapid walk from Berner-street to Aldgate, to find a fresh victim, the reckless daring of the deed – in itself the most dangerous and cunning of all the murderer's resources – these all point to some epileptic outbreak of homicidal mania. The immediate motive need not trouble us now, except so far as it suggests the invariable choice of the poor street-wanderers of the East-end. It may be, as Dr. SAVAGE supposes, a plan of fiendish revenge for fancied wrongs, or the deed of some modern Thug or Sicarius, with a confused idea of putting down vice by picking off unfortunates in detail. A slaughterer or butcher who has been in a lunatic asylum, a mad medical student with a bad history behind him or a tendency to religious mania – these are obviously classes on which the detective sense which all of us possess in some measure should be kept. Finally, there is the off-chance – too horrible almost to contemplate – that we have a social experimentalist abroad determined to make the classes see and feel how the masses live.

This rather insightful article contained many ideas that have been adopted by modern theorists. It considered possible methods of the murderer, including that he had some rough knowledge of anatomy, that probably only his hands would be smeared by blood, and that after doing the deed he would don gloves. It was thought that he must have done so to ensure Eddowes did not see the blood, if, indeed, the two deeds were the work of one hand. (This is an interesting reference to the fact that there may have been two murderers.) As a further precaution, the *Star* said, he might have put an overcoat on after the deed. As he apparently stopped nowhere to wash his hands, he probably did not live in a lodging house or hotel, but in a private house where he had 'special facilities – perhaps the chemicals and

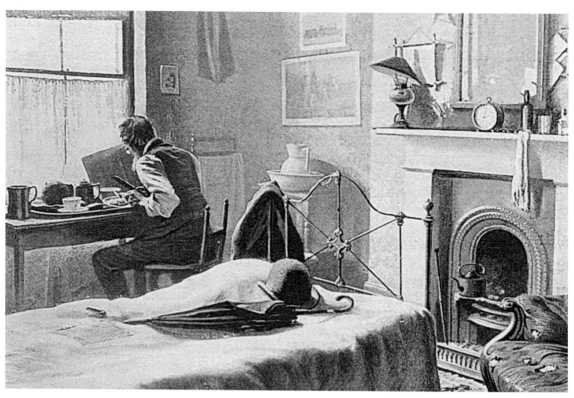

Many Ripper theories are built on the idea of the Ripper being a lodger living in the privacy of his own rented room. Here is an illustration of a Victorian lodger in his bed-sitting room in the East End.

Central News Agency (left), where the original Jack the Ripper letter was received. (*Guildhall Library, Corporation of London*)

a wash-hand stand communicating directly with a pipe – for getting rid of bloody hands and clothes'. The journalist thought that the murderer must be inoffensive, probably respectable in manner and appearance, or else how could woman after woman have been decoyed by him? Two theories had been suggested to the *Star*: that he wore women's clothes or that he was a policeman. These ideas appear repeatedly in letters to the police from the public.

A very significant development – from press, public and police points of view – occurred at this time. The 'Jack the Ripper' correspondence began with the publication of the infamous 'Dear Boss' letter. This letter, written in red ink, purported to have come from the murderer and was addressed to 'The Boss' at the Central News Agency in the City. It was dated 25 September 1888 and posted on the 27th. The agency forwarded the letter to the police on Saturday 29th, the eve of the 'double event' and on the Monday following it was made public. It read:

25 Sept: 1888.

Dear Boss

I keep on hearing the police have caught me but they wont fix me just yet. I have laughed when they look so clever and talk about being on the <u>right</u> track. That joke about Leather Apron gave me real fits. I am down on whores and I shant quit ripping them till I do get buckled. Grand work the last job was. I gave the lady no time to squeal. How can they catch me now. I love my work and want to start again. You will soon hear of me with my funny little games. I saved some of the proper <u>red</u> stuff in a ginger beer bottle over the last job to write with but it went thick like glue and I cant use it. Red ink is fit enough I hope <u>ha. ha</u>. The next job I do I shall clip the lady's ears off and send to the police officers just for jolly wouldn't you. Keep this letter back till I do a bit more work then give it out straight. My knife's so nice and sharp I want to get to work right away if I get a chance. Good luck.

Yours truly
Jack the Ripper
Dont mind me giving the trade name

[Then at right angles to above:]

wasnt good enough to post this before I got all the red ink off my hands curse it.
No luck yet. They say I'm a doctor now <u>ha ha</u>

This letter was forwarded to the police by Thomas John Bulling, a 42-year-old Central News reporter. The sensation created by the letter, coupled with the sale of the story to the newspapers, generated added income for the agency, a fact that was commented on at the time.

The 'Dear Boss' letter was quickly followed by the equally notorious 'saucy Jacky' postcard sent to the same agency on 1 October:

I wasn't codding dear old Boss when I gave you the tip. youll hear about saucy Jackys work tomorrow double event this time number one squealed a bit couldn't finish straight off. had not time to get ears for police thanks for keeping last letter back till I got to work again

Jack the Ripper

25. Sept. 1888.

Dear Boss

I keep on hearing the police have caught me. but they wont fix me just yet. I have laughed when they look so clever and talk about being on the right track. That joke about Leather apron gave me real fits. I am down on whores and I shant quit ripping them till I do get buckled. Grand work the last job was. I gave the lady no time to squeal How can they catch me now. I love my work and want to start again. You will soon hear of me with my funny little games. I saved some of the proper red stuff in a ginger beer bottle over the last job to write with but it went thick like glue and I cant use it. Red ink is fit enough I hope ha. ha. The next job I do I shall clip the ladys ears off and send to the

The Boss
Central News
    Office
London City.

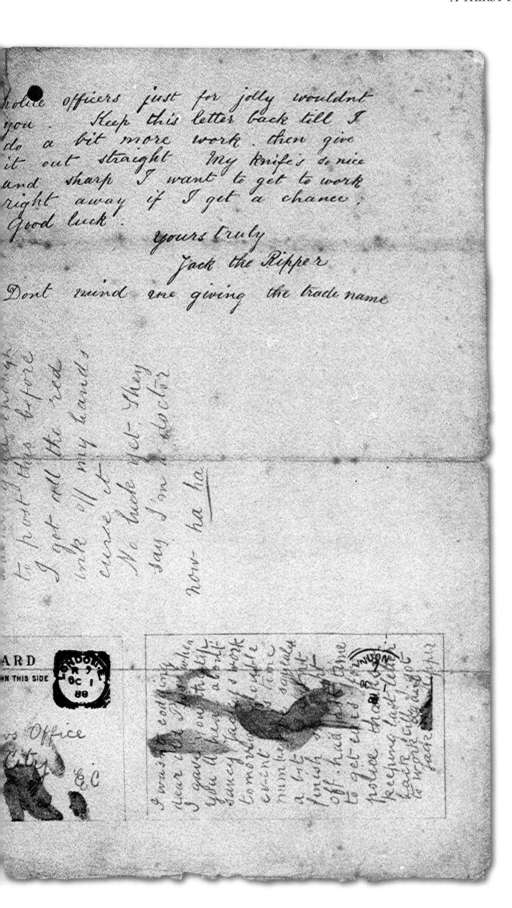

These two items of correspondence are the origin of the name 'Jack the Ripper' and this incredibly apt and sensational moniker for the unknown killer was immediately universally adopted. It has never been out of use since. If it was the work of the pressmen, which seems more than likely, it was a master stroke. According to Chief Inspector John George Littlechild, head of the Special Branch, senior officers at Scotland Yard believed Tom Bulling, and possibly his manager, Mr Moore, penned the letter.[9] Indeed, seasoned journalist George R. Sims wrote in his 'Mustard and Cress' columns in the *Referee* of 7 October:

> The fact that the self-postcard-proclaimed assassin sent his imitation blood-besmeared communication to the Central News people opens up a wide field for theory. How many among you, my dear readers, would have hit upon the idea of 'the Central News' as a receptacle for your confidence? You might have sent your joke to the *Telegraph*, the *Times*, any morning or any evening paper, but I will lay long odds that it would never have occurred to you to communicate with a Press agency which serves the entire Press? It is an idea which might occur to a Press man perhaps; and even then it would probably only occur to someone connected with the editorial department of a newspaper, someone who knew what the Central News was, and the place it filled in the business of news supply. This proceeding on Jack's part betrays an inner knowledge of the newspaper world which is certainly surprising. Everything therefore points to the fact that the jokist is professionally connected with the Press. And if he is telling the truth and not fooling us, then we are brought face to face with the fact that the Whitechapel murders have been committed by a practical journalist – perhaps by a real live editor! Which is absurd, and at that I think I will leave it.

The publication of the letter and the postcard heralded a flood of similar correspondence that was to plague the police investigation and further muddy the waters. There is no doubt that Warren himself viewed the 'Dear Boss' correspondence as a hoax. Writing to Lushington at the Home Office on 10 October, he said: 'At present I think the whole thing is a hoax but of course we are bound to try & ascertain the writer in any case.'[10]

The *Star* of Tuesday 2 October 1888 contained further lengthy coverage of the murders, including extracts from letters received concerning the case. 'A Laborer' suggested that the perpetrator of the murders might be a woman, a Kate Webster[11] who had gained anatomical knowledge while learning midwifery. Fred W. Ley suggested that the murderer was a religious fanatic. Mr T. Barry thought that the man must be one who, 'having been ruined by dissipation, was having his revenge'. 'A Reader' thought the murderer would be found 'among a class well known to the unfortunates themselves' because he escaped so easily. C.J. Solomons of Hanbury Street, Spitalfields, had come to the conclusion that the murders could not have been committed by any person living in a common lodging house because signs of blood would certainly have been noticed on him: it must be someone who had a room where he could go unnoticed at any time and make a change of clothing. 'Justice' thought the perpetrator might be a fanatical member of the Society for the Suppression of Prostitution or of a vigilance committee, who was murdering to frighten prostitutes from the streets.

— NINE —

Sleuth-hounds and Conspiracies

THE police response to the double murder on 30 September 1888 was swift. Within hours Warren had 10,000 leaflets printed asking for information about the killings between 31 August and 30 September. Clearly he did not consider the Smith and Tabram murders to be part of the pattern that was now developing. Next day, even before Eddowes had been identified, the lord mayor, on the recommendation of the City Police commissioner, offered a reward of £500 for information leading to the arrest of the unknown killer.

Just how the City Police investigation was shaping up did not become clear to the Home Office until it asked for a report from the City Police commissioner almost four weeks later. The reason for this lack of information was the unusual nature of the City's relationship with the Home Office: the cost of the force was borne entirely by the Corporation of the City of London. Because there was no government funding for the City Police, the Home Office had no say in how the force was run nor any authority over either it or its commissioner.

A lengthy report from Detective Inspector McWilliam[1] was received on 29 October giving details of the investigation to date and the coroner's inquest. He also told the home secretary that he had sent officers to all the

'Gog and Magog on their Mettle.' 'I say, matey, we've a share in this murder business now, and we'll have to act in a different way to those Metropolitan fellows', says one City of London Police constable to another in this *Funny Folks* cartoon of 6 October 1888. The Eddowes murder had brought the City Police into the investigation.

Two City of London Police constables check an old City graveyard at night. Similar scenes took place during the Ripper scare.

lunatic asylums in London seeking details of people recently admitted or discharged; because it was the opinion of many that the crimes were too revolting to have been committed by a sane person. The Home Office minute sheet accompanying this report[2] is particularly interesting as William Byrne, a Home Office clerk and a barrister, noted on it: 'This report tells very little' and: 'The printed report of the Inquest contains much more information than this. They evidently want to tell us nothing. ?Shall we ask them.' This is a little unfair as the City Police were under no obligation, unlike the Metropolitan Police, to report to the Home Office. Indeed, McWilliam's report is quite detailed and useful. (It is certainly fortunate that it was submitted in view of the later loss of the bulk of the City Police material.)

A detective, Sergeant Robert Sagar, was one of the liaison officers deputed to represent the City in meetings with senior detectives in nightly conferences with the Metropolitan force at Leman Street police station. A report from Chief Inspector Swanson explained that the investigations conducted by the two forces had merged into one another, 'each force cordially communicating with the other daily the nature and subject of their enquiries.'

So far the murders had been confined to one small area of the East End and City but on the afternoon of Tuesday 2 October a headless and limbless female

The Whitehall Mystery – the discovery of a female torso in the basement of New Scotland Yard on 2 October 1888. The building on the Victoria Embankment was then under construction. A mystery indeed, but not another Ripper murder. (*Penny Illustrated Paper*)

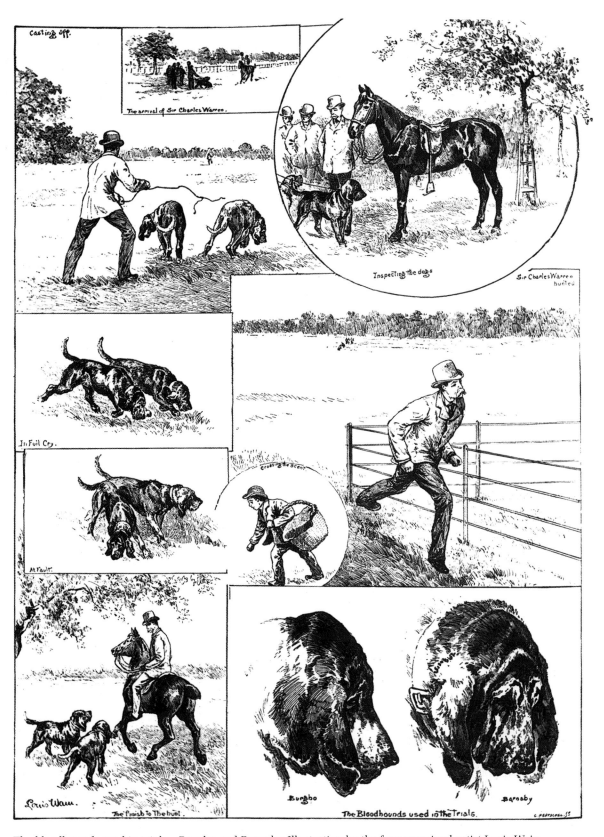

The bloodhounds used in trials – Burgho and Barnaby. Illustration by the famous animal artist Louis Wain.

The introduction of dogs into the hunt for the Ripper resulted in press cartoons of dogs as policemen, like this example from the *Penny Illustrated Paper*.

torso was found in the basement area of the new Norman Shaw building under construction on the Victoria Embankment. (It was to be the new Metropolitan Police headquarters – New Scotland Yard – to replace the old buildings at Whitehall Place.) The body's right arm and hand had been found in mid-September on the foreshore of the Thames. This case became known as the 'Whitehall Mystery'. Inevitably, the press became alarmist at the news, trying to forge links with the Whitechapel murders by suggesting that the killer had moved further west and was extending his boundaries, making no woman safe in London. There were even attempts to claim that the torso had been put into the basement as a way of taunting Warren and Matthews for their lack of success in catching the culprit. Some newspapers firmed up the connection with Whitechapel by claiming this unknown person was the Ripper's seventh victim. There was more embarrassment for the police when two amateur detectives using a sniffer dog dug up a human leg, severed just above the knee, in the cellar where the torso had been found. Constant rehashing of the Whitehall Mystery kept the newspapers busy until the story was knocked off the front page by more sensational news.

Suggestions had come from several sources that bloodhounds should be deployed to capture the killer and in the early hours of 9 October Warren witnessed a private trial of the dogs in Hyde Park. The bloodhounds belonged to Edwin Brough, who had been breeding the animals for several years. At the police's request he brought two bloodhounds, one named Champion Barnaby and the other a black-and-tan called Burgho, from Scarborough to London. They were tested over two days in Regent's Park and Hyde Park, with Warren himself acting as the hunted man on two occasions. The cost of the bloodhounds became something of a problem and Warren could give no definite assurance that the police would purchase the dogs. The intention was to take them to the site of the next murder, should it happen. Eventually they were returned to Scarborough but not before the newspapers had with great glee reported a totally fictitious story that they had been lost in a fog!

The double murder of 30 September prompted local demands for a further strengthening of police numbers in Whitechapel. Warren replied by return to the clerk of the Board of Works, which had passed a resolution to this effect, that he could not do more to guard against such murders 'so long as the victims actually, but unwittingly, connive their own destruction'. London, he went on, was the safest city in the world in which to live but increasing police strength would not help prevent this particular type of murder when the unfortunate victims appeared to take the killer to some isolated spot where they could be slaughtered without a sound being heard. He asked the board to try to dissuade women from going into these dark and lonely places with anyone, be they acquaintance or stranger. He pointed out the poor street lighting and resulting darkness, which did not help. Extra police had already been drafted into the area but only at the expense of other divisions – and normal police work still had to be done. He concluded by correcting a number of misconceptions which had arisen in the public mind and asked the board to dismiss 'as utterly fallacious, the numerous anonymous statements as to recent changes to have been made in the police force, of a character not conducive to efficiency'. There was no truth in the statement, which he had seen repeated many times, that constables were constantly being moved from district to district and therefore had no local knowledge. The system in use had existed for the last twenty years and constables were only moved on promotion or for some other reason. As far as the detectives were concerned, he had recently made arrangements which further reduced the necessity of transferring officers from one district to another. He ended by saying that one member of the board had said that a revision of police arrangements was necessary: perhaps the clerk would let Warren know what these necessary revisions were and he would give them every consideration.

A member of Parliament suggested to the home secretary that a cordon should be placed around Whitechapel and compulsory house-to-house searches made. When this idea was forwarded to Warren he threw it back, almost certainly tongue in cheek, saying that he was quite prepared to take the responsibility of adopting such drastic or arbitrary measures which would capture the murderer, 'however illegal they may be', but since the Home Secretary could not order him to do an illegal act, the responsibility must remain his. In the circumstances he wanted a government guarantee that there would be an indemnity for such an action: 'I have been accustomed to work under such in circumstances in what were nearly Civil wars at the [*missing*] & then the Government passed Acts of indemnity for those who have gone beyond the law.' He then went on to rub Home Secretary Matthews' nose in the suggestion by showing just how ludicrous it was. Of course, he said, in performing such an illegal act, Warren would be criticised if the murderer were not found. Such an illegal act might bond the Social Democrats together and he would then be accused of causing a riot. Houses 'could not be searched illegally without violent resistance & blood shed and the certainty of one or more Police Officers being killed'. There was the added possibility of a police officer being tried and hanged if a death resulted from an illegal search. Matthews sent a swift reply by return of post: the MP's suggestion was 'too sweeping'. In a postscript he pointedly asked if Anderson, absent now for a month and just returned from Paris, was well enough to resume his duties.

Warren had no intention of antagonising the people of Whitechapel. He needed their help and successfully arranged and carried out house-to-house searches in suspect areas with their cooperation. Two weeks later, after this exchange of letters with Matthews, Warren was able, through *The Times*, to thank publicly the people of the East End for the way they had helped the police with their inquiries. He felt that some acknowledgement was due 'on all sides for the cordial cooperation of the inhabitants'. He similarly acknowledged the immense volume of correspondence he had received and asked the writers to accept this statement in lieu of individual replies.

The *Pall Mall Gazette*, hostile as ever, now mounted a series of attacks in articles called 'The Police and Criminals of London' and with subtitles like 'The Headless C.I.D.' and 'Why Detectives Don't Detect'. They were very much pro-Monro and anti-Warren. Their tone was alarmist and they warned that unless a change was made (i.e. Warren and/or Matthews removed) there would be not only 'a widespread panic as to the growing insecurity of life and property in the metropolis' but a police strike resulting from disaffection over pay and pensions. 'All kinds of explanations, excuses, apologies had been made for the failure of the police to catch the murderer' except the obvious one that they had failed because the CID no longer had a head. In fact, Anderson had returned two days before the article appeared. Unaware of this, the reporter continued that Monro's position after four years had become

Police mocked in this *Punch* cartoon of
22 September 1888.

intolerable. But Dr Anderson, his successor, a millenarian and writer of books, was only there in spirit: 'You may seek for him in Scotland-yard, you may look for him in Whitehall-place, but you will not find him, for he is not there. Dr. Anderson, with all the arduous duties of his office still to learn, is preparing himself for his apprenticeship by taking a pleasant holiday in Switzerland!'

The article ended with a not unexpected attack on Warren who was blamed for decapitating the CID and making Scotland Yard a laughing stock. The police themselves were accused of destroying clues, in particular the grape stalks which had been recovered by the Vigilance Committee's private detectives and which, whether the newspaper knew it or not, were a part of Packer's fictional and discredited account of the Stride murder.

More laughable still, the writer complained of Warren's doubling of police patrols which meant the doubling of the sound of policemen's footsteps to warn the murderer of their approach! There was nothing but praise for Monro who had resigned because 'Sir Charles Warren would interfere, over-rule and dictate in matters which had heretofore been regarded as the legitimate province of the Assistant Commissioner' and who now had 'to face the situation which his overbearing and tactless interference had created'.

Warren replied to these and other charges in a statement to *The Times* on 10 October. The piece was headed 'Sir Charles Warren and the Detective Force'. Warren explained the basic height regulation, age limits, rules governing pensions and applications to the CID. He said that as a general rule it had been ascertained by the Criminal Investigation Department that candidates who had applied to be appointed directly to the CID without serving first in the uniform branch had not possessed any special qualities which would justify their acceptance. The tone of the statement was reasonable but it was not enough to stop the criticism. Newspaper coverage of the murders and the determination of some, including the *Gazette*, to exact revenge for the 'Bloody Sunday' riots had made of Warren a national hate figure. In Sheffield, where he had stood just a few years before as a Liberal candidate, the mention of his name at a Liberal meeting was received 'with hisses and cries of disapprobation'. Asquith was the speaker and reflected that 'he could not help thinking there were moments when the Chief Commissioner of the Metropolitan Police would look back with vain but unavailing regret to the time when, as one of the Radical candidates for Sheffield, he was the stalwart and outspoken champion of popular rights'.

Despite the £1,200 now being offered by the City, the *Financial News* and private individuals, the Home Office still refused to offer a reward for information or capture of the murderer. Until 1884 it had been policy to offer rewards from £200 to £2,000 – the highest ever was £10,000 for the Phoenix Park murders. The system of rewards was abandoned in early 1884 when a conspiracy was formed to cause an explosion at the German Embassy before planting papers on an innocent man to accuse him of the crime and obtain the expected reward. Such 'blood money conspiracies' had been a common feature of eighteenth- and early nineteenth-century law enforcement.

Warren was initially against offering a reward – in common with others he did not think that it would achieve much, except that the gesture might be a popular one. After thinking further he changed his mind, especially if in addition to the reward, a free pardon was offered to any accomplice who was not the murderer. Anderson, after taking soundings from the divisions and Williamson, agreed with him. Warren looked 'upon this series of murders as unique in the history of our country' and in a totally different category to anything that had gone before.

The suggestion of a pardon had been made by George Lusk of the Whitechapel Vigilance Committee in a letter to the home secretary. Warren had the idea at about the same time, his reasoning being that if the murderer was sane, with periodic fits of insanity, relatives and neighbours may have unwittingly slipped into the position of becoming accomplices with no way of escape from their predicament except by the offer of a pardon. Or, if the murders were being committed by a gang with only one person doing the killing, the free pardon might tempt an informer. Coincidentally, Warren was at this time in touch with someone who claimed to be such an accomplice and was asking for a free pardon; communication between the two men was through an advertisement in a journal. Warren thought the whole thing might be a hoax but felt it worth following up.

Matthews, however, was privately consulting with Monro who was against rewards. So, too, Matthews informed Warren, was the commissioner's predecessor, Colonel Henderson. Warren was having none of it and wrote back that while the home secretary had been given one set of views, he had a memoranda, which he enclosed, not only from both men but from Williamson too in favour of rewards. It may have been about this time that Warren discovered control of the CID had effectively moved from Scotland Yard to the Home Office. Every morning protracted conferences were held there between Monro, Anderson (Monro's protégé), Williamson and the principal detectives, including Abberline. Only information of the 'scantiest character' was passed back to the commissioner. All of this could only be done with the backing of the home secretary. Matthews was subsequently to admit that throughout this period he benefited from Monro's advice and discussed with him the organisation of the detective department. As Anderson was to say, the Home Office acted more like a blister than a plaster.

George Akin Lusk, c. 1885. (*Courtesy of the late Leonard Archer*)

The Letter Writers

BY October 1888 the murders were generating huge public interest and hundreds wrote to the press and the police to suggest ways of capturing the killer or to offer information about his identity.

Newspaper tales of suspects inspired many readers to write to the authorities. Typical of these reports was the widely published story about a 'suspicious' man who entered a cabman's shelter at Pickering Place, Westbourne Grove, Bayswater, on the afternoon of Sunday 30 September.[1] He asked the keeper, Thomas Ryan, to cook a chop for him. The man was about 5 feet 6 inches tall, round headed, with a thick moustache and clean white hands. He was wearing an Oxford cap and a light checked ulster with a tippet. He had very restless eyes and seemed to have been drinking. Several cabmen were in the shelter talking of the two murders discovered that morning. Ryan exclaimed, 'I'd gladly give a good deal if I could only find the fellow who did them.' The stranger looked into Ryan's face and said, 'Don't you know who committed the murders? I did them. I have had a lot of trouble lately. I came back from India and got into trouble at once. I lost my watch and chain and £10.' The cabmen did not take the man seriously because he had been drinking. He then signed a temperance pledge for them as 'J. Duncan; doctor, residence Cabman's Shelter; Sept. 30, 1888'. He stated that he had nowhere to live at present, ate his chop, left and was not seen again.

On Tuesday 2 October J. Trustram of Harpenden, Hertfordshire, wrote to draw the attention of the police to this report which appeared in the daily papers that morning:

> it is a singular thing this tale coincides with a man who escaped from Leaves[den] Asylum, some 12 months ago which cause a scare in this county and I have never heard he was captured it was report at the time he was a Doctor and came from India and was robbed his name was Macdonald, Now this man on Sunday signed his name Duncan if you have not already heard from Leavesden the authorities might give a description of Macdonald which may be serviceably . . .

The 'Cabmen's Shelter' story broke in the newspapers on 1 October 1888 and led to the identification of another suspect, John Davidson, who, according to Inspector Abberline, was seen by police and eliminated from inquiries. Shelters such as these were used by the hansom cab drivers for rest and refreshment and preserved examples may still be seen in London.

The Home Office received a suggestion that the same person be investigated from the governor of Newcastle Prison and requested a police inquiry. Inspector Abberline ordered the story thoroughly explored and the suspicious man was traced and interrogated. His real name was found to be John Davidson and he was able to account for his movements on the dates of the murders. He was thus cleared of suspicion.

As early as Monday 1 October, when maps of the murder sites were published in the newspapers, it was noticed that if the locations were joined together with crossed lines, a cross or dagger shape was formed. Writing to the *Daily Telegraph*,[2] 'Observer' noted:

London, W., Oct. 1.
To the Editor of the 'Daily Telegraph'.
Sir – In examining the chart representing the locality of the Whitechapel murders, published in your issue of to-day, it is curious to observe that lines drawn through the spots where the murders were committed assume the exact form of a dagger, the hilt and blade of which pass through the scenes of the sixth, second, first and third murders, the extremities of the guard making the fourth and fifth. Further, the spot where the portion of apron belonging to the victim of the Mitre-square tragedy was picked up lies in the imaginary line which forms the hilt of the dagger. Can this possibly afford a clue to the position of the next atrocity? –
I am, Sir, your obedient servant,

OBSERVER.

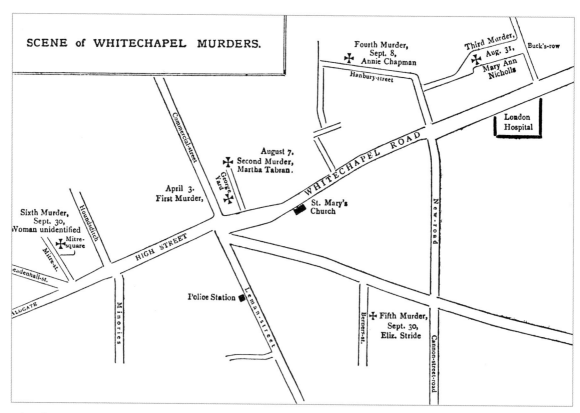

After the 'double event' of 30 September 1888 this basic map of the Whitechapel murders locations appeared in the *Pall Mall Gazette*. It shows the murder of Emma Smith on 3 April 1888 as the first killing and includes the murder of Martha Tabram on 7 August. Eddowes was shown as still unidentified when it was published.

A scene of cosy domestic life rudely intruded upon by the news of the horrible murders was painted by a Staffordshire lady signing herself 'xx'. She also wrote to the police on 2 October with her idea about the murderer's identity:

> While sitting sewing and listening to my husband reading the London atrocities last evening a renewed and strong Presentiment came to my mind as to who the man might possibly be as near as I can remember it is about a year since we read in the *Staffordshire Sentinel* of a man who was writing letters of a very immoral character to different young women residing in the same locality where he lived the authorityes were informed and he was caught and turned out to be a young Clergyman the authorities said that they should inform the bishop and how the case went on I cannot say but from the underminded and diabolical manner in which he wrote those letters I think he would do anything from a feeling of revenge and wherever he lives ore whatever his occupation he is still the same man and I believe in my heart that he is the man. You might get more particulars from the Editor of the *Staffordshire Sentinel*.

The detailed newspaper accounts of the murders repeatedly inspired amateur Victorian detectives to suggest suspects that the police may not have considered. 'E.C.' wrote to the City authorities on 2 October after reading the report of the Mitre Square murder in that day's paper:

it strikes me as strange the remark of the watchman, about the murderer – and also telling the constable who came up to his door to 'Keep himself cool' –

Now are you Sirs quite sure of this man's character being good etc.,

'E.C.' was not the only correspondent to suggest that George Morris of Messrs Kearley & Tonge might be the murderer. The watchman theory was also put forward by 'a maker and repairer of complicated repeater watches and chronometers, of Messrs. Swindon & Sons, Temple Street, Birmingham'. He wrote to the mayor of London stating that he had travelled in the United States and as a lad knew London very well. He felt that three things would allow him to 'think the "devil" out': first, a census of all lodgers returning home after 1.30 a.m. on the Sunday of the murders; second, whether the docks of London and the Commercial were open at night and whether there was a watchman who passed through in the early hours of that morning; and third, within a mile radius how many caretakers were in sole charge of premises from Saturday to Sunday last. If he could have this information he was prepared to identify the killer and to give all of the reward to 'the London Charities . . . except £100'. He also required two weeks' wages – he was paid £3.10 weekly – plus his train fare because he would need to be in London to carry out his investigation.

Edward Smith of 91 Upper Grange Road, Bermondsey, also felt that he knew who the murderer might be. To his mind the killer must have 'a wonderful control' over his victims. 'It might be a person who is throughly well acquainted with the powers of an Electre Biologist' as it would be easy for a man with such skills 'to put the poor persons under his influence while speaking to them'. Mr Smith went on to say that twenty-five years earlier he had heard two people lecturing on these powers in South London. They were Professors Reynolds and Audrade who used to lecture at two different halls and who, he believed, gave lessons to pupils. Professor Audrade was, he thought, a salesman at the Metropolitan Meat Market in the early part of the day and gave his lectures at night. It had been suggested that the murders were committed by someone used to using a knife, possibly a butcher, and Edward Smith believed it might be worth the police checking at the market to see if there was any person there acquainted with the powers of an 'Electre Biologist'.

There was also considerable correspondence purporting to come from the murderer – and not all of it was signed 'Jack the Ripper'. One letter dated 2 October ended 'M. Puddig Thrall [*sic* – Thrawl] Street, E.':

> You offer certainly a handsome reward but I have sworn that nobody shall earn it, this the one thousand eight hundred and eighty eighth year of our Lord. shall find me still at liberty untill its close, for not till I hear the first chimes of the church bells on watch night will I be tired of gloating over my work for hard work it has indeed been. thanks to my thorough proficiency in anatomical matters I gave them little or no pain, for humanity – they had to die, and at my hand. Still only a few more weeks and my task is done, when I shall ornament the scaffold that in short hours then and not till then shall you become acquainted with the motive of my crimes as you are pleased to style them [here there is a blot] was stern duty. They will forgive me when we meet in paradise, in celestial bliss. Amen.
>
> M= Puddig-

On the same date William Dickinson of 27 Zetland Street, South Bromley, was inspired to write to the inspector in charge of the City Police Detective Department, Mr McWilliam. He enclosed a sketch plan of the six murder spots (he included the killings of Smith and

Tabram) and indicated with dotted lines the murderer's possible escape routes. From this he deduced that the culprit must live in a house close to Chicksand Street Board School and incorporated the position of the house on the plan. Undoubtedly, the criminal 'devoured the accounts of his blood curdling work from the papers, which are supplied him by a near paper shop or lent by a publican close at hand'. He also felt that the killer was with his victims 5 or even 15 minutes before choosing a location for the murder and that he was well known to the women about the neighbourhood. He hoped that 'these ideas or surmisations may be of some little use in unearthing such a terrible fiend as the now notorious Whitechapel murderer'.

The case also intrigued retired policemen. An old officer who had 'been sent into Cornwall by the Lord Mayor of London in 1841' had developed a theory built upon past Fenian problems. Henry Armitage of Ludgvan, Penzance, wrote on 2 October to Colonel Fraser and the 'Chief Detective Department' to say that he felt 'an interest in the welfare of my country & anything I could do to throw light on this most dastardly case of murder':

> it has just occurred to me that you convicted an American Doctor for sending Dinamite, and by a person applying for the part of females inside they might possibly have wanted in America, by offering £20 for one if so if the Person who wrote that letter to the office which was stated in the newspaper on the Thursday before the last two murders was committed was the real murderer he was surely a Doctor and wrote it to throw you off the right scent and to deceive further by doing the daring deed again it looks more American than English was he an American Doctor or a Person connected with the one now in Prison and trying to Play off the Police for convicting one of their best men . . . there must be someone hiding this murderer is it a Catholic Dinamite or an American Doctor it was no madman that wrote that letter, it might have been an accomplice.

Henry Armitage was persistent and wrote again the following day to comment upon the use of the word 'Boss' and the 'daring exploits of the Irish American Dynamiters in London'. He thought that the letter signed 'Jack the Ripper' was written by an accomplice and wondered which Fenian dynamiters might be missing from New York. He was sure that the murders were all in revenge for the conviction of the American doctor 'some time since'.

Armitage wrote a third time on 8 October to thank the City Police for the acknowledgements they had sent him and to say that when the last letter signed 'Jack the Ripper' stated he was going to Brighton to 'kill a Dutchess', Armitage thought that he had made Whitechapel: 'too hot for him and perhaps he had gone back to America to show his trophies to the fenians & that we should not hear of any more murders just yet, and the one that writes the letters is writing now to deceive whilst the other the murderer gets away'. Three further letters from Henry Armitage on the subject, dated 28 November 1888, 19 July 1889 and 27 October 1889, are on file with the City force's correspondence. Checks by the police confirmed that the elderly Mr Armitage had indeed retired from the force in 1841.

Inspired by a letter written by Archibald Forbes and published that day in the *Daily News*, J.F. Boyd of 45 Bugle Street, Southampton, wrote to the City commissioner on 3 October. He thought that the murderer was 'the same gentleman who gave Mr. W.E. Baxter the Coroner the false information about an American who offered him £20. per uterus'.

The deluge of mail that followed in the wake of the 'double event' on 30 September brought with it many other putative suspects. Then, as now, theorists plucked names from the contemporary newspapers. Even the great self-appointed Ripper hunter Dr Forbes Winslow did not escape the attention of the amateur sleuths. C.J. Denny of Milestone House,

Blackwater, near Farnborough in Hampshire, medical officer for the Hartley Wintney Union, Rural Sanitary Authority, wrote on his headed stationery to Sir James Fraser to communicate his suspicions:

> I saw some weeks back a letter (in the *Globe* I believe) from Dr. Forbes Winslow dealing with the subject of insipient insanity. It struck me as strange that the night or the morning after this letter appearing one of these murders was committed, according to all accounts by some one possessing a knowledge of surgical anatomy. I have never spoken to nor do I know Dr. Winslow, even by appearance, but from letters I have seen as purporting to come from him & from what I have heard of him, I cannot but think that he must be a man of a very peculiarly constituted mind, & one who, possibly suffering from some incipient form of insanity himself, wd go any lengths to prove his case in order to bring about an alteration in the law. Should you consider my suspicions – wh I grant you may be far fetched – worth anything you will know just what to do. . . .

The hunter hunted! Denny suggested comparing the descriptions of parties allegedly seen with the murdered women to Winslow and perhaps even searching him. He ended by stating that he would, of course, claim the reward should his ideas bear fruit.

A most extraordinary suggestion as to the identity of the murderer was sent to the City Police on 3 October. Mrs L. Painter of Burlington Lodge, Strand, Ryde, wrote to say:

> No one seems to think of the possibility of the slayer of the six women at Whitechapel being other than a <u>man</u>, but it may be in fact woman or neither one nor the other. it may be a large animal of the Ape species belonging to some wild beast show. The animal would be swift, cunning, noiseless and strong, standing over its work until a footstep was heard and then vaulting over fence or wall, disappearing in a moment, hiding its weapon perhaps high up in a tree or other safe place, and returning home to shut itself up in its cage. There are, I have heard, a number of wild animals kept in a house in the heart of London, I think in Whitechapel, being allowed an extraordinary amount of liberty.

Mrs Painter went on to comment on the 'unfortunates' that 'nothing but fear for themselves' would remove from the streets. She commended her ideas to the police for consideration.

The idea that the killer might be making his escape via London's sewers occurred to more than one correspondent. On 3 October Frederick Allison of Gordon Street, Plaistow, wrote to Sir James Fraser with this suggestion; he added that the killer might also be 'dressed in the garb of a sewerman'. 'Supposing,' he went on, 'the murderer of last Sunday went down a grating say in Houndsditch or Aldgate & came up in Cheapside. . . .'

E.W. Clark of the post office, Addiscombe, Croydon, 'Like all English men', was 'shocked at reading of these horrible murders' and in a letter dated 3 October he gave his 'humble opinion' on the identity of the murderer to the City Police. He felt it was 'more the work of a Slaughterman' and thought that 'the evidence of the one who was examined at the Inquest about Sept 3 was very peculiar'. After all, such men 'understood exactly where to strike, and they would not be noticed so much if there was blood on them'. Mr Clark felt that it was worth watching slaughterhouses to see who went out after midnight and commended the police to read 'that evidence particularly the remark he made about the women of that part'. Clark was obviously referring to Henry Tomkins, employee of Harrison, Barber & Co. in Winthrop Street. During the inquest, Tomkins had been asked by the coroner, 'Are there any women about there?' He replied, 'Oh! I know nothing about them, I don't like 'em.' The coroner said, 'I did not ask you whether you like them; I ask you whether there were any about that night.' 'I did not see any,' Tomkins responded.[3]

Writing on 3 October, John S. Gordon of 9 Bridge Street, Aberdeen, informed Sir Charles Warren that:

> there is a Dr. Hartley, here selling a patent medicine named Sequah or Indian medicine, Now I believe this man and the Whitechapel Murderer & Mutilator have some connection. Set a watch on this patent medicine man. Examine all bottles & parcels that may be sent to him.

The *Star* of Thursday 4 October reported that the 'Whitechapel craze' had extended to the genteel neighbourhood between Upper Norwood and Croydon, where a belief was held by many people that the murderer found a hiding place in a dense wood skirting Leather Bottle Lane and leading on to Croydon. Gardeners in the employ of Mr Horne, the owner of the wood, had seen a man dressed as a woman lurking there at night. Since August, on each of the nights that a murder was committed, this person had been seen to enter the wood. The gardeners had duly armed themselves.

The *Star* also reported on the arrest on the night of Wednesday 3 October of an American suspect who refused to give his name or any account of himself. He was well dressed, rather tall, of slight build and clean shaven. He had accosted a woman in Cable Street and asked her to go with him. He had threatened that if she refused he would 'rip her up'. The woman screamed and the man rushed to a cab. The police gave chase, got on to the cab, seized the man and took him to Leman Street police station where he had asked the duty inspector, 'Are you the boss?' He was detained along with two others who were taken there the same evening. One of the men had gone up to an officer in the street and said he 'had assisted in the Mitre-square job'. The constable duly took him to Leman Street where it was found that he was suffering from delirium

Aspects of the murders, including sightseers at Mitre Square (centre), as reflected in *Pictorial World* in 1888.

tremens. The *Star* said he was held pending further inquiries and was released at 10 o'clock that morning, inquiries having shown that his account of himself was entirely satisfactory.

The *Star of the East* of Thursday evening, 4 October, reported a Press Association story that excitement continued to increase in Whitechapel. Should the miscreant fall into the clutches of a Whitechapel mob, it 'will go hard with him', the paper said. Late on the Wednesday night repeated reports had been received that the murderer was captured. Shortly before midnight a story circulated that the unidentified killer had been surprised in the act of 'attempting another outrage' on a woman in Union Street, Whitechapel. This was obviously another version of the American suspect story which stated that the woman was lured by the 'monster' into a side street, but the gleam of a steel blade alerted her to danger. Her screams brought to her assistance a man and two women who were said to have been watching the movements of the couple. The would-be murderer, it was stated, was pursued by a man who knocked the knife out of his hand. However, the unknown attacker then jumped into a passing cab, bidding the cabman drive wherever he liked. A howling mob swarmed after the fugitive and the police soon captured the vehicle, taking the occupant to Leman Street police station. The woman nevertheless declined to press any charge and left the police station. The man was described as 'an athletic determined fellow, of about 43 years of age'. No weapons were found on him. He gave a name, but refused to give his address. He conversed with a slightly American accent. When he was removed to the cells his attitude became defiant.

About 6 p.m. on Wednesday 3 October, a man, whose name was ascertained to be John Lock, a seaman, was rescued by the police from an excited crowd in the vicinity of Ratcliffe Highway. The crowd pursued him shouting 'Leather Apron' and 'Jack the Ripper'. When Lock was examined at the police station, his light tweed suit was found to have paint stains which the crowd had mistaken for blood. His explanation for his appearance was perfectly satisfactory, but it was some considerable time before the crowd dispersed and it was safe for him to depart.

While Eddowes' partner John Kelly was making his statement at Bishopsgate Street police station on 3 October, a man entered and confessed that he was the murderer. He strongly objected to being searched but had to submit when he was approached by two or three constables. He was detained and charged the next day at the Guildhall police court. He gave his name as William Bull, describing himself as a medical student at London Hospital. He appeared to have been drinking heavily. Inspector Izzard said that when Bull came into the station he claimed to have committed the murder in Aldgate, saying that the clothes he had worn were in the Lea and the knife had been thrown away. The prisoner was not known at the London Hospital but his parents were very respectable. In answer to the alderman at the police court, he said he was mad drunk when he made the statement and it was impossible for him to have committed the murder. He was remanded, the alderman refusing to grant bail.

Members of the public swamped the police with plans for how to trap the murderer and suggestions about who he might be. The most popular scheme was to dress police officers as women, arm them and thus lay a trap for the killer. Interest in the London crimes was truly national. On 4 October John S. Gordon of Aberdeen wrote again, this time to advise that information should be sought from all hotel porters and waiters regarding guests who had returned to their rooms about the time when the murders were committed. Mr Gordon also made the suggestion that detectives should dress as women and then added a postscript with his very own theory as to the identity of the killer – 'See where James Malcolm the Bigamist is, he is a Butcher and may have taken a hatred to women.'

'The Nemesis of Neglect',
Punch, 29 September 1888.

The same day Mary Heard of North London wrote to the City Police headquarters with the comment that the murderer was 'the Lunatic who escaped some time ago from Leavesden'. She added that the police might find him with the aid of the keeper who had been in charge of him at the asylum.

Another female correspondent wrote the same day to the Mayoress, Lady de Keyser, with an idea which she asked to be placed before the lord mayor. She was Mrs S. Luckett of 10 Somerford Grove and she had been scanning the letters pages of the newspapers. She suggested that A. Eberle Evans of Hillcote, Ilkeston, writing that day in the *Standard*, should be interviewed, as should C.H. Presgrave of the Conservative Club, Manchester. She further proposed that board schools and other educational establishments receive surprise visits from detectives. The children, she said, should be questioned class by class about where they lived, how many others lived there too and whether these people were relations or strangers to them. They should also be asked whether those who shared their house were of the same sex and what their habits were. Inquiries should be made as to the position of single-person households and the habits of their occupants. These homes should be particularly watched, Mrs Luckett thought. She then asked, 'Who is the author of 'Dr Jekyll & Mr. Hyde? Is he a capable & likely individual to be the perpetrator of dire offences?' – surely a first in suggesting Robert Louis Stevenson as the Ripper! She rounded off by stating that eight trained bloodhounds should be placed in pairs at police stations at the four points of the compass 'instead of only at Whitechapel for doubtless the ruffian will take hints & vacate other quarters'.

In the batch of suggestions sent on 4 October was a letter from 'Scotus' of Southampton to Sir James Fraser. It said that 'a clue for the perpetrator of the recent crimes' might be obtained if inquiries were made at the various London hospitals and of 'medical men about the East of London' as to whether any very bad case of 'phogdoena' was under treatment: 'My theory of the crimes is that the criminal has been badly disfigured by disease – <u>possibly had his privy member destroyed</u> – & he is now revenging himself on the sex by these atrocities. He has no doubt made up his mind also either to hang or to commit suicide if my conjecture is right.'

The idea that a police officer was the murderer was popular and on 2 October S.A. Ashby of 43 Acacia Road, Regent's Park, wrote to the City commissioner suggesting that the murders 'may have been committed by some human fiend in the disguise of a policeman' in order to evade detection. Then on 5 October an ex-patriot, John Hoyer, 'Artist Tailor' of 315 Broome Street, near Forsyth, New York, wrote to the lord mayor of the City of London:

> Nobody else can be the Villain but one of your Finest (as we call them) or may a Superior.
> Hoping the mystery be solved at a early Hour, and that I may be wrong.
> But you Oblige me by giving this a Investigation and oblige . . .

Also on 5 October 'M.P.' wrote to the City authorities having just been to see 34-year-old American actor Richard Mansfield[4] playing Dr Jekyll and Mr Hyde at the Lyceum. 'M.P.' was much impressed with the performance and had no doubt that Mansfield was none other than the murderer.

The popular idea that the murderer might be a Jewish slaughterman was explored by J.W. Causier of Yetminster near Sherborne in Dorset. In a letter to the City police dated 5 October he enlarged upon the suggestion which he had already made in a previous letter. He believed that such men were 'a sort of minor priesthood <u>holding a license to kill</u> from the Chief Rabbi'. They were therefore easily traced; some were foreigners and they were much more respectable than the majority of slaughterers. It was evident to Mr Causier that the murderer (or murderers) must be well acquainted with Whitechapel and Jewish slaughtermen could move about the area without rousing suspicion. He ended by asking, 'Have the offices connected with the Great Synagogue the one in Bevis Marks been searched?'

'W.G.' of Gloucester Walk, Kensington, wrote to the City authorities on 5 October after reading a letter by a Mr Evans published that day in the *Standard*. He recalled that some time ago there had been two individuals charged at separate times for disturbing the services at St Paul's Cathedral. They were evidently 'Religious monomaniacs' and were identifiable, he said. One was believed to be respectable, a solicitor – 'or called himself one'. The man was over 60 and had no practice. 'W.G.' stated:

> I have met the latter on 2 or 3 occasions and although at times very plausible his conversation often falls into boasting of his great strength inviting others to stand upon his bare breast &c I certainly dont believe he is capable of such villainy but thought I would mention these circumstances. He is an occasional frequenter of Turkish Baths and I may mention that walking is no trouble to him.

N. Hollander of 28 Stratford Road, Kensington, had been avidly scanning reports of the murders in the papers, including Bachert's account of his encounter with a suspicious man in the Three Nuns in Aldgate. Hollander had an idea that the individual Bachert saw was a local man and he wrote to Colonel Fraser about him on 6 October:

> There used to live a surgeon in the Abdingdon [Abingdon] Rd Kensington, or at least he had a surgery there. I think Doctor Sass or Sassy I cannot exactly say which he called himself – he was a Dr. of some club!! Now this man is the exact stereotype of a man seen by the man Baskert in the 3 Nuns Hotel Aldgate.
>   This Dr. is greatly reduced in circumstances, in fact, is loafing about like a tramp. I have seen him principally in the Parks of late; he is certainly a strange mannered man. I have seen him play with his bag like a big school boy. He always carries a black bag & wears black gloves.

It was about two years since this doctor kept a surgery. It seems very likely that he was eccentric or suffering from mild mental illness, but harmless. We do not know if the police made inquiries to trace him. Doctors were popular suspects and 'R.C.N.' of Bristol wrote to the City Police on 6 October with the information that:

> An American Doctor was in Bristol last Winter – he called himself 'Sequah' – he dressed like a Cowboy – he is not unlike the picture in the *Telegraph* of the 6th inst – Packer's description – square built – Height 5ft 7in age about 28 – full in the face, Dark complexion without moustache & alert looking – Black long hair – soft hat and long coat would just suit.

The police did not acknowledge this suggestion.

An interesting unsigned letter was sent to the City Police on 6 October asking if the London Hospital had been thoroughly searched:

> Is there no one there doing 'clerking' &c. who has acquired a little surgical knowledge. May have watched the use of the knife. May have access [to] certain knives and possibly drugs may know how to keep the victims silent by pressure on certain nerves in the neck and also how to preserve his own person and clothing comparatively unstained. It did not take a long time to return to his quarry from Mitre Square even[?] after scribbling a litt[?] via Goulston Street.

Another letter sent in the early part of October is undated. It is signed off by 'a stranger O.X.X.' and was sent to the City Police. The author stated that she had written to Scotland Yard regarding the facsimile of the original 'Jack the Ripper' letter which had been

A popular image of the Ripper.

published in the *Daily Telegraph*: she felt she recognised the writing. She now wrote again in order to give the man's name because 'some month back' he had said 'it was a very easy thing to do – what is now being done to the Poor women at the east end of London'. The correspondent went on:

> . . . he is a short man rather & I had to dry a jacket for him & women like I felt in his pockets while doing so & found his name was G<u>ale</u>r or G<u>ala</u>r & he often talk of the Brompton Hospital & a old nurse at the out Patients Part & what I now rember the number on the letter was either 13 or 31. South Place Chelsea.

The writer, wishing to remain anonymous, said that she would watch the *Daily Telegraph* for the letters 'O.X.X.' in the paper and she would answer any query. She committed to this against the advice of her friends who had told her to have nothing to do with it.

Not all suggestions received by the police were outlandish. On 6 October John Bland of 95 Sinclair Road, Kensington, wrote to the City Police commissioner suggesting that the murderer was:

> a watchman left in solo charge of one of Jewish houses in the City that are closed from Friday till Monday. If this were the case he would have plenty of time to wash away all traces of his crime. After he had done the Berner St murder he would probably make straight for his house so as to be out of sight before the 'hue and cry' was raised and the fact of his appearing in Mitre Square afterwards would tend to show that he lives in the direction of the City from Berners [*sic*] Street.

But Mr Bland also had a suggestion as to the actual identity of the killer, mentioning the widely discussed ideas that the murderer was a mad doctor and a religious fanatic:

> There is a poor lunatic named Herbert Freund who has been in the hands of the police several times for disturbances in St. Paul's. I do not know anything whatever against this man, whom I have never seen, except that he was educated for a doctor and he went mad on the subject of religion.

The Whitechapel Vigilance Committee had been formed on 10 September and its activities received wide publicity in the newspapers. The committee itself was to be the inspiration for further suspect stories and reports of odd incidents. The press pointed out that the murderer not only had to avoid uniformed and plain-clothed police officers but also had to 'reckon with a small, enthusiastic body of amateur detectives'. The duties of this band were twofold.

The Trafalgar Temperance hotel, headquarters of the Whitechapel Vigilance Committee.

It was to publicise far and wide its disagreement with the home secretary by offering a substantial reward to 'anyone – citizen or otherwise' who could give information that would bring the murderer or murderers to justice. In addition, its members patrolled the most secluded parts of the district in the dead of night with a view to running the criminal to earth. Unfortunately, those to whom they appealed for financial help were more ready to commend than to support. Excluding one or two substantial subscriptions, they were forced to admit that funds had not 'rolled in'. A suggestion that a large public meeting might be held to further the objectives of the 'Vigilants' was not responded to with alacrity. Undaunted by the disappointments, the committee worked persistently on. Night after night, at 9 o'clock, meetings were held in the upper room of a pub in the Mile End Road which had been placed at the disposal of the committee by the landlord, who was also its treasurer. The leaders of the group were principally tradesmen and included a builder, a cigar manufacturer, a tailor, a picture-frame maker, a licensed victualler and an actor.

Inexperienced in practical police work, they decided to call in professional assistance rather than rely solely upon their own resources. For this purpose they engaged the services of two private detectives, men who claimed to be 'experts in the unravelling of mysteries'.[5] About a dozen men with intimate knowledge of the neighbourhood of Whitechapel were placed at the disposal of those executive officers. Those selected were deemed to be 'physically and morally equal to the task they may any night be called upon to perform'. As they were drawn from the unemployed, it was not necessary to pay a high level of remuneration.

Shortly before midnight these 'assassin-hunters' were dispatched on their mission, their tread silenced by the use of galoshes and their own safety assured by carrying police whistles and stout sticks. The area they covered was divided into beats and each man was assigned his respective round. At 30 minutes past midnight committee rooms had by law to close and then the members who happened to be on duty emerged. Like police sergeants they made their tours of inspection, seeing that their men were faithfully performing their onerous duties and they themselves visited the most isolated and ill-lit spots. The volunteer policemen finally left their beats between 4 and 5 o'clock in the morning. It was not possible for members of the committee to supervise every night because most of them were engaged in their own businesses from early in the morning until late. Although the Whitechapel Vigilance Committee's men met with no success, it was claimed that they gathered much information that could be of future use. The regular police were not affected in their own endeavours to bring the criminal to justice. Suspicions, surmises and possible clues were notified to the nearest police station from time to time and it was reported that 'one member of the committee at least honestly believes that he is on the right track.'

Even without the help of the Whitechapel Vigilance Committee the police were not short of named suspects to either dismiss or investigate. On 6 October W.R. Collett of 104 Upland Road, East Dulwich, wrote to the City commissioner to name a man he had met the previous July while staying with his wife in a boarding house – Portland House, Havelock Road, Hastings. Mr Collett discovered that the man, who was named Willie Boult and aged about 30, had 'surreptitiously left' his employ with a firm of solicitors called Jacques in the WC district of London to move to the house in Hastings. According to Collett, it was apparent that he was deranged and in a few days he 'became an alarming lunatic'. His friends were called in to take him away to live with his mother in Fulham. The man's telling traits were that:

> He developed most tragedical ideas, reciting or singing things of that nature at all times of the day & night, accompanying his actions with a knife –
> He brought a small Gladstone Bag of black shiny leather with him, which he carried at all times, with his knife inside (an ivory handled one with a blade about 4 inches long) . . .

Such behaviour, said Mr Collett, made it possible that 'such a maniac would be a dangerous character if suffering from any injury inflicted on him (whether imaginary or real)' and he felt that the police should trace Boult as it was possible he might be guilty of the crimes.

Also on 6 October, 'Watchful' of the City of London wrote to Major Smith of the City Police with the warning to: 'Watch G. Weston & Cos, Electricians, 40 Burdett Rd., Mile End. There is one or more American employed there acquainted with life in Texas & other Western states.'

Sarah Fremlin of Park View, Loore Road, Maidstone, Kent, wrote to the lord mayor of London on 7 October to say that she suspected a person who was staying with an old gentleman, a doctor, she had known some years previously in a village where she then lived and kept a school. The man in question had approached her to ask if she would accommodate his three children and housekeeper for a few weeks because he wanted them to receive the benefit of the country air. She did this and then learned that the man's London address was Oxford Street, Whitechapel. She subsequently discovered that the man's wife was not dead but had left him, the fault being hers. The doctor died and the man arranged his funeral. After this, he left with his family and she had not seen him since. If he was still alive, the man would now be aged between 50 and 60 years. She could give his name 'if required & necessary for the furtherance of Justice'.

On 22 October, good as her word, Sarah Fremlin again wrote, to the City Commissioner, desiring 'to aid you all I can in the detection of the East end Miscreant'. Further to her previous communication, she could now name her suspect as John Davis, although the name appeared as Thomas Davis in a press cutting of a case in the Westminster Court where he was described as an elderly man, an agricultural worker, who had been charged with begging in the Fulham Road. She claimed that the doctor had referred to him as 'Jack & often Jackey', thus confirming her suspicions.

The *East Anglian Daily Times* of Saturday 8 October had further news on suspects:

THE

EAST END ATROCITIES.

ARRESTS AND DISCHARGES.

AN AMERICAN STORY.

[CENTRAL NEWS TELEGRAM]

NEW YORK, Friday Morning.

The atrocious crimes committed in Whitechapel have aroused intense interest here. The following statement has been made by an English sailor named Dodge. He says he arrived in London from China on August 13th by the steamship Glenorlie. He met at the Queen's Music Hall, Poplar, a Malay cook named Alaska. The Malay said he had been robbed by women of bad character in Whitechapel of two years' savings, and he swore that unless he found the woman, and recovered his money, he would murder and mutilate every Whitechapel woman he met. He showed Dodge a double edged knife, which he always carried with him. He was about 5ft. 7in. in height, 130lbs. in weight, and apparently 35 years of age. Of course he was very dark.

The 'Malay Cook' story had appeared in the *Daily Telegraph* on 6 October and there is little doubt that the name 'Alaska' was actually a misinterpretation of the ethnic description 'a Lascar' (an Indian sailor). This story had struck John Binny of 13 Tavistock Place, London, who wrote to the City Police superintendent on 6 October. Mr Binny felt that the story may be 'a ruse of the assassin or one of his friends' to put the detectives off the scent. He felt it was worth the police having inquiries made of Dodge in New York and told them they should obtain a description of the Malay. Binny had also read that a Malay was also among a group of men recently arrested and that he had been freed. Mr Binny compared descriptions of suspects given in connection with the Stride murder and the Malay. For the information of the police he enclosed a copy of the relevant newspaper article.

W. Cunliffe of 33 Harcourt Road, Brockley, SE, wrote to the City authorities on 8 October detailing suspicions he held in relation to a German man, H.C. Kromschroeder of St John's Wood, who had been employed as a draughtsman at Woodhouse & Rawson's, electrical engineers, Cadby Hall Works, West Kensington, until midsummer 1888. Just prior to leaving this employment the German had showed his fellow employees in the office 'a large & dangerous looking knife [apparently] of the Bowie type' which caused some interest. He then buckled it on to his waist to show how completely it was hidden. According to Mr Cunliffe, the man had openly declared that he was 'in the habit of associating with women of loose character', used phraseology that corresponded with the published letters of 'Jack the Ripper' and employed:

> the most vengeful & bitter expressions of hate & violence towards both Frenchmen & also loose women, and speak of 'ripping them up' – But on the other hand, once whilst I remonstrated with him for speaking & feeling so bitterly against such women – He admitted that they had helped him in needy circumstances, and therefore, he was under great obligation to them for that help.

However, the writer was still 'very forcibly struck' by the similarity between this man's words and the Ripper letters. Although Kromschroeder professed to be a German subject (Hanoverian), he spoke very good English without a German accent. In fact his accent seemed to hail more from Birmingham, the North or Lancashire. The man had tastes of 'a low & vulgar type' and his expressions were at times 'most disgustingly horrible and bloodthirsty'. His evident hate, malice and morbid character impressed Mr Cunliffe who also felt that his man resembled the first of the two suspect sketches reproduced in the *Daily Telegraph*. He said Kromschroeder wore a diagonal cloth coat, an overcoat similar to one described in the papers as worn by a suspect, and a stiff brown billycock hat. The man was a frequent visitor to the Hound & Flower pub near Addison Road station and the Beaconsfield near the Olympia. Cunliffe had become quite friendly with him and had visited both premises with him. Kromschroeder told Binny his mother was English and his father German.

The terrible murders had greatly affected B. Barraclough of 1 Woodview Terrace, Bradford. He wrote to the police on 9 October stating that his children had been experimenting with 'table rapping' and not only did the table respond with the words there would be 'more murders tonight in London', it also revealed the identity of the murderer. He was 'Tom Totson, 20 Wurt Street, W.C.'.

Another 9 October correspondent, W.J. Smith of Red Lion Passage, Holborn, had further suggestions for the police. His letter to Fraser identified a deep and dark motive behind the murders:

Motive

A week or two ago I noticed a poster of the Star saying, <u>War on Warren</u>, I have been daily looking for the outbreak in any form & I admit it is apparent in the Horrors they thought by Demoralising the Police force they would make government impossible that Lord Salisbury would resign and Gladstone come in and the ruin of the Empire certain – and their cherished object gained a (Republic) God <u>Forbid</u>.

Mr Smith had a suspect. In 1881 a 21-year-old Hungarian had applied to him for a lodging despite being unable to speak English. The man was very clever and soon learned the language. He had strong communist sympathies and knew that Mr Smith was 'a loyal Conservative' but wanted to 'be very intimate indeed'. He was propagating revolutionary literature in German and English with imported books. Many of his German customers were at the 'Lager Beer Distillery Tottenham & at Soho & Leicester Square & all over London . . . he has also had 2 or 3 Situations as Manager at a Salary from the Jews who I believe he hates & persecutes as well as the english workmen & Girls whom he is over & can sack or take on at his sweet will'. Mr Smith feared that the foreign socialists were taking over and that the situation was desperate. He then went on to list the suspicions he had regarding individuals:

THE
PALL MALL BUDGET

No. 1046.—Vol. XXXVI.   THURSDAY, OCTOBER 11, 1888.   *Weekly. Price Fourpence.*

WHERE IS JACK THE RIPPER?

SIR CHARLES (inveigled by the Whitechapel Will-o'-the-Wisp into the Morass of Muddle): "O!, dear! what a mess I am in."

Sir Charles Warren lampooned in the *Pall Mall Budget* of 11 October 1888.

no doubt you will pay some attention to the Tottenham address they have recently changed there [*sic*] Watchman the last I think his name was Lemon I heard he was to open a shop Eating house in Hollywell Lane E & doubtless these 2 friends found the substitute, there is a Hungarian Club in Burt St opposite the British Museum, do you know anything about it I think the caretakers name is Hoot he has been a great traveller in his time, since April to September this year he has been travelling & visited Dublin I have some doubts about him also a Man Travelling for Henry Pound Bag Maker Leadenhall St. his name is Garrod, if you could find all the places he went to in England & Ireland between April & Sept last, & if all his business was legitimate. I fear he was agent for the socialists at the same time I know he received a good deal of money & I thought his movements very suspicious I would like to add I know a Mr Mac Sweeny I hear he cost his father 600 Pounds for his Education he was educated at university college Hospital. Previous to his present situation 4 years ago he was in America, some time, and always uses the dialect Boss &c. might not a man with his education instruct others in dissection.

It is interesting to note that Mr Smith's theorising encompasses all the popular themes of foreign anarchists, Irish links and an American connection.

Writing to the City authorities, also on 9 October, J.J. Beckett, a barge owner and contractor of Union Wharf, East Greenwich, informed the police that he believed he knew the identity of 'the person who is likely to have committed the late <u>murders</u> in <u>Whitechapel</u>'. Mr Beckett was at Greenwich police station on Friday 5 October and there he saw a copy of the letters said to have been written by the Whitechapel murderer. The writing and language of the letters struck him as familiar and:

in pondering over the matter it came forcibly to my mind that one James David Lampard was the party whose writing and language they represented. I was the Proprietor of the house known as the <u>Ram</u> & <u>Magpie</u>, Fleet Street, Shoreditch and he was one of my most frequent customers and I have been often alone in his company and have had both time & opportunity to study this man and know him well. In former years this man was in affluent circumstances and had travelled both the European and American Continents he had stayed some little time in America and often addressed me as the Boss and other slang American terms. He led a life of great profligacy and this had brought him to a condition little better than beggary. He was most excitable and was fond of causing fierce excitement at one time he broke his arm, and set it again himself tearing the sleeve of his shirt for bandages. He had a great taste for anatomy & had dissected and stuffed different animals & birds. He was a good scholar and I have heard him speak of the human body in a very learned manner.

So struck was Beckett by the likelihood of Lampard being the murderer, he made inquiries about the man in Whitechapel on Saturday 6 October among people who knew him well. They told him that Lampard had been 'out of his mind' and had been a patient at the London Hospital, from whence he had been sent to a convalescent home. However, since his return he had been leading a life as dissipated as before. He had, apparently, ruined his father, who was now destitute. Mr Beckett felt that Lampard fitted the description of the murderer, given by a doctor in the *Chronicle*, as an educated man who had been insane but had been discharged from a hospital supposedly cured. Also, Lampard knew 'every corner in Whitechapel', and had lodged in most of the lower-class lodging houses in the area. Beckett

An early photograph of City of London Police officers checking the security of doors while on night duty. Note the old bull's-eye oil lanterns attached to the officers' belts.

described his suspect as about 5 feet 8 inches in height, well knit and broad-shouldered. He had the appearance of a military man with 'a very authoritative tone of voice'. He had a red face, pointed moustache, no whiskers, dark hair, a high forehead and was bald in front. Even when badly dressed, he still retained a gentlemanly appearance, sometimes wearing a high hat and frock coat, and at other times a round felt hat, long coat or dress coat and sometimes a peaked cap. Lampard had been seen going through Fleet Street, Shoreditch, on the night of Thursday 4 October much the worse for drink. It was believed that he lived somewhere in the neighbourhood and was well known to residents.

An anonymous accusation against an ex-police officer was sent to Sir James Fraser on 12 October. 'I am about to make a <u>serious</u> accusation,' the writer began, 'but, if followed up, I am certain with good result.'

There was a man in your force Stationed at Se<u>ething</u> Lane for some considerable time as Constable, but he has been discharged I think about 12 months –
When he joined, I am possitive there was a screw loose with regards a child –
Then again, he was on duty in the neighbourhood of Al<u>dga</u>te very often and would know very inch of it – When he left he was about going in for wi<u>ndow cleaning</u> at Private Houses etc and I am possitive he was living, (if not now) in the im<u>mediate</u> neighbourhood, where all these Chrimes have been committed,–He is a stout man I should say about 5 feet 8 and 30 years.of.age. no whiskers & slight moustache and corresponds exactly with the man Pack<u>er the fruiterer</u> describes of course you will know best how to go about the matter but if he was confronted with the man that sold the grapes. I feel certain he would recognize him as the man.–It will be remembered that the unfortunate woman that was killed should say that she used to keep company with a policeman.

The writer pointed out that the suspect was often on that particular beat and would know the exact time it took for the patrolling officer to get round his beat before returning again, and he would know the warehouseman's duty on a Saturday night.

On 12 October Major-General E.R.C. Wilcox of 27 Ashburnham Road, Bedford, wrote to Sir Charles Warren with his deductions about the case, having reflected on evidence reported in that day's issue of the *Standard*:

1st Three doctors certify that the murderer is no skilful anatomist and therefore not the Whitechapel murderer.

2nd That a Thomas Conway exists, a pensioner from the 18th R. Irish, and that this man is not recognised as the original Thomas Conway, also a pensioner from the same regiment, the missing husband of Catherine Eddowes. Can this man be personating the original Thomas Conway and drawing his pension? If so, what more natural than that the personator should meet with & destroy the only living being who could expose his identity & lose him his pension, ergo, he is the murderer!

Chief Inspector Swanson initialled the letter on receipt and forwarded it to the City Police as it related to the Eddowes murder.

The same day 'An Observer' posted a letter, in London, to Scotland Yard, also having read the Eddowes inquest evidence in his paper. Again the correspondence related to Conway and the City murder and the letter was also duly forwarded. The writer noted the evidence of Eddowes' daughter, Annie Phillips, that Tom Conway had two sons aged about 20 and 15. He had suspicions relating to them. He said that four or five months previously two young men styling themselves as 'the Conway brothers' had played at Dauntless' Main Hall in Sisson Grove, Marylebone. One was certainly Tom Conway who hailed from the East End; the other actor he did not know. They played female characters and used to walk about Piccadilly in the evening, between Piccadilly Circus and Bond Street, and even as far as Hyde Park Corner. Tom Conway, who rejoiced in the local alias of 'Eliza Armstrong'[6] was aged about 20, usually rouged and powdered, and had an effeminate walk and speech. 'An Observer' had no doubt that he was well known to the Vine Street police as would be his mate, 'Baby Kate'. Their gang, which included Preston White an ex-convict (alias Madge Wildfine), Poll, Alice the Betrayer, Esmeralda and others, usually met on Sunday nights at Hadkin's public house, Green Street, Leicester Square. A visit to that hostelry, by a detective, should reveal some information about Tom Conway 'for he is known to the society there as well as the Church Clock'. 'An Observer' had been informed of the existence of this 'infamous clique' by a young male relative who had foolishly nearly allowed himself to be 'inveigled into their clutches', and who had, out of curiosity, watched their movements about Piccadilly for several evenings. This sounds like an example of an anonymous writer with some personal agenda who wished to put the police on to a group who had upset him, using a suggestion about the murders as an excuse.

Alese Brown of 26 Caledonian Place, Aberdeen, had some years previously been engaged in business in Whitechapel and claimed to know the locality and 'class of people living there well'. In a letter to the mayor of the City of London on 15 October he stated:

I have all along believed the murderer to be a Jew, as I know that a number of Jews, believe in the literal meaning of the law as laid down in their Bible, which says that a woman who is a prostitute shall be put to death. Now a Jew if a monomaniac would naturally reason that he was doing according to that law, if he was clearing the streets of these unfortunates, and he would have no difficulty in finding out that class, from other women, as all these poor victims must have lain down before him for an immoral end, and they were then at his mercy.

I beleive [sic] that he is either a Jewish minister, or some of the higher functionaries belonging to that Religion, and if a strict watch was kept upon the movements of that class of persons, I have not the slightest doubt but that the murderer would be arrested.

One of the Ripper letters
sent to Sir Charles Warren.

Among the various suggestions that the murderer was a police officer was an unsigned letter on 15 October to the Metropolitan Police from Trowbridge, Wiltshire. It was addressed to Sir Charles Warren but was forwarded to the City Police because it referred to PC Watkins who had found Eddowes' body. It was received on 18 October:

> i feel i must for reasons which i will tell you another time if the man should prove to be the one that did the murders i mean the policeman Watkins that found the body of the woman in mitre square i want you to keep an eye on him you may think it strange i should pick out a man in the service but if he was in the ploice service or my own brother i would for the sake of the peopel try and find him out Dear Sir if he should prove to be the man or lead to the discovery you will hear from me again.

On the back page, written at an angle, was:

> please be careful and keep this quiet not let him know you are watching him.

On 16 October the most sensational item of correspondence, allegedly from the killer, was received by builder and decorator George Lusk of 1 Alderney Road, Mile End, President of the Vigilance Committee. The small cardboard box contained half a human kidney that had been longitudinally divided and a letter:

> From hell
> Mr Lusk
>   Sir
>   I send you half the
> Kidne I took from one women
> prasarved it for you tother piece I
> fried and ate it was very nise I
> may send you the bloody knif that
> took it out if you only wate a whil
> longer.
>   Signed   Catch me when
>   You can
>   Mishter Lusk.

This must have been like manna from heaven for the press who were still printing sensational and blood-curdling stories even though October was proving a rather uneventful month in the absence of further murders in Whitechapel. Lusk, after initially regarding it as a joke, finally took the letter and piece of kidney to a local doctor and then to Dr Thomas Horrocks Openshaw, the pathological curator at the London Hospital, who pronounced it to be human. From there the items were taken to Leman Street police station on 18 October. The kidney was forwarded to the City Police office at Old Jewry and the letter to Scotland Yard. On 20 October Swanson loaned the letter to McWilliam who had it photographed and returned it to Scotland Yard on 24 October. Dr Brown examined the section of kidney and he too declared it to be human. The combined medical opinion was that it was the kidney of an adult human. It was not charged with fluid (formalin) as it would have been in the case of a cadaver used for dissection in teaching, but was from a body which had been autopsied and, as such, could be obtained by any student or mortuary porter. Every effort was made to trace the sender but to no avail. McWilliam felt that it might turn out to be the act of a medical student, who would be in a position to obtain such a specimen. There was cooperation between the City and Scotland Yard and James McWilliam and Donald Swanson met daily to confer on the subject.

There is a popular misconception that Eddowes was suffering from a kidney condition known as Bright's disease, but there is actually no evidence to show that she did. The person responsible for starting the myth is Henry Smith of the City Police. In his entertaining book *From Constable To Commissioner* (1910) Smith relates the story of the Lusk letter and kidney, telling how he passed the portion of kidney to Dr Gordon Brown, instructed him to consult with the most eminent men in the profession and asked him to send a report as soon as possible. Smith then went on to give the main points of the report, stating that the renal artery was 3 inches long and that 2 inches remained in Eddowes' corpse while 1 inch was attached to the piece of kidney. However, when Dr Brown was interviewed by the press about his examination of the kidney he stated that the renal artery had been trimmed off. Smith then went on to say: 'The kidney left in the corpse was in an advanced stage of Bright's Disease; the kidney sent me was in an exactly similar state.' This was simply untrue. Dr Gordon Brown said no such thing as is clear from the surviving detail in his inquest evidence. Present at the post-mortem examination on Eddowes was Dr William Sedgwick Saunders, the Analyst for the City of London, who inspected the stomach contents. In an interview with the *Manchester Evening News* on 19 October, he said:

> You may take it that the right kidney of the woman Eddowes was perfectly normal in its structure and healthy, and by parity of reasoning you would not get much disease in the left. The liver was healthy and gave no indication that the woman drank. Taking the discovery of a kidney and supporting it to be human my opinion is that it was a student's antic. It is quite possible for any student to obtain a kidney for the purpose.

Bright's disease, named after Richard Bright (1789–1858) of Guy's Hospital does not exist as a named illness today; the modern equivalent would be glomerulonephritis, which has many variants. In 1888 it was customary to describe a non-suppurative inflammation of the kidneys (nephritis) as Bright's disease, and nearly all forms of nephritis would come under this heading. There is no evidence that Eddowes was suffering from such a condition. That having been said, it was not an uncommon illness in 1888.

The newspapers of 1888 mentioned that Dr Openshaw stated the kidney belonged to a female, that it was part of a left kidney and that the woman had been in the habit of

The infamous 'From hell' letter, sent to George Lusk of the Whitechapel Vigilance Committee on 16 October 1888 together with a section of human kidney. Initially worried about it, Lusk came to regard it as a 'joke' by someone at the London Hospital.

Letter, envelope and enlarged detail of Jack the Ripper correspondence sent to Dr Thomas Openshaw.

Dr Thomas Openshaw, who examined the 'Lusk kidney' and pronounced it human.

drinking (it was reported he said it was a 'ginny' kidney). '[T]he kidney is evidently that of a person who had been a considerable drinker, as there were distinct marks of disease,' said the *Daily Telegraph*. Such Sherlockian deductions could not be made from the piece of organ and Dr Openshaw was quick to deny that he had made such comments, stating that he was merely able to say that it was half of a left human kidney.[7] Alcohol does not damage the kidneys and there was no such thing as a 'ginny' one. No doubt Smith elaborated his tale using the erroneous press reports rather than drawing on anything resembling evidence.

The third point Smith raised in his efforts to prove that the letter and piece of kidney were genuine was a statement that according to the medical experts, specifically Mr Sutton of the London Hospital, the specimen 'had been put in spirits within a few hours of its removal from the body – thus effectually disposing of all hoaxes in connection with it'. He went on to explain that the body of anyone who had died violently was not taken direct to the dissecting-room but must await the inquest and this was never held sooner than the following day. This is simply incorrect and irrelevant. All bodies which had met with a sudden death were autopsied at a mortuary in order to establish cause of death – even if it was obvious. These examinations were carried out daily and were easily accessible to many medical men or others with permission to attend, as well as the mortuary attendants who dealt with the bodies for the doctors. It is a procedure that has led to a misunderstanding among some modern theorists who have confused these usually fresh bodies, dealt with almost every day, with the formalin-preserved cadavers used for dissection by students. The piece of kidney sent to Lusk had been steeped in spirits of wine, which was the standard medium for preserving specimens in the short term. Therefore, the kidney could easily have been obtained by any medical student, for example, from a fresh corpse. The natural way to keep it before posting would be in spirits of wine. Smith's own man, Inspector McWilliam, allowed the possibility that it was a hoax. He said, 'It might turn out after all, to be the act of a Medical Student who would have no difficulty in obtaining the organ in question.' The view was endorsed by Swanson who stated that:

> the result of the combined medical opinion they have taken upon it, is, that it is the kidney of a human adult, not charged with fluid, as it would have been in the case of a body handed over for the purposes of dissection to an hospital, but rather as it would be in a case where it was taken from the body not so destined. In other words similar kidneys might & could be obtained from any dead person upon whom a post-mortem had been made from any cause by students or dissecting room porter.

This, combined with the opinion of Dr Gordon Brown and Lusk, who later stated he was known at the London Hospital and believed that the kidney was sent to him as a practical joke,[8] leads the authors to doubt that the 'From hell' communication was genuine. We can only assume that Lusk had good reason for his belief and may even have had an idea who the culprit was.

'An Accessory', writing on 19 October 1888 to the inspector of the Detective Department of the City Police, was another correspondent who accused an ex-policeman:

> The crime committed in Mitre Square City and those in the district of Whitechapel were perpetrated by an Ex Police Constable of the Metropolitan Police who was dismissed the force through certain connection with a prostitute. The motive for the crimes is hatred and spite against the authorities at Scotland Yard one of whom is marked as a victim after which the crimes will cease.

The City Police marked this letter as having sent a copy to Scotland Yard on 20 October.

The chalking of messages on walls was obviously popular in 1888, especially after the publicity accorded to the Goulston Street writing. Even the toilet walls of the Guildhall were not spared. On 25 October 1888 Josiah E. Boys of 41 Commercial Street, E, reported in a letter to Sir James Fraser that:

> whilst in the Guildhall this afternoon I had occasion to go into one of the water closets, and, upon the wall I saw written the following words, I am Jack the Ripper and intend to do another murder at the Adelphi Arches at 2. a.m. at first I was inclined to think it an hoax he also adds I will send the Ears to Colonel Frazer – I have compared the handwriting and find a striking resemblance In the formation of the letters.

On Sunday 26 October Florence Forbes Winslow, wife of the celebrated Ripper-hunting doctor, wrote from Rivercourt, Hammersmith, to make the suggestion that 'Jack the Ripper' lived in the north of London. She enclosed a cutting from the *People* of that day which reported that some two weeks previously two ladies who disembarked the train at Finchley Road had been much frightened by a well-dressed young man in their railway carriage. He had taken out a knife and conducted himself like a madman. He got out at the same station but quickly disappeared. She should not have thought much about the latest 'Strange Affair on the North London Railway' were it not for this incident. She felt that it was very likely that the man went to and fro to Broad Street, which, she believed, was not far from Whitechapel and she ended, 'As I often travel alone to Finchley Road I am naturally rather alarmed.'

The enclosed cutting was entitled 'WAS IT JACK THE RIPPER?' and related to an incident that had occurred on the night of 25 October. A young lady, on her own, had caught a train at about 8 p.m. at Broad Street station and was alarmed by 'a tall, gentlemanly-looking man, who wore a silk hat and carried a black bag' who tried to enter her carriage but was put into the next one by a porter. She heard strange noises in the next carriage near Shoreditch and between there and Haggerston she was 'much startled by the appearance of a thin white hand at the carriage window on the right side of the train'. To her further alarm 'a few seconds later a man's face, pale and startled looking, peered in through the glass on the opposite side, and almost petrified the young lady with fright'. She recognised him as the passenger from the next carriage and had the presence of mind to pull up the window by the strap and hold on to the leather. Apparently, as he was in a perilous position outside on the narrow footboard he was unable to enter. The train began to brake at Haggerston station and 'the haggard and wild-looking face' left the window. She alighted from the train, as did the stranger with his bag. She said to him, 'You coward, to try and frighten me!' He looked at her in a 'dazed sort of fashion' and slipped off among other passengers leaving the station. She burst into hysterical tears and was helped by a gentleman and his wife who listened to her story and tried to find the man without avail. The piece ended with another story of an incident that had occurred at a house in the north of London. A 16-year-old girl retired to bed with her elder sister at nearly 11 p.m. and at about 6 the next morning she awoke to find that her hair had been plaited and then cut through. A piece about 8 inches long, still plaited, was found lying on the pillow and next to it was a note: 'This is just to show you that I am about.–The Barber.' The bedroom door was still locked but the window, on the second floor, was open. The elder girl denied all knowledge of the affair and seemed more frightened than her sister.

Such were the bizarre incidents reported as the month drew to a close but the mystery of the murders remained as impenetrable as the October fog that drifted against the windows of Scotland Yard. The parlous state of the investigation's affairs was summed up by Anderson in a report to the Home Office dated 23 October:

The Whitechapel Murders

At the present stage of the inquiry the best reply that can be made to the Secretary of State's request for a report upon these cases is to send the accompanying copy of detailed reports prepared by Chief Inspector Swanson, who has special charge of the matter at this office.

I wish to guard against its being supposed that the inquiry is now concluded. There is no reason for furnishing these reports at this moment except that they have been called for.

That a crime of this kind should have been committed without any clue being supplied by the criminal, is unusual, but that five successive murders should have been committed without our having the slightest clue of any kind is extraordinary, if not unique, in the annals of crime. The result has been to necessitate our giving attention to innumerable suggestions, such as would in any ordinary case be dismissed unnoticed, and no hint of any kind, which was not obviously absurd, has been neglected. Moreover, the activity of the Police has been to a considerable extent wasted through the exigencies of sensational journalism, and the action of unprincipled persons, who, from various motives, have endeavoured to mislead us. But on the other hand the public generally and especially the inhabitants of the East End have shown a marked desire to assist in every way, even at some sacrifice to themselves, as for example in permitting their houses to be searched as mentioned at page 10 of the last report.

The vigilance of the officers engaged on the inquiry continues unabated.

R.Anderson
Oct 23/88

Clearly the police were at a loss to explain their lack of results and were painfully aware that there was still an unknown killer at large. It was not a good start for Anderson's career as head of the CID and, unknown to him at this time, he was already being viewed by the Home Office as a potential scapegoat for failure to solve the crimes.

Things were to get worse.

—— ELEVEN ——

Whitechapel is Panic Stricken

AS some had already noted, the killer was apparently working to a timetable of his own. The past four murders had occurred on 31 August, 8 and 30 September. October had been a blank although the weather had been in the murderer's favour. There was fog. This was the only month when these conditions prevailed, all the others had been clear. If the crimes followed a date pattern then logically 8 and 30 November were the days when he might strike again. If this supposition was correct, the timing could not have been worse for the police. On 8 November both London forces were heavily involved in final planning for the Lord Mayor's Show, which was to take place the next day and faced threats of disruption from further demonstrations against poverty and employment conditions. This was the day when the new lord mayor would be sworn into office and drive through cheering crowds in a great gilded and painted coach to the Royal Courts of Justice in the Strand.

By then, Warren's letter of resignation would be in the home secretary's hands. Not the 'Bloody Sunday' riots, his quarrels with Monro or even his failure, to date, to capture the Whitechapel killer had brought Warren down. It was an article in the current issue of *Murray's Magazine*. Ironically it had been written by Warren himself.

During his time as commissioner, Warren had published other articles, including one on dogs, but this piece was provocative to say the least. It was no coincidence that publication had been timed just before the Lord Mayor's Show. The title was innocuous enough, 'The Police of the Metropolis', but it turned out to be more than an account of how the force worked. It was a stinging attack on governments past and present who had failed to get to grips with the London mob (this 'noisy minority') or who had sided with them when in opposition. The piece began dramatically, 'London has for many years been subject to the sinister influence of a mob stirred up into spasmodic action by restless demagogues.' Signs had not been wanting that another attack on the police was approaching, 'being directed not so much against the individual police constables, as against the police administration, and if successful, it would effectually cripple the power of the Executive to keep peace and order on the approaching Lord Mayor's Day'. The 1886 riots, which had brought down Warren's predecessor, had let the mob feel its strength and powers, the article said. Had it not been for the vigorous police handling of the November ('Bloody Sunday') riots of 1887, London might have faced ruin. But for the first time that century the power of the London mob had been broken; it had failed in its ascendancy over the capital and in coercing the government. Since then, there had been frequent attempts to vilify the police and circulate exaggerated and incorrect reports about its internal administration. No minister, past or present, was exempt from Warren's accusations. He also turned his wrath on public opinion which had veered from praising and petting the police to vilifying and abusing them, depending on the level of fear of riots on the streets.

Warren was on the defensive about a number of issues on which he tried to answer the critics. He asked for understanding. It was

> quite impractical within the limits of a short article to do more than show in a few import-ant instances that the hostile criticism levelled at police administration is based upon absolutely incorrect premises; probably enough has been said to assure the reader that no attempt has been made to drill and train the police as a military force, that more attention is being paid to the detective duties than the service has ever bestowed upon it before.

He concluded, if Londoners would 'keep cool, and recognise the fact that the police are doing their duty in an admirable and exemplary manner, so far as is in the power of flesh and blood, among all the temptations to which the citizens subject them, they will come forward and assist the police'.

All sounded reasonable enough but no home secretary, even putting other objections aside, would like to be told in such a manner that it was the commissioner's rough wooing, and not his actions, which had saved London from mob rule. The *Star*, one of Warren's fiercest critics, regarded the article as 'an impeachment of democracy'. It added, 'What he calls the mob is only his insolent military fashion of speaking of the efforts of the people – whose servant he is – to enlarge their democracies.'

The offending article was shown to Home Secretary Matthews who fired off a hurried letter to Warren on the morning prior to the show. He forwarded a copy of a Home Office ruling sent to Henderson in 1879, seven years before Warren's appointment, which the commissioner had now breached by publishing his piece. The circular said that to avoid embarrassment no officer should publish any work relating to the department without first obtaining the home secretary's approval. This applied to every policeman from the commissioner downwards and in

'Drumming Them Out'. A *Funny Folks* cartoon of Saturday 29 September 1888, the day before the 'double event', shows Matthew and Warren being drummed out 'to oblivion' by the police with posters of the unsolved murdered arrayed on the wall behind them.

future was to be strictly complied with. Warren had not even known that such a directive existed and his reply was swift and uncompromising. Had he known that the ruling was in force, he wrote back, he would never have accepted the post of commissioner: the document's existence, if enforced, would make it possible for everyone to anonymously attack the police without the commissioner being allowed to challenge false statements, which he had been in the habit of doing for nearly three years. Clearly some way could have been found out of this impasse but Warren was in no mood to compromise. His duties, he insisted, were governed by statute and under statute the home secretary did not have the power to give orders to the police force. He absolutely refused to accept such instructions and yet again offered his resignation as he had done twice before in March and early summer. Matthews, probably glad to get rid of such a quarrelsome subordinate, accepted almost at once. His letter of acceptance, sent two days later on 10 November, gave just a one-line acknowledgement to the services Warren had rendered as commissioner over nearly three years.

The crime generally regarded as the Ripper's last was the murder of Mary Jane Kelly, aged 25 years, whose horrendously mutilated body was discovered lying on her bed in room 13, Miller's Court, at the rear of 26 Dorset Street, Spitalfields. She was found on Friday 9 November, the morning of the Lord Mayor's Show.

Large crowds had gathered in the City. Rain had fallen heavily in the early morning but had cleared away by 10 a.m. leaving the streets dirty and slippery. The skies were still heavy and threatening. Many streets were decorated with flags, banners and floral streamers. There were rumours of demonstrations planned to disrupt the pageant and reporters noted a great many roughs in the crowd and a good deal of jeering. The route was lined with foot police and the streets in front of the lord mayor's Mansion House were patrolled by forty mounted Metropolitan policemen. At Trafalgar Square, where the mayoral procession made its turn to re-enter the City, Warren had placed a strong force of foot and mounted police. The lord mayor's coach had a mounted escort of 19th Hussars. The procession was formed up at the medieval Guildhall and was timed to commence at 12.30 p.m. By then Kelly's body had been discovered.

Initial press reports of the case were sensational and contained many errors and false stories. To piece together the events of that fateful night we have to examine the evidence of various witnesses who appeared at the inquest. It was held on Monday 12 November at Shoreditch Town Hall, presided over by 47-year-old Coroner Dr Roderick Macdonald.

Joseph Barnett, a 30-year-old fish porter of 24/25 New Street, Bishopsgate, had been unemployed for three or four months and had been living with 25-year-old Mary Jane Kelly for about eighteen months at room 13, 26 Dorset Street. Then the couple fell out with each other. On Tuesday 30 October 1888 they separated because Barnett was not earning money and Kelly had had to resort to prostitution as a result. He left between 5 and 6 p.m. He told the inquest that he left because Kelly had taken in a person who was a prostitute and he objected to this. In a contradiction to his earlier evidence he said he had not left her because he was out of work. However, Barnett claimed to have remained friendly with Kelly and had, in fact, visited her between 7 and 8 p.m. on the eve of her murder. He told her that he was sorry that he had no work and could not give her any money. They did not drink together and she was quite sober. In fact, he said, she did not drink when she was with him. It was, he stated, the last time he saw her alive. He was now living with his sister at 21 Portpool Lane, Grays Inn Road, presumably because he could not afford to pay for his bed at his registered address in New Street.

THE INQUEST AT SHOREDITCH TOWN HALL

A contemporary sketch of the coroner, Dr Roderick Macdonald, presiding over the inquest into the death of Mary Jane Kelly, held at Shoreditch Town Hall on Monday 12 November 1888. (Pictorial News, *Saturday 17 November 1888*)

J BARNETT THE FRIEND OF THE DECEASED

The *Pictorial News* of Saturday 17 November 1888 carried this sketch of Joseph Barnett, ex-partner of Mary Jane Kelly, giving evidence at her inquest at Shoreditch Town Hall. He has been suggested as her murderer and as the Ripper himself.

All that is known of Kelly's antecedents was furnished by Barnett – and that was only what, he said, she had told him. He had lived with her for eighteen months and her name was Marie Jeannette Kelly, which seems to indicate that she preferred to use the French version of her first names. He said that Kelly was her maiden name and it was the one she always went by. The police had shown him her body and he was able to recognise it by 'the ear and the eyes'. Having been intimate with the woman for the past eighteen months, we must assume that Barnett did indeed recognise the victim. The reference to 'the ear' seems to indicate that there was some old injury or peculiarity there.

Barnett had met Kelly in Commercial Street and on their first night together they had a drink. They arranged to meet again the next day, a Saturday. At their second meeting they agreed to remain together and he took lodgings in George Street where he was known. They stayed together until the separation at the end of October 1888. On several occasions she had asked him to read to her about the murders and she seemed afraid of someone, he said. If that was the case it seems odd that Barnett did not ask her of whom she was afraid. However, he qualified his statement in a strange way: he said she did not express fear of any particular individual except when they had a row – presumably she then expressed fear of him – but they always made up quickly. According to Barnett, Kelly had become drunk several times in his presence. This appears to contradict his earlier statement that 'she did not drink when she was with him' but it seems likely he meant she was sober when the two were living together and took to drink after they split up. By this point she obviously did not control her drinking very well, and the drink cost money that would have been better spent on her rent. A report in the *Daily Telegraph* said that Barnett described Kelly as being an 'unfortunate' when he met her. He told the inquest she never had any children.

Kelly had told Barnett that she was born in Limerick and that she was aged 25. If this was true, she was born in about 1863. She said she moved to Wales when she was still very young. Her father's name was John Kelly and he was a gauger at an ironworks in Caernarvonshire. She had a sister who was a traveller in materials, selling from market place to market place. She also had six brothers at home and one in the army. One was called Henry. Barnett had never spoken to any of them. Kelly claimed that she was married in Wales when she was only 16 to a collier whose name was Davis or Davies, probably the latter. She lived with him for two or three years until he was killed in an explosion. She then went to Cardiff when she was about 19 and was in an infirmary there for eight or nine months. She had followed 'a bad life' with a cousin in the city and left for London in about 1884.

In London she was first in 'a gay house' (a euphemism for a brothel) in the West End and a 'gentleman' there asked her to go to France. She went to France but did not like it and returned after a couple of weeks. She then lived in Ratcliffe Highway for some time, and then near Stepney Gas Works with a man named Morganstone, and then in Pennington Street. She also lived in Bethnal Green Road with one Joseph Fleming, a mason's plasterer, of whom she was very fond. Barnett was not sure whom she had lived with last but Fleming used to visit her.

Maria Harvey, a laundress, of 3 New Court, Dorset Street, slept with Kelly on Monday 5 and Tuesday 6 November, the week of her murder. About 6.55 p.m. on Thursday 8 November she saw Kelly in room 13 – Harvey took her new room in New Court that night. Harvey was in room 13 when Barnett called and she left noting that the couple appeared to be on good terms. She left some clothes with Kelly – an overcoat, two dirty cotton shirts, a boy's shirt, a girl's white petticoat and a black crêpe bonnet. The police showed her an overcoat which she identified as the one she had left. According to Barnett, he had stayed about an hour and departed shortly after Harvey.

Admission tickets for
the Providence Row
Night Refuge in Crispin
Street, off Dorset Street.

The Providence Row Night Refuge, whose frontage can still be seen. There are reports that Mary Jane Kelly was once taken in here by nuns, but these are modern stories and have no historical foundation. However, she would most certainly have known the building.

Mary Ann Cox, a widow aged around 30 and a self-confessed 'unfortunate', lived at 5 Miller's Court, which was the last house at the top of the court. About 11.45 p.m. that night she entered Dorset Street from Commercial Street and saw Kelly and a man walking ahead of her. Kelly and her companion turned into the Miller's Court passage and Cox followed a few steps behind them. She saw the couple entering Kelly's room, which was on the right. Cox said, 'Good night, Mary Jane.' Kelly was very drunk and could scarcely answer her, but did manage to say, 'Good night' and 'I am going to have a song.' The man banged the door shut as soon as she spoke. Cox noticed that he was carrying a quart can of beer. Shortly afterwards Cox heard Kelly singing 'A violet I plucked from my mother's grave when a boy'. Cox went back on to the streets just after midnight and returned at 1 a.m. She could hear Kelly still singing and there was a light in room 13 though the windows were covered on the inside so she saw nothing. A few minutes later Cox went out again and did not return until 3 a.m. when Kelly's light was out and all was silent. She did not undress that night and heard no noise. It was raining hard. She claimed that she did not sleep but heard no cry, only several men going in and out. She said she definitely heard someone go out at 5.45 a.m. but she did not hear a door shut and could not tell which house he left. He did not pass her window. It should be remembered that Cox's house was situated at the top of the court, the furthest away from Kelly's room, which may account for the fact that she did not hear the cry to which two other witnesses testified, even though she felt she should have heard it. She told the inquest she very often saw Kelly drunk.

Cox described the man she saw with Kelly as aged about 36 years and 5 feet 5 inches tall. He had a fresh complexion but possibly blotches on his face and a thick, carroty moustache but a clean-shaven chin. He was dressed in shabby dark clothes, a 'longish' dark overcoat and a hard black felt billycock (bowler) hat. Kelly was wearing a dark linsey (coarse inferior wool weave) frock and a red knitted crossover or pelerine (a long narrow cape or shawl) around her shoulders, but no hat or bonnet.

Elizabeth Prater was the wife of William Prater, a boot machinist who had deserted her five years previously. She lived in room 20, which was up the stairs and above Kelly's lodging. She knew that Kelly had been living with Barnett until about ten days previously when they had had a quarrel and separated. She was an 'unfortunate', like Kelly, and it was 'a common thing for the women living in these tenements to bring men home with them, they could do so as they pleased'. Undoubtedly landlord John McCarthy, who occupied 27 Dorset Street, adjoining the west side of no. 26, was aware of this and realised that at least the women were raising some cash to pay him as rent. The police carefully watched for premises being used as brothels so this arrangement was a less risky option for him as a way of generating income.

Prater had last spoken with Kelly on the Thursday. She went out that evening about 5 o'clock and returned at 1 a.m., possibly just after the hour because she did not mention seeing Cox. She stood for about 30 minutes at the bottom of Miller's Court and for a short time chatted with McCarthy at his chandler's shop. She saw no one pass up the court. Prater's room was accessed through a door on the right of the entrance passage, just before Kelly's door. The staircase inside this door had only a wooden partition between it and Kelly's room to the left. The flimsiness of the construction is testified to by the fact that Prater could tell if Kelly still had a light on because she could see a glimmer through the boards. This night she saw none. In fact, the partition was so thin that Prater was usually able to hear Kelly when she walked about in her room. Prater went to bed at around 1.30 a.m. after barricading her door with two tables, presumably because she had no key. She fell asleep straight away and slept soundly. However, around 3.30 or 4 a.m. she was

This Victorian street scene shows Dorset Street, narrow and surfaced with cobblestones, looking east, with Miller's Court on the left near the parked carriages.

woken by a kitten walking across her neck. At the same time she heard screams about two or three times in a female voice, later noted at the inquest as a cry of 'Oh, murder!' in a faint voice. The sound seemed to come from the court. She took little notice as she frequently heard such cries at the back of the lodging house where the windows looked into Miller's Court.

She woke at 5 a.m. and was downstairs at 5.30 but saw no one other than two or three carmen (drivers) harnessing their horses in Dorset Street. She went across Commercial Street to the Ten Bells public house where she had some rum. After that she returned home to bed, slept until about 11 a.m. and saw Kelly's body through the window after she got up.

Sarah Lewis, a laundress, lived at 34 Great Pearl Street, Spitalfields. After having an argument with her husband, between 2 and 3 a.m. she went to room 2, Miller's Court, to stay with the Keylers. When she went up the court she noticed a man standing against the lodging house on the opposite side of the road. She was unable to describe him.[1] Shortly before 4 a.m. she heard a scream not far away. It sounded like a young woman, who called out 'Murder'. Lewis heard it only once. She added a bit of colour to her statement at the inquest when she told the court that she and another woman were accosted by a suspicious man carrying a black bag in Bethnal Green on the previous Wednesday evening.

The cries heard by Prater and Lewis have often been trivialised by those seeking to place the time of death at a different hour. The usual way of doing this is, of course, to quote Prater who said she took no notice because such cries were frequently to be heard. But to qualify this, surely such a cry was not quite so common between the hours of 3.30 and 4.00 a.m. and, more significantly, the body of a murdered woman *was* found at the location the next morning.

Right: View up Miller's Court from the rear of Kelly's room towards the north.

Below: A sketch from the *Pictorial News*, Saturday 17 November 1888, of the crowd gathered outside the entrance to Miller's Court on the morning of the murder of Mary Jane Kelly, Friday 9 November 1888. Inset is a sketch of Thomas Bowyer discovering the body by looking through the window. The shed on the right is where Catherine Eddowes is alleged to have slept at one time.

Julia Venturney, a widow and charwoman of room 1, Miller's Court, where she was then living with a man named Harry Owen, was unable to sleep that night. Her room was opposite Kelly's and she had known her for about four months. She knew Barnett and said that she had heard him say he did not like Kelly going out on the streets. He frequently gave her money and was very fond of her, but could not live with her while she led that course of life. Kelly occasionally got tipsy and had broken her windows a few weeks previously while drunk. Kelly told Venturney that she was very fond of another man named Joe, but he often 'ill-used' her because she was living with Barnett. From this it would seem that Kelly had been conducting parallel relationships with the two Joes.

The hideous crime was discovered by Thomas Bowyer of 37 Dorset Street who was employed by John McCarthy. Bowyer served in McCarthy's chandler's shop and McCarthy had instructed Bowyer to call on Kelly for her rent, which was 29s in arrears. (Her rent was 4s 6d per week, so she owed for just under six weeks.) At 10.45 a.m. Bowyer knocked at the

door of room 13 but received no reply. He went around to the rear. The window was broken and he drew the curtain aside. He was appalled by the sight that met his eyes. He saw two lumps of flesh on the bedside table and when he looked again he realised a body was lying on the bed. A copious amount of blood was visible on the floor. Bowyer immediately went to inform McCarthy who returned with him and looked through the window into the room. McCarthy dispatched Bowyer to fetch officers from Commercial Street police station, a few minutes away. The on-duty divisional inspector, Walter Beck, quickly donned his hat and coat and, with constables, went to the scene with Bowyer.

McCarthy, who later saw the body, had no doubt as to the woman's identity. His and Barnett's identifications alone should put paid to any fanciful ideas that the body was not that of the woman known as Mary Jane Kelly. According to McCarthy, she and Barnett had lived comfortably together 'but once broke the two windows', presumably during the row when he left her. All the furniture in the room belonged to McCarthy who confirmed to the inquest that Kelly had a real problem with drink, something that Barnett seemed reluctant to do. McCarthy was explicit, 'I very often saw deceased worse for drink she was a very quiet woman when sober but noisy when in drink, she was not ever helpless when drunk.' So it seems Kelly was not prone to become paralytic, but was often drunk and noisy, despite her normal quiet character.

A discordant note among the witnesses called to give evidence at the inquest was sounded by Caroline Maxwell, the wife of Henry Maxwell, a lodging-house deputy, who lived almost opposite Miller's Court at 14 Dorset Street. Her evidence was not only contrary to both doctors' estimates of the time of death, it also went against other accounts, such as the reports of cries of 'murder'. She claimed to have known Kelly for some four months past and also knew that since Joe Barnett left, Kelly had been 'living as an unfortunate'. She claimed to be on speaking terms with the victim but had not seen her for the past three weeks – that was until the morning of 9 November at 'about half past 8 o'clock'. If she was correct then Maxwell was the last witness to see Kelly alive. Maxwell claimed that she was standing in Dorset Street at the corner of Miller's Court when she saw Kelly and said to her, 'What brings you up so early?' Kelly replied, 'I have the horrors of drink upon me, as I have been drinking for some days past.' Maxwell said, 'Why don't you go to Mrs. Ringer's,[2] and have half a pint of beer?' Kelly replied, 'I have been there and had it, but I have brought it all up again.' And she pointed to some vomit in the roadway.

Mrs Maxwell left to do an errand in Bishopsgate and returned to Dorset Street about 9 a.m. It was then, she claimed, that she saw Kelly standing outside the Britannia pub talking to a man aged about 30 years, 5 feet 5 inches tall and dressed as a market porter. This was at some distance, about 25 yards, and she doubted that she could recognise him again. Kelly was wearing a dark dress with a black velvet body and a coloured wrapper round her neck.

Maxwell's evidence was considered so contrary by the coroner that he felt it necessary to warn the woman to be careful before she gave it. There were no other witnesses who could show that Kelly might still have been alive at so late a time and in Dorset Street; it is difficult to believe no one else saw her in such a busy location.

What is the explanation for Maxwell's odd claims? Some have suggested that she was mistaken as to the day, but this is unlikely. Her statement was taken too soon after the event and she backed it up with reasons for her perambulations that day. It is more likely that she did not know who Kelly actually was. She must have been on nodding terms with many such women in the neighbourhood and by her own admission had spoken to Kelly (or the woman she believed to be Kelly) only twice in the past. This makes her claim of first-name familiarity rather hollow. There is little doubt that she thought she saw Kelly that morning. Once she was committed to stating this, she felt that she needed to give her account extra authority by exaggerating the conversation side of the sighting and restating her certainty about the identity of the woman she had spoken with.

Dr George Bagster Phillips gave evidence at the inquest stating that he was called by the police about 11 a.m. and entered Miller's Court at 11.15 to find Inspector Beck in charge of the scene. Phillips produced a photograph of the exterior of room 13 showing its door in the passage and the two windows facing into the court.[3] He said that two panes nearest the passage were broken and that because the door was locked he looked through the lower broken pane and satisfied himself that the mutilated corpse lying on the bed was 'not in need of any immediate attention from me'. He decided 'probably it was advisable that no entrance should be made into the room at that time' and remained outside until about 1.30 p.m. when the door was broken open by McCarthy under Superintendent Arnold's instructions.

Dr Phillips was the first person to enter the room. The door knocked against a table when it was opened. This table was close to the right-hand side of the bed and the bed was close up against the wooden partition that formed the wall at that side of the room. The mutilated female remains were lying two-thirds over towards the edge of the bed that was nearest the door and the woman was clothed in only her linen undergarment. Phillips made an examination and was sure that the body had been moved after the fatal injury was inflicted. He said she had been lifted across from the side of the bed nearest to the partition. The large

quantity of blood that he found under the bed, the saturated condition of the palliasse, pillow and the sheet at the top corner nearest the partition led him to the conclusion that the severance of the right carotid artery was the immediate cause of death. He said the injury was inflicted while the victim was lying on the left side of the bed with her head and neck in the top left-hand corner. According to the *Daily Telegraph* of 10 November, that evening Bagster Phillips visited the House of Commons where he had a conference with the Under Secretary of the Home Office, Mr Stuart-Wortley.

No detailed account of what the medical men found in the room was available until November 1987 when a large brown envelope bearing a Croydon postmark was sent anonymously to New Scotland Yard.[4] The envelope contained old official

In about 1966/7 Donald Rumbelow discovered some old glass-plate negatives in the photographic room at Old Jewry, the City of London Police headquarters. One of them was this fine Victorian photograph of the exterior of room 13, Miller's Court, the scene of the murder of Mary Jane Kelly. It is the only known photograph of the location.

Mary Jane Kelly, murdered in room 13, Miller's Court, Dorset Street, Spitalfields, on 9 November 1888. She is regarded by many as the last Ripper victim but others now feel that she was killed by another hand. This photograph was discovered by Donald Rumbelow in the City of London Police archives in the 1960s.

documents relating to the Dr Crippen case of 1910 and the Whitechapel murders of 1888. These included the famous 'Dear Boss' letter and envelope, and, more importantly from a historian's point of view, Dr Thomas Bond's account of what he found in his examination of the Kelly murder scene.[5] Despite fingerprint tests on the envelope the sender was never identified.

Bond was the police surgeon for A (Whitehall) Division. His report stated that the body was 'lying naked', which contradicts Dr Phillips' inquest statement that she had 'only her linen undergarment on her'. However, inspection of the primary Kelly crime scene photograph appears to show some sort of chemise around her left shoulder, thus giving greater credence to Dr Phillips on this point. Bond said she was lying in the middle of the bed, the shoulders flat but with the axis of the body inclined to the left side of the bed. The head was turned on to the left cheek. The left arm was close to the body, flexed at a right angle at the elbow and lying across the abdomen. (The photograph shows the left hand was actually partly in the stomach cavity.) The right arm was slightly away from the body and resting on the mattress, bent at the elbow and with the forearm and palm lying upwards with the fingers clenched. Both 'arms and forearms' had extensive and jagged wounds. The right thumb had a small superficial incision about 1 inch long with bleeding in the skin and several abrasions on the back of the hand which had also bled into the skin. The legs were wide apart, the left thigh at right angles to the trunk and the right forming an obtuse angle with the pubes. The whole of the surface flesh of the abdomen and both thighs was removed and the abdominal cavity emptied of its viscera. The breasts had been cut off with more or less circular incisions leaving the muscles down to the ribs attached to the breasts. One was placed under the head and the other by the right foot.

The face had been hacked beyond recognition of the features, with gashes in all directions; the nose, cheeks, eyebrows and ears were partly removed. The lips were blanched and cut by several oblique incisions that ran down to the chin. There were also numerous cuts extending irregularly across all the features. The tissues of the neck were severed all round, dividing the windpipe through the lower part of the larynx and the cricoid cartilage and cutting down to the vertebrae, the fifth and sixth of which were deeply notched. The skin cuts at the front of the neck showed distinct discolouration of the skin resulting from bleeding underneath.[6] The muscles between the fourth, fifth and sixth ribs had been cut through and the contents of the thorax were visible through the openings. The skin and tissues of the abdomen from the arch of the ribs down to the pubes had been removed in three large flaps. The right thigh was denuded in front to the bone and the flap of skin removed included the external sex organs and part of the right buttock. The left thigh was stripped of skin, fascia and muscles as far as the knee. The left calf had a long gash through the skin and tissues to the deep muscles; the incision reached past the knee to 5 inches above the ankle. The viscera were found in various places: the uterus and kidneys with the breast under the head, the liver between the feet, the intestines by the right side of the body and the spleen by the left. The flaps removed from the abdomen and thighs were on a table.

The lungs were still inside the ribcage although the lower part of the right one was broken and torn away. The left lung was intact. The membranes enclosing the heart were open below and the heart was absent. The abdominal cavity contained some partly digested fish and potatoes. Similar food was found in the remains of the stomach which were attached to the intestines found by the right side of the body.

The right-hand corner of bed clothes was saturated with blood and on the floor beneath was a pool of blood about 2 feet square. The partition wall next to the bed, in line with the neck, was marked by blood that had struck it in a number of separate splashes.

Inspector Walter Beck stated that he was the first police officer on the scene and that on his arrival he had closed the court to all persons and had summoned Dr Phillips. Inspector Abberline told the inquest that he had charge of the case and arrived at the scene of the murder at 11.30 a.m. Inspector Beck told him that the bloodhounds had been sent for and Dr Phillips asked him not to force the door so that the dogs could be tested. Superintendent Arnold arrived at 1.30 p.m. and told him that the order to call in the dogs had been countermanded and gave directions for the door to be forced. Abberline took an inventory of the contents of the room and discovered that there had been a fire in the grate that was 'so large as to melt the spout off the kettle'.[7] He went through the ashes in the grate and found nothing of consequence except that articles of a woman's clothing had been burnt. He presumed this had been done to generate light because there was only one piece of candle, on top of a broken wine glass, in the room. Barnett informed Abberline that the key to the room had been missing for some

A view of the lower part of Kelly's body on the bed in room 13, Miller's Court, taken from the opposite side of the bed to the better known full view. This photograph was in an album returned to Scotland Yard in 1988 by the family of the late Deputy Assistant Commissioner Ernest Millen, which also contained photographs of Nichols, Chapman, Eddowes and Stride. (*S.P. Evans/Metropolitan Police*)

time and that they opened the door by reaching through the window and moving back the catch. There was also a clay pipe found in the room and Barnett said it was his.

In addition to his duties as police surgeon for A (Whitehall) Division, 47-year-old Dr Thomas Bond was also attached to the Commissioner's Office. He had attended the scene 'in obedience to special instructions' given by Anderson, and was accompanied by his assistant Dr Charles A. Hebbert MRCP.[8] According to the *Daily Telegraph*, Dr Gordon Brown and Dr John Rees Gabe were also called. The medical men were reported to have remained at the scene until gone 4 p.m. making their 'on the spot' examinations. Warren was informed of the discovery by Superintendent Arnold and placed the investigation into the hands of Anderson who, it was reported, drove up in a cab at about 1.50 p.m. and remained in Miller's Court for some time. Detectives searched the adjacent houses for suspicious persons without result, all the occupants being able to account for their whereabouts, and a general house-to-house inquiry was conducted. In their search for witnesses, Sergeant Thick and other officers were fully engaged in taking statements from potential witnesses in the lodging houses in Dorset Street. An estimated 1,500 people lived in this short stretch with several houses accommodating over 200 and one upwards of 260. Although Warren did not visit the scene, Colonel Bolton Monsell, the Chief Constable for the eastern district, attended, as did Chief Constables Howard and Roberts. They all inspected the room.

On 10 November, the day after the murder, Dr Bond wrote an assessment of the preceding cases, none of which he had attended. He did so in response to a request from Anderson sent on 25 October. Anderson wanted Bond's opinion because of the difficulty the police were experiencing in conducting their investigation as a result of having no reliable expert assessment of the amount of surgical skill and anatomical knowledge 'probably possessed by

The front of 26 Dorset Street on the day of the Kelly murder as police control the crowds.

the murderer or murderers'. Sir Charles Warren had authorised Anderson to ask Bond to examine all the medical evidence. Warren felt that his 'eminence as an expert in such cases' would render Bond's opinion especially valuable. This is also the reason that the Kelly murder was referred to Bond although it was a significant slight upon the other doctors, especially the vastly experienced Phillips. Little wonder that this high opinion of Bond's status resulted in conflict with his H Division colleague.

Bond responded with gusto, producing a report that included a psychological profile of the murderer that Dr Krafft-Ebing would have been proud of.[9] Bond read the notes on the murders of Nichols, Chapman, Stride and Eddowes, and included his own first-hand knowledge of the Kelly murder. He immediately proclaimed all five to have been committed by the same hand thus marking out what today are called 'the canonical five' Ripper murders.

All the women must have been lying down when they were murdered and in every case the throat was cut first. Bond admitted that in the four cases he had not attended he was unable to give a definite opinion as to how long the victims had been dead when they were found. His reading of the case notes led him to conclude that Stride had been found immediately after her murder, and in the cases of Nichols, Chapman and Eddowes 'three or four hours only could have elapsed'. Any reader with the barest knowledge of the facts of this case will know how wrong this statement is. Bond's conclusions regarding Kelly's time of death are examined below and again he appears to have been very wide of the mark. He concluded that in none of the cases had there been a struggle and that Kelly's face may have been covered with the sheet when she was attacked. In the first four crimes the killer had attacked from the right side of the victim, but in the case of Kelly from the left because there was not enough room between her body and the wall. The murderer would not necessarily have been deluged with blood but would at least have had blood smeared on his hands, arms and parts of his clothing.

The mutilation in every case except that of Stride, where there was none, were all of the same character and showed clearly that mutilation was the killer's objective. This mutilation had been inflicted by someone who had no scientific or anatomical knowledge. In fact, in Bond's opinion, 'he does not even possess the technical knowledge of a butcher or horse slaughterer or any person accustomed to cut up dead animals'. Moving on to the murderer's weapon, it 'must have been a strong knife at least six inches long, very sharp, pointed at the top and about an inch in width. It may have been a clasp knife, a butcher's knife or a surgeon's knife. I think it was no doubt a straight knife.'

After these pronouncements Bond went on to describe the murderer. He must have possessed physical strength, great coolness and daring. There was no evidence of an accomplice. In Bond's opinion he must have been a man who was 'subject to periodical attacks of Homicidal and erotic mania'. The character of the mutilations indicated that the man may be in a sexual condition called satyriasis.[10] Bond thought that it was possible the homicidal impulse may have 'developed from a revengeful or brooding condition of the mind, or that Religious Mania may have been the original disease, but I do not think either hypothesis is likely'. By now Bond felt that he could physically describe the man. His report continued:

The murderer in external appearance is quite likely to be a quiet inoffensive looking man probably middleaged and neatly and respectably dressed. I think he must be in the habit of wearing a cloak or overcoat or he could hardly have escaped notice in the streets if the blood on his hands or clothes were visible.

Assuming the murderer to be such a person as I have just described he would probably be solitary and eccentric in his habits, also he is most likely to be a man without regular occupation, but with some small income or pension. He is possibly living among respectable persons who have some knowledge of his character and habits and who may have grounds for suspicion that he is not quite right in his mind at times. Such persons would probably be unwilling to communicate suspicions to the Police for fear of trouble or notoriety, whereas if there were a prospect of reward it might overcome their scruples.

Bond's letter made its way through the hands of Anderson to the Home Office. Despite its obvious shortcomings, its errors and the fact that some of what Bond deduced was fairly obvious, it seems to have greatly influenced senior police and government officials. The last reference to people the killer might be living with was later to be echoed by Anderson when he described certain 'low-class Polish Jews' as being unwilling to give up one of their own to Gentile justice. Later, in 1894, Chief Constable Melville Macnaghten was to espouse Bond's 'canonical five' victims.

Long regarded as the Ripper's 'ultimate act of barbarity' and 'his defining moment', the Kelly murder has been much discussed, analysed and endowed with great mystery. This has been deepened by the fact that Mary Jane Kelly has never been positively identified in a genealogical sense. The facts of her background are far from clear and mystery shrouds all aspects of the crime. Even the time of death is far from certain.

Dr Bond's estimate of the time of death was reached as follows:

In the Dorset Street case the body was lying on the bed at the time of my visit, 2 o'clock, quite naked and mutilated as in the annexed report –

Rigor Mortis had set in, but increased during the progress of the examination. From this it is difficult to say with any degree of certainty the exact time that had elapsed since death as the period varies from 6 to 12 hours before rigidity sets in. The body was comparatively cold at 2 o'clock and the remains of a recently taken meal were found in the stomach and scattered about over the intestines. It is, therefore, pretty certain that the woman must have been dead about 12 hours and the partly digested food would indicate: that death took place about 3 or 4 hours after the food was taken, so one or two o'clock in the morning would be the probable time of the murder.

Dr Phillips' estimate of the time of death was not given at the inquest and no written report made by him has survived. However, if *The Times* of 12 November is correct, his estimate was quite different to Bond's:

the opinion of Dr. George Bagster Phillips, the divisional surgeon of the H division, that when he was called to the deceased (at a quarter to 11) [*sic* – it was 11.15] she had been dead for some five or six hours. There is no doubt that the body of a person who, to use Dr. Phillips's own words, was 'cut all to pieces' would get cold far more quickly than that of one who had died simply from the cutting of the throat; and the room would have been very cold, as there were two broken panes of glass in the windows. Again, the body being entirely uncovered would very quickly get cold.

So Dr Phillips' estimate of time of death would appear to have been around 5.15 or 6.15 a.m. If the witnesses Elizabeth Prater and Sarah Lewis, who heard the cry of 'murder', were correct then the crime was probably committed between 3.30 a.m. and 4 a.m. – a time

Dr Roderick Macdonald, coroner at the inquest
into the death of Mary Jane Kelly. (Pictorial News,
Saturday 17 November 1888)

DR MACDONALD. M.D
CORONER

roughly half-way between the estimates
given by the two medical men. It seems
highly probable that the evidence of the
two women indicates the time of murder more accurately than the opinions
of the doctors.

The inquest was a hurried affair that
opened and closed on 12 November.
Dr Roderick Macdonald was the Coroner for the North Eastern District of
Middlesex and his being put in charge
of proceedings caused some controversy
because it was claimed the murder was
committed in Coroner Wynne Baxter's
South Eastern District. However, the
body had been taken to Shoreditch
mortuary which was certainly under
Macdonald's jurisdiction. Unlike Wynne
Baxter, Macdonald seemed to be less concerned with drawn-out and detailed proceedings
and was happy to obtain the jury's verdict at the one sitting, which must have been a great
relief to both the police and the Home Office. At least that way it drew less press attention
and gave less scope for controversy and debate. However, it has to be said that to open and
close an inquest on a murder victim at the same sitting is most unsatisfactory, and it was a
mere three days since the murder. The point is proved by the fact that a further relevant
witness, George Hutchinson, presented himself to the police just after the inquest closed.
The usual verdict of wilful murder by some person or persons unknown had been
returned.[11]

The *Daily Telegraph* of Saturday 10 November had carried a long report on the murder,
although this did contain errors like most of the early accounts.[12] It described the premises
of Miller's Court, which contained six houses let out in tenements chiefly to women, the
rooms being numbered. The passage giving access to Miller's Court had two doors on the
right, the first of which opened on to a staircase to the upper floor and Prater's room, and
the second the door to Kelly's room. The ground-floor front room, between Kelly's room
and Dorset Street, was described as a 'shed or warehouse used for the storage of costers'
barrows'. So, strictly speaking, the room was not a 'shed' at all but was called such because
it was used for storage.

There has always been much speculation as to whether the victims knew each other. They
lived in a small geographical area and were of the same class so it would not be unusual if
some of them were acquainted. Although stories in the press cannot always be
corroborated by other sources, the *People* of Sunday 11 November clearly indicated that
Kelly and Chapman knew each other. As both women lived in Dorset Street this is not
surprising. The *People* piece ran:

Annie Chapman a Friend of Hers.

The murdered woman is said to have been a person of extremely quarrelsome tendencies. She was, it is hardly necessary to say, extremely poor. She belonged, morally, and in every other respect, to the class to which Annie Chapman belonged. Singular to relate, the murdered woman, Annie Chapman, was a friend of this very Mary Jane Kelly.

Another newspaper account claimed that Eddowes had slept in the 'shed' at 26 Dorset Street and, if this is correct, it could be suggested that she, too, may have known Kelly.

The rather controversial witness, George Hutchinson, of the Victoria Home, Commercial Street, appeared during the Kelly murder investigation, but not until after the inquest. He attended Commercial Street police station at 6 p.m. on Monday 12 November and provided a statement which was written down by Sergeant 31H Edward Badham.

Hutchinson had returned from Romford in the early hours to find the Victoria Home locked, leaving him stranded on the streets for the night. He stated that at 2 o'clock on the morning of the murder he was in Commercial Street where he encountered Kelly, who was known to him, between Thrawl Street and Flower and Dean Street. She asked him if she could borrow sixpence and he said that he had spent all his money going down to Romford. She simply said, 'Good morning. I must go and find some money', walking off towards Thrawl Street. It was then that a man coming in the opposite direction tapped her on the shoulder and said something that resulted in both of them laughing. She said, 'Alright', and the man said, 'You will be alright for what I have told you', and placed his right hand

A scene in the kitchen of the Victoria Home, Whitechapel, where the witness in the Kelly murder, George Hutchinson, lived. He was unable to gain access on the night of the murder.

The entrance to Miller's Court.

around her shoulders. Hutchinson was obviously within hearing distance and he could see that the man had 'a kind of a small parcel in his left hand with a kind of strap round it'. Hutchinson 'stood against the lamp of the Queen's Head Public House' and watched the man. The couple then came past Hutchinson and the man 'hung his head with his hat over his eyes' so Hutchinson stooped and looked him in the face. The man regarded him sternly and passed on with Kelly. They went into Dorset Street. The curious Hutchinson followed and saw the couple stand at the corner of the court for about 3 minutes. The man said something to her and she replied, 'Alright my dear, come along you will be comfortable.' The man put his arm on her shoulder and gave her a kiss. She said that she had lost her handkerchief and the man pulled out his, a red one, and gave it to her. They then both went into Miller's Court together.

Hutchinson went to the court to see if he could see them but they had vanished from view. He waited for about 45 minutes 'to see if they came out' and when they did not he left. The account Hutchinson provided of the man described him as aged about 34 or 35, 5 feet 6 inches in height with a pale complexion, dark eyes and eyelashes, a slight moustache curled up at each end and dark hair. He was very surly looking. He wore a long dark coat with collar and cuffs trimmed with astrakhan, a dark jacket under that with a light waistcoat and dark trousers, a dark felt hat turned down in the middle, button boots and gaiters with white buttons. He also had a very thick gold chain, a white linen collar and a black tie with a horseshoe pin. He was of very respectable appearance, walked 'very sharply' and was of Jewish appearance. Hutchinson stated that he could identify the man if he saw him again.

There has been much speculation as to why Hutchinson waited for so long outside Miller's Court. However, the explanation could be quite simple. As we know, he had arrived home too late to get into his lodging house and had seen Kelly out and about in Commercial Street. Having known her for three years, longer even than Barnett, perhaps he felt that when she had 'finished with' her client he might be able to scrounge shelter on what was a particularly unpleasant night. When the 'client' did not reappear from Kelly's room he gave up his vigil. A report in the *Weekly Dispatch* of 18 November quotes him as saying, 'After I left the Court I walked about all night, as the place where I usually sleep was closed.'

From a modern police point of view Hutchinson's statement is not particularly good and lacks much relevant detail and qualification. It has been suggested by modern theorists that it is in fact *too* detailed, particularly in regard to the description of the man. However, the basic physical description is not really out of the ordinary and as a working man Hutchinson would be bound to notice signs of affluence such as a gold chain, pin, collar and tie, and gaiters. It has also been suggested that Hutchinson must have been lying because he would not have been able to tell the colour of the man's handkerchief in the darkness of the night. We simply do not know enough about the ambient lighting conditions to be able to say this categorically. Was the handkerchief visible, tucked into a top pocket when he passed Hutchinson under the pub lamp and what was the quality of lighting in Dorset Street outside Miller's Court? In his evidence at the Stride inquest, witness Edward Spooner stated, 'I could see that she had . . . a red and white flower pinned on to her jacket', and this by the light of a match. The witness Lawende described a man he saw with Eddowes as having a 'reddish' neckerchief, and that at 1.35 a.m. in poor lighting. Were these witnesses lying too?

Inspector Abberline was a greatly experienced CID officer and he 'interrogated' Hutchinson the same night at Commercial Street police station, armed with the statement

The pardon signed by Sir Charles Warren.

Hutchinson had already provided. In a written and signed report Abberline said unequivocally that George Hutchinson's statement was important, and in his opinion it was true. The mere fact that Abberline states that he interrogated Hutchinson indicates that he had not accepted the man's account on face value.

Hutchinson also told Abberline that he occasionally gave Kelly a few shillings and had known her for about three years. He explained that he was surprised 'to see a man so well dressed in her company which caused him to watch them'. This comment alone accounts for the fact that Hutchinson had taken in all the man's trappings of wealth. In view of the fact that Hutchinson said he could identify the man, Abberline made immediate arrangements for two officers to accompany him around the district for a few hours that very night. Hutchinson was not then in employment and he promised to go with a police officer at 11.30 a.m. the next morning, Tuesday 13 November, to Shoreditch mortuary to identify the body as Kelly.

As in the case of Schwartz, the press interviewed Hutchinson and printed a report of his account that varied in some aspects from the police statement. However, the truly puzzling fact is that after his brief appearance in mid-November Hutchinson seems to disappear totally from the story of the Whitechapel murders. The only real answer to this mystery is that over the years much of the basic paperwork in relation to the ongoing investigation has been lost. It may be that within days Hutchinson identified a man to the police as the one he had seen and that it was proved beyond doubt that he was wrong, thus destroying his value as a witness. Or, perhaps, some other fact came to light in relation to the sighting by Hutchinson. We simply do not know, but the questions surrounding this intriguing witness have resulted in his becoming a suspect himself.

On 10 November the Cabinet decided, possibly under pressure from the Queen who had been petitioned for help by the women of Whitechapel and had now taken a direct interest, to offer a royal pardon 'to any accomplice, not being the person who contrived or actually committed the murder, who shall give such information & evidence as shall lead to the discovery and conviction of the murderer or murderers'. Notices were distributed to that effect. A reward would not be offered. On 23 November a question was raised in the House of Commons by Mr Hunter, MP for Aberdeen North, as to whether the home secretary was prepared to offer a free pardon to anyone who was not the actual murderer but who offered conclusive information about the other Whitechapel murders. To this Matthews replied:

> I should be quite prepared to offer a pardon in the earlier Whitechapel murders if the information before me had suggested that such an offer would assist in the detection of the murderer. In the case of Kelly there were certain circumstances which were wanting in the earlier cases, and which made it more probable that there were other persons who, at any rate after the crime, had assisted the murderer.

This is a strange comment for it indicates that the Kelly murder was different from the others and there was an increased likelihood of there having been an aider-and-abetter. The reason for Matthews' words seems to lie in Dr Bond's 10 November letter submitted to the Home Office where he indicated the possibility of 'respectable persons' with whom the murderer might be living and who might have suspicions about him.

Thus ended the series of murders generally accepted as being committed by 'Jack the Ripper', although his name would live on in infamy. A legend had been created alongside the reality of the crimes – and legends do not die easily.

Uneasy Aftermath

TWO days after the discovery of Kelly's body, the first anniversary of 'Bloody Sunday' was marked in Hyde Park with a gathering of close upon 4,000 people. A considerable number of policemen were deployed but there were no disturbances. The Kelly murder coincided with Warren's departure from office although it was five days before the resignation was presented to Parliament, where the news was greeted with loud cheers by the opposition. The coincidence between the crime and the end of Warren's time as commissioner inevitably led to speculation that the two events were linked. They were not.

Warren was to remain in office until the end of the month and his resignation was formally announced in Metropolitan Police Orders on 1 December 1888. The Home Office had wanted someone to blame for the CID's failure to capture Jack the Ripper and Anderson had seemed the obvious scapegoat. Anderson's relationship with Warren had always been 'easy and pleasant' and he was unaware, until later, of how seriously his position had been threatened. He subsequently learned that it was Warren who had been his unseen protector and who had prevented him from losing his job.

If the opposition was delighted by Warren's resignation, the lower ranks of the Metropolitan Police felt quite differently. A deputation of superintendents representing the whole force waited upon him at his home to express their regret at his resignation. The men paid tribute to his thoughtfulness and care for those under his command; discipline, they said, had been improved and the regulations had been

The fall of Sir Charles Warren, as depicted in a contemporary cartoon.

'In Memory of Sir Charles Warren.' After Warren's resignation the press soon began to publish satirical cartoons of him. This example recalls the main reason for his vilification – the Trafalgar Square riots and his subjugation of the mob by force. (Funny Folks, *Saturday 17 November 1888*)

IN MEMORY OF SIR CHARLES WARREN.

A SUGGESTION FOR THE UTILIZATION OF TRAFALGAR SQUARE, BY WHICH MEANS NOT ONLY WILL MEETINGS OF THE UNEMPLOYED BE PREVENTED, BUT THE NAME OF THE LATE CHIEF COMMISSIONER, WHOSE STATUE OCCUPIES A SOMEWHAT ELEVATED POSITION IN THE CENTRE, WILL BE HANDED DOWN TO POSTERITY, AND KNOWN TO FUTURE AGES BY HIS FONDEST TITLE, THAT OF –" 'IGH CHARLES WARREN "

administered with the 'fairness and equity which had characterised' the commissioner's tenure of office. The superintendents felt that Warren had always been willing to support them in what they did which had enabled them to work more efficiently, knowing that they always had his backing. There were only two matters which had prompted some ill-will, one relating to new regulations for dealing with drunkenness and the other to pensions for men injured on duty. In reply, Warren said that although he had strong views on drunkenness he was not responsible for the new regulation. The Home Office had thought that the penalties for inebriation were too light and had ordered him to stiffen them. As for the pensions due to men injured on duty, he had made recommendations but the Home Office had taken the opposite view. He concluded by saying that the work he had done on consolidating orders had taken up much of his time but he had at last succeeded in clearing the decks and hoped to visit the men on divisions, which he could do now in the short time left to him before he

James Monro. As Assistant Commissioner he headed both the CID and the Special Irish Branch but resigned in August 1888 over his differences with Sir Charles Warren. On Warren's resignation he became the new Commissioner of the Metropolitan Police in December 1888.

officially retired on 30 November. He thanked them for their kindness 'and assured them that their willing and cordial co-operation in such reforms as he had ventured to propose would be one of his pleasantest recollections of his Commissionership'.

In a private letter to Edwin Chadwick dated 19 November, Warren said that he would not have resigned if it had not been for the difficulties placed in his way by the home secretary. The statements about him were not true 'but the public do not want to know the truth they only want to sacrifice someone'. Even after his resignation, Warren continued to be a subject of press speculation, and on 21 December he was forced to write, 'There is no truth whatever in the statements in the papers that I have been asked to go to the Soudan. I have heard nothing from the Government since I left the Police.'

It was inevitable that Monro would replace Warren as commissioner. Although temporarily shelved at the Home Office, he still controlled Special Branch Section D, for which he was answerable direct to the home secretary. Moreover, despite Matthews' assurances to Parliament that he was involved only in discussion of a reorganisation of the CID, Monro had continued to influence the day-to-day running of the CID. He was presumably also using its manpower, which would explain the meetings and conferences at the Home Office between Monro, Anderson and senior detectives, to which Warren objected and about which he had been given very little information.

On his appointment as commissioner Monro seems to have retained control of Section D instead of surrendering it to Anderson as might have been expected because Anderson was Monro's protégé. In June 1889 Williamson's bad health enabled Monro to appoint one of his other protégés, Melville Macnaghten, as Assistant Chief Constable. Warren had rejected Macnaghten, but Macnaghten's legacy, although he was never part of the original investigation, is arguably the most important of all surviving documents pertaining to Jack the Ripper suspects. For a short time in 1889 Macnaghten was Williamson's understudy. Williamson told his younger colleague that the 'Yard' was a funny place to work: he would be blamed if he did his job and blamed if he didn't. Williamson's disgruntlement may in part have been due to Monro's earlier attempt to get the completely inexperienced Macnaghten promoted over his head to the newly created rank of chief constable CID which, according to the recommendation of 1886, was to be filled only by 'gentlemen', preferably from the army or navy. The vastly more experienced Williamson had risen up through the ranks and the prospect that this Indian tea planter might be promoted over his

Sir Melville Leslie Macnaghten. An overseer in the family tea plantations in India, he returned to England and took office as Assistant Chief Constable CID at Scotland Yard on 1 June 1889. He was promoted to Chief Constable in 1890 and was second in command to Anderson. He retired in 1913 as Assistant Commissioner, Crime. He was responsible for the 1894 memorandum naming Druitt, Kosminski and Ostrog as Ripper suspects.

head may have prompted him to threaten to resign. It seems likely that this was one of the reasons why the offer to Macnaghten was withdrawn and Williamson promoted to the rank instead. His was to be the only such appointment from the ranks for the next thirty years.

November 1888 saw an increase in the number of letters sent to press and police. Some purported to be from the killer while many advised the police on how to capture the criminal or suggested his identity. An interesting example was published by the *Star* on 19 November. It made a suggestion as to the killer's motive and incorporated the other high-profile topic of the day, the Irish problem:

A 'Unionist' Theory

We are on the track of the murderer at last! No one will be surprised to hear that all those who ought to know – police, journalists, doctors, and the rest – are on a false scent. It has been reserved for a lowly Scotch 'Meenister' to evolve the truly new and the newly true theory from his inspired cranium. 'The EMISSARIES OF THE IRISH-AMERICAN SECRET SOCIETIES,' says this ingenious scribe, 'were thwarted in all their efforts to terrorise London with dynamite, &c., but no one who knows their creed and aims is likely to believe that they have abandoned their fiendish schemes. May it not be possible that one of their most dare-devil agents has taken this plan to annoy and engross the Metropolis? By waging war on a class of practically helpless and unknown waifs, he is more likely to accomplish his work with impunity, needing only the inevitable knife, which can be easily concealed.' This worthy Scotch cleric considers the fact that 'Jack the Ripper' carries a black bag, wears a black moustache and a wideawake hat (if it be a fact), suspicious, and triumphantly declares that there are several Americanisms in the letters attributed to him. Here is some ground for Warren's successor to work on, and if he wants the name of the author of the theory the editor of the (of course) Unionist *Scotsman* will no doubt give it him.

The days following the horrendous murder of Mary Kelly threw up a spate of suspect stories in the press, just as the other killings had done. The *East Anglian Daily Times* of Monday 12 November, the day of the Kelly inquest, reported:

the public appear anxious to assist them in every way. This was seen by an incident which occurred to-day, and which resulted in the arrest and detention of a strange man at Bishopsgate Street Police Station. Some men were drinking at a beerhouse in Fish Street Hill. One of them began conversing about the Whitechapel murderer, and a man named Brown living at 9, Dorset Street, thought he detected blood marks on the coat of a stranger. On the latter's attention being called to it he said it was merely paint, but Brown said it was blood. Similar stains were seen on the man's shirt, and he then admitted that they were blood stains. Brown followed him from the house, and when opposite Bishopsgate Police Station gave him into custody. The prisoner gave the name of George Compton. On being brought before the Inspector on duty he excitedly protested against being apprehended in the street, alleging that in the present state of public feeling he might have been lynched. The same man had been arrested at Shadwell on Saturday, by a police-constable, who considered his behaviour suspicious, but he had been discharged. It transpired that before he left the Fish Street Hill beerhouse he had, so Brown alleged, made contradictory statements respecting his place of residence and the locality in which he worked. Compton does not bear any personal resemblance to the published description of the man who is supposed to be the murderer.

Considerable importance is attached to an arrest which was effected at an early hour this morning, through the exertions of two young men living in the neighbour-hood of Dorset Street. Like many others in the neighbourhood, they appear to have transformed themselves into amateur detectives, and have been perambulating the streets on the look-out for suspicious persons. About three o'clock this morning their attention was drawn to two men in Dorset-street, who were loitering about. The two men separated, and one of them was followed by the two youths into Houndsditch. They carefully observed his appearance, which was that of a foreigner, about 5ft. 8in. in height, and having a long pointed moustache. He was dressed in a long black overcoat and deerstalker hat. When near Bishopsgate Street the young men spoke to a policeman, who at once stopped the stranger and took him to Bishopsgate Street Police Station. Here he was searched and it was found he was carrying a sort of pocket medical chest, containing several small bottles of chloroform. In rather imperfect English he explained that he lived in Pimlico, where he was well known. After this preliminary examination he was taken to Commercial Street, Police-station, in which district the murder was committed. He was detained on suspicion, but subsequently was taken to Marlborough Street Police-station, for the purpose of facilitating his identification. Another man is detained at Commercial Street Station on account of his suspicious movements.

A man named Peter Maguire says that about eleven o'clock on Saturday night he was drinking at the public-house kept by Mrs. Fiddymont in Brushfield Street, when he noticed a man talking very earnestly to a young woman. He asked her to accompany him up a neighbouring court, but she refused, and afterwards left the bar. Maguire followed the man, who, noticing this, commenced running. He ran into Spitalfields Market, Maguire following. The man then stopped, went up a court, took off a pair of gloves he was wearing, and put on another pair. By a roundabout route he arrived at Shoreditch, and got into a 'bus. Maguire also followed. A policeman was asked by Maguire to stop this 'bus, but it is said he refused, and Maguire continued the pursuit until he met another constable, who at once stopped the vehicle. The man was inside huddled up in a corner. Maguire explained his suspicions, and the man was taken to Commercial Street Police Station, where he was detained pending inquiries. . . .

A later despatch says:– The man Compton has since been discharged. The police telegraphed to the authorities at King David Lane Station, Shadwell, and found the man's statement to be true. He was detained no longer. Still later information from the East End states that all the men who were in custody to-day have given satisfactory explanation of their movements, and have been released.

The Times of Monday 12 November carried the story that great excitement was caused shortly before 10 p.m. the night before by the arrest of a man with a blackened face who had publicly proclaimed himself to be 'Jack the Ripper'. This occurred at the corner of Wentworth Street and Commercial Street. Two young men, one a discharged soldier, had immediately seized him and a great crowd that always paraded the neighbourhood on a Sunday night raised a cry of, 'Lynch him.' The *Daily News* reported:

Fortunately for him, there were a large number of policemen about, both in uniform and plain clothes, by whom he was at once surrounded on the first alarm being given. He at first resisted capture, but, happily for himself, soon recognized his position and consented to go quietly to Leman-street Police-station. Meanwhile, the officers who had him in charge had the greatest difficulty in saving their prisoner from the fury of the mob, who amid the wildest excitement made the most desperate endeavours to lynch him. As it was, he was very roughly handled and considerably bruised by the time he reached the police-station, where he gave his name and address which are withheld by the police authorities. He stated that he was a medical man, and had disguised himself in the absurd manner above described in order to endeavour by what he thought were detective means to discover and apprehend the perpetrator of the Whitechapel horrors. He also gave such particulars of himself as enabled the police to quickly substantiate their accuracy, and to discharge him after a short detention in the cells.

The man was Dr William Holt, aged 34 years, of St George's Hospital. He was lucky to emerge from this incident unscathed.

On 13 November an unsigned letter written in red ink and identifying the murderer was received by the City of London Police. In the writer's opinion:

The Man That Wrote The Letter from folks stone Is The Man that Commited the Last 3 Murders and that Man Is William Onion he as Been In Coney Hatch Asylum & Wakefield twice last time in Wakefield Asylum in 1887 Come But with new suit of clothes on ½ sovering and money Is fare paid to Leicester where he has friends smashed a Plate Glass Window in London for fun got 12 months for

A suspect is escorted by a police officer to the steps of Leman Street police station, headquarters of H Division.

It he as only Been out of Prison long enough to have done the last 3 crimes That R. Sect that sent him from London to Wakefield Asylum is Paying him for Those murders he is a man About 5 ft 5 stout Built Ginger wiskers a Crucked flatish nose he will have a faint mark on his nose that was made with a Pepper Box about where the mark is he his Between [here there are two crude sketches of a face in profile and full showing the nose] 40 & 50 years The womens opinion of him & descriptions of his Letter from folkstone its Nobody else.

Policemen were once again the subject of an amateur detective's suspicions. On 13 November Charles Palmer of 57 Gracechurch Street, London EC, wrote to Sir James Fraser to suggest that:

it is my opinion that it might be worth your trouble to compare the time of each of these murders with the time of the Policemen that were off duty, for it is evident the murderer is fully cognizant of the beats of the Policemen as well as the habits of his victims, & there is the possibility that a Policeman when in uniform might make a rendezvous with each of these unfortunates when he would be of duty, & the mere fact of being in uniform would inspire confidence with the women, besides the idea of searching a Policemans lodgings would possibly be looked upon as unnecessary . . . for a maniac of the class this murderer is might be found even in the Police Force.

Victorian Metropolitan Police constables filing out on patrol in King's Road, London SW. Their duty armbands are visible on their left arms and the heavy-duty overcoats protected them against adverse weather conditions. Some suggested that the Ripper was a policeman.

The idea that Mary Jane Kelly may not have been a Ripper victim is not a new one and was espoused by some at the time, including police officers. An unsigned letter of 15 November gave the writer's reason for discounting Kelly as a Ripper victim and pointed out certain suspicions regarding landlord McCarthy. It is an intriguing piece of reasoning:

> Hon Sir having looked over the evedence given at the Coroners Inquest of the last Victim in Whitechapel)Kelly(I am off openion that it was not the work off Jack the ripper but some one who wanted it to appear as if it was him, for by the evedence she appears to have been in her naked Bed when murdered, now its Questionable whither the man she was last seen with was her murderer, was it not rather by some one that knew her to open the door by the broken Window Pain. now the key has been ammising. Did MCarthy know it was ammising. Was he not in the habet off looking in to see if all his belongings were there if so did he not know that the door could be opened by the Window if he did why did he need to force the door What reason was there for him and his man Both going for the Police X over Would it not have been more reasonable for one of them to have Watched the House while the other was away for the Police did the young man ever call for the rent Before and at such an early time off the morning. that should be Inquierd into Why was MCarthy so Put about when his man told him what he had seen, 29/ she was due to him had she got notice to Quit the House and would not, after he discovered they were not married Why was the letter addrest to his wife and not to him Rather strange aint it depend upon it twas some one who knew the Broken Window and not Jack the Ripper that done the deed. Look at the case in County Durham)Weddell(twas made to appear as if it was Jack the Ripper)my( )Private opinion(

The spiritualists were still at work trying to identify the killer. A letter written in French and dated 19 November came from 'Charton (& Lagrange)' of the Royalty Theatre, Dean Street, London, to the City Police. It was the sequel to an earlier communication on the subject of the murders. The medium in a séance held on Sunday 18 November revealed that the complete name of the suspect was 'Bluendenwall' and that 'at half past ten last night it appears the Criminal was lying in the room over his shop (a Butcher's) occupied in reading the different journals speaking of his crimes'. The medium had also informed them that: 'three Police agents instructed by you Sir were keeping observation outside the suspected shop. Two of these men in ordinary attire were sitting on the ground in front of the suspected shop the third keeping watch at the corner of the street.' The writers closed by offering further guidance and putting themselves at the disposal of the police. One is tempted to wonder whether, since police observations may have been noticed, the medium might have had knowledge that the City force was so engaged.

International interest in the murders resulted in lengthy reports in foreign newspapers, those published in the USA being particularly detailed. George Hanmer of Garrett, DeKalb County, Indiana, was appointed to the City Police in May 1866 but resigned in January 1870 to emigrate to the USA. He wrote to Sir James Fraser on 28 November:

> this is from PC765, resigned 1870 I have rendered your City some valuable Service on Two occasions and may bee I could help on the third occasion. I mean the whitechaple out rage, I am informed through the newspapers that all efforts fail to catch the Fiend therefor I am willing to leave my home & family and render you some assistance as I know my ability for Business of that kind I am not the young precocious youth nor the

old crank, but I am George Hanmer in manhood and honorable in every letter if you think my knowledge servicable please send pass and I will be on hand.

The City Police were unimpressed, and possibly a little ungracious – the top of the letter is marked 'No notice need be taken of this.'

Another November correspondent wrote to Colonel Fraser suggesting his own highly unlikely suggestion for a suspect for the murders. In an unsigned letter posted in London he stated:

> You seem to have no proof of the outrages in Whitechapel. The man seen with the black bag in Mitre Court corresponds by description with the man Parnell. The waiter describes him he is suspected of wearing a knife by a strap from his neck. Why do not the police watch him to see if he has any house where he keeps his clothes with any marks of blood.

A sensation was caused on Wednesday 21 November when a 'dissolute' woman was allegedly attacked by a man at 19 George Street, Spitalfields. The incident occurred at around 9.30 a.m. in a room at that address and was probably a prostitute–client dispute in which the woman, one Annie Farmer aged about 40, suffered only minor injuries. (These may even have been self-inflicted.) The man ran away but the alleged assault was good enough for the papers and the next day they reported 'another murderous outrage'.

A suspect named Joseph Isaacs was revealed by the house-to-house search after the Kelly murder. Mary Cusins, the deputy-keeper of a common lodging house in Paternoster Row, reported that Isaacs, a Polish Jew cigar-maker, had stayed at the house for three to four days prior to the murder and had disappeared immediately afterwards. He fitted the description given by Hutchinson and published in the newspapers. Cusins had heard the man walking around his room on the night of the murder and another lodger, Cornelius Oakes, stated that Isaacs often changed his clothes and was heard to threaten all women over the age of 17. Isaacs, who in the meantime had stolen a customer's watch in a Drury Lane shop, returned to the lodging house to collect a violin bow. He was arrested and taken to Bow Street police station. There he was collected by Inspector Abberline in a strongly escorted cab. One newspaper reported that Abberline was heard to say to one of his subordinates, 'Keep this one quiet; we have got the right man at last. This is a big thing.' However, it was subsequently found that Isaacs had no connection with the murders, although he was suspected of the attack on Annie Farmer.

Metropolitan Police Orders for Tuesday 27 November carried an interesting reference under the 'Commendation and Rewards' heading:

> The Commissioner desires to place on record the conduct of the following officers, who, by zeal and activity in the discharge of their duties, effected the apprehension of persons wanted for offences committed:–
>
> | A (4th inst). | Insp. | (C.I.D.) | Marshall |
> |---|---|---|---|
> | " (4th inst). | Ch. Insp. | (C.O.–C.I.D.) | Littlechild |
> | " (4th inst). | Ch. Insp. | (" ") | Swanson |
> | " (4th inst). | Insp. | (" ") | Andrews |

All were recommended for a reward. We have no details of the arrest for which these officers were responsible, but it is notable that the award was made at the height of the

Ripper investigation and shows three notable figures, Littlechild, Swanson and Andrews, were all apparently working together at this time. Inspector Walter Andrews of Scotland Yard was said by Walter Dew[1] to have been allocated to work on the Whitechapel murders inquiry with Inspectors Abberline and Moore.[2] In December 1888 Andrews went to Canada to escort a prisoner, Roland Gideon Israel Barnett, to Toronto. He was then, apparently, detained there to make inquiries into the whereabouts of the suspect Dr Tumblety who had fled back to New York in November. Andrews failed to locate Tumblety.[3]

On 7 December 1888 the new Metropolitan Police Commissioner, James Monro, submitted a report to the Home Office which sheds light on the status of extra police patrols deployed at that time. He said that in connection with the recent murders 1 inspector, 9 sergeants and 126 constables of the uniform branch had been sent out in plain clothes to patrol the neighbourhood of the murders in an effort to prevent a repetition of the crimes. This involved the additional expense of a plain-clothes allowance of 1s 11d per week for each of the sergeants and constables and 3s 11d for the inspector. Many of these men were from other divisions and these special duties necessitated their patrolling some distance from home and on continuous night duty, which was very trying as winter set in. Monro described the work as 'specially irksome and unpleasant'. The officers were practically doing the duty of permanent patrols, he said. The additional allowance was insufficient to cover the extra wear and tear these protracted duties involved on their clothing and Monro requested an increase of 1s per day for each of the men deployed to bring them into line with the payments granted to permanent patrols. This amounted to an additional expense of £5 per day in total, contributing to the heavy cost of the investigation and the drain on dwindling police financial reserves.[4]

On 20 December 1888 the body of Rose Mylett, a known prostitute, was discovered by a patrolling constable and a sergeant in Clarke's Yard, off Poplar High Street. The corpse was still warm and the woman's face was 'placid'. Her clothes were not disarranged and there was a handkerchief loosely folded, but not tied, around her neck. No marks of violence were immediately noticeable. Mylett (apparently pronounced Millett) was 26. The lack of obvious signs of a struggle led the police to think initially that this was a case of suicide or death from natural causes. Over a month had passed since the Kelly murder and this body, albeit that of a prostitute, presented no evidence of a violent death, let alone the Ripper-trademark severed throat and mutilation. It is therefore understandable that the police wanted to play the case down rather than be burdened by another unsolved prostitute murder. It was certainly not a Ripper killing; that much is obvious. However, thanks to Robert Anderson there is a question mark over whether it was a murder at all (see chapter 16).

There is an enduring and misleading myth that after the Kelly murder police inquiries were wound down and the additional strength of men deployed in Whitechapel in response to the murders was reduced or stood down entirely. This is usually quoted in connection with a theory supporting a favoured suspect or an idea that the police knew the identity of the killer. After the McKenzie murder on 17 July 1889 (see chapter 13), the police again came under scrutiny and questions were raised about their conduct. The Jewish MP for the Whitechapel Division of Tower Hamlets, Samuel Montagu, asked the home secretary about the question of a reward and 'whether he will sufficiently increase the number of detectives so as to prevent, if possible, further atrocities in East London'. Henry Matthews passed his questions, via his private secretary Evelyn Ruggles-Brise, to the chief commissioner. In his reply Monro stated:

The force of men in plain clothes (additional) in H. and J. Divisions has been increased & decreased. Since Sep. 88. – till February .89

Since February .89 the additional plain clothes men have been dispensed with. but about 60 additional men in uniform have been retained, and Whitechapel up to the present moment has been deriving the benefit of these additional mens service.

The figures showing the gradual increase & decrease of men in plain clothes up to February are given as under.

Sep.	1888.	–	27.
Oct	"		89.
Nov.	"		143.
Dec	"		143.
Jany.	1889.		102.
Feby.	"		47.

The strength of Whitechapel Division is 585. of all ranks.

As I said before I give these figures for the information of S. of S. not for publication.

Jmonro
18.7.89

This report alone shows that there was no immediate scaling down of police strength in the area following the murder of Kelly. The real influences in the number of officers on the streets were, in fact, a cut in police expenditure and the apparent inactivity of the murderer.

The Metropolitan Police commissioner's report for 1888 summed up the year's activity in the light of the Jack the Ripper killings:

Crime during the year has shown a decided tendency to increase. This fact may be accounted for, to a certain extent, by circumstances which affected the administration of the Force in a peculiar manner at different periods of the year. The agitation which centred in Trafalgar Square, and the murders in Whitechapel, necessitated the concentration in particular localities of large bodies of police, and such an increase of force in one quarter of the Metropolis, it must be remembered, is only procurable by diminishing the number of men ordinarily employed in other divisions. In the present state of the force increase of protection in the East End means diminished numbers of police in other quarters, and so long as the available force is hardly sufficient, as it is just now, for the performance of the ordinary and every day duties of the Police, any additional drain on its resources leads to diminished protection against, and consequent increase of, crime. There has been no relaxation of effort on the part of the Police to cope with crime; the fact is that the Force is overworked, and under such circumstances crime cannot be met or coped with in a satisfactory and efficient manner. . . . I need not do more than merely allude to the extraordinary series of murders which occurred in Whitechapel, which gave rise to the greatest excitement in London. I regret to say that in spite of most strenuous efforts on the part of the Police, the criminal has up till now remained undiscovered.

These remarks by Monro should be borne in mind when making any assessment of the state of the Whitechapel murders investigation at the end of 1888. In particular he makes the unequivocal statement that 'the criminal has up till now remained undiscovered'.

—— THIRTEEN ——

The Ripper Again?

EARLY in 1889 it was briefly mooted in the press that one William Henry Bury might be Jack the Ripper. Bury had just moved to Scotland from London's East End and was arrested in Dundee for the murder of his wife in February 1889. He was tried and hanged at Dundee in April 1889 and never admitted committing the Ripper crimes. The hangman, James Berry, later claimed that two Scotland Yard detectives had attended the execution and thought that Bury was the Whitechapel murderer. There is no official documentation to back up this story and no evidence to support it.

Back in London another savage crime rekindled fears that the Ripper had not yet finished with the women of the capital. At 12.15 a.m. on Wednesday 17 July, PC 423H Joseph Allen stopped under a street lamp in Castle Alley, Whitechapel, to eat some food. At that time the alley was deserted and he left about 5 minutes later. About 5 minutes after that PC 272H Walter Andrews patrolled through Castle Alley and he, too, found it to be deserted. At about 12.50 a.m. Andrews was in the alley again, trying doors to make sure they were secure. This time he saw a woman lying on the footpath with her throat cut; the body was still quite warm. There was no one else in the street. Andrews blew his whistle and then saw Isaac Lewis Jacob of 12 New Castle Place walking in the direction of Wentworth Street with a plate in his hand. Jacob told the officer that he was going to get something for his supper and Andrews asked him to wait because a woman had been murdered there and he might be required to answer questions.

Andrews' whistle blast had been heard by Sergeant Badham, who immediately ran to join him. In fact, Badham had already met Andrews some 2 minutes earlier at a rendezvous point in Castle Alley and had walked only 150 yards or so before he heard the whistle. Andrews showed the sergeant the murder scene. The woman was lying on the right side of the footpath, close to two parked vans. She was on her right side and her clothing had been drawn half up to her waist exposing her genitals and abdomen upon which there were several cuts. There was a quantity of blood on the footpath under her head. Andrews said, 'Here's another murder' – presumably as memories of the series some seven months earlier were still fresh. Badham instructed Andrews to stay with the body and to prevent anyone

A contemporary sketch of the discovery of 'Clay Pipe Alice' McKenzie in Castle Alley on 17 July 1889.

touching it before the doctor arrived. Badham secured the assistance of PC 101H George Neve and PC 423 Allen, directing the former to make a search and the latter to fetch the doctor and duty inspector. Badham then returned to assist with the search. Shortly afterwards other constables arrived along with Detective Inspector Edmund Reid. Badham hailed a passing cab and went to inform the superintendent of the murder. Several officers were sent to lodging and coffee houses and other establishments to inquire whether any suspicious men had recently been seen. Dr Bagster Phillips was called at 1 a.m. and arrived at the scene at 1.10, when it was 'raining sharply'. An old clay pipe smeared with blood and a farthing were found under the body when it was moved. The body was conveyed on an ambulance to the mortuary in the Pavilion yard by Sergeant Badham accompanied by Superintendent Arnold and Chief Inspector West, who had both attended the scene. The body was searched at the mortuary by Inspector Reid.

The woman appeared to be aged about 40 years, 5 feet 4 inches tall, with a pale complexion and brown eyes. The top of her left thumb was missing, an old injury, and a tooth was missing from the lower jaw – it had also been gone for some time. She was dressed in a red stuff bodice (patched under the arms and sleeves with maroon), one black and one maroon stocking, a brown stuff skirt, kilted, a brown Lindsey petticoat, a white chemise and apron, a paisley shawl and button boots.

Inquiries were made by Sergeants Record and Kuhrt. She was quickly identified as Alice McKenzie, a prostitute living at a lodging house at 52 Gun Street, Spitalfields. She lived with

Alice McKenzie, murdered 17 July 1889 in Castle Alley, Whitechapel. She was initially regarded as another Ripper victim but it was later thought that she was killed by another hand.

John McCormack, a labourer, and they had been together for six or seven years. He had last seen her about 4 p.m. on the previous day when he came home from work. He gave her some money, 1s 8d, and then went to sleep. When he awoke between 10 and 11 p.m. he found she had gone out. He next saw her when he identified the body at the mortuary on the afternoon of 17 July. Betsy Ryder, the deputy at the lodging house, stated that she had seen McKenzie go out between 8.30 and 9 p.m. on the 16th and noticed that she had some money in her hand. Ryder also went to the mortuary, at 2 p.m., and identified the body. She believed that McKenzie was aged 39. She said the woman used to go out at night but she did not know if this was as a prostitute. The police certainly regarded McKenzie as such. She was also known to be 'much addicted to drink'. The last known sighting of her was made in Brick Lane at about 11.40 p.m. by Margaret Franklin, a friend. Franklin was sitting with two friends, Catherine Hughes and Sarah Mahoney, on the step of a barber's shop at the junction with Flower and Dean Street. At that time McKenzie was hurrying past in a southerly direction and in response to an inquiry by Franklin said that she was all right but, 'I can't stop now.'

At 5 p.m. the same day, 17 July, Coroner Wynne Baxter opened the inquest at the Working Lads' Institute in Whitechapel Road and several witnesses were called. A post-mortem examination had been made at 2 p.m. by Dr Phillips with Chief Surgeon Alexander MacKellar and Dr Gordon Brown, the City Police surgeon.[1] Also in attendance were Phillips' assistant Percy Clark, a friend of MacKellar's and a Mr Boswick who gained admission for a short time but not with Dr Phillips' permission. The inquest was adjourned to the next day to await the results of the autopsy. The police had made 'careful' inquiries at coffee and lodging houses without result and the investigation was continuing. Two suspects had been detained but were subsequently released when inquiries revealed their stories to be satisfactory.

Reporting to the Home Office the same day Commissioner James Monro forwarded the details of the crime. The occurrence of a prostitute murder similar to the earlier series was obviously regarded seriously by the police. Monro had received notification of the crime at home by telegraph in the early hours and had set out for the scene at 3 a.m. In his initial report Monro stated:

> I need not say that every effort will be made by the Police to discover the murderer, who, I am inclined to believe is identical with the notorious 'Jack the Ripper' of last year.

It will be seen that in spite of ample Police precautions and vigilance the assassin has again succeeded in committing a murder and getting off without leaving the slightest clue to his identity.

The significance of this unequivocal statement by the chief commissioner should not be underestimated. Clearly on this date, 17 July 1889, Monro did not believe that the murderer of 1888 had died or been incarcerated, or that there was any good clue as to his identity.

Phillips' full written report on the death of McKenzie was completed on 22 July. He had found the cause of death to be severance of the left carotid artery. There were two jagged wounds on the left side of the neck, but they were no longer than 4 inches and the windpipe was not severed as in previous cases. There was some bruising high on McKenzie's chest. The wounds to the abdomen were not deep and several were only superficial. The most severe of the wounds, about 7 inches long, only divided the subcutaneous tissues and did not open the abdominal cavity or even injure the muscles. Five superficial marks on the left side of the abdomen might have been caused, Phillips thought, by the pressure of the fingers and thumb of the killer's right hand, perhaps indicating that he was left-handed. A sharp, pointed weapon had been used. Phillips did not feel that it was the work of the previous killer:

> After careful & long deliberation I cannot satisfy myself, on purely anatomical & professional grounds that the Perpetrator of all the 'Wh'Ch'l. murders' is one man.
>
> I am on the contrary impelled to a contrary conclusion. This noting the mode of procedure & the character of the mutilations & judging of motive in connection with the latter.
>
> I do not here enter into the comparison of the cases neither do I take into account what I admit may be almost conclusive evidence in favour of the one man theory if all the surrounding circumstances & other evidence are considered.
>
> Holding it as my duty to report on the P.M. appearances and express an opinion solely on Professional Grounds, based upon my own observations. For this purpose I have ignored all evidence not coming under my own observation.

Phillips showed his objectivity by ignoring points that might have indicated a Ripper killing, such as location, the fact the deceased was a prostitute and recent history. He based his judgement solely on his own expertise in assessing the method of killing and the nature of the injuries inflicted.

Moonshine, 28 September 1889, cartoons James Monro, the Commissioner of the Metropolitan Police, as a dummy of the Home Office.

Dr Bond was also called in to examine McKenzie, presumably because he had reported on the earlier murders, although he had resigned his attachment to the Commissioner's Office in November 1888.[2] Bond disagreed with Phillips and stated in a letter to Anderson:

> I see in this murder evidence of similar design to the former Whitechapel murders viz. sudden onslaught on the prostrate woman, the throat skilfully & resolutely cut with subsequent mutilation, each mutilation indicating sexual thoughts & a desire to mutilate the abdomen & sexual organs.
>
> I am of opinion that the murder was performed by the same [hand – <u>deleted</u>] person who committed the former series of Whitechapel murders.

Dr Bond was introduced again at the instigation of Anderson, to whom he reported direct. Oddly, Anderson did not appear to agree with Bond's conclusion, writing in his later memoirs that he 'assumed' the murder was 'by another hand' because Monro had decided that it was 'an ordinary murder, and not the work of a sexual maniac'. The disagreement of the two doctors is a prime example of how two expert professionals in the same field may come to two completely opposing conclusions.

Another minor mystery emerged with the murder. It involved the clay pipe found with the body, rather appropriately as McKenzie rejoiced in the nickname 'Clay Pipe Alice'. This object assumed significance only because of a later statement by Anderson who described a lost clay pipe as a clue to the identity of the killer.[3] In the autopsy report Dr Phillips stated:

> **Discovery of & subst. loss of short clay pipe.**
> While searching the clothing one of the attendants found a short pipe, well used, which he thoughtlessly threw onto the ground & broke it. I had the pieces put on one side meaning to preserve them but up to the time of writing this report they have not been recovered by me.

At the resumed inquest on 18 July Inspector Reid gave evidence of finding a broken clay pipe and a farthing, both of which had blood on them, under the body when it was moved. The pipe contained tobacco that had not been lit and was believed to have belonged to the woman herself, although she also borrowed pipes to smoke the tobacco she purchased.

The police arrested a drunken criminal named William Wallace Brodie who gave himself up as the murderer at Leman Street police station on 19 July 1889. Brodie was eventually cleared of all suspicion with regard to the murders but was rearrested on a warrant for fraud. McKenzie's killer was never found but the overall impression created by the crime is that her murderer, having killed her with the cuts to the throat, decided to try to make it look like another Ripper killing to deflect suspicion. Perhaps he was a regular client, or knew her anyway. The general *modus operandi* of the killing leads the authors to believe that this was not the work of Jack the Ripper.

In view of a discovery that was to be made just six days later, an unsigned letter to the City Police, dated 4 September 1889 and postmarked London SE5, seems strangely coincidental. It ran:

> I think a murder was committed last night at 65 Gt Prescot St. It may have been the young servant who I was told had been made to one of the daughters in the day. I heard another was to be killed to day if <u>some one</u> told. The mistress told me in the afternoon if

young servants did not please her she sent them away, some in the house wanted me to be killed but the eldest daughter would not allow it. I think some one was brought in and his [?] of one night before. I am very sorry to say this and am sorry that the family should be Jewish. I would ask if it would not be possible for a detective from London not known here to take the furnished bedroom and by God's help put a stop to what I fear is a practice of young women brought in and then murdered. I am very sorry to have to give information but I must please God. This is strictly private & only for the eyes of those in authority–

If I did not tell it would it seem as if I connived at the shedding of blood and I will by Gods help have nothing to do with it.

Station Sergeant Donald Calder reported on the letter and had it forwarded to the duty Inspector at Leman Street police station. An entry to that effect was made on the station occurrence sheets at 10.25 p.m. on 5 September. The City Police liaison officer, Robert Sagar, reported that he had shown the anonymous letter to Detective Inspector Reid at H Division of the Metropolitan Police. Reid told Sagar that the woman responsible was known to him and she was insane. Detective Sergeant White of Leman Street station was allocated to make inquiries about the correspondence.

Six days after the letter arrived, the Pinchin Street torso case gripped London. On Tuesday 10 September 1889 unidentified female remains were found under a railway arch. This case bore no resemblance to a Ripper killing. On the contrary, it appeared that the murderer had cut up a body to prevent its identification and then dumped it away from the scene of his crime. At 5.15 a.m. that day PC 239H William Pennett was on patrol when he discovered a headless and legless female body underneath a railway arch at the Backchurch Lane end of Pinchin Street. There was a gash on the abdomen but this appeared to have been inflicted when the dismemberment had taken place. Dr Bagster Phillips' assistant, Dr Percy J. Clark, attended the scene at about 6 a.m. and examined the remains. He then went to the St George's-in-the-East mortuary and further examined the corpse. As he and Divisional Inspector Pinhorn were on their way back to Leman Street police station, they were called by some men to a piece of waste ground in Hooper Street where a bloodstained petticoat had been found. It was a false clue and appeared to be old; the garment seemed to have been folded and used for absorbing menstrual blood.

Inspector Reid again led the initial investigations. Sergeant Thick conducted inquiries at sheds, houses and barrow-parking areas, and also at butchers' premises in the neighbourhood. Detective Sergeant George Godley carried out research on missing persons in an effort to identify the remains. All stations were alerted to search for the other body parts and several officers were engaged in local inquiries on a similar quest. Reid asked the inspector of dustcarts for the parish of St George's-in-the-East to check if any of his men had collected bloodstained clothing from any house. Some had been found in Batty Street but were revealed to be totally innocent in nature, being the result of a pregnancy.

The inquest was concluded at St George's Vestry Hall, Cable Street, on 24 September and a verdict of wilful murder against person or persons unknown was returned. There is nothing at all to suggest that this was a Ripper victim and such was the opinion voiced by Donald Swanson in a report to the Home Office dated the day of the murder. In it he stated:

What becomes most apparent is the absence of the attack upon the genitals as in the series of Whitechapel murders beginning at Bucks Row and ending in Miller's Court. Certainly if it be a murder there was time enough for the murderer to cut off the head

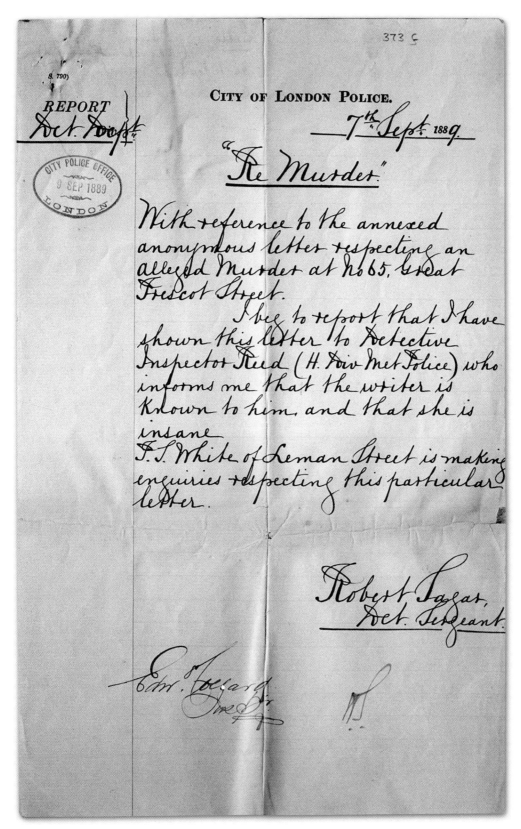

S. 790)

REPORT
Det. Dept

CITY POLICE OFFICE
9 SEP 1889
LONDON

CITY OF LONDON POLICE.

7th Sept. 1889

"Re Murder."

With reference to the annexed anonymous letter respecting an alleged Murder at No. 65. Great Prescot Street.

I beg to report that I have shown this letter to Detective Inspector Reed (H. Div Met Police) who informs me that the writer is known to him, and that she is insane

P.S. White of Leman Street is making enquiries respecting this particular letter.

Robert Sagar,
Det. Sergeant.

Sergeant Sagar's report.

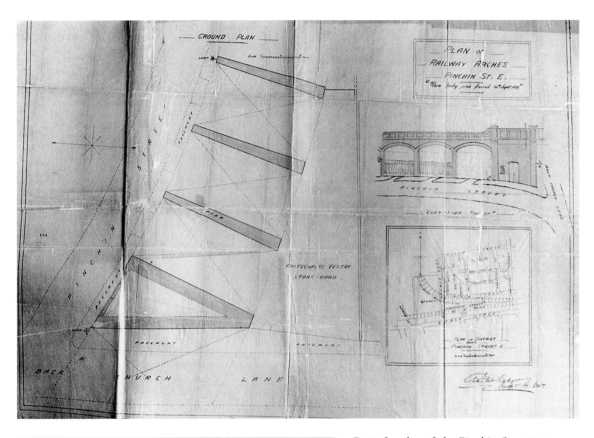

Part of a plan of the Pinchin Street torso crime scene drawn by Inspector Charles Ledger of G Division. A similar plan was made of the Miller's Court murder scene but has apparently not survived. (*S.P. Evans/Metropolitan Police*)

Sergeant Pennett. As a PC, he discovered the Pinchin Street torso.

and limbs there was time to mutilate as in the series mentioned. It appears rather to go side by side with the Rainham, Whitehall and Chelsea murders.[4]

It should be noted here that Swanson wrote as a man who believed that the Ripper was still at large and noted the Ripper murders as beginning with Nichols and ending with Kelly.

On 11 September Monro reported to the Home Office, giving the full circumstances of the Pinchin Street case. He dismissed any idea that it might be another Ripper killing and leaves us in no doubt that he too believes the Ripper still had his liberty:

> If this is a fresh outrage by the Whitechapel murderer known by the horribly familiar nickname of Jack the Ripper the answer would not be difficult, altho' this murder, committed in the murderers house wd. be a new departure from the system hitherto pursued by this ruffian. I am however inclined to believe that this case is not the work of the 'Ripper', which has characterized the previous cases has been a/. Death caused by cutting the throat, b/. Mutilation c/. Evisceration d/. Removal of certain parts of the body. e/. Murder committed in the street, except in one instance in Dorset Street. In this last case there were distinct traces of furious mania, the murderer having plenty of time at his disposal slashed and cut the body in all directions, evidently under the influence of frenzy.

Fresh newspaper talk of Jack the Ripper appears to have prompted H.T. Haslewood of White Cottage, High Road, Tottenham, to write to the Home Office on 10 September. He said he had 'very good grounds to believe' that Detective Sergeant William Thick had committed the Whitechapel murders and that he should be watched and his whereabouts at the times of the previous murders be ascertained. His allegation was regarded as 'rubbish' and was undoubtedly malicious.

The newspapers mentioned a possible identification of the Pinchin Street victim as Lydia Hart.[5] The woman was thought to be missing but was quickly located by her sons at the local infirmary where she was receiving medical attention after a 'bit of a spree'.

The renewed press speculation about Jack the Ripper included a clever colour cartoon by Tom Merry on the front cover of *Puck* newspaper of Saturday 21 September.[6] It depicts the back of a leather-apron-wearing Ripper gazing into a large oval mirror in which are reflected the images of various suspects. There is a lawyer, a Jew, a cleric, a woman, a bandit and, just above the Ripper's arm, the top of a policeman's helmet. The caption read: JACK THE RIPPER. WHO IS HE? WHAT IS HE? WHERE IS HE???

On 30 September the *Morning Advertiser* reported that there had been another possible identification of the torso. It was said to be Emily Barker of Northampton, who had led a 'wild life', had been found semi-nude on a doorstep in London by a missionary and had escaped from his charge just two days before the discovery in Pinchin Street. Her mother was convinced Emily was the victim and that she had made the chemise found wrapped around the remains. She further claimed that her suspicions were confirmed by a mark on a finger. Emily Barker was, however, under 20 years of age and the remains appeared to be those of an older woman. On 1 October the *Morning Advertiser* was able to report that Scotland Yard had investigated the claims and that the remains were definitely not Emily Barker, who was shorter than the estimated height of the Pinchin Street victim. The torso was never identified.

The idea that Jack the Ripper was a woman was explored in a letter written by Max Kamthun of Misdroy, Pomerania, Germany, dated 16 October 1889, to the superintendent of the City Police. Kamthun wrote:

This Tom Merry cartoon from the front cover of *Puck* of 21 September 1889 was inspired by the fresh outrage of the Pinchin Street torso case, which was not the Ripper's work. It reveals the great public fascination with Jack the Ripper and his identity. In the picture the Ripper looks at reflections of who he might be – a doctor, a cleric, a female, a Jew, a bandit – and just above his right arm can be seen the top of a policeman's helmet. (*British Library*)

All the world believes that the murderer is a man, Jack the Ripper, as, if I am not mistaken, that individual has called himself several times in his letters. I should not entertain any doubt whatever regarding the sex of the perpetrator, if it was a murder committed in lust. But as only a simple murder has been committed, and the perpetrator has never been apprehended, I feel persuaded with the greatest certainty that the murderer is not a man, but a mad woman, suffering from a mania of murder, who always manages to escape the hands of the police, as men only are carefully watched, and women are left free to pass. A woman approaches another woman in the dark without making her suspicious and without causing her to arouse the neighbourhood with her cries. A man would moreover know how to kill his victim otherwise than by cutting her throat, which is known to be an extremely easy way of killing. Besides, according to all newspaper reports, all the murders have been executed with the cunning so peculiar to madmen, and it is not at all impossible that the woman tries to put the police on the wrong scent by giving herself out as a man. [*Translated from the German original.*]

There is no evidence the police seriously considered that the murderer could have been a woman and it was not a popular idea among the theorists.

Monro's report for the Metropolitan Police force for 1889 made for slightly happier reading than the previous year's. In part it ran:

The criminal returns for the year . . . show a marked improvement upon the statistics for 1888. A few points only claim notice. That 17 murders are recorded without a single conviction having been obtained may seem to need explanation. In 8 of these cases the persons actually causing deaths were made amenable, but escaped the capital penalty; 2 of them on the ground of insanity, and the others because the homicides were held not to amount to murder. In 4 of the 9 remaining cases the persons against whom coroners' juries found verdicts of wilfil murder had committed suicide before their crimes were discovered. In one, the murderer was tracked to New York, and arrested there, but committed suicide in prison. There are four cases only, therefore, to be accounted for. One of these was the case of a prostitute found lying in Algernon Road, Lewisham, on the 10th February, and who died on the 14th from a fracture of the skull, supposed to have been caused by a blow. The second was the case of Elizabeth Jackson, also a prostitute, portions of whose dismembered body were found, some in Chelsea, some in Battersea, and some in the Thames. The next was the case of Alice McKenzie, whose death in Castle Alley, on the 17th July, was the last of the crimes known as the Whitechapel murders. And the last was a case where a portion of a woman's body was found in a railway arch in Pinchin Street, St. George's East, on the 10th September.

It was now almost twelve months since the recognised Ripper murders had ended with the killing of Kelly, although Monro's criminal returns for the year showed the McKenzie case as the last of the Whitechapel murders. It was an unhappy record of undetected crimes and another was to be added to the list over a year later.

The End of the Whitechapel Murders

GIVEN his status as former head of CID, and in view of the criticism levelled at Warren, it would have been surprising if Monro had not kept an anxious eye on Assistant Commissioner (Crime) Anderson's handling of the Whitechapel murders and the constant press speculation about Jack the Ripper. Such matters, however, must have been on the periphery of his concerns. There is a certain irony in the fact that on appointment as commissioner he found himself in conflict with the home secretary on some of the same issues that had eventually forced Warren's resignation. Monro's term in office lasted less than two years and proved to be the shortest on record.

The initial conflict between Matthews and Monro was over a clothing contract which had been entered into by the Home Office against the advice of both Warren and the receiver, for once apparently in agreement. Monro found it impossible to get clothing for the force and after ten months was forced to disclaim any responsibility for the contract. Repeated complaints to the Home Office were ignored or marked by the lack of action which was also apparent in other matters affecting the force, such as pay, overtime, pensions and other legitimate grievances. Monro soon found, like Warren, that obstacles were constantly put in his way by the Home Office and Matthews was as indecisive as ever. Large numbers of policemen were constantly tied up in dealing with meetings, strikes and processions by the unemployed. The force was in a mutinous condition and there were threats of strike action. Ironically, some of the younger members of the force, who were advocating the formation of a union, were accused of being under the influence of the socialists whom they had truncheoned so vigorously less than four years before.

The crisis point was reached in 1890 when Assistant Commissioner Lieutenant-Colonel Pearson died unexpectedly and Monro wanted to replace him with Chief Constable Charles Howard. Matthews, however, wanted to appoint a civil servant, his own secretary, to the post. Monro resisted, saying that the man had no police, military or legal training and that such an appointment could only demoralise the force which was expecting some senior promotions to come from the lower ranks. This was a case of the biter bit: Monro and Warren, implementing the 1886 Committee's recommendations, had tried to put

Home Secretary Henry Matthews portrayed as a 'fantastic failure' in this cartoon from the *Pall Mall Budget* of 27 September 1888.

THE

PALL MALL BUDGET

No. 1044.—VOL. XXXVI.   THURSDAY, SEPTEMBER 27, 1888.   *Weekly. Price Fourpence.*

MR. MATTHEWS AS "THE FANTASTIC FAILURE."

The DAILY TELEGRAPH says that it "cannot shrink from the painful but imperatively necessary task of warning Lord Salisbury that the public are altogether discontented with, and will soon become uncontrollably impatient of, the presence at the Home Office of Mr. Matthews. The fact can be no longer disguised that the Home Secretary now in office is a source of miserable weakness and discredit to the present Administration. In the House of Commons he has been nothing more or less than a fantastic failure."

Macnaghten in over the head of the vastly more experienced Williamson. Monro had had his way but it was a short-lived victory.

After becoming commissioner, Monro became deeply involved in the issue of police pensions. It was a major grievance among the men. When a Police Pensions Bill was to be submitted to Parliament Monro did not think it went far enough and submitted his resignation, which was accepted on 12 June 1890. Yet when Matthews' Bill was published on 17 June, it apparently met all of Monro's demands. Whether Monro actually saw the final bill is open to question. It is possible that Matthews deliberately misled him with the draft and by this duplicity was able to rid himself of a second troublesome commissioner within two years. Monro returned to India where he established a medical mission some 40 miles from Calcutta. He retired eventually to England in 1905 but resurfaced five years later when he denied that he had given Anderson permission (as Anderson was then claiming) to publish the series of anonymous articles in *The Times* in 1887.

Monro's replacement was another old India hand, Sir Edward Bradford, who since 1887 had been secretary of the political and secret departments in the India Office. Instead of taking up Monro's old office in Whitehall Place, he moved into the new Norman Shaw

The well-remembered New Scotland Yard of early B movies opened in 1890 and was the scene of the Whitehall Mystery of 2 October 1888.

Colonel Sir Edward Bradford who succeeded James Monro as Metropolitan Police Commissioner in 1890 and retired in 1903.

headquarters on the Embankment, close to Westminster Bridge, which Monro had named New Scotland Yard. He had been in office some months when another Whitechapel murder occurred, a case that caused the police to think initially that the Ripper had begun to kill again after a break of more than two years.

On Friday 13 February 1891 a 27-year-old police officer, PC 240H Ernest Thompson, was on his first tour of night duty in H Division. PC Thompson had joined the force on 29 December 1890 and no doubt he was still feeling rather nervous and vulnerable. His patrol took him along Chamber Street, off the southern end of Leman Street. As he approached Swallow Gardens (off to his left under the railway arches and separating Chamber Street from Royal Mint Street) he heard the sound of footsteps, apparently those of a man, proceeding in a westerly direction towards Mansell Street. However, he saw no one and at this time,

Coles and Sadler in the doss-house prior to her murder. She was the worse for wear after an epic pub crawl.

about 2.15 a.m., was not aware that anything was amiss. He then immediately turned under the railway arch into Swallow Gardens and saw a woman lying on the ground. He went to the body and found that the woman was bleeding from a throat wound. She was still warm. Indeed, he claimed that there was a movement of one of the woman's eyelids when he first saw her. The victim was Frances Coles, a 25-year-old prostitute, and the similarities between the case and the previous Whitechapel murders were obvious.

Later that day Anderson forwarded the H Division report on the murder to Commissioner Sir Edward Bradford, noting that the case had been reported to him in the middle of the night and he had authorised all aid that Superintendent Arnold might require. He stated that officers who had investigated the earlier murders were quickly on the spot and every effort was being made to trace the criminal. As in former cases, the criminal had left nothing and carried away nothing that might afford a clue. A Home Office note by Godfrey Lushington[1] on Anderson's minute stated that he had shown the report to Henry Matthews and explained that he thought it would be premature for them 'to venture taking opinion as to now for this case may obviously not be connected with any previous cases'. Anderson's final annotation was: 'As in former cases I wish to have a report each morning for the present.' This is relevant as it shows that Anderson relied on reports submitted to him on the murders for his updates, as opposed to being a part of the actual

James Sadler at Thames Police Court.

investigation. Indeed, as an assistant commissioner, he would not expect to be involved in the inquiry directly.

A suspect was already known. He was James Thomas Sadler who had been with the murdered woman the previous day when the two had been on an epic pub crawl together. Sadler had been assaulted and robbed by some men – the attack, he alleged, was at Coles' instigation. Sadler was quickly arrested by Sergeant Don and PC Gill, who found him in the Phoenix public house in Upper East Smithfield. On being arrested and told of the offence Sadler replied, 'I expected this.' He was taken to Leman Street police station. As in the previous cases Chief Inspector Swanson submitted reports, the first on the day of Sadler's arrest. Sadler was described as aged about 50 but looking older. He was 5 feet 6 inches tall, 'stoops a little, fair and even ruddy when washed'; he had a moustache and goatee beard. He was wearing a pilot cloth pea jacket, serge trousers and a black cap with a leather peak. There was some blood on the lining of the cap but this was explained by the beating he had taken. There can be no doubt that the police attached great importance to the arrest of Sadler as a full statement was taken from him by Swanson himself. It is beyond doubt that Sadler was initially believed to be a potential suspect for the earlier murders for Swanson included in Sadler's statement all his discharge dates from ships back to March 1887. They included the fact that he was engaged on 24 March 1887, next 5 May 1887, engaged 17 August 1888, next 2 October 1888 (London), next discharge 1 October 1889 (London), and so on.[2] He was also later put on an identification parade in front of the Mitre Square witness – although the witness was not named it must have been Lawende.[3]

Images of Sadler in court and various scenes from the Coles murder.

Frances Coles was the last Whitechapel victim to be realistically considered a Ripper victim.

On 21 February 1891 Swanson went to Chatham to obtain full details of Sadler from his wife at 3 Skinner Street. Swanson took a detailed history of Sadler from the woman, including details of his work and residence in 1888. The couple had separated after a quarrel in August 1888. He left her at the beginning of the month and she moved from the residence off Commercial Road two weeks later, the 15th, to go to Chatham to live with her mother. She had resided there ever since. She did not hear from Sadler again until about March 1889. Further detailed inquiries about Sadler's previous employment and addresses were carried out by Inspector Henry Moore, who submitted a report on the subject on 2 March 1891. Special inquiries were also made by Sergeant Kuhrt as to Sadler's whereabouts between 16 and 20 July 1889. (The McKenzie murder took place on 17 July that year).

On the evening of Saturday 15 February, the Coles inquest was opened at the Working Lads' Institute where Coroner Wynne Baxter was having a busy day – it was his eleventh inquest that day. Albert Bachert, now described as the chairman of the Whitechapel Vigilance Committee, was in attendance and had been rejected as a jury member by Baxter. Bachert asked why he had been refused. Baxter replied, 'Because I decline to allow you to serve.' Bachert replied, 'You know I will inquire into the case; that's why you refuse me. I am a ratepayer, and pay my rates.' Baxter retorted, 'Why should you be so anxious to serve? I decline to accept you.' The jury then went off to view the body which was lying in a shell in the makeshift mortuary in the parish dustyard.

They returned to the institute to begin the inquest hearing and Bachert again inquired on what grounds Baxter had refused him. Annoyed with the interruption Baxter said, 'You be quiet, sir; if you are not I shall have you ejected.' A juror was then heard to remark, 'That settles his little game.'[4]

The inquest was adjourned until the following Tuesday. In the meantime the press commented on the importance that was being attached to this murder and its possible connection with the Whitechapel cases of 1888. In a lengthy report in the *Daily Telegraph* of Wednesday 18 February, a list of all the previous murders was drawn up and comparisons were made with the dates of Sadler's voyages. The inquest was protracted and was not concluded until Friday 27 February when the jury returned the familiar verdict of 'wilful murder against some person or persons at present unknown'.

There was ultimately no evidence adduced by the police to connect Sadler with the murder of Coles, nor with any of the previous Whitechapel killings, and he was discharged at the Thames police court on 3 March 1891. There is no doubt that he was, for a short time, strongly suspected by the police of committing the Ripper murders, and this has important ramifications in relation to the later theory that the killer was a Polish Jew (see

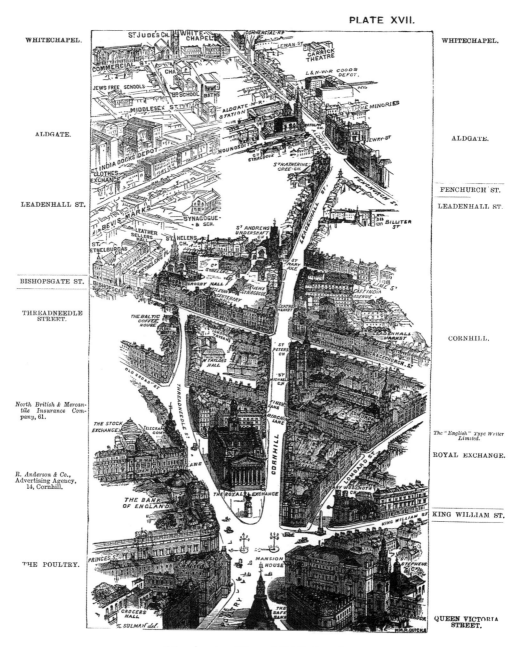

Map showing City and Whitechapel.

chapter 15). According to J. Hall Richardson,[5] Sadler went on to take legal action against a newspaper that had discredited him and won damages. After that he allegedly became involved with a 'gentleman' who was planning a gun-running expedition to South America where two republics were at war. It was then that Sadler disappeared from the pages of history.

After the murder of Frances Coles there were no more killings even loosely attributed to the elusive Jack the Ripper. The people of the East End settled down as the fears of 1888 gradually faded and the murders became a memory.

Was there a Police Solution?

ERMANE to the importance of any suspect is the quality and source of the evidence giving rise to the suspicion. From the police files we know that no hard evidence ever existed against any suspect, and if the evidence could not be adduced in 1888 then it certainly will not be discovered at this remove in time. It must be recognised that if there was ever a true indication that any suspect was the killer, then the best, and only really valid, source for this must be the official police records or, at the very least, the words of the senior police officials involved.

It has been stated that the police files on the Ripper crimes were closed in 1892, this date usually being arrived at by the fact that on deposit at the Public Record Office they were marked as 'Closed until 1992', that is subject to the 100-year closure rule. This date, however, is rather arbitrary because official police files on undetected crimes of this nature were not generally closed when the case was still quite recent. They were merely stored when active investigation ceased but were there, ready to use, should any new evidence or possibly connected incident come to light. Although the generally recognised Ripper crimes ceased at the end of 1888, it was several years before the files were put away and additions were made from 1889 to 1892. The last papers were placed with the files in 1896 when another letter purporting to be from 'Jack the Ripper' was received by the police.

Among the senior police sources of information on the crimes are Sir Charles Warren, James Monro, Robert Anderson, Donald Swanson (who reported on the murder investigation direct to Anderson), Anderson's second-in-command Melville Macnaghten, the Inspector of HM Prisons, Major Arthur Griffiths (a personal friend of both Anderson and Macnaghten) and John George Littlechild of the Special Branch. Comments made by senior policemen, or senior officials connected with the police, concerning whether the Ripper case could ever be solved are listed here chronologically.

23 October 1888

Assistant Commissioner Dr Robert Anderson – That a crime of this kind should have been committed without any clue being supplied by the criminal, is unusual, but that five

Whitechapel Murders.

	Date	Time	Person Murdered	Where	
1	Tuesday 3.4.88	12.15 & 5 AM	Emma E. Smith	Osborn Street	
2	Tuesday following Bank Holiday 7.8.88	11.45 pm 6th & 4.50 AM 7	Martha Tabram	37 George Yard	
3	Friday 31.8.88	3.45 am	Mary Ann Nicholls	Bucks Row	201
4	Saturday 8.9.88	6 AM	Annie Chapman	29 Hanbury St.	201
5	Sunday 30.9.88	1 AM	Elizabeth Stride	Berner Street	
6	" "	1.45 AM	Catherine Eddowes	Mitre Square	
7	Friday 9.11.88		Mary Janet Kelly	Dorset Street	
	Wednesday 17.7.89	12.40 AM	Alice McKenzie	Castle Alley	
	Friday morning 13.2.91	2.15 am	Frances Coles	Swallow Gardens	

Alleged Attempted Murder

21.11.88   9.30 AM   Annie Farmer.   19 George St.

Alleged Murder

20.12.88.   Rose Mylett alias Catherine Milett alias — Davis   } High St. Poplar

This contemporary list was retained by Chief Inspector Donald Swanson. (*Courtesy of the late Jim Swanson*)

successive murders should have been committed, without our having the <u>slightest clue of any kind</u> is extraordinary, if not unique, in the annals of crime.[1]

27 October 1888

Inspector James McWilliam, City of London Police – Every effort has been made to trace the murderer, but up to the present without success. Enquiry has been made respecting persons in almost every class of society & I have sent officers to all the Lunatic Asylums in London to make enquiries respecting persons recently admitted or discharged, many persons being of opinion that these crimes are of too revolting a character to have been committed by a sane person.[2]

August 1889

Dr Robert Anderson – 'I am sorry to say on your account and quite satisfied on my own that we have very few criminal "show places" in London. Of course, there is the Scotland Yard Museum that visitors consider one of the sights, and then there is Whitechapel. But that is all. You ought to see Whitechapel. Even if the murders had not taken place there it would be still the show part of the city for those who take an interest in the dangerous classes. But you mustn't expect to see criminals walking about with handcuffs on or to find the places they live in any different from the other dens of the district. My men can show you their lodging houses and can tell you that this or that man is a thief or a burglar, but he won't look any different from any one else.' The American journalist interviewing Anderson suggested at this point that he had never found they looked any different from any one else. 'Well, I only spoke of it because they say, as a rule, your people come over here expecting to see dukes wearing their coronets and the thieves of Whitechapel in prison-cut clothes, and they are disappointed. But I don't think you will be disappointed in the district. After a stranger has gone over it he takes a much more lenient view of our failure to find Jack the Ripper, as they call him, than he did before.'[3]

May 1892

Chief Inspector Frederick George Abberline – 'Theories! we were lost almost in theories; there were so many of them.' Nevertheless, he has one which is new. He believes, from the evidence of his own eyesight, that the Miller's Court atrocity was the last of the real series, the others having been imitations, and that in Miller's Court the murderer reached the culminating point of the gratification of his morbid ideas.[4]

June 1892

Dr Robert Anderson – 'I sometimes think myself an unfortunate man,' observes the C.I.D. chief, 'for between twelve and one of the morning of the day I took up my position here the first Whitechapel murder occurred.'

The mention of this appalling sequence of still undiscovered crimes leads to the production of certain ghastly photographs.

'There,' says the Assistant Commissioner, 'there is my answer to people who come with fads and theories about these murders. It is impossible to believe they were acts of a sane man – they were those of a maniac revelling in blood.'[5]

February 1893

Superintendent Thomas Arnold – I still hold what you may consider some curious opinions on that subject. For instance for reasons which I am sure you would consider sufficiently convincing, but which are too long to detail now, I still hold to the opinion that not more than four of those murders were committed by the same hand. They were the murders of Annie Chapman in Hanbury Street, Mrs. Nicholls in Buck's Row, Elizabeth Stride in Berner Street, and Mary Kelly in Mitre Square.[6] We police came in for a very large share of blame at the hands of the public at that time for not acting as some people considered we ought to have acted in the matter, but I can assure you that no stone was left unturned by the police in endeavouring to detect the criminal.[7]

Arnold described how the police had used bloodhounds and considerably augmented both the detective department and the general force at that time: 'We had some of the very finest men from all parts of London, but all their efforts were useless.'

23 February 1894

Chief Constable Melville Macnaghten – The last murder is the only one that took place in a room. . . . A much more rational theory is that the murderer's brain gave way altogether after his awful glut in Miller's Court, and that he immediately committed suicide, or, as a possible alternative, was found to be so hopelessly mad by his relations, that he was by them confined in some asylum.[8]

No one ever saw the Whitechapel murderer, many homicidal maniacs were suspected, but no shadow of proof could be thrown on any one. I may mention the cases of 3 men, any one of whom would have been more likely than Cutbush[9] to have committed this series of murders:–

(1) A Mr. M.J. Druitt, said to be a doctor [*sic*][10] & of good family who disappeared at the time of the Miller's Court murder, & whose body (which was said to have been upwards of a month in the water) was found in the Thames on 31st. Decr., or about 7 weeks after that murder. He was sexually insane and from private inf. I have little doubt but that his own family believed him to have been the murderer.

(2) Kosminski, a Polish Jew, & resident in Whitechapel. This man became insane owing to many years indulgence in solitary vices. He had a great hatred of women, specially of the prostitute class, & had strong homicidal tendencies; he was removed to a lunatic asylum about March 1889. There were many circs connected with this man which made him a strong 'suspect'.

Montague John Druit. He was one of three suspects named by Macnaghten in his memorandum of February 1894. A barrister and teacher, he committed suicide in December 1888 and was Macnaghten's favoured suspect of the three.

Michael Ostrog, the third Jack the Ripper suspect named by Macnaghten. Osrog was a Russian-born thief and confidence trickster who lived in England for many years. Research by author Philip Sugden has now eliminated him as a suspect: he was in custody in Paris at the time of the murders.

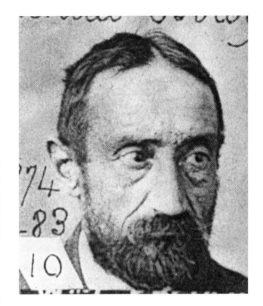

(3) Michael Ostrog, a Russian doctor, and a convict, who was subsequently detained in a lunatic asylum as a homicidal maniac. The man's antecedents were of the worst possible type, and his whereabouts at the time of the murders could never be ascertained.[11]

1895

Inspector of Prisons Arthur Griffiths (on Anderson)
– Although he has achieved greater success than any detective of his time, there will always be undiscovered crimes, and just now the tale is pretty full. Much dissatisfaction was vented upon Mr. Anderson at the utterly abortive efforts to discover the perpetrator of the Whitechapel murders. He has himself a perfectly plausible theory that Jack the Ripper was a homicidal maniac, temporarily at large, whose hideous career was cut short by committal to an asylum.[12]

May 1895

Chief Inspector Donald Swanson, as reported in the *Pall Mall Gazette* – Since the cessation of the Whitechapel murders there has been no lack of theories accounting for the disappearance of the author of those crimes, 'Jack the Ripper,' as he is called, in consequence of a series of letters so signed, purporting, rightly or wrongly, to come from the murderer. The theory entitled to most respect, because it was presumably based upon the best knowledge, was that of Chief Inspector Swanson, the officer who was associated with the investigation of all the murders, and Mr. Swanson believed the crimes to have been the work of a man who is now dead. Latterly, however, the police have been busy investigating the case of William Grant Grainger, who was caught in the act of wounding a woman in the abdomen, in a street close by Buck's-row, the scene of the first of the real series of Whitechapel murders, those outrages in which the victims were killed and left horribly mutilated in the streets. Grainger's crime so much resembled the former outrages that infinite pains were taken to trace his antecedents. Nothing was found, however, to warrant placing him upon his trial for any previous outrage, and on March 27 last he was brought up at the Old Bailey charged with feloniously wounding Alice Graham.[13]

1898

Arthur Griffiths – The outside public may think that the identity of that later miscreant, 'Jack the Ripper', was never revealed. So far as actual knowledge goes, this is undoubtedly true. But the police, after the last murder, had brought their investigations to the point of strongly suspecting several persons, all of them known to be homicidal lunatics, and against three of these they held very plausible and reasonable grounds of suspicion. Concerning two of them the case was weak, although it was based on certain colourable facts. One was a Polish Jew, a known lunatic, who was at large in the district of Whitechapel at the time of the murder, and who, having afterwards developed homicidal tendencies, was confined in an asylum. This man was said to resemble the murderer by the one person who got a glimpse of him – the police-constable in Mitre Court. The second possible criminal was a Russian doctor, also insane, who had been a convict both in England and Siberia. This man was in the habit of carrying about surgical knives and instruments in his pockets; his antecedents were of the very worst, and at the time of the Whitechapel murders he was in hiding, or, at least, his whereabouts were never exactly known. The third person was of the same type, but the suspicion in his case was stronger, and there was every reason to believe that his own friends entertained grave doubts about him. He also was a doctor in the prime of life, was believed to be insane or on the borderland of insanity, and he disappeared immediately after the last murder, that in Miller's Court, on the 9th of November, 1888. On the last day of that year, seven weeks later, his body was found floating in the Thames, and was said to have been in the water a month. The theory in this case was that after his last exploit, which was the most fiendish of all, his brain entirely gave way, and he became furiously insane and committed suicide. It is at least a strong presumption that 'Jack the Ripper' died or was put under restraint after the Miller's Court affair which ended this series of crimes. It would be interesting to know whether in this third case the man was left-handed or ambidextrous, both suggestions having been advanced by medical experts after viewing the victims. Certainly other doctors disagreed on this point, which may be said to add another to the many instances in which medical evidence has been conflicting, not to say confusing.[14]

February 1901

Sir Robert Anderson – Or, again, take a notorious case of a different kind, 'the Whitechapel murders' of the autumn of 1888. At that time the sensation-mongers of the newspaper press fostered the belief that life in London was no longer safe, and that no woman ought to venture abroad in the streets after nightfall. And one enterprising journalist went so far as to impersonate the cause of all this terror as 'Jack the Ripper,' a name by which he will probably go down to history. But all such silly hysterics could not alter the fact that these crimes were a cause of danger only to a particular section of a small and definite class of women, in a limited district of the East End; and that the inhabitants of the metropolis generally were just as secure during the weeks the fiend was on the prowl as they were before the mania seized him, or after he had been safely caged in an asylum.[15]

March 1903

Frederick George Abberline – In March 1903 at the time that the 'Borough Poisoner' George Chapman (Severin Klosowski), aged 38, was lying under sentence of death for the murder of three women by poison Abberline, then living in retirement in Bournemouth, was interviewed by a reporter from the *Pall Mall Gazette* about the idea that Chapman and the Ripper could be one and the same person. This theory seems initially to have evolved in the same way that similar stories emerged about convicted women-killers Dr Neill Cream and Frederick Deeming at the time of their trials. Abberline seemed enthusiastic about the idea, stating that he had been about to write to Assistant Commissioner Macnaghten to suggest this very thing.

Poisoner George Chapman, hanged in 1903 and
named at the time by ex-Inspector Abberline as a
possible Ripper suspect.

Abberline stated that he had been
struck by the coincidences in the two
series of murders. He was reported as
saying, 'We have never believed all those
stories about Jack the Ripper being dead,
or that he was a lunatic, or anything of
that kind.' He went on to explain the
various coincidences linking Chapman
to the cases, such as the date of his
arrival in England at the beginning of
the series of Whitechapel murders; that
the murders ceased in London when
Chapman went to America (this is not
true – he went at a later date); that
similar murders began to be perpetrated
in America after he landed there (not
true); that Chapman studied medicine
and surgery in Russia before coming to
England and the Ripper murders were 'the work of an expert surgeon' (not true – the
Ripper showed no particular medical knowledge or skill); that Chapman 'attempted to
murder his wife with a long knife while in America' (not true – he threatened her during
a 'domestic' and had a knife under his pillow); that Chapman had lodgings in George
Yard 'where the first murder was committed' (not true – he later worked in the White
Hart at the bottom of that street); that Chapman's height and the peaked hat he wore
tallied with descriptions of the Ripper (there was no reliable description of the Ripper and
thousands were that height and wore peaked hats); he was a 'foreign-looking man', and
so on.[16]

If this report truly reflects Abberline's words, it shows he was working with some
pretty shaky 'facts'. Chapman was a totally different sort of murderer, a surreptitious
poisoner who killed his common law wives, so little credence can be given to these
'revelations'. This story was adopted by H.L. Adam when he edited and wrote the
introduction to *The Trial of George Chapman* (William Hodge, April 1930), which included
a large section about Chapman as the Ripper. Adam quoted Abberline as saying to
Detective Inspector George Godley, when he arrested Chapman, 'You've got Jack the
Ripper at last!' There is no other reference to this nor any confirmation of it, nor is there
any evidence that Abberline had contact with Godley when Chapman was arrested. In
fact, Abberline's alleged statement that he was writing to Macnaghten with the
information in March 1903 would tend to indicate that he had no contact with Godley
or Scotland Yard by that time.

January 1905

The *City Press* of 7 January 1905 reported on the retirement of Detective Inspector Robert
Sagar of the City of London Police force. He had served twenty-five years with the force and

was promoted to sergeant at the time of the murders. A Lancashire man by birth, Sagar was once a medical student attached to St Bartholomew's Hospital and had an apartment in Bartholomew Close where a noted City detective named Potts also lived. Described as 'a first edition of Sherlock Holmes', Potts, it seems, influenced young Sagar's mind to become 'diverted from the study of surgery and medicine to the fascinating problem of criminology, and the varied means which a quick intelligence offered for the detection of crime'. He appeared for the prosecution in a large number of cases at the City police courts and at the Old Bailey. This was brought to the attention of the Commissioner, James Fraser, and he called for a report 'with respect to the many cases in which the young medical student had been involved'. The result was that it was suggested that Sagar join the police force which, of course, he did, in January 1880. He was promoted to sergeant in December 1888, to detective sergeant in June 1889 and to detective inspector in November 1890. It was said that he never donned a uniform, which was unique in the history of the force. The relevant part of the report regarding Sagar's association with the Ripper investigation ran:

> His professional association with the terrible atrocities which were perpetrated some years ago in the East End by the so-styled 'Jack-the-Ripper' was a very close one. Indeed, Mr. Sagar knows as much about those crimes, which terrified the Metropolis, as any detective in London. He was deputed to represent the City police force in conference with the detective heads of the Metropolitan force nightly at Leman Street Police Station during the period covered by those ghastly murders. Much has been said and written – and even more conjectured – upon the subject of the 'Jack-the-Ripper' murders. It has been asserted that the murderer fled to the Continent, where he perpetrated similar hideous crimes; but that is not the case. The police realised, as also did the public, that the crimes were those of a madman, and suspicion fell upon a man, who, without a doubt, was the murderer. Identification being impossible, he could not be charged. He was, however, placed in a lunatic asylum, and the series of atrocities came to an end. There was a peculiar incident in connection with those tragedies which may have been forgotten. The apron belonging to the woman who was murdered in Mitre Square was thrown under a staircase in a common lodging house in Dorset Street [*sic*], and someone – presumably the murderer – had written on the wall above it, 'The Jewes are not the people that will be blamed for nothing.' A police officer engaged in the case, fearing that the writing might lead to an onslaught upon the Jews in the neighbourhood, rubbed the writing from the wall, and all record of the implied accusation was lost; but the fact that such an ambiguous message was left is recorded among the archives at the Guildhall.

This piece does not really give an indication of what Sagar might have thought in relation to the identity of a suspect, unlike an article that appeared many years later and long after Sagar's death in 1924. On 15 September 1946 *Reynold's News* published number 7 in a 'Great Unsolved Mysteries' series – 'WHO WAS JACK THE RIPPER?' by Justin Atholl. It mentioned the idea that George Chapman was the murderer and, more interestingly, touched on a theory linked with Sagar:

> More probable is the theory that the police knew the identity of the Ripper but were never able to get evidence to arrest him. The crime committed by a maniac, completely without motive, is the most difficult on which to get evidence the law will accept. The police made a number of arrests, but none of them 'stuck'.

Inspector Robert Sagar, who died in 1924, played a leading part in the Ripper investigations. In his memoirs he said: 'We had a good reason to suspect a man who worked in Butcher's-row, Aldgate. We watched him carefully.

'There was no doubt that this man was insane, and after a time his friends thought it advisable to have him removed to a private asylum. After he was removed, there were no more Ripper atrocities.'

Unfortunately Sagar's 'memoirs', if ever they existed, have never come to light. Atholl, who wrote popular pieces and books on crime, was prone to errors and he gives no source for the information. However, this short and intriguing piece is essentially little different from the story given in 1905 at the time of Sagar's retirement, and does not disagree in any relevant detail with ex-Inspector Harry Cox's account in 1906 (below). It should be noted that the later suspect, Aaron Kosminski, had not worked for years, which does not tie in with either Cox or Sagar's accounts.[17]

December 1906

Harry Cox, Detective Inspector, City of London Police – The first crime took place on August 6, the second on the last day of the month. The third occurred in the beginning of the following month, this time two days later, and the fourth and fifth were once again on the last day of the month. The final murder was again on the opening days of the month.

This, as I say, seems to point to the murderer having a system, but it also considerably strengthens the theory that the man was a sailor, and timed his murders so that he could board his vessel just as it was on the point of sailing.

We had many people under observation while the murders were being perpetrated, but it was not until the discovery of the body of Mary Kelly had been made that we seemed to get upon the trail.

Certain investigations made by several of our cleverest detectives made it apparent to us that a man living in the East End of London was not unlikely to have been connected with the crimes.

To understand the reason we must first of all understand the motive of the Whitechapel crimes. The motive was, there can be not the slightest doubt, revenge. Not merely revenge on the few poor unfortunate victims of the knife, but revenge on womankind. It was not a lust for blood, as many people have imagined.

The murderer was a misogynist, who at some time or another had been wronged by a woman. And the fact that his victims were of the lowest class proves, I think, that he was not, as has been stated, an educated man who had suddenly gone mad. He belonged to their own class.

Had he been wronged by a woman occupying a higher stage in society the murders would in all probability have taken place in the West End, the victims [would] have been members of the fashionable demi-monde.

The man we suspected was about five feet six inches in height, with short, black, curly hair, and he had a habit of taking late walks abroad. He occupied several shops in the East End, but from time to time he became insane, and was forced to spend a portion of his time in an asylum in Surrey.

While the Whitechapel murders were being perpetrated his place of business was in a certain street, and after the last murder I was on duty in this street for nearly three months.

City of London Police officers on the roof of Snow Hill police station, probably in 1887. The men are wearing their jubilee medals for service on Queen Victoria's Golden Jubilee. Unfortunately they are not captioned but most of the officers involved in the Mitre Square murder investigation are probably here. Superintendent Foster can be seen, seated, second row, fourth from left, and PC Harvey of Mitre Square fame can also be identified, second row from top, third from left.

There were several other officers with me, and I think there can be no harm in stating that the opinion of most of them was that the man they were watching had something to do with the crimes. You can imagine that never once did we allow him to quit our sight. The least slip and another brutal crime might have been perpetrated under our very noses. It was not easy to forget that already one of them had taken place at the very moment when one of our smartest colleagues was passing the top of the dimly-lit street.

The Jews in the street soon became aware of our presence. It was impossible to hide ourselves. They became suddenly alarmed, panic-stricken, and I can tell you that at nights we ran a considerable risk. We carried our lives in our hands so to speak, and at last we had to partly take the alarmed inhabitants into our confidence, and so throw them off the scent. We told them we were factory inspectors looking for tailors and capmakers who employed boys and girls under age, and pointing out the evils accruing from the sweaters' system asked them to co-operate with us in destroying it.

They readily promised so to do, although we knew well that they had no intention of helping us. Every man was as bad as another. Day after day we used to sit and chat with them, drinking their coffee, smoking their excellent cigarettes, and partaking of Kosher rum. Before many weeks had passed we were quite friendly with them, and knew that we could carry out our observations unmolested. I am sure they never once suspected that we were police detectives on the trail of the mysterious murderer; otherwise they would not have discussed the crimes with us as openly as they did.

We had the use of a house opposite the shop of the man we suspected, and, disguised, of course, we frequently stopped across in the role of customers.

Every newspaper loudly demanded that we should arouse from our slumber, and the public had lashed themselves into a state of fury and fear. The terror soon spread to the provinces too. Whenever a small crime was committed it was asserted that the Ripper had shifted his ground, and warning letters were received by many a terror-stricken woman. The latter were of course the work of cruel practical jokers. The fact, by the way, that the murderer never shifted his ground rather inclines one to the belief that he was a mad, poverty-stricken inhabitant of some slum in the East End.

I shall never forget one occasion when I had to shadow our man during one of his late walks. As I watched him from the house opposite one night, it suddenly struck me that there was a wilder look than usual on his evil countenance, and I felt that something was about to happen. When darkness set in I saw him come forth from the door of his little shop and glance furtively around to see if he were being watched. I allowed him to get right out of the street before I left the house, and then I set off after him. I followed him to Lehman [sic] Street, and there I saw him enter a shop which I knew was the abode of a number of criminals well known to the police.

He did not stay long. For about a quarter of an hour I hung about keeping my eye on the door, and at last I was rewarded by seeing him emerging alone.

He made his way down to St George's in the East End, and there to my astonishment I saw him stop and speak to a drunken woman.

I crouched in a doorway and held my breath. Was he going to throw himself right into my waiting arms? He passed on after a moment or two, and on I slunk after him.

As I passed the woman she laughed and shouted something after me, which, however, I did not catch.

My man was evidently of opinion that he might be followed at every minute. Now and again he turned his head and glanced over his shoulder, and consequently I had the greatest difficulty in keeping behind him.

I had to work my way along, now with my back to the wall, now pausing and making little runs for a sheltering doorway. Not far from where the model lodging-house stands he met another woman, and for a considerable distance he walked along with her.

Just as I was beginning to prepare myself for a terrible ordeal, however, he pushed her away from him and set off at a rapid pace.

In the end he brought me, tired, weary, and nerve-strung back to the street he had left where he disappeared into his own house.

Next morning I beheld him, busy as usual. It is indeed very strange that as soon as this madman was put under observation the mysterious crimes ceased, and that very soon he removed from his usual haunts and gave up his nightly prowls. He was never

Leman Street at Whitechapel High Street, showing the heavy traffic at this busy junction which Commercial Street also joined from the north.

arrested for the reason that not the slightest scrap of evidence could be found to connect him with the crimes.

Long after the public had ceased to talk about the murders we continued to investigate them.

We had no clue to go upon, but every point suggested by the imagination was seized upon and worked bare. There was not a criminal in London capable of committing the crimes but was looked up and shadowed.

The mystery is as much a mystery as it was fifteen years ago. It is all very well for amateur detectives to fix the crime upon this or that suspect, and advance theories in the public press to prove his guilt. They are working upon surmise, nothing more.

The mystery can never be cleared up until someone comes forward and himself proves conclusively that he was the bloodthirsty demon who terrorized the country, or unless he returns to his crimes and is caught red-handed. He is still alive then? you ask. I do not know. For all I know he may be dead. I have personally no evidence either way.[18]

September 1908

Sir Robert Anderson – Something of the same kind happened in the Ripper crimes. In two cases of that terrible series there were distinct clues destroyed – wiped out absolutely – clues that might very easily have secured for us proof of the identity of the assassin.

In one case it was a clay pipe. Before we could get to the scene of the murder the doctor had taken it up, thrown it into the fire-place and smashed it beyond recognition.

In another case there was writing in chalk on the wall – a most valuable clue; recognized as belonging to a certain individual. But before we could secure a copy, or get it protected, it had been entirely obliterated. . . .

I told Sir William Harcourt, who was the Home Secretary [*sic*], that I could not accept responsibility for non-detection of the author of the Ripper crimes, for the reasons, among others, that I have given you.[19]

March 1910

Sir Robert Anderson – My last article brought down my story to my appointment, in September 1888, as Assistant Commissioner of Police and head of the Criminal Investigation Department. . . .

But I told Mr Matthews, greatly to his distress, that I could not take up my new duties until I had had a month's holiday in Switzerland. And so, after one week at Scotland Yard, I crossed the Channel.

But this was not all. The second of the crimes known as the Whitechapel murders was committed the night before I took office, and the third occurred the night of the day on which I left London. The newspapers soon began to comment on my absence. And letters from Whitehall decided me to spend the last week of my holiday in Paris, that I might be in touch with my office. On the night of my arrival in the French capital two more victims fell to the knife of the murder-fiend; and next day's post brought me an urgent appeal from Mr Matthews to return to London – and of course I complied.

On my return I found the 'Jack-the-Ripper' scare in full swing. When the stolid English go in for a scare they take leave of all moderation and common-sense. If nonsense were solid, the nonsense that was talked and written about those murders would sink a *Dreadnought*. The subject is an unsavoury one, and I must write about it with reserve. But it is enough to say that the wretched victims belonged to a very small class of degraded women who frequent the East End streets after midnight, in hope of inveigling belated drunkards, or men as degraded as themselves. I spent the day of my return to town, and half the following night, in reinvestigating the whole case, and next day I had a long conference on the subject with the Secretary of State and the Chief Commissioner of Police. 'We hold you responsible to find the murderer,' was Mr Matthews' greeting to me. My answer was to decline the responsibility. I hold myself responsible, I said, to take all legitimate means to find him. But I went on to say that the measures I found in operation were, in my opinion, wholly indefensible and scandalous, for these wretched women were plying their trade under definite Police protection. Let the Police of that district, I urged, receive orders to arrest every known 'street woman' found on the prowl after midnight, or else let us warn them that the Police will not protect them. Though the former course would have been merciful to the very small class of women affected by it, it was deemed too drastic, and I fell back on the second.

However the fact may be explained, it is a fact that no other street murder occurred in the 'Jack-the-Ripper' series [Footnote – I am here assuming that the murder of Alice M'Kenzie on 17th July 1889 was by another hand. I was absent from London when it occurred, but the Chief Commissioner investigated the case on the spot. It was an ordinary murder, and not the work of a sexual maniac.] The last and the most horrible of that maniac's crimes was committed in a house in Miller's Court on the 9th November. And the circumstances of that crime disposed of all the theories of the amateur 'Sherlock Holmses' of that date.

One did not need to be a Sherlock Holmes to discover that the criminal was a sexual maniac of a virulent type; that he was living in the immediate vicinity of the scenes of the murders; and that, if he was not living absolutely alone, his people knew of his guilt, and refused to give him up to justice. During my absence abroad the Police had made a house-to-house search for him, investigating the case of every man in the district whose circumstances were such that he could go and come and get rid of his blood-stains in secret. And the conclusion we came to was that he and his people were low-class Jews, for it is a remarkable fact that people of that class in the East End will not give up one of their number to Gentile justice.

And the result proved that our diagnosis was right on every point. For I may say at once that 'undiscovered murders' are rare in London, and the 'Jack-the-Ripper' crimes are not within that category. And if the Police here had powers such as the French Police possess, the murderer would have been brought to justice. Scotland Yard can boast that not even the subordinate officers of the department will tell tales out of school, and it would ill become me to violate the unwritten rule of the service. The subject will come up again, and I will only add here that the 'Jack-the-Ripper' letter which is preserved in the Police Museum at New Scotland Yard is the creation of an enterprising London journalist [Footnote – Having regard to the interest attaching to this case, I should almost be tempted to disclose the identity of the murderer and of the pressman who wrote the letter above referred to, provided that the publishers would accept all responsibility in view of a possible libel action. But no public benefit would result from such a course, and the traditions of my old department would suffer. I will only add that when the individual whom we suspected was caged in an asylum, the only person who had ever had a good view of the murderer at once identified him, but when he learned that the suspect was a fellow-Jew he declined to swear to him.][20]

March 1910

Sir Robert Anderson – When I stated that the murderer was a Jew I was stating a simple matter of fact. It is not a matter of theory. I should be the last man in the world to say anything reflecting on the Jews as a community, but what is true of Christians is equally true of Jews – that there are some people who have lapsed from all that is good and proper. We have 'lapsed masses' among Christians. We cannot talk of 'lapsed masses' among Jews, but there are cliques of them in the East-end, and it is a notorious fact that there is a stratum of Jews who will not give up their people.

In stating what I do about the Whitechapel murders, I am not speaking as an expert in crime, but as a man who investigates the facts. Moreover, the man who identified the murderer was a Jew, but on learning that the criminal was a Jew he refused to proceed with his identification. As for the suggestion that I intended to cast any reflection on the Jews anyone who has read my books on Biblical exegesis will know the high estimate I have of Jews religiously.[21]

'Mentor', writing on 11 March in the *Jewish Chronicle*, responded angrily to Anderson, saying if he felt the identity of the murderer was a 'fact' Anderson would have done better to keep it to himself in view of the anti-Semitism prevalent in society. No good purpose was served by revealing it, 'Mentor' added. It would have sufficed merely to say that he was 'satisfied the murderer was discovered'. 'Mentor' felt that the murderer was a lunatic and thus, it was irrelevant whether he was also a Jew. However, his main objection was Anderson's claim that 'Jews who knew that "Jack the Ripper" had done his foul deeds, shielded him from the police, and guarded him so that he could continue his horrible career, just because he was a Jew.' It was also significant to note that despite Anderson's assertion that the 'man was "proved" to be the murderer, and upon that point he spoke facts'. the suspect was never tried; 'Mentor' 'would hesitate to brand even such a creature Sir Robert describes as the author of the Ripper crimes upon the very strongest of evidence short of a conviction after due trial'.

April 1910

Edmund Reid, ex-Detective Inspector – What should we do if it could be proved beyond all doubt that 'Jack the Ripper' was dead? We should have to fall back upon the big gooseberry or the sea serpent for stock. Some years ago the late Major Arthur Griffiths, in his book, 'Mysteries of Crime and Police' [*sic*], endeavoured to prove that 'Jack's' body was found floating in the Thames seven weeks after the last Whitechapel murder on the last day of the year 1888. Considering that there were nine murders said to have been committed by 'Jack the Ripper', I think it wonderful that the man's body should have been found in the Thames before the first of the murders were committed [*sic*]. I carried on a correspondence through the newspapers with a writer who signed himself 'Unofficial', who tried to prove that 'Jack the Ripper', Neill Cream, and Klosowski, alias Chapman, were all the same individual. I pointed out that both Neill Cream and Klosowski were poisoners, and that to compare their work with 'Jack the Ripper's' was like comparing the work of a watchmaker with that of a bricklayer. 'Unofficial' finished up by stating that he obtained his information from Major Griffiths' book, and expressed a wish to hear about what the Major, who was then alive, had to say about it. There was no response. Thus the matter ended. Now we have Sir Robert Anderson saying that 'Jack the Ripper' was a Jew. That I challenge him to prove; and, what is more, it was never suggested at the time of the murders.

Next we have a solicitor stating that 'Jack the Ripper' was an Irishman, who had been educated for the medical profession, worked as a fireman on a cattle boat, and was arrested in the very act of mutilating a woman. That is news indeed. Then we come to a statement from Dr. Forbes Winslow, who professes to know all about 'Jack the Ripper', and states that the last Whitechapel murder committed was that of Alice McKenzie in July, 1889. The Doctor is a bit out in his statement; the last murder was Frances Coles in Swallow Gardens on 13th February, 1891. Much has been said and written which is not true about certain mutilations having characterised these murders, and if Dr. Baxter [*sic*] Phillips, who held the post-mortems in conjunction with Dr. Percy Clark, was still alive, he would confirm my statement. Dr. Clark, who resides in Spital-square, is still alive, and knows what I write is true. The number of descriptions that have been given of 'Jack the Ripper' are truly astonishing, but I challenge anyone to prove that there was a tittle of evidence against man, woman or child in connexion with the murders, as no man was ever seen in the company of the women who were found dead.[22]

Reid was a very important police player in the Ripper investigation and it is a great pity that his own statement is so flawed and error strewn, reducing the authority of the valid points he makes. His mistake about the body being found in the Thames 'before the first of the murders were committed' is inexcusable – his own words give the lie to that. It is also strange that he identified the last Ripper victim as Coles when the police appear to have dismissed that possibility at the time. Could this be a confusion of 'the Ripper murders' with the total of eleven Whitechapel killings contained in the police files, or did he really feel she was the last victim?

Reid's statement dismisses Anderson's claim that the murderer was a Jew, saying that this was 'never suggested at the time'.[23] He states that there was never any proof against anyone and adds that 'no man was ever seen in the company of the women who were found dead', ignoring or dismissing such witnesses as Elizabeth Long, Israel Schwartz, Lawende, Levy and Harris, and Hutchinson, without so much as a mention. Reid's statement merely serves to add to the overall impression that there was no police consensus on the facts of the murders and that many senior police officials had their own ideas on the Ripper's identity. Reid was honest enough to admit that he had no clue about who the killer was.

May 1910

The *East London Observer* of Saturday 14 May 1910, the time when Anderson's revelations were enjoying publicity, carried an article with the title 'The Whitechapel Murders – Theories as to the Perpetrator – Interview with Dr. Percy Clark'. Clark was an interesting local figure who had been in the East End for many years. During the Whitechapel murders he was assistant to Dr Phillips, the divisional police surgeon, and was based then, as he continued to be in 1910, at 2 Spital Square. He assisted at the post-mortems Phillips carried out on the victims. On the death of Phillips in 1897 Percy Clark took over the practice. According to the newspaper's representative Dr Clark had spoken freely on the subject:

> At the time of the murders, however, both Dr. Phillips and he were, naturally, reserved on the subject, and even now Dr. Clark thinks it better to let the matter rest. In view of the recent publicity given to the theories as to the perpetrator of the crimes, our representative called on Dr Clark, who in this interview for the first time gives his views on the matter.
>
> He pointed out that during the scare all sorts of stories were spread through the newspapers, and every murder that was perpetrated was attributed to 'Jack the Ripper'. For instance, a headless and armless woman was found and her death was attributed to him. But this case, Dr. Clark points out, in no way resembled those in Dorset-street and Hanbury-street.
>
> 'All the Ripper murders,' he said, 'were similar in character, and they were all the work of a homicidal maniac. The victims were unfortunate women of the lowest type. It is my idea that the perpetrator was a man who had become insane – probably a man of the lowest class.'
>
> 'One of the suppositions was that he was a medical student, or something of that sort?'
>
> 'There was nothing of a professional character about these wounds. The bodies were simply slashed about from head to foot.'

Dr Clark was in possession of a photograph of Mary Kelly's body, which he showed to the pressman to prove his case:

> 'Mr. Phillips,' said Dr. Clark, 'did not believe in publishing details of these cases. The reporters never got the least information from him, so that a great many of the details were pure imagination.

'I say he was a man not in a decent position in life, because, however low a man of that kind sinks, he would be chary of consorting with these women. If he were a sailor or a man on a cattle boat – as has been suggested – he would not be. In one case there was exhibited a certain knowledge of butchery or of killing animals, judging from the way the body was disembowelled. But there was never any justification for the suggestion that the culprit was a professional man. The Dorset-street murder was done inside a room, so that he had plenty of time. The others were committed in a court or street.'

'Do you think they were all the work of one man?'

'I am not so certain of that. You see, if you publish details of cases of that kind – and all the evidence at the inquests appeared in the papers – a weak-minded individual will be induced to emulate the crime, which was evidently done with a butcher's knife or a table. Because of this it was thought the deeds were perpetrated by a butcher or someone acquainted with the killing or cleaning of animals. It need not necessarily have been a butcher, because so many people can do that work.'

Asked if he thought one man was responsible for all the murders, Dr. Clark said: 'I think perhaps one man was responsible for three of them. I would not like to say he did the others.'

'It is surely a remarkable thing that the police could get no clue.'

'Not in the least. No one is more cunning than a maniac. Then, again, he would be one of the low type, of which you see thousands loafing about the streets.'

'Isn't it rather curious that he should not have revealed himself in some way since?'

'No. Anything may have happened to him. He may have died or got shut up in a lunatic asylum.'

'Possibly he may have no recollection of having done the deeds?'

'Possibly not.'

'Nothing like that kind of slashing as done by the murderer has ever occurred before or since.'

'No; I don't think so.'

'Mr. George R. Sims states that the man committed suicide.'

'That is really supposition. As far as I heard – and I think I heard most about the cases – there was never the slightest clue to anybody. The whole thing was theory.'

'And I suppose it will remain so?'

'It will remain so, because you could not believe the word of the man who committed these crimes even if he told you. You have only to look at that photograph to see that it is the work of a homicidal maniac.'

Clark had been with Dr Phillips and had seen most of the bodies. It is therefore interesting to note he felt that as few as three victims could be attributed to the Ripper.

June 1912

Hargrave L. Adam, a criminological writer of some note, had many police contacts, including Sir Robert Anderson – Sir Rbt. Anderson has assured the writer that the assassin was well known to the police but, unfortunately, in the absence of sufficient *legal* evidence to justify an arrest, they were unable to take him. It was a case of moral versus legal proof. . . . Sir Robt. Anderson states confidently that he was a low-class Jew, being shielded by his fraternity. . . .

Sir Henry Smith pooh-poohs this, declaring with equal confidence that he was a Gentile. He further states that the writing on the wall was probably a mere 'blind', although the writing itself might have afforded a valuable clue. One thing is certain, namely, the elusive assassin, whoever he was, possessed an anatomical knowledge. This, therefore, leads one pretty surely to the conclusion that he was a medical man, or one who had formerly been a medical student.[24]

1912

Sir Robert Anderson – So again with the 'Whitechapel murders' of 1888. Despite the lucubrations of many an amateur 'Sherlock Holmes', there was no doubt whatever as to the identity of the criminal, and if our London 'detectives' possessed the powers, and might have recourse to the methods of Foreign Police Forces, he would have been brought to justice. But the guilty sometimes escape through the working of a system designed to protect innocent persons wrongly accused of crime. And many a case which is used to disparage our British 'detectives' ought rather to be hailed as a proof of the scrupulous fairness with which they discharge their duties.[25]

June 1913

Sir Melville Macnaghten – Sir Melville confessed that the greatest regret of his life was that he joined the force six months after 'Jack the Ripper' committed suicide. 'That remarkable man,' he said, 'was one of the most fascinating of criminals. Of course he was a maniac, but I have a very clear idea who he was and how he committed suicide, but that, with other secrets, will never be revealed by me.

DESTROYED SECRETS.

'I have destroyed all my documents, and there is now no record of the secret information which came into my possession at one time or another.'[26]

September 1913

John George Littlechild, ex-Detective Inspector, Special Branch – Amongst the suspects, and to my mind a very likely one, was a Dr. T. . . . He was an American quack named Tumblety and was at one time a frequent visitor to London and on these occasions constantly brought under the notice of police, there being a large dossier concerning him at Scotland Yard. Although a 'Sycopathia Sexualis' subject he was not known as a 'Sadist' (which the murderer unquestionably was) but his feelings towards women were remarkable and bitter in the extreme, a fact on record. Tumblety was arrested at the time of the murders in connection with unnatural offences and charged at Marlborough Street, remanded on bail, jumped his bail, and got away to Boulogne and was never heard of afterwards. It was believed he committed suicide but certain it is that from this time the 'Ripper' murders came to an end.

It is finished – except that I knew Major Griffiths for many years. He probably got his information from Anderson who only thought he knew.[27]

June 1929

The *Sunday News* of 2 June 1929 reported on the memoirs of another retired police officer. This time it was ex-Chief Inspector Tom Divall of New Scotland Yard who had just published *Scoundrels & Scallywags & some honest men*. The piece was headed 'MEMOIRS OF A C.I.D. MAN. Chief Inspector Who Tried To Solve "Jack the Ripper" Mystery'. Despite the prominent mention of the name, there is very little in the book about the Ripper. Divall was a very junior officer at the time of the Whitechapel murders and does not appear to have played

Dr Francis Tumblety, the American quack doctor named by
ex-Chief Inspector Littlechild as 'amongst the suspects' and
to his mind, 'a very likely one'.

any part in the hunt for the Ripper. He
was involved in the investigation of the
murder of PC Thompson and made the
mistaken claim that Thompson was
'the only constable who ever saw Jack
the Ripper'. It was Thompson, of
course, who discovered the body of
Frances Coles in Swallow Gardens in
February 1891 and, as a brief perusal
of the police documents will show,
Thompson saw no one at all, but had
merely heard footsteps hastening away
just before he discovered the body. Also,
this murder was never seriously regarded as
a Ripper crime. Divall's work is an example of
how misleading some police officers' memoirs can
be. He mentions the Ripper murders on pages 126–7
of his book, noting that:

> The 'Ripper' murders gave us no end of worry and anxiety. They caused the greatest
> sensation throughout the civilized world and, I think, frightened the general public more
> than any other crimes yet known. . . . It seemed to me that this madman was obsessed
> with the idea that these corrupted women were spreading disease to other persons, and
> in order to prevent this he undertook this foul work, which I believe resulted in the death
> of seven of these unfortunates within the space of about three years. We have never
> found any trace of this man, or of any connection of his, nor have we been able to
> ascertain definitely the end of him. The much lamented and late Assistant Commissioner
> of the C.I.D., Sir Melville Macnaghten, received some information that the murderer had
> gone to America and died in a lunatic asylum there. This perhaps may be correct, for
> after this news nothing was ever heard of any similar crime being committed.

1956

In August 1888 the situation was warming up in the political sense as sections of the press
took every opportunity to attack officialdom. The Parnell Commission was looming and the
Irish problem was still the main topic of the day. The police were about to experience an
unprecedented spate of unsolved murders on the streets and word of an American Fenian
assassination plot had just been received. Queen Victoria wrote in her journal from her
secluded and pleasant surroundings on the Isle of Wight:

> OSBORNE, 11th Aug. 1888. – A very hot night, but the day cooler than yesterday. Saw
> Lord Salisbury and talked with him of many things, of Germany, Russia, Ireland, but
> he was sorry to say the Government had had notice from America of a plot to kill
> Mr. Balfour, which is terrible, and he has to be well watched.

This is particularly significant in view of a remark contained in Douglas G. Browne's book *The Rise of Scotland Yard* (1956),[28] in which he commented on suspects for the Ripper murders: 'A third head of the C.I.D., Sir Melville Macnaghten, appears to identify the Ripper with the leader of a plot to assassinate Mr. Balfour at the Irish Office.' Detail contained in Browne's book makes it apparent that he had access to the closed Scotland Yard files on the murders at a time when much material that later went missing was still in the archive. In view of Macnaghten's publicly stated preference for M.J. Druitt as a suspect, this could indicate that he had in fact noted another view as to the identity of the killer and that this was recorded in the official files. Littlechild was head of the Special Branch from 1883 to 1893 and had particular interest in Irish matters so it may be significant that he disclosed the name of Tumblety, an Irish-American with Fenian sympathies, as a 'very likely' suspect. Littlechild stated that there was a 'large dossier' on Tumblety at Scotland Yard. This would probably have been a Special Branch file that was never released to the public archives and it could be the location of the Macnaghten reference quoted by Browne. It is also important to note that there are Special Branch files relating to the Whitechapel murders that are closed 'in perpetuity'. They are not likely to contain evidence that proves the identity of Jack the Ripper but they must include some very interesting and enlightening information.

SIXTEEN

Did Anderson Know?

PERHAPS the most enigmatic, and certainly one of the most important, senior police officers involved in the investigation of the Whitechapel murders was Assistant Commissioner Robert Anderson. Many theorists have long regarded him as the best source offering an identification of Jack the Ripper and, to a degree, this may be true. Appointed head of the Metropolitan Police CID at the very start of the Ripper scare, he was, and remains, the only high-ranking officer actually to claim that the identity of the Ripper was known to the police. Anderson was absent from the country when most of the Ripper-related murders were committed. He left on 7 September 1888, the day before the Chapman murder, and did not return until 6 October, after the Stride and Eddowes murders. He took charge of the investigation on his return.

Anderson's claims have received additional support since 1987 as a result of the publication of annotations, now popularly known as 'the Swanson Marginalia', made by ex-Chief Inspector Donald Swanson in his copy of Anderson's book, *The Lighter Side of My Official Life* (1910). (Now deposited in New Scotland Yard's Crime Museum.) There are one or two discrepancies but, by and large, Swanson's notes appear to agree with what Anderson says, and even confirm that Anderson's Polish Jew suspect was 'Kosminski'. (Anderson mentions no name, though, of course, Kosminski was also identified as a suspect by Chief Constable Macnaghten in 1894.) This results in supporters of Anderson's theory claiming that Swanson endorsed Sir Robert's opinion that the Ripper case was solved. However, it is not quite as simple as that.

In view of his claims, Anderson's character, reliability and truthfulness have been subjected to close scrutiny. Those who have based their theorising on Anderson's words have, of course, sought to establish that he was beyond reproach. Therefore, anything he said must be able to be regarded as fact, or at least as what Anderson genuinely believed. A very religious man to the point of bigotry, Anderson was dogmatic, inclined to be pompous, a name-dropper and not above boasting. But the crucial question is, can we accept his bold claim that the Ripper was a poor Polish Jew? Should we believe that this is as close as we may ever hope to come to identifying the killer?

A nice portrait of Donald Swanson during his retirement in later years. It was in this period that he wrote his famous 'marginalia' naming Anderson's suspect. (*Courtesy of the late Jim Swanson*)

Those who do not accept Anderson's credentials as flawless, and who do not believe in the guilt of Anderson's suspect, usually indicate that Sir Robert was suffering from a faulty memory and inhabiting a world of wishful dreams.[1] Some have suggested that Anderson was suffering from self-delusion or even lying. Anderson's supporters say that he may have been dogmatic but he was not a liar, that statements in his published 'memoirs' are demonstrably correct and that he 'had a peculiarly scrupulous regard for the truth and would never have lied directly'.[2] Given all the secret service work Anderson was involved in over the years, it is hard to imagine that he did not frequently resort to deception and untruths of one sort and another.

In the case of the Whitechapel murders, it is his published works that are quoted in support of his truthfulness and accuracy. So it is to Anderson's semi-autobiographical *The Lighter Side of My Official Life* of 1910 that we must turn to assess these claims. In his book Anderson repeated most of what he had published in serial form earlier in the year in *Blackwood's Magazine*, although there were some minor variations. It will be remembered that it was in *Blackwood's* that Anderson made the specific claim that the identity of the Ripper was known and that the murderer had been identified by a Jewish witness who had refused to testify.

Significantly, the book contains an important example of Anderson's ability to make misleading statements. In late December 1888 Anderson went to extraordinary lengths, including a personal visit to the mortuary to see the body, to try to influence the medical men to state that the death of Rose Mylett was one of 'natural causes' rather than another unsolved murder. There was little reason to suppose that she was another Ripper victim, although certain newspapers tried to suggest she was, and the cause of death, strangulation, lent itself to the possible interpretation of 'accidental choking'. However, the divisional surgeon, Dr Matthew Brownfield of 171 East India Dock Road, who carried out the post-mortem examination, remained adamant that this was a case of murder by strangulation. The scene had been attended by Dr Brownfield's assistant, Dr Harris, who also assisted at the post-mortem. The surgeon-in-chief for the Metropolitan Police, Dr Alexander O. MacKellar, agreed with the conclusions drawn. But there followed an extraordinary sequence of events: Anderson, and doctors called at his request, all attended the mortuary to examine the body.

At the inquest, doctors Brownfield, Harris, Hebbert (A Division Surgeon Dr Thomas Bond's assistant) and MacKellar all gave evidence supporting the fact that the woman had been murdered. Sole dissentient in their ranks was Dr Thomas Bond who, although he initially believed this to be a case of strangulation, made a further late examination under Anderson's direction and changed his opinion. Although Coroner Wynne Baxter complained of the involvement of so many doctors and the police, he appeared to favour the idea that it was a death from 'natural causes'. The jury, no doubt influenced by the preponderance of medical evidence, returned a verdict of 'wilful murder against some person or persons unknown'. The Mylett file was then added to the Whitechapel murders series and remained on Scotland Yard's books as an unsolved killing.

On 11 January 1889 Anderson submitted a six-page report to James Monro about the inquest and its verdict. Anderson dogmatically pronounced:

> The Supt. has come to this Office to ask instructions in view of this verdict. I have thought it only fair to him and his officers to tell him plainly that neither the evidence given at the inquest, nor the verdict arrived at, affects the judgment I formed when I personally investigated the case on the 22nd ult:, and that I did not intend to take any further action in the matter.
>
> Having regard to the Coroner's strictures upon the action of the Police, it may be well to place the facts on record. . . .
>
> Mr. Brownfield made a P.M: on the morning of the 21st and formed the opinion that the woman had been murdered; but this was not communicated to the Police. The first intimation I had of it was derived from the report of the inquest in the Evening Paper, which I took up after midnight on the 21st on my return from a surprise visit to Whitechapel.
>
> Next morning I brought the matter before you, and by your desire I went to Poplar to investigate the case personally, writing to Mr. Bond to meet me there. Mr. Bond, however, was unfortunately out of town for the day.

The statements of the officers who found the body, and especially of P.S. Golding, who impressed me as being an exceptionally safe and reliable witness, seemed so incompatible with the theory of murder that I brought them to the scene of the death, and finally undertook the distasteful task of going on to the mortuary and examining the body myself.

As the result I came to the conclusion that the death had not been caused by homicidal violence.

It is interesting to see that Anderson had personally viewed the already autopsied body and convinced himself that it was a case of 'death by natural causes'. He totally ignored the opinions of the medical men involved and decided to call in his own favoured police surgeon, Dr Bond. Anderson wrote:

Mr. Bond's assistant, Mr. Hibbert [*sic* – Hebbert], had opened my note to Mr. Bond, and (unfortunately I think) decided to act for him in the case. He thus arrived at Poplar soon after I left the mortuary, and made a second P:M: on the body.

In ignorance of this, I made such representations to you on my return to Whitehall that you asked the Chief Surgeon to go down himself; and he reached Poplar just after Mr. Hibbert had left. Finally Mr. Bond went down next day to verify Mr. Hibbert's notes.

All three Doctor's confirmed Mr. Brownfield's view of the case, and Mr. Bond and Mr. Hibbert called on me on the 24th with a report to that effect.

Anderson was dissatisfied with the doctors' conclusions. Although Bond agreed with the others that this was a case of murder, Anderson was having none of it:

After a long conference, in which I pressed my difficulties and objections, I referred them to you. But that same afternoon Mr. Bond went again to Poplar to make a more careful examination of the woman's neck, and he returned to tell me he had entirely altered his view of the case, and was satisfied that though death was due to strangulation, it was produced accidentally and not by homicidal violence.

This is the basis of the Coroner's complaint that 'the Asst. Comr. Sent down Doctor after Doctor without his sanction'; and this claim on the part of the Coroner to control the action of the Police in cases of supposed homicide raises a question of such great practical importance that I think an authoritative decision upon it should be obtained.

Moving forward to 1910 and the publication of *The Lighter Side of My Official Life*, Anderson states in a footnote on page 137: 'And the Poplar case of December, 1888, was a death from natural causes, and but for the "Jack the Ripper" scare, no one would have thought of suggesting that it was a homicide.' Anderson was clearly still firm in his belief that the Mylett case was not one of wilful murder. Is this a case of faulty memory, confusion of facts or wishful thinking? Or is it, more seriously, a case of deliberate falsehood? Perhaps an unshakeable faith in his own thought processes led him to regard his interpretation as the correct one. It is hard to imagine that Anderson had completely forgotten the almost farcical comings and goings at the mortuary in 1888. Anyone who uses his book as their reference for information on the Poplar crime will come away believing that it was not a crime at all. This example alone shows that Anderson's word in his published works should not be accepted as accurate without corroboration.

With regard to the possibility that he was suffering from faulty memory, confusion due to age or wishful thinking in 1910, Anderson has again been assessed. The argument is put forward that he had stated his Polish Jew theory as far back as the early 1890s. However, the early references do seem to refer only to a theory; the more dogmatic claim that the Ripper case was solved and the killer's identity known did not appear until 1910. So did Anderson's theory change into hard fact in his mind when he was aged about 70? Well, we are at least able to show that at that time his memory had begun to fail him.

In the early twentieth century Hargrave Lee Adam, a criminological author of some note, wrote extensively on celebrated cases and police matters. He knew Anderson well and often quoted him. Anderson also wrote the introduction to Adam's 1912 work, *The Police Encyclopaedia*. One of Adam's later books, *C.I.D.: Behind the Scenes at Scotland Yard* provides a unique insight into Anderson the man:

Sir Robert Anderson, the only police officer to claim that the identity of the Ripper was known to him. Some say that he was telling the truth and actually did know of a positive identification of the killer. But was he mistaken, indulging in wishful thinking, suffering from bad memory or confusion in old age, or simply deceiving his readers?

The first figure that comes into my mind's eye is that of a tall, vigorous-looking man, with a determined expression of countenance and a Victorian habit of dressing. He is emphatic in speech and prolific in delivery. His rugged face is enlivened by his superabundant energy. He is rather deaf and challenges you in a declamatory voice to 'Speak Up!' He has a keen, rather a grim sense of humour which, when he indulges it, is accompanied by a demure and self-satisfied grin.[3]

Highly relevant to Anderson's supposed identification of Jack the Ripper was his pet theory on the difference between moral and legal proof. Adam continues:

He was never tired of referring to this, because he said that he felt keenly the injustice done to the police when they failed to catch and convict a criminal against whom there was a lack of legal proof. He said that the public did not understand this. He was right. They don't. . . .

I remember on one occasion how Sir Robert positively thrilled me while relating an incident which occurred during his term of office, and which illustrated his argument as to the difference between moral and legal proof. There had been a mysterious murder in the West End, and as no clue had been left behind by the culprit the police were at a loss. A woman had been strangled in bed. A certain man, a relation of the dead woman, was very abusive towards the police for failing to arrest the murderer. In fact he was so active in his hostility that he aroused Sir Robert's suspicions. So he decided to apply a test. He gave orders that this man should be summoned to Scotland Yard, and that he should be shown into his, Sir Robert's, private room. Then, with the man seated in front of him, and nobody but their two selves in the room, the Commissioner, fixing a steady gaze upon his visitor, declared that the murderer had been found.

The man turned deathly pale and trembled in his chair, but said nothing. Then Sir Robert went on to describe how a test had been applied to the eye of the dead woman. A photograph, a 'close-up' photograph, had been taken of one of the eyes, with the result that a clear image of the murderer was found imprinted upon the dead woman's retina! It was partly an invention. Such an experiment had in fact been made, but proved futile. However, the man did not know. 'Then', exclaimed Sir Robert, 'I was morally certain that I had the murderer before me!'

Nothing, however, unfortunately could be done. It was merely moral and not legal evidence. So the murderer went unpunished. Of course the police were blamed. But were they to blame?[4]

It may come as a surprise to those with a legal background to hear that a qualified lawyer, and high-ranking police officer, could speak in such terms. Merely by observing a man's reaction, Anderson had found him categorically guilty. Anyone sitting in the presence of an assistant commissioner of Scotland Yard who was implying he was a murderer would surely be uneasy, even frightened. There could have been several reasons for the man's reactions, not least the fact that he was close to the dead woman and may have been very upset by the words he was hearing.

Anderson frequently stated, apropos of the failure to bring the Ripper to justice, that if the English police had powers such as their French counterparts possessed, then 'the murderer would have been brought to justice'. He enlarged on the French method:

it sometimes happens that the murderer is known, but evidence is wholly wanting. In such circumstances the French Police would arrest the suspected person, and build up a case against him at their leisure, mainly by admissions extracted from him in repeated interrogations.[5]

Perhaps more relevant to the subject of this chapter are the following remarks of Adam in relation to Anderson's memory and apparent confusion when recalling past cases. This, in addition to the 1908 *Daily Chronicle* article (see chapter 15), seems to add strength to the idea that Anderson's memory may have been unreliable:

> Sir Robert was sometimes rather mysterious. For instance I find in one of his letters to me the following curious paragraph: 'You have no idea how I am watched and criticised as regards my acts and words. And if your new book should contain (as it seems likely to do) matter such as made me shy of your *Woman and Crime*,[6] I should be swamped by the correspondence it would bring me.'
>
> I had asked Sir Robert to write a Preface for a book in which I had dealt with a certain phase of the sex question, although, I trusted, with discretion and reserve, I have never been able to quite understand what his words meant. His memory also apparently began to fail him, and he fell into the error of mixing cases. For instance, in reference to the Penge murder which I was discussing with him, he said, or rather wrote, 'I am too tired to-night to recall it. But I think it was a nightdress that the officer was put to watch –its hiding-place having been discovered, and when he awoke it was gone, carried off, they supposed, by Alice Rhodes.'
>
> He was clearly mixing up the Penge case with that of the Road murder, in which a woman's nightdress figured prominently.[7]

Here we have positive evidence that Sir Robert Anderson's memory may have been flawed and untrustworthy. It is evidence from someone who knew the man and must surely indicate that less reliance should be placed on Anderson's word when assessing the value of his thoughts about a suspect for the Whitechapel murders. This reference can be dated to 1914 – the remark that Anderson makes as to 'how I am watched and criticised as regards my acts and words' can be explained in the light of the 1910 controversy in the House of Commons over his admission that he wrote the anonymous *Times* Parnell articles in 1887 which nearly led to his losing his pension. All this is not intended to vilify Anderson, nor to show him in a bad light. Indeed, most of what he wrote can be shown to be correct and of value to the historian. But the admixture of accuracy and assumed facts can be dangerous.

One of the most crucial aspects of Sir Robert Anderson's claim that the identity of Jack the Ripper was a 'definitely ascertained fact' is the alleged identification of the 'poor Polish Jew' suspect by a Jewish witness who then refused to give evidence. As unlikely and extraordinary as this claim may sound, the nature of its source means we should treat it seriously. It is therefore necessary to identify both the suspect and the witness.

It is difficult to believe that the attempted identification of a suspect as Jack the Ripper could take place with no surviving official record and with no mention ever being made by anyone who was party to that identification. Anderson never named his Polish Jew but there seems to be little doubt that the suspect he referred to was Kosminski, mentioned by Macnaghten in his 1894 report concerning Cutbush. Ascertaining the identity of the witness is not so easy. Two men have been suggested as fitting the bill. They are: Israel

Schwartz, the Hungarian Jew who witnessed an attack on Elizabeth Stride in Berner Street some 15 minutes before her body was found; and Joseph Lawende, the German Jew who allegedly saw Catherine Eddowes with a man at the Duke Street entrance to Mitre Square (Church Passage) shortly before her murder. Both qualify for consideration because both saw a suspect with a victim (assuming both women were Ripper victims) shortly before a murder. In the case of Schwartz, it is not known whether he could have recognised his man if he had seen him again, but Lawende stated he did not think he would be able to make an identification. In relation to both men, it is the closeness of the sighting to the known time of the discovery of a body that makes it possible both, or either, saw the killer. Schwartz saw his man at 12.45 a.m. at the site of the murder and the body was found about 1 a.m.; Lawende made his sighting at about 1.37 a.m. near to the site of the murder and the body was found at 1.45 a.m.

The validity and reliability of a modern witness's account are judged against the following criteria: ambient visibility, distance of subjects from the witness, duration of the sighting, attention paid to the subjects, health and reliability of the witness, and quality of the witness's memory. Unfortunately, at this remove in time these factors cannot be accurately estimated – the surviving record is all that remains to judge them by. However, there is one piece of evidence which, if it is correct, suggests the witness Anderson referred to was Lawende. It dates from February 1891 and involves the victim Frances Coles and the suspect for her murder, James Sadler. Crucially, the police at first thought this murder might be another in the Ripper series and, therefore, that Sadler might be the Ripper.

On Saturday 14 February 1891, the day of Sadler's arrest, the *Daily Chronicle* reported: 'At three o'clock the authorities circulated an announcement that the crime was supposed to be the work of "Jack the Ripper", and ordered all docks, wharves, and stairs to be searched.' The *Evening News and Post* of the same date enlarged on the story:

> In the minds of the police officials who have been summoned to investigate the murder there is now practically no doubt that it is the handiwork of the terrible miscreant who has earned the name of 'Jack the Ripper'. All important details correspond, and the absence of fiendish mutilation is only to be accounted for by the supposition that the murderer was interrupted before the completion of his full intentions. The selection of the scene of the tragedy, the appearance of the victim, and the way in which her death was brought about all correspond with the series of mysterious and as yet totally unexplained crimes which was thought to have been closed with the discovery in September, 1889, of the trunk of a woman in Pinchin-street. It should be stated, however, that there was some doubt as to whether this discovery had any connection with the previous murders; and making allowance for this uncertainty, the record of the crimes included eight outrages. The one brought to light this morning is therefore the ninth. So far as can be ascertained, the facts upon which the police are at present able to base their inquiries are of a meagre character.

It is unlikely that the police would have risked causing another panic in London if they did not seriously think that the Ripper might have been at work again. Sadler was soon subjected to a series of identification parades where he was seen by various witnesses.

The report of a Jewish witness and a failed attempt to identify Sadler as Jack the Ripper is to be found on page 4 of the *Daily Telegraph* of Wednesday 18 February 1891. The story ran thus:

It was yesterday proved that the Treasury authorities attach the greatest importance to the arrest of the ship's fireman, Sadler, who is in custody for the murder of Frances Coles, aged 25, in Swallow-gardens, on Friday morning last. At the resumed inquest Mr. Charles Mathews, instructed by Mr. Pollard, was present to examine the witnesses, with the permission of the Coroner, Mr. Wynne Baxter, who whilst assenting to arrangement, seemed impressed with its unprecedented character. Further, it is certain that the police are not neglecting the facts which came to light in connection with the previous murders. Probably the only trustworthy description of the assassin was that given by a gentleman who, on the night of the Mitre-square murder, noticed in Duke-street, Aldgate, a couple standing under the lamp at the corner of the passage leading to Mitre-square. The woman was identified as one victim of that night, Sept. 30, the other having been killed half an hour previously in Berner-street. The man was described as 'aged from thirty to thirty-five; height 5ft 7in, with brown hair and big moustache; dressed respectably. Wore pea jacket, muffler, and a cloth cap with a peak of the same material.' The witness has confronted Sadler and has failed to identify him.

This report leaves no doubt that the witness referred to, and used, was Joseph Lawende, and that he failed to identify the suspect. No hard evidence against Sadler, either for the Coles murder or the Ripper crimes, was ever found and he was released on 3 March 1891. Another point to bear in mind is that on 7 February, less than a month earlier and less than a week before Coles died, the putative Ripper suspect Aaron Kosminski entered permanent incarceration when he was detained as an imbecile.

The events of 7 to 17 February throw up a remarkable series of coincidences. Anderson's suspect was almost certainly Kosminski and *a* Kosminski *had* been detained very shortly before Sadler's arrest and investigation as a possible Ripper suspect. Aaron Kosminski was permanently 'caged in an asylum' and shortly after his detention there was a failed attempt to identify a suspect (Sadler) as Jack the Ripper by a Jewish witness, Joseph Lawende. These circumstances tally very closely with Anderson's words:

> I will only add that when the individual whom we suspected was caged in an asylum, the only person who had ever had a good view of the murderer at once identified him, but when he learned that the suspect was a fellow-Jew he declined to swear to him.[8]

And:

> I will merely add that the only person who had ever had a good view of the murderer unhesitatingly identified the suspect the instant he was confronted with him; but he refused to give evidence against him.[9]

It may benefit the reader to pause and consider the implications of this coincidence. Over two years after the last generally accepted Ripper killing (Kelly) we have a Polish Jew lunatic named Kosminski locked up and within a week a Ripper suspect is subjected to a failed identification as the Ripper by a Jewish witness. If the attempted identification took place as described by Anderson, then it is interesting to note that he used the word 'confronted' as opposed to a reference to picking the suspect out of a formal line-up. Identification by confrontation was employed by the police but was not as evidentially valuable as identification from a line-up of usually twelve or more people.

Some who adhere to the theory that the identification took place *exactly* as Anderson described it say that there must have been another witness and that he (probably Schwartz) had been used to identify Kosminski, but was not used again because of his refusal to testify against the Polish Jew. This idea is not tenable. First, as Lawende was used in the attempt to identify Sadler he would, naturally, also have been used in any other attempted identification of a Ripper suspect. Secondly, a witness cannot simply 'refuse to give evidence' if it is required.

Another telling point is the fact that the police believed Sadler was indeed the murderer of Frances Coles (*vide* Macnaghten). We do not know if Lawende at first identified him, but then backtracked and refused to sign a sworn statement to this effect. We know he was not certain that he could identify the man he saw with Eddowes and perhaps he did not want to risk a suspect being convicted on his evidence alone.

Another ingredient is added to the concoction by an odd reference to the attempted identification of Sadler and the refusal of the witness to give evidence. The comment appears in Swanson's annotations to Anderson's book:

> because the suspect was also a Jew and also because his evidence would convict the suspect, and witness would be the means of murderer being hanged which he did not wish to be left on his mind. . . . And after this identification which suspect knew, no other murder of this kind took place in London . . . after the suspect had been identified at the Seaside Home where he had been sent by us[10] with difficulty in order to subject him to identification, and he knew he was identified. On suspect's return to his brother's house in Whitechapel he was watched by police (City CID) by day & night. In a very short time the suspect with his hands tied behind his back, he was sent to Stepney Workhouse and then to Colney Hatch and died shortly afterwards – Kosminski was the suspect – DSS

Swanson's poor grammar here adds another complication. If he was referring to Aaron Kosminski, then the identification in question appears to have taken place in July 1890 whereas Anderson's reference relates to February 1891, the time of Kosminski's final incarceration. And Swanson's suspect died soon after incarceration.[11] So here we have a discrepancy between the two men's stories.

At this juncture it is as well to point out another possibility that exists regarding this confusing issue. Anderson was an assistant commissioner and he did not 'dirty his hands' with 'on the ground' police work. He was based in an office in Scotland Yard and was essentially a supervisor and department head. All his knowledge and information regarding the crimes came direct from his subordinate Donald Swanson. So the whole Polish Jew suspect/failed identification story may have originated with Swanson in the first place. And when Anderson wrote the story in his book his source may well have been Swanson. If this was the case, the one can offer no corroboration of the other, merely repetition. This would also explain Swanson's annotations, in that he was simply correcting, and adding to, his own story as published by Anderson.

Swanson's reference to the man being watched by the 'City CID' is also interesting because the suspect described by Inspector Cox of the City Police (see chapter 15), although apparently a Jew, was clearly not Aaron Kosminski, who had not worked for years, did not occupy a shop, and, so far as we know, did not enter a Surrey asylum.

The mention of an identification at the Seaside Home is truly baffling, and the annotation on the rear flyleaf of Swanson's copy of Anderson's book is the only reference to this incident. It has been assumed Swanson was referring to the Convalescent Police Seaside

Home in Sussex – in police circles this establishment was always referred to as 'the Seaside Home'.[12] But what factors should be considered in relation to this interpretation? After all, there was a similar Jewish Seaside Convalescent Home and many others. Indeed, the usefulness of the statement depends entirely on the flyleaf entry being accurate.

Is there another way that 'the Seaside Home' could have entered the equation? Well, allowing for faulty memories, confusion or deliberate invention, the idea of a 'home' is also to be found in the story of Sadler and his identification. Two of the witnesses who attended identification parades for Sadler were from the Sailors' Home (or Seamen's Home) and here is another telling coincidence. A bedraggled Sadler had finally gravitated to the Sailors' Home in Wells Street while seeking shelter on the morning after the murder of Coles. There he sold a foreign clasp knife to a witness, Duncan Campbell. Campbell attended the police station and identified Sadler as the man who had sold him the knife from a line-up of fifteen or sixteen men dressed as seamen. A second witness from the home, Thomas Johnson, similarly identified Sadler.[13] So even a Sailors' (or Seamen's) Home figures in the Sadler identification scenario (albeit not the failed identification by Lawende) – and Seamen's Home could easily translate to Seaside Home.

Allowing for genuine confusion of memories on the part of Anderson (and/or Swanson), or the possibility of deliberate invention, it is easy to see how the failed attempt to identify Sadler as Jack the Ripper could have evolved into Anderson's identification story. These important considerations have been totally ignored in the past but, as may be seen here, they are very relevant to the potential veracity of Anderson's claims. At best, the story is very unsatisfactory. It certainly cannot, and should not, be taken to mean that the police knew the identity of Jack the Ripper – surviving police files indicate there was no certainty. Anderson's claim is rendered even more unlikely by the fact that his second-in-command, confidential assistant and, ultimately, successor as assistant commissioner, Sir Melville Macnaghten, makes no mention of an identification. In fact, he reached an entirely different conclusion to Anderson and felt that Montague John Druitt was the most likely of the unlikely suspects in his list. This hardly enhances the view that the Polish Jew's guilt was a definitely ascertained fact. And it cannot be claimed that Macnaghten did not know of the Polish Jew Kosminski theory as it is his report in which it is first outlined in the surviving records.

It should also be noted that theorists have suggested 'Anderson's witness' was not Joseph Lawende at all but was in fact Israel Schwartz, the non-English-speaking Hungarian Jew who witnessed an attack on Elizabeth Stride at the murder site in Berner Street. Appealing as this idea may seem, it is apparently negated by the fact that, according to the *Daily Telegraph*, it was Lawende who was used in the attempt to identify Sadler as the Ripper in February 1891. If Schwartz was regarded as a good witness and was still available, there can be no reason why he would not have been called upon, even if he had been used in a previous unrecorded and unsuccessful identification attempt. And, as we have seen, Swanson clearly dismissed both witnesses, Schwartz *and* Lawende, believing them unable to make a positive identification of the Ripper because their sightings did not contain proof that it *was* the killer they saw. In any event an identification by either of them would have amounted merely to supporting circumstantial evidence and not direct evidence of the fact to be proved.

Despite years of research, speculation and writing there has been no satisfactory answer to the conundrum of Anderson's 'identification' of Jack the Ripper. It has to be said that such important an identification of a suspect could not have been conducted with no other official source making mention of it; nor could it have been carried out in such

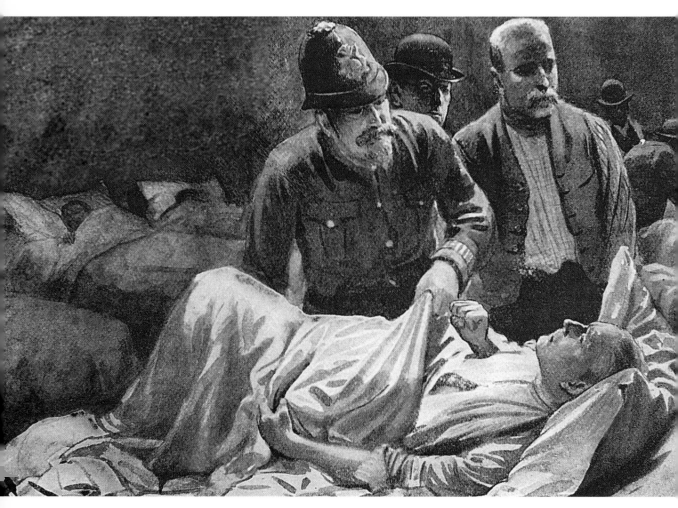

A police constable checking an inmate in a common lodging house as suspects were questioned in the house-to-house search.

secrecy that all the senior police officers of the day (other than Swanson) knew nothing about it. Given that we know no witness saw the Ripper in the act of killing, Anderson's story cannot be taken as a fact, even if what he (and Swanson) says is accepted without qualification.

In Anderson's memoirs, as we have seen, he makes the following statement with regard to his suspect:

> During my absence abroad the Police had made a house-to-house search for him, investigating the case of every man in the district whose circumstances were such that he could go and come and get rid of his blood-stains in secret. And the conclusion we came to was that he and his people were certain low-class Polish Jews; for it is a remarkable fact that people of that class in the East End will not give up one of their number to Gentile justice.

This passage has led some modern theorists to argue that the house-to-house search must have yielded evidence as to the identity of the killer. Anderson was wrong on one point here, for the search was conducted *after* his return from the continent in early October 1888, and not during his absence abroad.[14] We know from the comments of senior officers such as Swanson and Monro, and arguably Anderson himself in 1889, that the police had no clue as to the identity of the murderer. However, it is obvious from Anderson's words that the officers carrying out the house-to-house inquiries, who had been issued with special notebooks for the purpose, must have compiled lists of all males that fitted the criteria given. And there must have been many. It is very likely that Kosminski's name appeared among those listed, but without any special reason to distinguish it from the many others. It is not known exactly when the name Kosminski emerged as a suspect, but it is first mentioned, by Macnaghten, in February 1894. So we must assume that sometime before early 1894, possibly in 1890–91, 'Kosminski' did come into the frame and the lists compiled in October 1888 would then have been checked for his name. This seems to be the most reasonable interpretation of Anderson's words.

Turning to Macnaghten and the witness question, he stated in his 1894 official report that 'No one ever saw the Whitechapel murderer.' This totally contradicts Anderson's later claim that there was a witness who 'had a good view of the murderer'. And of the suspects the police were investigating, Macnaghten says, 'no shadow of proof could be thrown on any one'.[15] This again contradicts Anderson's claim of a positive identification and, for that matter, suggests there was no other sort of evidence either. Moreover, these words appear in an official report that stayed on the police file; Anderson must have seen and been aware of it. In view of this it is impossible to say that Macnaghten supported Anderson's claim in any way.

It is interesting to note that many modern theorists cite Macnaghten's memorandum in its draft version (usually called the Aberconway version) and the almost certainly apocryphal third version quoted by Philip Loftus, which he said he had seen in the early 1950s. Loftus's story was written in 1972 in a review of a new Ripper book, by Daniel Farson.[16] It seems very likely that Loftus had seen the Aberconway version but had misremembered it. His memory appears to have been contaminated by having read Tom Cullen's 1965 book in the interim. (This was based on the Aberconway version.) A comparison of the documents reveals that the majority of errors and anomalous statements by Macnaghten appear in the draft (Aberconway) version and that he apparently removed several of them from the final (official) version. In any final analysis, only the official version of the memorandum should be taken as a true reflection of Macnaghten's considered opinion. It is also relevant to note here that the account of Macnaghten's suspects published by Major Arthur Griffiths in his 1898 *Mysteries of Police and Crime* appears to be taken from Macnaghten's draft version, as the 'police-constable in Mitre Court' witness reference indicates. This reference is missing from the official memorandum so perhaps Macnaghten gave Griffiths the information from his draft version after the official one had been filed away, or merely gave him the details verbally from memory. The mention of a police constable witness in Mitre Court rather than Mitre Square is an obvious error.[17] Yet, some modern writers still attempt to suggest that there was such a police witness and that the official records relating to him are now missing. A reading of all the surviving official reports on this murder plainly shows that no such witness ever existed.

That Anderson chose not to name his suspect, his witness and the reason for his emphatically stated belief (in private or official papers that would have remained confidential for 100 years) is one of the greatest frustrations encountered by researchers and historians interested in this fascinating case. He clearly had his reasons but the only one he would publicly state was, 'Scotland Yard can boast that not even the subordinate officers of the department will tell tales out of school, and it would ill become me to violate the unwritten rule of the service . . . no public benefit would result from such a course, and the traditions of my old department would suffer.' These are very odd statements: they would not, of course, be relevant to private or official records, neither of which Anderson appears to have left in relation to this mystery. He also enlarged on the secret aspect of his work at Scotland Yard:

> The outside working of the machine is public property, and may here be explained, for the knowledge may possibly be both interesting and useful to the public. But if any one takes up these pages in expectation of learning the secrets of the department, he may throw them down at once. For I cannot speak too highly of the sense of honour which prevails, not only among the officers, but among the pensioned officers, of the C.I.D. in regard to all matters of which they have official knowledge.[18]

This still does not explain the total absence of any other official or private reference to, or confirmation of, his claims regarding the identification of the Ripper, other than the notes in Swanson's personal copy of the book in which these sentiments appear.

—— SEVENTEEN ——

Popular Ripper Myths

AN obvious result of what is now popularly claimed to be the greatest unsolved murder mystery of all time is the accumulation of much myth and fantasy. Popular myths began to emerge in 1888 and have been added to in a seemingly never-ending stream over subsequent years. Certain questions are raised time and again about the case. Why the name Jack the Ripper? What did he look like? Did he really write the letters allegedly sent by the killer? Who was he? How did the victims actually die? Was it all a conspiracy? And so on. It is, of course, impossible to answer any of these questions with certainty and this is where the myths begin. From 1888 onwards public fascination with the unknown killer escalated and books, then films, joined in the fun. Here are a few of the more enduring and plausible theories about the case.

COMMISSIONER JAMES MONRO HAD SOME SORT OF 'INSIDE KNOWLEDGE' ABOUT THE IDENTITY OF THE RIPPER

In view of Monro's importance and the fact that he was involved both at the Home Office and Scotland Yard during the crucial years it is suggested that he may have had ideas regarding the identity of the killer. This belief has been bolstered by the contents of a memo from Home Secretary Matthews to Evelyn Ruggles-Brise, his Private Secretary, dated 22 September 1888. In many Ripper publications[1] Matthews has been reported as writing: 'Stimulate the police about the Whitechapel murders. Monro might be willing to give a hint to the CID people if necessary.' This alleged statement has prompted endless speculation as to exactly what Monro knew of the possible identity of the killer and the nature of the hint he might have been able to give. The simple answer is, however, that Monro knew nothing of the identity of the killer and the accurate wording of the memo actually ran: 'Stimulate the Police about Whitechapel murders. *Absente* Anderson, Monro might be willing to give a hint to the C.I.D. people if needful.' So the true meaning of the memo is that Matthews, concerned about the absence of Anderson as head of the CID at this crucial time in the investigation, suggested that the former head of the CID, Monro, might be able to give the leaderless detectives some sort of direction if it were needed.

THERE WAS A WITNESS WHO ACTUALLY SAW THE KILLER

It is often asked, 'Did a reliable witness ever see the killer and if so do we have a good description of the Ripper?' The first and most important fact to remember is that no one actually saw a killing taking place – therefore, no person seen, whether with a victim or not, can be categorically stated to be the killer. Therefore, however good any witness, it is impossible to prove that it was the murderer they saw, and this alone allows theorists to dismiss witnesses if they do not suit their case. There are only a few witnesses who may be argued to have actually seen the killer with a victim. These are Mrs Elizabeth Long (Annie Chapman); Israel Schwartz (Elizabeth Stride); Joseph Lawende, Joseph Levy and Harry Harris (Catherine Eddowes); and George Hutchinson (Mary Kelly).

Mrs Long identified the body of Chapman as the woman she had seen with a man near 29 Hanbury Street.[2] Schwartz identified the body of Stride as the woman he had seen with a man outside Dutfield's Yard. Lawende identified the clothing only as that of Eddowes whom he saw near Mitre Square; his two companions did not take as much notice as Lawende and were not able to give a good description. Hutchinson actually knew Kelly and saw her with a man in Commercial Street. He followed them to Miller's Court around 2 a.m. on the morning of her murder, although even this is disputed by those who seek to portray Hutchinson himself as the Ripper.

DR DUTTON'S *CHRONICLES OF CRIME*, THE OLD NICHOL GANG AND OTHER 'MCCORMICK MYTHS'

Many enduring Ripper myths have been created by popular authors down the years and among them Donald McCormick surely reigns supreme in the field of invented Ripper history. His literary devices included such undying myths as Dr Thomas Dutton's 'three volumes of handwritten *Chronicles of Crime*' (no evidence for the existence of which has ever been found), owned by Hermione Dudley (no evidence for the existence of whom has ever been found). He also wrote of 'the Old Nichol Gang' (for which no mention prior to McCormick's 1959 book has ever been traced); a Klosowski/Pedachenko link; various rhymes and ditties; the deliberate placement of 'two brass rings, a few pennies and two farthings . . . neatly laid out' at Chapman's feet; Elizabeth Long and 'a woman Darrell' as two separate witnesses (they were one and the same); the bloodhounds getting lost; the 'ginny' kidney of Eddowes; the two Liverpool 'Jack the Ripper' letters (it was one letter – McCormick found it in J. Hall Richardson's *From the City to Fleet Street*, undated, and turned it into two letters with a date); the 'Eight Little Whores' verses; Abberline's consultations with Dr Dutton; Abberline's tracking of Klosowski; the *Ochrana Gazette* report on 'KONOVALOV, Vasily, alias PEDACHENKO, Alexy, alias LUISKOVO, Andrey'; and many others.

One of his most audacious inventions, after Cullen's Druitt theory was published, was that the police gave Albert Backert (*sic*) information in confidence in about March 1889. McCormick alleged that the police told the leading member of the Whitechapel Vigilance Committee: 'The man in question is dead. He was fished out of the Thames two months ago and it would only cause pain to relatives if we said any more than that.' There is no evidence for this whatsoever. Nor is there any evidence that Druitt, the man fished from the Thames, was a suspect at this early date nor that Albert Bachert (noted for his earlier 'man with a shiny black bag' in the Three Nuns Hotel story) was ever told any such thing. On the contrary, later statements by Bachert indicate quite the opposite.

ABBERLINE STATED THAT THE RIPPER WAS 'ONE OF THE HIGHEST IN THE LAND'

Unfortunately McCormick was not alone in the art of inventing tales that posed as factual events. Nigel Morland, a journalist, novelist, author and self-proclaimed criminologist, has also added to the mythology. Frank Spiering's abysmal 1978 Ripper effort, *Prince Jack*, most inappropriately subtitled *The True Story of JACK THE RIPPER*, includes an introduction by Nigel Morland. Leaping into the 'Royal Ripper' frenzy of the 1970s, Spiering concocted an error-filled fantasy proposing the hapless Prince Albert Victor as the Ripper and telling tales of his own research into the case involving an otherwise untraceable and unrecorded set of notes belonging to Sir William Withey Gull and cryptic exchanges with British officialdom still involved in the royal cover-up. Apparently getting carried away with all this, in the introduction Morland staked his claim to being the originator of the royal nonsense in 1970 when he, as editor of the *Criminologist* magazine, published the unlikely story of an elderly English surgeon named Thomas E.A. Stowell. Getting into the spirit of the fantasy, Morland divulged a gem of invention with the story of how he became interested in the Ripper 'in a purely academic way'. As a youngster, a remark made to him by Sir Arthur Conan Doyle that the Ripper was 'somewhere in the upper stratum', although he did not enlarge on the comment, was enough to ignite his interest.

Morland had met just about anyone who was anybody in his day and this, of course, included the redoubtable ex-Chief Inspector Abberline. The well-travelled Morland was at this time, the early 1920s, at home on leave from his job as a crime reporter on a newspaper in Shanghai. Hearing that Abberline had retired to 'the elegant seaside resort of Bournemouth', Morland hastened there to locate the former policeman. Eventually Morland found Abberline working in his garden, just as all good retired policemen should. To Morland's disappointment Abberline was not pleased to see him and refused to answer any questions about Jack the Ripper. Morland's last ditch ploy was to say that he was about to return to Shanghai and this, coupled with the tale that he was making notes for a future book on the Ripper, caused Abberline to relent and provide an illuminating (and convenient for Spiering's book) statement about the identity of the Ripper. According to Morland, Abberline said, 'I cannot reveal anything except this – *of course* we knew who he was, one of the highest in the land.' This alleged statement flies in the face of everything that Abberline had reliably been reported to have said about the case in the past. And why? The answer must be obvious. Morland had made the whole thing up but the damage was done. This alleged statement by Abberline is now often quoted.

CATHERINE EDDOWES MAY NOT HAVE BEEN A PROSTITUTE

Catherine Eddowes was clearly a casual prostitute although it has now become popular to suggest that she was not. The influential *Jack the Ripper A–Z* states:

> we have no direct evidence that she did prostitute herself: only the suggestive facts that shortly before she died she was talking to a strange man at a dark corner in a direction leading away from the lodging house where she was staying; and that she had, apparently, no money at 2.00 p.m. on 29 September, but had acquired enough to make a drunken scene six hours later.

This idea has been taken up by some other students of the case, but it is not, in the opinion of the authors, a very likely suggestion. The facts are that she was murdered in an area frequented by casual prostitutes, away from where she lived, in the early hours of the morning and this surely points as to what she was doing when she was killed. We also have the remarks made by her partner Kelly at the inquest and the statement made by Inspector McWilliam of the City of London Police that:

> she had lived with a man named Thomas Conway, a pensioner for about twenty years & had three children by him – two sons & a daughter, but Conway was eventually compelled to leave her on account of her drunken and *immoral habits*. [*Authors' italic*.][3]

All things considered, it seems obvious that Eddowes was not that much different from the other victims and was surely engaged in casual prostitution to raise money in order to survive.

JACK THE RIPPER HAD FIVE VICTIMS AND FIVE ONLY

This statement may not be recognised as a myth at all since 'the canonical five' – Nichols, Chapman, Stride, Eddowes and Kelly – have been generally accepted as the Ripper victims for many years. Dr Bond and then Melville Macnaghten were the first to specify these five women as *the* Ripper victims. But, of course, unless a killer is caught and his tally proven there is absolutely no way that specific victims can be categorically stated to be the work of one hand. No Whitechapel murderer was ever identified or convicted and we simply cannot say with certainty which ones fell to the Ripper. Both authors feel that on grounds of *modus operandi* at the very least, Nichols, Chapman and Eddowes were almost certainly victims of the same killer. There must be less certainty, on the same grounds, that Stride and Kelly were. Doubt must exist that Tabram was a Ripper victim, the circumstances ostensibly indicating a soldier client as her most likely killer. Almost certainly Emma Smith (attacked in the street by a gang of three according to her own testimony), Rose Mylett, Alice MacKenzie, the Pinchin Street woman (never identified) and Frances Coles (probably murdered by James Thomas Sadler) were all victims of different killers.

Authors' Epilogues

INVESTIGATING WITH HINDSIGHT

STEWART EVANS

MANY of today's popular Ripper suspects emerged many years after the murders. They were not contemporary suspects in any shape or form and never featured in the police investigation at all. Indeed, 'suspect' seems rather too strong a word to use in relation to them for, seemingly, anyone can point the accusing finger at whomsoever he wishes without the need for any supporting historical evidence to validate his claim.

A favourite source of suspects in the years immediately following the Ripper crimes were cases where actual murderers were brought to justice. These included such infamous names as Mrs Mary Pearcey, Dr Thomas Neill Cream, Frederick Deeming and George Chapman. Today, the list of Ripper suspects includes many of the witnesses and characters who actually appeared in the accounts and records of the murders, such as Timothy Donovan, Michael Kidney, John Kelly, Joseph Barnett, George Hutchinson and John McCarthy. At the ridiculous end of the suspect spectrum we find such individuals as Dr Thomas Barnardo, Sir William Withey Gull, HRH Prince Albert Victor Christian Edward (Eddy), Walter Sickert, Lewis Carroll and the 1889 alleged murder victim James Maybrick.[1]

Since the 1988 centenary of the murders it has been increasingly popular to add 'criminal profiling' to the list of aids deployed in an attempt to solve the Ripper murders.[2] It is questionable whether modern profiling is relevant to a series of Victorian murders for which we have very little hard evidence and no certainty about which killings were committed by the same individual. Popularised in America by the FBI and dramatised in films, profiling has, however, attracted a great following. It is looked upon by most seasoned police officers as of dubious value, many of them arguing that its methods are merely common sense and provide conclusions about murders that they would arrive at themselves anyway without outside help. So although it may be interesting to apply modern profiling techniques to the Whitechapel murders of 1888–91, we feel that it is of little real value and most certainly will not result in the identification of the murderer.

As retired police officers with joint service experience of around sixty years, we felt that readers would, naturally, want to know exactly what opinions and conclusions we have reached as a result of our long-standing interest in this mystery. We both visited the scenes of the crimes in the 1960s, when much remained unchanged and radical rebuilding had yet to begin. We thus gained a good idea of how the area looked at the time the unknown killer prowled those streets.

The loss of official documents over the years has greatly hindered Ripper research and has become the stuff of legend. Often too much is read into this and it provides a useful aid for those who wish to promote 'official conspiracy' theories. The truth is more mundane. Much of the material held by the City of London Police was simply lost during the Blitz in

London. Scotland Yard itself did not escape totally unscathed but the bulk of the Metropolitan force's archived records survived the war.

The police are not renowned for their sense of history and stored records can take up an awful lot of space. There was a tendency simply to destroy documents that were out of date and no longer required. The late Mr Heron, Scotland Yard's first archivist, told Donald that until 1959, when the Yard's files came under the control of the Public Record Office (now the National Archives) it was customary for the porters to dispose of handfuls of paper to make room for newer material. In 1970, while engaged upon research for his history of the City of London Police, Donald consulted the old files at Scotland Yard. He was allowed to take documents, including the Ripper files, home and he photocopied several of them.

Writing to researcher Keith Skinner in 1992, Norman Fairfax, another Scotland Yard archivist, said that when he first started work in the registry on the third floor of the famous New Scotland Yard building on the Embankment, the old files were kept in the 'P.A.', the loft of the building. No one was permitted upstairs except the registry staff and, 'curiously', certain visitors. The Ripper documents were then kept in long green trays with the papers folded into four and tucked in so that three-quarters of the documents were visible. The trays were on the end of industrial shelving. According to Mr Fairfax, it became apparent that as the number of visitors increased so the number of papers decreased until around 1948 when it was decided that visitors should no longer be allowed in the PA.

This would seem to indicate that as early as the 1940s material was being taken from files and not returned. The visitors involved, one must assume, were the friends or guests of high-ranking police officers who were able to break through the red tape that then existed. It was not until the 1970s, with greater official laxity, that researchers were allowed access to the still closed Scotland Yard files. In 1972 researchers for BBC television's Barlow and Watt docu-drama 'Jack the Ripper' were allowed to view the files. In notes made during his research, series producer Paul Bonner recorded that the Scotland Yard file Mepol 3/141 contained reports 'that seem to have been called for by Scotland Yard in January 1889' and that 'they include a range of colourful suspects (mostly from outside Whitechapel)'. These included:

> September 27th 1887 'Mary' – the male barber from Bremen (discovered, subsequently, to have been in prison in Osterhausen on the Ripper dates).

> October 5th 1887 – Dick Austen – sometimes a sailor and more recently in 'R' Troop of the 5th Lancers.

> January 14th 1889 – Pierce John Robinson reported by his business partner, Richard Wingate of Edgware Road.

These were followed by various police reports of suspects pointed out to the police by members of the public, and included:

> November 22nd 1888 – James Connell, a 36-year-old Irish draper from New Cross Road, Greenwich, picked up a married woman at Marble Arch and took her into Hyde Park. There, while walking and talking with her, he started speaking of 'Jack the Ripper and lunatic asylums'. This so upset Mrs. Martha Spencer that she called PC 271A Fountain who was passing by. He took both of them to Hyde Park Police Station where Inspector Bird sent a telegram of inquiry to Greenwich 'as to the correctness of his address and

his respectability; a satisfactory reply having been received, he was then allowed to go as nothing further suspicious transpired'.

December 9th 1888 – Antoni Pricha of Hatton Garden who was drawn to the attention of PC 61A, Thomas Maybank, by Mr. Edward Knight Larkins of H.M. Customs.[3]

Edwin Burrows, aged 45, of Victoria Chambers, Whitechapel, a common lodging house, of whom Inspector Rutt of 'A' Division said 'has been sleeping on seats for 12 months and is evidently doing his best to exist on the pound a week his brother allows him'.

December 17th 1888 – Douglas Cow, met by Mrs. Fanny Drake of the Conservative Club, Clerkenwell Green, while she was crossing Westminster Bridge. His behaviour led her to report him to Inspector Walsh on his horse beneath Westminster Abbey. Mr. Cow produced letters and business cards proving his identity and that he worked for Cow and Co., India Rubber Merchants of 70 Cheapside. Walsh took them both to 'A' Division station at Rochester Row where the information was 'imparted to the lady when she at once apologized to Mr. Cow for having caused him inconvenience and both parties then left the station'.

All these are no longer to be found in the records. Paul Bonner noted that the theme that ran throughout these reports appeared to be that if the 'suspect' could show that he was a respectable citizen, he was alright and that if he could prove his identity, he was 'fairly o.k.'. It appeared that no alibis for the preceding September and November dates were given, nor, indeed, asked for. At least 100 men in the file were taken to police stations for carrying black bags, having foreign accents, accosting women or talking about the Ripper in pubs. They were released when they were able to prove their identity. At least two suspects, one Dutch and one American, gave their addresses as Bacon's Hotel, Fitzroy Square. Significantly there was no mention in this file, nor any other, of Macnaghten's named suspects, Druitt, Kosminski and Ostrog. Other files present at this time but now missing were reports by Inspector Edmund Reid and Chief Inspector West on the murder of Emma Elizabeth Smith in April 1888.

The late Stephen Knight, while carrying out research for his influential 1976 book *Jack the Ripper: the Final Solution*, also accessed the Scotland Yard files and was assisted by Donald Rumbelow who supplied him with some of the photocopies he had made earlier. We are also told, by Robin Odell, that the late author, publisher and criminologist Joe Gaute borrowed the files and actually had them at home. Stories are told that researchers accessing these files in pre-Public Record Office days were shown into a garret room at New Scotland Yard where they were left to peruse the material, unsupervised, at their leisure. What went missing during this period we do not know.

From notes and photocopies made by these early researchers we know that other documents later disappeared from the files that were finally handed over to the Public Record Office in the 1980s. Among these were the papers relevant to a suspect suggested by a Mr Callaghan, via Dr Forbes Winslow – G. Wentworth Bell Smith.[4] This suggestion was investigated and disposed of by Chief Inspector Donald Swanson himself. The missing documents also related to the suspect Roslyn D'Onston (Robert Donston Stephenson). D'Onston, a patient in the London Hospital, had suggested a suspect of his own, Dr Morgan Davies of the hospital. D'Onston was himself linked with the murders in December 1888 by a pub acquaintance, George Marsh, but was dismissed as a suspect by Inspector Roots who saw him when he attended Scotland Yard on Boxing Day 1888. Roots stated he had known

D'Onston, an excessive drinker, for twenty years. It is not known who stole this material or where it now reposes.

Other relevant documents would have been routinely destroyed by the police themselves, as was their practice. These would have included the bulk of the written statements taken at the time, police officers' pocket books (and notebooks specifically issued during the investigation of the murders), station occurrence books, station detention and bail records, arrest warrants, dockets and many other valuable references.

Fortunately police reports on the investigation were sent to the Home Office and these have survived, some of them lengthy and detailed. The Home Office files were not pillaged over the years and are, essentially, complete. They comprise overview reports on the investigation. Filed under the HO 144/220 and 144/221/A49301 series, these records are now held in the National Archives and guaranteed safe for future generations. They put the lie to much false theorising about suspects and incidents in the Ripper story.

The Home Office did, however, once have items that have been missing almost since the time of the murders. A note on file A49301 shows that out of forty-eight items, twenty-two were destroyed or missing when filed in 1893.

Possibly the question most frequently asked of Ripper authorities is 'Will Jack the Ripper ever be positively identified?' We have different views on this. I feel confident in saying that the case will never be solved. This may not be the answer anyone wants to hear but I believe it is an honest and accurate one. The evidence as to the identity of the killer could not be adduced by the police at the time of the murders and it is therefore possible to say that, at this remove, it certainly will not be found. If the evidence was not obtained in the first place, no matter how many 'lost' papers may be discovered none will identify the murderer. There may be new material to add, such as finds of recent years have proved – for example, the case of Francis Tumblety whose status as a contemporary suspect was revealed in the letter written by ex-Chief Inspector Littlechild and found in 1993. We may, at best, add to the list of viable suspects but this is a far cry from proving the identity of the Ripper.

Another interesting and relevant point as regards Tumblety is that Littlechild stated that there was a 'large dossier' concerning him at Scotland Yard. This dossier has never been located nor is there any mention of Tumblety in the extant official files at the National Archives. However, Littlechild was head of the Special Branch and Tumblety was an Irish-American with Irish Nationalist sympathies, maybe even a Fenian. It is more than likely that the documents comprised a Special Branch file and these have never been released to the archives for reasons of secrecy. They are held confidential in perpetuity. There is a Special Branch index book listing records that were compiled by the likes of Monro, Anderson, Williamson and Littlechild during the crucial and formative years 1880 to 1910. The book reveals a Fenian/Whitechapel line of inquiry of some sort. Should the relevant Special Branch files ever be made available for public scrutiny, they might precipitate more progress in Ripper research than has been achieved at any other time, save possibly when the main police and Home Office files were made public in the 1970s.

Peripheral mysteries may also be cleared up and more information on known suspects will almost certainly be discovered. We have seen new research by Philip Sugden positively eliminate Michael Ostrog, who was listed as a suspect by Macnaghten – he was incarcerated in Paris at the time of the murders. So in the final analysis the student of the Ripper mystery is left to weigh the pros and cons of each viable suspect and decide who his own favoured 'culprit' is.

Many reach the conclusion that Jack the Ripper was a total nonentity who has never been named – and this may well be true.

NOTES FOR THE CURIOUS

DONALD RUMBELOW

One of the problems I faced when I researched the early history of the City of London Police was the lack of documentation in the possession of the City Police themselves. Had it not been for the Police Committee papers lodged at the Corporation of the City of London, no history would have been possible. There are two major explanations for the loss of such documentation. The Blitz began with bombs on the City itself in 1940. All of the City Police stations took direct hits during this time. Moor Lane A Division, present-day Barbican, was completely destroyed and never re-formed. The second reason for the lack of records is the carelessness or indifference of police generally to the keeping and storing of such documentation. City Police photographs taken after the IRA bombing of the Old Bailey (1973) and the Moorgate Tube disaster (1975) were thrown away after five years. Such destruction is not peculiar to the City; this is a police scandal which still continues to this day. All police forces should be compelled to have a resident archivist.

I joined the City Police in 1963 and, being a Londoner by adoption, soon immersed myself in the capital's history. Within a short time I was teaching London history to police proba-tioners at Bishopsgate police station's School of Instruction. It was here on the sixth floor that there had once been a force museum. One of the exhibits was the 'From hell' letter to Mr Lusk.[5] About 1959 the museum was broken up. The two constables in charge, Vic Wright and 'Jock' Watt, were away at the time. The police inspector in charge of the school decided that he wanted another classroom and sent in the cadets to clear out the museum. When Wright and Watt returned they found that the exhibits had just been dumped in another room; some things were broken or torn, others were missing and the letter had gone. Understandably the two men were angry and would never have anything to do with the museum again.

Fast forward to 1966 when a new police station was built at Wood Street close to the City's Guildhall. The building was near completion when I was told to report to the inspector overseeing the project and asked when I was going to do something about the museum. I did not even know there was to be a museum in the new building but apparently I was in charge. I had been scavenging around the stations for some time and was horrified to see items such as letters to the governor of Newgate Gaol and parish records dating back to the eighteenth century. For some reason these had found their way into police hands and were now being thrown out. I recovered what I could and placed the material in the Guildhall Library and Records Office. Other items I retained for the police museum. On one collecting expedition I came across some filthy card boxes containing photographs and papers relating to the Siege of Sidney Street and awaiting destruction. I knew something about this case involving the murder of three City policemen in 1910 and thought the destruction of such papers absolutely wrong. I managed to squirrel them away and eventually took them home bit by bit. Only several years later did I think of using them to write a book, *The Houndsditch Murders* (revised edition 1988). The bulk of these papers, like so many other photographs and documents, I deposited in the Corporation of London Records Office. This is where I have always thought such papers should be stored. Eyebrows were raised when I took the Dr Openshaw letter from someone calling himself Jack the Ripper to the National Archives at Kew in 2004. Such items are not for sale. I have enjoyed them while they have been in my possession and I want others to enjoy them equally.

I found a cache of over 300 Jack-the-Ripper-related letters from the public to the City Police commissioner in a broken cupboard in the basement of Old Jewry headquarters. I had not expected to find anything because the cellar had just been emptied out. The correspondence was in some very old and torn cardboard boxes. Some people knew that they were there but did not rate them of any value, which is why they had been left for throwing out. The only individuals who had shown any interest in the collection were stamp collectors who had taken many of the envelopes for the Victorian stamps. This is why some of the letters cannot now be exactly dated. I eventually deposited these letters in the Records Office too, having kept them at home for a number of years and referred to them in the original edition of *The Complete Jack the Ripper*.

In about 1966/7, after I had been told about the proposed museum, I was in the photographic department in the upstairs room of Old Jewry when I spotted some glass plates. Picking them up, I found one of them to show Metropolitan policemen; it was dated about 1870. The other I instantly recognised as an image of the exterior of Miller's Court. Being a young uniform constable in the City of London Police in the 1960s was like being the lowliest private in a Guards regiment from which so many of my colleagues had been recruited. We were the first of those who had just escaped two years' National Service and had not had any military training so it is hard to explain the atmosphere except in such terms. When I asked about the photographs I was told by the detective sergeant, Ken Poole, that they came from an album that contained more images. His response, like that of so many others, was that he would not tell me the whole story or let me see everything he knew about because he wanted the material for an autobiography when he retired or to sell to the newspapers. More I never found out.

I found the photograph of Mary Kelly's body, along with the Eddowes images, in the filthy attic room at Snow Hill police station where the remains of the old museum had been dumped. At some point the Kelly picture had been fixed to something with a drawing pin: the holes at the top are still visible on reproductions. In about 1969 I began to write a history of the City Police (published in 1971 by Macmillan as *I Spy Blue*). I was given access to the Metropolitan Police files relating to the Siege of Sidney Street and Jack the Ripper. Both sets of files I took home at different times and photocopied a number of them. When my book was published in 1975 I considered that I had no further use for the Ripper files and, to the best of my recollection, gave the photocopies to Stephen Knight, which explains in part the very fulsome thanks I receive in his book. With the commissioner's approval, and as a thank you, I placed a set of the Kelly and Eddowes photographs in the Scotland Yard files which were empty of images except for those of Tabram, McKenzie and Coles.

It was through my involvement with the museum that I first met Professor Francis Camps and his assistant Sam Hardy, who had found the drawings of Eddowes' body *in situ* and of Mitre Square in the basement of the London Hospital. I contacted him, told him of the Eddowes and Kelly photographs, and went to see him. I gave him a set of the photographs and in return borrowed the Mitre Square drawings, which I had framed and hung in the museum for several years. I had asked Camps to keep the photographs to himself and so was annoyed to discover that he had a number of sets printed off, one of which he gave to Dan Farson who then published them for the first time in his 1972 book *Jack the Ripper*.

As I have explained elsewhere, I understand that the City Police were in possession of the Miller's Court photographs because in the delay before authorisation was given for the door to be opened, City officers arrived, forced an entry and then took the pictures as their justification for doing so. This, of course, is completely contradicted by the evidence that McCarthy broke open the door with a pickaxe. I am perfectly willing to be persuaded by this but there are references to Superintendent Arnold ordering one of the windows to be taken out prior to McCarthy's entry, which might just explain the City Police photographs.

Dr Bagster Phillips, we know, had a photograph taken of the exterior of Kelly's room and he produced it for the coroner at the inquest. I think it worth pointing out, too, how conveniently near at hand the City Police were. Bishopsgate police station was not a 5-minute walk from Miller's Court and it would have been surprising, during the wait to effect entry, if City detectives had not made their way to the murder scene.

It is not clear what the police procedures were for taking photographs. In Metropolitan Police Orders of 1 January 1889 yearly returns were requested for 'The number of Bodies of Persons unknown to be photographed during the year 1888, the number identified, and the number remaining not identified.' Although this was for identification purposes, only this instruction would explain the photographing of Nichols, Chapman, Stride, Eddowes, McKenzie and Coles. Presumably, like the Metropolitan Police, the City force used a professional photographer. In the City Police Order Book for Bishopsgate police station dated 5 September 1887 to 7 May 1889, and now kept in the basement safe of the station, there is an order from John Whatley, the Chief Clerk at Old Jewry, dated 23 October 1888. It is addressed to the chief inspectors and inspectors of each division and states that, 'The Commissioner orders that whenever it may be necessary for future identification to obtain the photograph of a body found dead or otherwise. Application is to be made at once to this office.' In the same book an order dated 31 October 1888 says, 'The Commissioner orders that the accompanying patterns of "Silent Boots" be sent for the Inspection of members of the Force, should any boots of the same pattern be required they may be obtained on application at this office.' Obviously the Star's criticisms that criminals could hear the police approaching in their regulation boots had been taken to heart.

In the City Police museum, at least when I was curator, there was a large loose-leaved album containing not only mortuary photographs but prisoner photographs also, of men, women and children, dating mostly from the 1870s. Among them were photographs of the Bidwell brothers and their two accomplices who famously tried to rob the Bank of England in 1873. I published these in an article written for the Bank of England in 1973 and later in a City of London Police 150th anniversary booklet published in 1989. Full-length photographs were originally taken of the prisoners; a few survived, but the majority had been cut down to head-and-shoulders portraits which had then been mounted on a card recording the individual's name, age, date of arrest, offence and sentence. How long this practice continued is impossible to determine. A professional photographer was used to take photographs of the Houndsditch murderers in 1910.

One has to assume that this practice of using professional photographers continued throughout the interwar period, although there is no documentary evidence to confirm this. Certainly there is no evidence for a photographic department. It took two City Police amateur photographers to bring this about. Between 1939 and 1945 Arthur Cross and his assistant Fred Tibbs, photographed the effect of the Blitz on the square mile. Tibbs lived at Bishopsgate police station because his family had been evacuated to Wales and was frequently on scene within minutes of the 'All Clear' sounding. His image of the falling front of the Salvation Army headquarters in Queen Victoria Street is internationally famous. The shot is slightly blurred because he pressed the button at the same instant as he fell backwards into a pot-hole. I managed to recover a complete collection of Cross and Tibbs' work which I deposited in the Museum of London, which subsequently published a small pamphlet on it.

The two men had a small basement room in Bishopsgate police station which they were allocated just prior to the outbreak of war in 1939. In 1959 a new Commissioner, Sir Arthur Young, was astounded by what he saw and on leaving this black hole commented, 'If the officer took from this room the equipment belonging to himself, the force would be in a mess photographically.' In fact, the only equipment belonging to the force at this time were some dishes and trays and a flat-bed glazing machine. Cross was paid 10s a month for the use of his small plate camera. He was not allowed to spend more than £10 a year on materials and was allowed 4 hours to complete each photographic assignment before returning to uniform duty. The commissioner radically transformed the photographic department. A stunned Arthur Cross soon found himself spending not £10 a year, but over £1,000. Two rooms at Old Jewry were converted into a studio and darkroom and photographic, a much expanded department, was located here when I first joined the force.

'On the Day of Judgement, when all things shall be known, when I and other Ripperologists ask for Jack the Ripper to step forward and call out his name, we shall look at one another as he does so and say, "Who?"' These words from the original edition of my book have often been taken to assume that I do not believe we will ever know the Ripper's real name. Possibly not. The opinion most frequently voiced to support the claim that there will never be a solution to the Ripper crimes is that too many documents are missing. Despite this, the spark still lingers that somewhere some of those hundreds of discarded Scotland Yard documents may still exist and with them the necessary clues to provide an answer. It may be just a question of looking in the right place. I often quote the example of the American scholar Dr Leslie Hotson who, back in the 1920s, looked for a true account of the death of Christopher Marlowe, Shakespeare's great contemporary. The crude outlines of his death had been known for nearly four centuries, that he had been stabbed to death in a tavern brawl in Deptford. By asking the right questions and pushing the right buttons Hotson found the complete inquest papers and witness statements in archives where they had sat undisturbed and waiting. For several centuries writers and scholars had argued and guessed at the truth. Again, by asking the right questions and pushing the right buttons, he went on to unearth an unknown cache of letters written by Shelley to his first wife.

So, and this is said very frankly, there just might be a solution out there. Will it be my favoured suspect, Timothy Donovan, Annie Chapman's lodging-house keeper in Dorset Street? The best that I can say here is that it may be so. I doubt it, but reason goes out of the window and this is where instinct, unreasoning instinct takes over. As I have explained elsewhere, Mary Kelly has to be excluded from the Ripper equation because Donovan died shortly before she was murdered. Here I find myself agreeing with Superintendent Arnold that there were only four victims. Donovan fits neatly in the frame – he was the right age, he was deputy at the lodging house where he could hide and clean up after each killing, he knew Chapman and almost certainly some of the other victims, and he conveniently died just before the Kelly murder which has to be attributed to some other unknown.

But proof? That's something else.

Divisions of the Metropolitan and City Police, 1888

In 1888 the Metropolitan Police area comprised the following divisions:

CO or Commissioner's Office, also known as Central Office: Charles H. Cutbush, Superintendent Executive Branch; Edward Ware, Superintendent Public Carriage Branch; John Shore, Superintendent Criminal Investigation Department. 43 inspectors, 63 sergeants, 120 constables. Total 229

A or Whitehall Division: Joseph Henry Dunlap, Superintendent, also Charles Fraser, King Street, Westminster. 38 inspectors, 60 sergeants, 835 constables. Total 935

B or Chelsea Division: Charles W. Sheppard, Superintendent, Walton Street, Brompton. 22 inspectors, 52 sergeants, 560 constables. Total 635

C or St James's Division (smallest division, $\frac{7}{10}$ square mile area): William G. Hume, Superintendent, Little Vine Street, Piccadilly. 17 inspectors, 37 sergeants, 386 constables. Total 441

D or Marylebone Division: George Draper, Superintendent, Marylebone Lane. 23 inspectors, 40 sergeants, 467 constables. Total 531

E or Holborn Division: Richard W. Steggles, Superintendent, Bow Street. 17 inspectors, 50 sergeants, 447 constables. Total 515

F or Paddington Division: Philip Giles, Superintendent, Paddington Green. 21 inspectors, 41 sergeants, 377 constables. Total 440

G or Finsbury Division: Charles Hunt, Superintendent, King's Cross Road, Clerkenwell. 23 inspectors, 46 sergeants, 480 constables. Total 550

H or Whitechapel Division: Thomas Arnold, Superintendent, Leman Street, Whitechapel. 30 inspectors, 44 sergeants, 473 constables. Total 548

J or Bethnal Green Division: James Keating, Superintendent, Bethnal Green Road. 38 inspectors, 56 sergeants, 522 constables. Total 617

K or Bow Division: George Steed, Superintendent, Bow Road. 48 inspectors, 71 sergeants, 619 constables. Total 739

L or Lambeth Division: James Brannan, Superintendent, Lower Kennington Lane. 22 inspectors, 35 sergeants, 346 constables. Total 404

M or Southwark Division: Denis Neylan, Superintendent, Blackman Street, Southwark. 28 inspectors, 43 sergeants, 429 constables. Total 501

N or Islington Division: William J. Sherlock, Superintendent, Stoke Newington High Street. 37 inspectors, 66 sergeants, 536 constables. Total 640

P or Camberwell Division: Thomas Butt, Superintendent, High Street, Peckham. 44 inspectors, 68 sergeants, 599 constables. Total 712

R or Greenwich Division: Christopher McHugo, Superintendent, Blackheath Road, Greenwich. 38 inspectors, 71 sergeants, 476 constables. Total 586

S or Hampstead Division (largest division, 79 square miles area): William Harris, Superintendent, Albany Street, Regent's Park. 42 inspectors, 80 sergeants, 613 constables. Total 736

T or Hammersmith Division: William Fisher, Superintendent, Broadway, Hammersmith.
   52 inspectors, 75 sergeants, 623 constables. Total 751

V or Wandsworth Division: David Saines, Superintendent, West Hill, Wandsworth. 36 inspectors,
   59 sergeants, 561 constables. Total 657

W or Clapham Division: Stephen Lucas, Superintendent, Brixton Road. 39 inspectors, 72 sergeants,
   571 constables. Total 683

X or Kilburn Division: Frederick Beard, Superintendent, Carlton Terrace, Harrow Road. 40 inspectors,
   53 sergeants, 469 constables. Total 563

Y or Highgate Division: William J. Huntley, Superintendent, Kentish Town Road. 46 inspectors,
   73 sergeants, 607 constables. Total 727

Thames Division: George Skeats, Superintendent, Wapping, near the river. 49 inspectors, 4 sergeants,
   147 constables. Total 201

The City of London Police divisions were:

Police Office (City) 26 Old Jewry: Colonel Sir James Fraser, KCB, Commissioner; Major Henry Smith,
Chief Superintendent; J.W. Carlyon-Hughes, Receiver; John Whatley, Chief Clerk
Divisions:
   1.   Cripplegate, Moor Lane
   2.   Snow Hill
   3.   Bridewell Place
   4.   Cloak Lane, Queen Street
   5.   Tower Street, Seething Lane
   6.   Bishopsgate, Bishopsgate Street

List of Letters Sent to the City Police

The letters and associated correspondence regarding the murders received by the City of London Police were recovered and rescued by Donald Rumbelow. He later donated the collection to the Corporation of London Record Office. The CLRO, on acquisition, listed and indexed the letters in a brief fashion and roughly alphabetically. They were later passed to the London Metropolitan Archives. As these letters are accessed by the references then allocated, we have adhered to this numbering. Virtually all the letters received refer either to suggestions for capturing the murderer(s), or suspicions as to the identity of the killer. A basic breakdown of these numbered entries reveals about 301 correspondents and 345 letters. The remaining documents comprise police letters and acknowledgements, envelopes, visiting cards and news cuttings. They range from the sensible to the eccentric to the apparently insane.

No.	Date	Sender/Address	Content/Remarks
1	3 Oct. 1888	Fred. J. Allinson, Baythorne House, Gordon Street, Plaistow, E	Murderer escapes through sewers theory. Possibly dressed as a sewerman.
2	2 Oct. 1888	S.A. Ashby, 43 Acacia Road, Regent's Park, London NW	Suggests the murderer is disguised as a policeman to escape detection.
3	26 Oct. 1888	John L. Bagg Junior, Corscombe Mills, Dorset	Suggests a knife is visible in an illustration of the 'Lord's Supper'.
4	1 Oct. 1888	J. Baker, 221 Upper Brook Street, Manchester	Suggests dressing policemen as women resembling the ones attacked and arming them.
5	9 Oct. 1888	B. Barraclough, 1 Woodview Terrace, Bradford, Yorkshire	His children were playing at 'table rapping'; murderer's name is Tom Totson of Wurt St.
6	25 Dec. 1888	Revelation, c/o Delia Bass, Minneapolis, Minnesota, USA	Writer is a 'see-er' and could catch the man. Religious tone to letter.
7	16 Oct. 1888	Mrs Melinda Bate, Anns Cottage, Friendly Street, Deptford.	Wants to explain 'my ideas' to catch the murderer.
8	13 Oct. 1888	"	Had a presentiment there would be another murder. Has idea of a plan.
9	"	"	Envelope.
10	4 Oct. 1888	John Binny, 13 Tavistock Place, London	Suggests a gang may be responsible.
11	6 Oct. 1888	"	Regarding tracking, mentions Red Indians and bloodhounds.
12	5 Oct. 1888	Walter Biss, 23 Maclise Road, London W	Acknowledgement from police.
13	6 Oct. 1888	John Bland, 95 Sinclair Road, Kensington	Suggests that murderer is a watchman in a Jewish house or Herbert Freund, a lunatic.

No.	Date	Sender/Address	Content/Remarks
14	3 Oct. 1888	J.F. Boyd, 45 Bugle Street, Southampton, Hampshire	Mentions Archibald Forbes' letter and man who gave Wynne Baxter false information.
15	25 Oct. 1888	Josiah E. Boys, 41 Commercial Street, London E	Has seen wall-writing in Guildhall toilets, a message from 'Jack the Ripper'.
16	n.d.	"	Police envelope.
17	26 Oct. 1888	"	Police acknowledgement.
18	1 Oct. 1888	Thomas Bolas, Cursitor Street, London EC	Has had no reply from Met. Police to letter, re 'Burke and Hare' theory on murders.
19	2 Oct. 1888	John Brand, 22 & 23 Newbury Street, Cloth Fair, London EC	Suggests using dogs to catch the murderer and checking uninhabited houses.
20	15 Oct. 1888	Alese Brown, 26 Caledonian Place, Aberdeen, Scotland	Has theory that the murderer is a Jew and a monomaniac, perhaps a Jewish minister.
21	2 Oct. 1888	J.O. Byrne, 20 Winterwell Road, Brixton Hill, London SE	Murderer accesses his hiding place by climbing with a rope into a small house.
22	4 Oct. 1888	W.A. Bridge, Parsons Town, Kings Co., Ireland	Suggests disguising detectives as unfortunate women.
23	2 Oct. 1888	W. Bryn, 43 Sunderland Road, Forest Hill, London	Suggests dressing figures as women and placing them in dark and lonely places.
24	1 Oct. 1888	W. Bryant, Runcorn	Suggests disguising 'small but active' men as unfortunates.
25	3 Oct. 1888	W.F. Bunger, 3 Sydney Terrace, Mitcham Road, Croydon, Surrey	Suggests dressing police as women, and wearing metal collars, bloodhounds, photos.
26	2 Oct. 1888	Harry S. Caldecott, 130 Gower Street, London WC	Cites a case of unsolved South African murders near Pretoria.
27	"	"	Second page of above letter.
28	3 Oct. 1888	A. Calverley, 38 Furnival Street, Holborn, London	Suggests stop and search in area of White-chapel Church and using rubber-soled boots.
29	12 Nov. 1888	Geo. Cant, 8 Fergusons Lane, Carlisle	Suggests plan to dress 300 to 500 police in 'womans garment'.
30	n.d.	William Cargill, Buckminster, Grantham, Lincolnshire	Suggests women wear tin collars.
31	n.d.	Mrs Carey, 2 Stanley Street, Bedminster, Bristol	Suggests murderer is a black man wearing 'dark trowsers' and 'no shirt'.
32	6 Oct. 1888	Dr A. Casserini, Barbican, London and Switzerland	Has plan to catch murderer.
33	n.d.	"	Visiting card.
34	1 Oct. 1888	John Castle, The Hoo, Sydenham Hill	Suggests dressing police as women.
35	10 Oct. 1888	T. Cathrey, Church Street, Bolton	Suggests murderer is a steam printer. Has also written to Sir C. Warren.
36	3 Oct. 1888	J.W. Causier, Sherborne, Dorset	Murderer is a Jewish slaughterman.
37	23 Oct. 1888	H. Cavanagh, 3 Northumberland Street, Charing Cross	Suggests murderer is a caretaker or night-watchman.
38	19 Nov. 1888	J.R. Clark, Cleveland, Ohio, USA	Suggests using electric alarms and police dressed as women.
39	"	"	Plan for above.

No.	Date	Sender/Address	Content/Remarks
40	18 Oct. 1888	T. Cleare, 2 South Grove, Bow, London E	Suggests murderer is 'Barber the Chemist of Walthamstow notoriety'.
41	6 Oct. 1888	W.R. Collett, 104 Upland Road, East Dulwich	Suggests murderer is Willie Boult, who had been employed by Jacques Solicitors, W
42	3 Oct. 1888	J. Constant, Post Restant, Gloucester	Mentions Irish problems, gives advice.
43	n.d.	A.T. Coppen, Alameda, Spain	Visiting card.
44	6 Oct. 1888	"	Cites Spanish murders of four or five women in Vitoria/Tarragona. Is murderer a Spaniard?
45	n.d.	W. Cunliffe, 33 Harcourt Road, Brockley, London SE	Visiting card.
46	n.d.	H.C. Kromschroeder, 4/ ? Hill, St John's Wood, London NW	Visiting card.
47	8 Oct. 1888	W. Cunliffe, as above	Suggests murderer is a German, H.C. Kromschroeder, a draughtsman (as above).
48	"	"	PS to above. Suspect.
49	3 Oct. 1888	W.A. Curnock, Moorgate Street, London EC	Suggests dressing detectives as females.
50	2 Oct. 1888	'E.C.'	Suggests murderer is watchman Morris, use bloodhounds.
51	n.d.	'P.C.', Queen's Park, London, W	Scheme to find suspect who may be newspaper buyer who is reading of murders.
52	3 Oct. 1888	A. Davidson, Edinburgh	Has 'news'.
53	27 Jul. 1889	J. James Davis, Highbury, N	Suggests murderer uses sewers and is left-handed.
54	n.d.	A. Davidson, Edinburgh	Envelope.
55	10 Oct. 1888	"	Police acknowledgement.
56	10 Oct. 1888	John Davison, Hawthorn Grove, Birkbeck Estate, Enfield	Has a suspect who uses word 'Boss' and is left-handed.
57	12 Oct. 1888	H. Day, The Elms, Tunbridge, Kent	Suggests photography may make wall-writing reappear.
58	2 Oct. 1888	Dennocks, Sevenoaks, Kent	A burglar may have witnessed the Aldgate murder.
59	3 Oct. 1888	"	Re grapes, murderer may have given sweetmeats.
60	4 Oct. 1888	Joseph Diagree, City of London Union, 42 Clifton Rd, Clapton	Believes Mitre Square victim may be his wife, wants to view body.
61	1 Oct. 1888	H.R. Eason, 16 Dalston Lane, Kingsland, London E	There is an 'American twang' in the Jack the Ripper letter.
62	3 Oct. 1888	Chas. Egersdorff, 40 Camden Street, Walworth, SE	Suggests using couples and marking of suspects who accost them.
63	n.d.	J. Enser, 22 Wyndham Road, Camberwell	Suggests murderer is a doctor, described, who has passed his shop.
64	"	"	Doctor suspect, as above, more sightings.
65	18 Oct. 1888	Fannie M. Fletcher, Ivy Bank, Park Road, Leytonstone	Saw suspicious foreigner on train, Liverpool Street to Leytonstone who spoke to her.

No.	Date	Sender/Address	Content/Remarks
66	22 Oct. 1888	Sarah Fremlin, Park View, Loore Road, Maidstone, Kent	Names suspect John Davis, called 'Jack' and 'Jacky', aged nearly 60.
67	"	"	Newscutting, with Westminster court case of Thomas Davis for begging.
68	5 Dec. 1889	J. Fogarty, Dublin, Ireland	Re: telegram to police.
69	6 Dec. 1889	"	Re: fictional suspect Polermo Negro.
70	n.d.	W. Geary, 33 Adys Road, East Dulwich, SE	Encloses 'a scheme'.
71		"	The Plan, employ female detectives, to walk streets.
72	12 Oct. 1888	James B. Gibbins, Percy Lodge, Wood Green, London N	Graphologist, will analyse writing in letters. See also no. 276.
73	3 Oct. 1888	"	Re: graphology, postcards and 'Jack the Ripper'.
74	16 Oct. 1888	George Goodwin, 13 Auckland Road, Battersea Rise	Has some 'most startling evidences'.
75	n.d.	"	Newscutting (missing).
76	19 Oct. 1888	"	Unable to keep appointment to see police, aged 78, will try tomorrow.
77	4 Oct. 1888	John S. Gordon, 9 Bridge Street, Aberdeen, Scotland	Suspects hotel guest is murderer, names James Malcolm, 'the Bigamist', 'a Butcher'.
78	3 Oct. 1888	William Gow, Black Burn Road, Alyth, Perthshire	States female organs are used for amulets by Hill Tribes. Suggests a gang of them.
79	9 Oct. 1888	"	Sends pamphlets on East Indian tribes.
80	"	"	Booklet 'Apocalypse Unveiled'.
81	11 Oct. 1888	Sarah Goulding, High Street, Lincoln	Suggests using a mesmerist friend.
82	1 Oct. 1888	Harry B. Green, 34 Compton Road, London N	Suggests police use of galoshes at night to silence steps.
83	2 Oct. 1888	"	Suggests use of bloodhounds.
84	2 Oct. 1888	Nurse Groom, 7 Fourth Avenue, West Brighton, Sussex	Suggests dressing detectives as unfortunates, armed and carrying whistles.
85	2 Oct. 1888	Gunthorpe, 24 Castlegate Street, Gainsborough, [Lincs.?]	Suggests second police patrol to follow the first, wearing India-rubber soles.
86	4 Oct. 1888	Irvine Harle, Solicitor, 31 Furnival Street, Holborn	Question the unfortunates re clients they have spoken to.
87	26 Nov. 1888	William Harrison, Moulton, Newmarket, Suffolk	Clergyman, dreamt that Pat Murphy and Jim Slaney are the murderers at 22 Gresham Street.
88	3 Oct. 1888	Albert Hartshorne, Bradbourne Hall, Wirksworth, Derbys	Suggests dressing detectives as females with extra protection round the throat.
89	3 Oct. 1888	E. Haskell, 18 Baker Street, Portman Square, London	Thinks murderer is foreign medical student.
90	4 Oct. 1888	Mary Heard, London N	Murderer is escaped lunatic from Leavesden some time ago.
91	n.d.	J.H. Heath, 82 Barry Road, Hemel Hempstead, Herts.	Offers assistance to police and wishes for issue of protective clothing and warrant.

No.	Date	Sender/Address	Content/Remarks
92	n.d.	"	More of above.
93	22 Jan. 1889	N. Heeney, Rockery Pond Gdns, Ballarat, Victoria, Australia	A medium.
94	"	"	'spiritist' nonsense.
95	"	"	Envelope.
96	20 Oct. 1888	L.C. Ingham, West Vale, near Halifax	Wants lock of victim's hair or item of clothing 'worn close to the skin'.
97	6 Oct. 1888	N. Hollander, 28 Stratford Road, Kensington, London W	Believes murderer is a Dr Sass or Sassy, a surgeon from Kensington.
98	1 Oct. 1888	W. Hope, Naval and Military Club, 94 Piccadilly, London W	Will provide 'specials' to assist the police. Friends of his who 'will respond to the call'.
99	30 Sep. 1888	"	Suggests attaching detectives to paid prostitutes.
100	2 Oct. 1888	Edw. M. Hore, Dulwich Common, London SE	Suggests that murderer(s) dresses in a woman's garb to 'delude the police'.
101	8 Oct. 1888	John F. Hunt, Biggleswade. Bedfordshire	Is a 'sensitive', has advice for police. A fantasist.
102	6 Oct. 1888	"	Enrol me as a candidate (for reward).
103	22 Oct. 1888	"	Has messages from spirits.
104	"	"	With 103 above.
105	3 Oct. 1888	"	'Sensitive' thinks murderer is an Italian sculptor.
106	13 Nov. 1888	"	Wants a reward poster, supplies descriptions of suspects.
107	28 Nov. 1888	"	Thanks police for 'placard'. More nonsense.
108	7 Dec. 1888	"	Has name and address of murderer!
109	8 Dec. 1888	"	Is unhappy that police are not receptive to his suggestions.
110	26 Dec. 1888	"	Wants to assist police.
111	2 Jan. 1889	"	Has spirit messages, details available.
112	4 Mar. 1889	"	Another spiritual message, William Hinton, a butcher, is the murderer.
113	"	"	Part of above.
114	"	"	Part of above.
115	3 Oct. 1888	T.S. Jolly, 324 Commercial Road, London E	Police must hit murderer on head if he is caught as he is dangerous.
116	16 Oct. 1888	'Justitia', a Jew, London	The fire in Hooper Street, may have been the murderer burning his clothes.
117	29 Nov. 1888	Mary Kidgell, 6 Via Gioberti, Turin, Italy	Murderer(s) might be Buddhist(s).
118	"	"	Part of above letter.
119	3 Dec. 1888	W. Kilsby, 1 Harewood Terrace, Southall	Sketch and description of murderer, a man seen in High Holborn.
120	6 Dec. 1888	"	Police report re above.
121	7 Oct. 1888	E. Jay Klinck, 207 Genessee, Utica, New York, USA	Suggests use of spiritualism.

No.	Date	Sender/Address	Content/Remarks
122	"	"	Part of above letter, description.
123	1 Oct. 1888	Maj Samuel Knight, City Carlton Club, London EC	It is the work of two men, suggests reward.
124	5 Oct. 1888	Alfred J. Kyle, 130 Pilgrom Street, Newcastle	Mr Victor Wyldes, a 'Psycometer', may be able to assist.
125	n.d.	"	Press cutting, 'Thought Reading Applied to the Detection of Crime', 5 Oct. 1888.
126	6 Oct. 1888	John Laver, 592 Old Ford Road, Bow, London E	Use female decoys with men waiting.
127	8 Oct. 1888	Rob. H. Lawrence, 6 St George's Road, London SE	Journalist has plan to entrap killer, using outcasts as bait with police hiding.
128	1 Oct. 1888	J.S. Levin, Steam Printing Works, 75 Leadenhall Street EC	Has premises opposite Aldgate Pump, suggests closing gateways at night.
129	3 Oct. 1888	Percy Lindley, 123/125 Fleet Street, London	Regrets being out when police called, is testing the hound tomorrow.
130	12 Oct. 1888	"	Re offer of bloodhound for City Police does not think country-trained hound suitable.
131	3 Oct. 1888	W. Longley, Yalding, Kent	Has had hop-pickers down and has heard the murderer may be a slaughterman.
132	2 Oct. 1888	J. Lovell, Chyandour, Penzance, Cornwall	Suggests making copies of Jack the Ripper letters and distributing them.
133	1 Oct. 1888	Selina McCaul, St Magnus Rectory, London EC	Suggests the murderer may be disguised as a policeman.
134	1 Oct. 1888	L.M. MacReady, 3 Dawson Street, Dublin, Ireland	Suggests employing prostitutes as detectives with steel or chain armour collars.
135	1889	P. McGaw	Writes re fire at Dumfries.
136	1 Oct. 1888		Address of 'Jane Kelly 6 Dorset Street is no doubt Dublin not London.'
137	1 Oct. 1888	James S. Mason, Carnoustie, NB	Suggests disguising police as women, armed and with means to raise alarm.
138	2 Oct. 1888	R.H. Merrett, 61 Lime Place, Higher Broughton, Manchester	Suggests use of bloodhounds kept in readiness at police stations.
139	3 Oct. 1888	C. Morgan, 58/60 Cannon Street, London EC	Murderer may be a woman, or disguised as a woman.
140	2 Oct. 1888	Francis H. Morgan, Rector, Gisborough Rectory, Yorks	Suggests murderer 'is occupying a much higher position' and may stay in a hotel.
141	4 Oct. 1888	Herbert Morris, Haslemere, Lansdowne Place, Upper Norwood	Murderer may be hiding in old Jews' cemetery (includes sketch).
142	2 Oct. 1888	Charles McPhater, 144 Berkeley Street, Glasgow, Scotland	Suggests dressing detectives as women, with metal collars.
143	n.d.	"	Visiting card.
144	n.d.	E.M.	Suggests dressing man in armour as a woman.
145	2 Oct. 1888	'Nemesis', Dumfries (postmark)	Suggests using a hound attached to every police office.
146	2 Oct. 1888	'Nemo'	Suggests the murderer may give his victims sweets, possible clue if traced where bought.

No.	Date	Sender/Address	Content/Remarks
147	9 Dec. 1888	'Nemo', London	Has given description of two men, previous letters refer. Different writing to no. 146.
148	27 Sep. 1889	Robert S. Owen, Milldale, Tuscalovsa Co., Alabama, USA	Suggests murderer, once respectable, has a disease caught from women and is ruined.
149	n.d.	Mrs. L. Painter, Burlington Lodge, Strand, Ryde, SU	Visiting card.
150	3 Oct. 1888	"	Suggests murderer may be a woman, or an ape. There are wild animals in London.
151	5 Oct. 1888	Sid J. Paull, 11 Luard Street, Caledonian Road, London N	Suggests using an electric light attached to a building and bellringer to warn of crimes.
152	5 Oct. 1888	B. Pearse, 4 Town Hall Avenue, Bournemouth, Hampshire	Suggests ambush by three powerful men in lonely places in wait.
153	9 Oct. 1888	H. & R. Powell, 17 Bayswater Terr., Lancaster Gate, London W	Suggests murderer is a medical man and placing advert in *The Lancet*.
154	2 Oct. 1888	M. Puddig, Thrall Street, London E	Religious tone, letter allegedly from the murderer, gloats, will carry on a few weeks.
155	5 Oct. 1888	M.P.	Thinks murderer is Richard Mansfield, the actor, an American.
156	3 Oct. 1888	W.P.	Suggests supplying prostitutes with whistles to call for help.
157	3 Oct. 1888	A. Blandy, Chief Constable, Reading., Berkshire	Reports on Captain Rathbone's suspect, a Dr Duncan, the man in the cabmen's shelter.
158	n.d.	Capt. St G. Rathbone, Reading, Berkshire.	Newscutting re the above suspect.
159	2 Oct. 1888	"	Re suspect Dr Duncan, above, met him in Bombay in army.
160	3 Oct. 1888	Joshua Rowe, 8 Bryneaeran Terrace, Llanelly, Carms, Wales	Has theory, or clue, and wants reward.
161	17 Oct. 1888	T. H. Rundle, North Parade, Camborne, Cornwall	Suggests photographing victims' eyes for image of killer's likeness.
162	"	"	Part of above letter.
163	30 Jul. 1889	Dr P.J. Ross, Washington DC and New York, USA	Envelope.
164	"	"	Suggests murderer is a woman and dressing up a man as a lady to catch her.
165	12 Oct. 1888	'Saccharince', West Ham	Suggests murderer works in a sugar house as there is one in Hanbury Street and Berner Street.
166	4 Oct. 1888	'Scotus', Southampton	Suggests murderer is a diseased medical man working in a local hospital.
167	n.d.	E.L. Sellon, 3 Glazbury Road, West Kensington, London W	Suggests dressing female detectives as street walkers, wearing armour and armed.
168	2 Oct. 1888	James Carter Shepherd, Lainel Bank, Ambleside, Westmorland	Murderer is a female or is dressed as a female. Dress detectives as women.
169	1 Oct. 1888	J.N. Smart, St James Street, Walthamstow	Man followed him into coffee house where a fight and attempted assassination took place.

No.	Date	Sender/Address	Content/Remarks
170	2 Oct. 1888	Edward Smith, 91 Upper Grange Road, Bermondsey	Suggests murderer is 'Electre biologist', Professor Reynolds or Audrade.
171	3 Oct. 1888	N. Smith, Stancombe Villa, Howard Road, Penge, SE	Suggests searching roofs, lofts and stables in the neighbourhood.
172	9 Oct. 1888	W.J. Smith, 13 Red Lion Passage, Holborn, London WC	Has a motive and suspect, a Hungarian or a Mr MacSweeny.
173	"	"	Re a Mr Sweeney he has suspicions about.
174	n.d.		Printed form to prize fund of Polytechnic Young Men's Christian Institute.
175	n.d.	"	
176	2 Oct. 1888	G. Stainburn, 177 Stanhope, Street, London NW	Suggests disguising 'several young men' as women, armed.
177	1 Oct. 1888	Frank Standage, The Village, Blackheath, London	Has plan to catch killer using decoys.
178	28 Oct. 1888	Edwin Court, Eliza Street, Adelaide, Australia	Apparently mad, says murderer is men in false faces.
179	2 Oct. 1888	Messrs. Swindon & Sons, Temple Street, Birmingham	Problem solver, suggests census of lodgers returning home late, watchman or caretaker.
180	1 Oct. 1888	Edward Terry, Terry's Theatre, London WC	Suggests dressing detectives as women and using coded signals to other police.
181	3 Sep. 1888	'A Thinker'	Suggests murderer has venereal disease, details murderer's method of using knife.
182	"	"	Part of above letter.
183	28 Jan. 1889	'J.O.F.' C.C., City Police	Police acknowledgement re woman's letter of 27 January naming a man.
184	13 Nov. 1888	Unsigned	Murderer is William Onion late of Colney Hatch and Wakefield Asylums.
185	27 Jan. 1889	Richard Whittington The Second, Thornton Street, Leeds	References letter posted 13 November 1888 and asks for acknowledgement.
186	2 Oct. 1888	J. Trustram, Harpenden, Hertfordshire	Man in cab shelter is Dr MacDonald an escapee from Leavesden Asylum a year ago.
187	1 Oct. 1888	J.C. Tucker, 7 Holborn Street, Plymouth, Devon	Suggests dressing detectives as women. Murderer waits until after pub closing time.
188	2 Oct. 1888	J. Tullidge, Patent Steam Carpet Beating Works, King's Cross, N	Suggests murderer's method of killing is from behind.
189	3 Sep. 1888	William Turner, 4 Paternoster Row, Brushfield Street, London E	Has plan to catch murderer.
190	1 Oct. 1888	Mary Ann Waite, Wisbech, Cambridgeshire	A plea for fallen women.
191	3 Oct. 1888	William Watkins, 60 Cobbold Road, Shepherd's Bush, W	Police should wear silent boots.
192	18 Aug. 1889	"	Policemen to whistle and telegraph each other.
193	8 Oct. 1888	W.G. Watts, Blackheath Road, Greenwich	Murderer is a Hebrew butcher and left-handed.
194	10 Oct. 1888	Unsigned	Written in pidgin English, watch house 51 King Street, Gt Yarmouth for suspect.

No.	Date	Sender/Address	Content/Remarks
195	3 Oct. 1888	Chas. Wilkinson, Lonsdale Street, Stoke-on-Trent, Staffordshire	Dress men as women and wear iron collars.
196	"	"	Dress young men as girls.
197	2 Oct. 1888	Dr Forbes Winslow, 70 Wimpole Street, London	Telegraph, offers his services to the police.
198	3 Nov. 1888	W. Aston, 47 Pearson Road, Stockton-on-Tees	Suggests using unfortunates as detectives, 'Pro tem', use 300 of them.
199	9 Oct. 1888	Francis Witt, 28a Basinghall Street, City of London	Plan to capture the murderer by advertising meeting in papers to discuss his capture.
200	13 Nov. 1888	F. Wontisette, Thanet College, Margate, Kent	Suggests the murderer is a monomaniac.
201	3 Oct. 1888	'C. Wy'	Set women with men waiting nearby in ambush.
202	8 Oct. 1888	Mrs A.W., 99 Rendlesham, Road, Upper Clapton	Has seen the murderer in Cavendish Court. Has religious tone. See also no. 206.
203	4 Oct. 1888	'A Well Wisher', Knowle Road, Brixton	Brixton is infested with loose women. Brixton police cannot do a thing.
204	2 Oct. 1888	Unsigned	Suggests taking a thumb print from the postcard sent to Central News.
205	2 Oct. 1888	'xx', Staffordshire	A young clergyman who was in the papers is the murderer, was writing immoral letters.
206	4 Oct. 1888	Unsigned	Re suspicious man exposing himself in Cavendish Court. See also 202 and 207.
207	n.d.		Newscutting – description of suspect circulated.
208	4 Oct. 1888	'A Sane Woman'	Saw a suspicious man in Bond Street 'last week', 'un-English' in appearance.
209	"	"	Part of above letter.
210	7 Oct. 1888	'A Friend', Liverpool	Suspects the watchman George Morris of being the murderer.
211	12 Oct. 1888	Unsigned	Suspects Herbert Freund of being the murderer, a religious fanatic. See also no. 13.
212	15 Oct. 1888	A.F. Williamson, Chief Constable, Scotland Yard	Metropolitan Police letter sending two letters to City Police.
213	8 Oct. 1888	'May-Bee', Edinburgh Scotland	States that murderer lives at 29 Fleet Street, a supposition.
214	9 Oct. 1888	Anon	States that 24 Duke Street is connected with the murders.
215	15 Oct. 1888	Unsigned, Trowbridge (post-mark)	States that PC Watkins is the murderer, 'Watch him.'
216	13 Oct. 1888	"	Envelope for above letter.
217	17 Oct. 1888	R. Anderson, Assistant Commissioner, Scotland Yard	Metropolitan Police letter re the above, no. 215.
218	20 Oct. 1888	'Common Sense', London	What happens to the suspects who have been arrested?
219	5 Nov. 1888	'andy-handy', London	Has seen suspicious man in Fleet Lane, had a bag with two feet and a head in it.

No.	Date	Sender/Address	Content/Remarks
220	15 Nov. 1888	Unsigned	The Kelly murder was not the work of Jack the Ripper but wanted it to appear so.
221	n.d.	'a stranger O.X.X.'	A man named Galer is the writer of the letters.
222	n.d.	Unsigned	Letter re using bloodhounds.
223	n.d.	'Feather Few'	Suggests dressing men as women and wearing steel collars.
224	n.d.	'Jack the Ripper'	Postcard, drawing, has 'Annie's' rings, 'I mean doing more.'
225	19 Oct. 1888	'Jack the Ripper', Dublin	'I intend to murder one in Dublin.' Postcard Messrs. BENSDORP, see no. 226.
226	23 Oct. 1888	Messrs. Bensdorps (Cocoa), St Paul's Churchyard, London	Covering letter from Bensdorps with above.
227	2 Oct. 1888	Unsigned, 30 Melville Road, London NW	Suggests murderer hides near scene of his deeds.
228	3 Oct. 1888	Unsigned, Eastbourne, Sussex	Suggests that murderer dresses as a woman to escape.
229	23 Jul. 1889	R. Anderson, Assistant Commissioner, Scotland Yard	Metropolitan Police acknowledgement, receipt of letter dated 20th.
230	6 Mar. 1889	T.N. Abbott Bros., 25 Austin Friars, London EC	Having seen 'Inspector' McWilliam today requests any update re suggestion made.
231	2 Oct. 1888	Henry Armitage, Ludgvan, Penzance, Cornwall	Suspects American Fenian doctor of being the murderer. Ex-police constable.
232	3 Oct. 1888	"	Second letter re Fenians, Americans and the dynamite outrages.
233	8 Oct. 1888	"	Re American doctor.
234	28 Nov. 1888	"	Re murder near Dover, tall man seen, who lodged at a village near Havant.
235	19 Jul. 1889	"	More on Fenians, Le Caron, etc.
236	27 Oct. 1889	"	"
237	28 Nov. 1888	'Astrologer'	See the *Astrologer* for November for a description of the murderer.
238	12 Nov. 1888	E. Ballon, 114 E. 10th Street, New York, USA	The murderer is a religious monomaniac. Perhaps relative was led into a life of shame.
239	3 Oct. 1888	S.G. Batting, 98 Calverly Road, Tunbridge Wells, Kent	Suspects travelling gypsies he saw go by.
240	9 Oct. 1888	J.J. Beckett, Union Wharf, East Greenwich, London SE	Suspects that the murderer is James David Lampard, described.
241	4 Oct. 1888	N.A. Benelius, 30 Aldgate Street, London EC	Writes re meeting a lady, Miss Wilkinson.
242	18 Oct. 1888	N.A. Benelius, 19 Goswell Road, London	Wants to get to know the mayor.
243	29 Jun. 1889	W. Benton, Beaconsfield House, Earith, Huntingdonshire	Saw a suspicious man while on a trip to London.
244	n.d.	Charles Berkley, Granville Road, South Fields, Wimbledon Park, SW	Suggests dressing policemen as women.

No.	Date	Sender/Address	Content/Remarks
245	18 Nov. 1888	Chas. B. Billinge, New Mills, Derbyshire	Suggests employment of 'intelligent females' from asylums.
246	6 Oct. 1888	John Binny, 13 Tavistock Place, London	The Malay cook and Dodge the sailor theories are a ruse by the murderer.
247	2 Oct. 1888	Webster Biss, 23 Maclise Road, Addison Road, London W	Look for a 'velvet-footed' man.
248	6 Oct. 1888	J.W. Boyd, Lee, Kent.	Look after American in cab who was arrested.
249	6 Oct. 1888	R.C.N., Bristol	Suspects American doctor, Sequah, dressed like a cowboy.
250	3 Oct. 1888	J. Burke, New Hartley, Northumberland	I should dress as a street girl, 'I would like to become a young detective.'
251	19 Nov. 1888	H. Carr, Maryborough, Main Street, Queen's Co., Ireland	Arrest women and dress police in women's clothing at night.
252	5 Oct. 1888	J.W. Causier, Yetminster, Sherborne, Dorset	Suggests the murderer is a Jewish slaughter-man.
253	19 Nov. 1888	Charton (& Lagrange), Royalty Theatre, Dean Street, London	Name suggested in a séance was Bluendenwall, a butcher.
254	3 Oct. 1888	E.W. Clark, Post Office, Addiscombe	Murderer was one of the slaughtermen at the Nichols inquest.
255	5 Oct. 1888	R.B.B. Clayton, 88 Bishopsgate, London EC	Encloses cutting from the *Standard* on a missing doctor.
256	10 Oct. 1888	T. Cleare, 2 South Grove, Bow Road, London E	Suggestions re murderer hiding in model dwellings.
257	3 Oct. 1888	H.O. Cooke, 88 Lugard Road, Peckham, London SE	Suggests distributing handbills with description of the murderer, etc.
258	16 Nov. 1888	James Coutts, 21 Jopps Lane, Aberdeen, Scotland	Suggests photographing victims' eyes for image of murderer.
259	1 Oct. 1888	H.E. Curtis, A.P.S., 1 Croft Villas, Lower Croft, Hastings	Suggests dressing men as women.
260	27 Sep. 1888	H. Darley, 30 Melville Road, Stonebridge, London NW	Suggests murderer is an assistant or porter at a hospital.
261	2 Oct. 1888	G.M. Dartnell, 272 High Street, Plumstead	Suggests the murderer is a 'she' instead of a 'he'.
262	16 Jan. 1890	Thos. H. Dawson, Corning Observer, Tehama, Calif., USA	Suspects a French butler from a lady's house in Paris is the London murderer.
263	15 Nov. 1888	John Dean, Hill Side, Strood, Kent	Suggests using prostitutes to catch murderer.
264	12 Sep. 1888	A. deBorra, Elsinore, San Diego, California, USA	Murderer is a practising physician and is insane.
265	3 Oct. 1888	C.J. Denny, Milestone House, Blackwater, Farnborough, Hants	Suspects Dr Forbes Winslow of committing the murders, 'who has a peculiar mind'.
266	2 Oct. 1888	William Dickinson, 27 Zetland Street, South Bromley, London E	Thinks the murderer lives near to Chicksand Street Board School. Includes sketch plan.
267	3 Oct. 1888	J.J. Durrant, Watchmakers, 40 Cheapside, London EC	Thinks the murderer is a left-handed butcher or slaughterman.

No.	Date	Sender/Address	Content/Remarks
268	2 Oct. 1888	A.H. Edwards, St Albans, Hertfordshire	The cabman's shelter suspect, a doctor, is the murderer, escaped from Leavesden.
269	2 Oct. 1888	John Forbes, Hertford	Suggests use of posters of the Jack the Ripper letter.
270	5 Oct. 1888	James Ford, 112 Commercial Road, Bournemouth, Hants	Thinks that his missing wife is the Mitre Square victim.
271	3 Oct. 1888	Fred C. Friend, Peckham, London SE	The murderer is a ship's cook or steward. Watch sailors' lodging houses.
272	7 Oct. 1888	Sarah Fremlin, Maidstone, Kent	Thinks a doctor she once knew may be the murderer. Suspect, see also no. 66.
273	16 Nov. 1888	J.M. Fry, 1 Denham Villas, Surbiton, Surrey	Thinks the press publish too many details and get in the way of police capturing killer.
274	2 Oct. 1888	H.B. Garling, 25 Clifton Crescent, Folkestone, Kent	Suggests dressing armed men as women.
275	16 Jul. 1889	Charles Geary, 3 Wood Street, Spitalfields, London E	Complains of state of Middlesex Street.
276	13 Oct. 1888	James B. Gibbins, Percy Lodge, Wood Green, London N	Graphologist. Regrets police unwilling to accept his proposal. See nos 72 and 73.
277	3 Oct. 1888	John S. Gordon, 9 Bridge Street, Aberdeen, Scotland	Suspects Dr Hartley, a patent medicine man selling Indian medicine. See also no. 77.
278	1 Nov. 1888	J.S. Gordon, 52 Loadside Road, Aberdeen, Scotland	Murderer is connected with the medical men.
279	1 Oct. 1888	Harry R. Green, 34 Compton Road, Canonbury, London N	Suggests watching the slaughterhouses. See also nos 82 and 83.
280	20 Jul. 1889	H.O. Breen, Wieringen, Holland	A magistrate, thinks the murderer is a woman.
281	5 Oct. 1888	W.G., Gloucester Walk, Kensington, London W	Murderer is a religious monomaniac at St Paul's.
282	4 Oct. 1888	S. Hacker, 7 Boyne Street, Willington, Co. Durham	Suggests photographing image in women's eyes.
283	3 Oct. 1888	Frank Hall, 16 Stratford Place, Camden Square, London NW	Suggests that murderer has a key to sewers.
284	28 Nov. 1888	George Hanmer, Garrett, DeKalb Co., Indiana, USA	An ex-police constable offering to help. (PC 765, resigned in 1870).
285	14 Jan. 1889	H. Harriss, Bolton Street, Newcastle, NSW, Australia	Offers to guide police, also see no. 293. Mentions Mr. F.A. Inglis and J.A. Garrick.
286	2 Oct. 1888	John Harris, Hungerden, Frittenden, Staplehurst, Kent	Has plan to involve prostitutes.
287	10 Sep. 1889	Attewart S. Harrison, 105 Cannon Street, London EC	Thinks that the murderer is a butcher and has washable clothes.
288	2 Oct. 1888	Gilbart Harry, 112 North End, Croydon, Surrey	Suggests dressing detectives as women. Murderer may be disguised as a woman.
289	4 Oct. 1888	Harry Hime, 14 Castle Street	Thinks murderer is a maniac and a medico, may be a student.
290	5 Oct. 1888	John H. Hoyer, 315 Broome Street, Near Forsyth, New York, USA	Artist tailor, thinks murderer is a police officer.

No.	Date	Sender/Address	Content/Remarks
291	2 Oct. 1888	John E. Humfrey, 149 Southwark Park Road, Bermondsey, E	Suggests a plan involving observations by hidden men with night glasses.
292	24 Dec. 1888	J.F. Hunt, Biggleswade, Bedfordshire	Unhappy with police, wants the reward. See also nos 101–14.
293	4 Jan. 1889	F.A. Inglis, Pitt Town, Wallsend, NSW, Australia	Offers his help. See also no. 285.
294	8 Oct. 1888	A.H. Jackson, Bishopbriggs, near Glasgow, Scotland	Religious tone re poor women.
295	12 Nov. 1888	A. James, 2 Therland Place, Station Road, Twickenham	Suspects a man he saw in Richmond. Gives description.
296	27 Oct. 1888	G. Gerring, Great Barrington, Massachusetts, USA	Offers to act as 'bait' for killer.
297	2 Oct. 1888	W.H. Jones, Surbiton House, Redhill, Surrey	Thinks murderer finds refuge in a vacant house in the neighbourhood.
298	16 Oct. 1888	Max Kamthun, Pomerania, Germany	Thinks the murderer is a mad woman. It is simple murder and not committed in lust.
299	29 Oct. 1888	Herbert H. Lane, Mount Pleasant, Chepstow, Monmouth	Suggests photographing victims' eyes for image of the murderer.
300	11 Jan. 1889	E.K. Larkins, Custom House, London EC	Propounds his seaman theory.
301	12 Mar. 1889	"	Re ship movements.
302	3 Oct. 1888	Maj Charles Latham, 4th Battalion, Royal Fusiliers	Murderer is a medical man and has a plan to capture him.
303	3 Oct. 1888	George Letts, The Chase, Kislingbury, Northants	Suggests dressing police as old women and loitering. Article re photographing eyes.
304	2 Oct. 1888	Percy Lindley, 123 & 125 Fleet Street, London EC	Re bloodhounds, see also nos 129–30.
305	22 Nov. 1888	John Loomey, 42 Pownell Street, Stretford Road, Manchester	Plan circulated printed information for women, wants to work as amateur detective.
306	22 Nov. 1888	Arthur Lowe, Thoroughfare, Saxmundham, Suffolk	Has a scheme to catch murderer.
307	4 Oct. 1888	Mrs S. Luckett, 10 Somerford Grove	Suggests suspects, including Richard Mansfield, the actor.
308	10 Nov. 1888	A. Mason, Union Bank of Scotland, Chancery Lane, London	Saw a repulsive man at Smith's bookstall at Cannon Street station last evening.
309	19 Sep. 1888	John Moore, Central News Agency, 5 New Bridge Street, City	Requests a copy of a bill from City Police.
310	2 Oct. 1888	T.S. Nettleship, 434 Oxford Street, London W	Suspects a socialist speaker at Hyde Park.
311	15 Nov. 1888	Eduard Neuberger, 82 Colvestone Crescent, St Mark's Square, Dalston	The police should be given every possible information.
312	26 Sep. 1889	Cesarine Kestelout de Noyelles, Rue de Bernay, Orbec en Auge, Calvados, France	Murderer(s) is/are student(s) in medicine or surgery.
313	n.d.	H. Obermuller, Neptune Place, Risdon Street, Rotherhithe, London	Suggests dressing men as women, wearing boots with India-rubber soles.

No.	Date	Sender/Address	Content/Remarks
314	1 Oct. 1888	Edward O'Brien, The Financial News, 11 Abchurch Lane, EC	Offers £50 cash towards a reward.
315	5 Oct. 1888	"	Acknowledgement from police re above.
316	13 Nov. 1888	Charles Palmer, 57 Gracechurch Street, London EC	Suspects an off-duty PC is the murderer.
317	3 Dec. 1888	Jetze Posthuma, Harlingen, The Netherlands	Believes he has a 'means' to cause the murderer to betray himself.
318	4 Oct. 1888	John Powell, High Street, Winslow, Buckinghamshire	Has a plan to catch the murderer.
319	2 Oct. 1888	Richard Pybus, Wyton House, Crouch Hill, London N	Suggests disguising policemen as women, armed with revolvers and whistles.
320	10 Sep. 1889	James Quinn, c/o John Taylor, 14 Meanwood Road, Leeds	Offers services to discover the murderer.
321	20 Jul. 1889	Dr P.J. Ross, Washington DC and New York, USA	Murderer is dressed as a woman or as a policeman.
322	n.d.	Eliza Rowland	Change the police beat times etc., police stations should communicate by telegraph.
323	3 Oct. 1888	Mrs. E.H. Russell Davies, 44 Lady Maynard Road, Kentish Town	Has clairvoyant power, see below.
324	3–4 Oct. 1888	R.H. Davies, Kentish Town, London NW	Wife is a clairvoyant, would be able to get contact through hair or clothing.
325	8 Nov. 1888	Jessie Scorgie, Mill of Fochel	'Protection Take and Return.'
326	2 Oct. 1888	Henry H. Selby Hele, Holy Trinity Vicarage, Rotherhithe, London SE	A bloodhound might be found useful.
327	12 Nov. 1888	H. Serret, Paris, 19 Rue de Richelieu, Paris, France	A hypnotist, offers his services.
328	26 Nov. 1888	J. Davies Sewell, Chamberlain's Court, Guildhall, London EC	Writes re offer of £100 reward by Sir Alfred Kirby.
329	2 Oct. 1888	W. Simmonds, The Ferns, Fair field, Farnham, Surrey	Wants photographs of Stride and Eddowes. Re missing girl from 9 Brick Lane.
330	12 Sep. 1889	Ernst Spetman, 105 Am Alten Hafen, Bremerhaven, Germany	Suggests photographing the victims' eyes for image, details methodology.
331	2 Oct. 1888	J. Horatio Smith, Oakendean Park, Crofold, Horsham, Sussex	Suggests disguising a detective as a woman.
332	22 May 1890	J.T.S.	A photograph of a man outside Ward's photographers is his suspect.
333	8 Oct. 1888	Richard Taylor, Public Baths, Endell Street, Long Acre, London	Has suggestions of means of catching the criminal, women to wear steel protection.
334	30 Jul. 1889	John Thompson, Belmont House, 28 Clarence Parade, Southsea	'I am on the right track with God's help . . .'
335	3 Oct. 1888	Lizzie Tunnicliffe, Market Street, Penkridge, Nr Stafford	Some woman should act the part of a fallen woman and be followed by police.
336	6 Sep. 1888	W. Turner, 4 Paternoster Row, Brushfield Street, London EC	Suggests detectives keep observations in passages of lonely houses.
337	2 Oct. 1888	E.T.	Religious letter, a prayer has been offered.

No.	Date	Sender/Address	Content/Remarks
338	8 Nov. 1888	C.J. Van Vessem, Wermeldinge, The Netherlands	Impracticable suggestions to trace murderer.
339	8 Oct. 1888	William Walton, Kingsley, Cheshire	Suggests women carry a marker to identify an accoster, bird lime.
340	Oct. 1888	N. Watts, 11 Young Street, Kensington, London W	Suggests method for silent boots for police.
341	n.d.	Alfred Wayles, 7 Roman Road, Bedford Park, London	Suggests employing women with nerve and intelligence as unfortunates.
342	14 Nov. 1888	George West, Kingstone, near Hereford, Herefordshire	Suggestion re identity of Mary Jane Kelly. Mad Jack Ryan may be the murderer.
343	4 Oct. 1888	E.J. Whitefern, 337 City Road, London	Suggests murderer is disguised as a woman. Details clothing.
344	26 Oct. 1888	Florence Forbes Winslow, Rivercourt, Hammersmith	Jack the Ripper lives in North London and was seen on a train, encloses press cutting.
345	19 Nov. 1888	Thomas Woodgate, 100 Conway Street, West Brighton, Sussex	Offers services of wife and himself to help, 'we have an idea'.
346	2 Oct. 1888	Geo. Young, 15 St Dunstan's Hill, London EC	Asks for a poster (reward £500 Aldgate murder) for his shop (give to bearer).
347	15 Mar. 1890	Francis Zysler, 75 Bishops Road, Cambridge Heath	Claims he has stopped the murders and wants the reward.
348	15 Nov. 1888	Mrs M. Bate, Anns Cottage, Friendly Street, Deptford	Acknowledgement from City Police, see nos 7–9.
349	29 Nov. 1888	J.R. Clark, Cleveland, Ohio, USA	Acknowledgement from City Police, see nos 38–9.
350	23 Jul. 1889	Metropolitan Police	Letter of acknowledgement.
351	1 Oct. 1888	Unsigned	Suggests dressing detectives as women and varying police hours.
352	3 Oct. 1888	'A Working Man', 5 Rothbury Road, Victoria Park	Suggests dressing men as women.
353	2 Oct. 1888	Unsigned	Suggests dressing police as women.
354	6 Oct. 1888	'Watchful,' City	Suspects an American working at G. Weston & Co., Electricians, Mile End.
355	7 Oct. 1888	'Homo Sum', Bromley, Kent	Suggests dressing detectives as women.
356	9 Oct. 1888	'One that has had his eyes opened'	Critical of police, 'advertising your doings in the Papers'.
357	9 Oct. 1888	Unsigned	Suspects a lodger at 44 Holly Terrace, Hammersmith. Resembles likeness in *Telegraph*.
358	12 Oct. 1888	Unsigned	Suspects a discharged City Police constable who was stationed at Seething Lane.
359	19 Oct. 1888	'An Accessory'	States an ex-Metropolitan PC (dismissed) is murderer.
360	12 Nov. 1888	'One of the Public'	Thinks the murderer is a caretaker or house-keeper in charge of offices City area.
361	15 Nov. 1888	Unsigned	Suggests watching the seaside resorts Folke-stone, Hastings and Brighton.

No.	Date	Sender/Address	Content/Remarks
362	15 Nov. 1888	Unsigned	The murderer may be a butcher, in locality of Buck's Row.
363	11 Nov. 1888	Unsigned (USA?), (resident of Philadelphia)	Keep guard on those who have been arrested and lately discharged.
364	27 Dec. 1888	J.R.	Letter allegedly written by the murderer, 'I will put away with her Sunday.'
365	7 Jan. 1889	Louisa Gooding, Newton Poppleford, Devon	Rambling religious letter, 'I was removed from the Asylum insanity has done its work.'
366	22 Jan. 1889	'Nemo', London	Suspects the two foreigners seen with Rose Mylett.
367	29 Jan. 1889	"	The two men above seen again.
368	16 Feb. 1889	"	Re steamer times, *Calderon*, ex-Bilbao, entered on 28 September.
369	22 Jan. 1889	'Jack the Snicker', London. Lombard Street postmark	Suspects a man seen on a train journey to Wimbledon, described.
370	4 Jul. 1889	R. Anderson, Scotland Yard	Metropolitan Police pro-forma letter.
371	24 Jul. 1889	'Qui Vire', Liverpool	Murderer may be a single man living alone, a butcher or shoemaker.
372	30 Jul. 1889	Unsigned	Suggests that labels are put up where the women were found dead – religious.
373	4 Sep. 1889	Unsigned, London SE 5 postmark	A murder was committed at 65 Great Prescot Street last night, report by Sgt Sagar.
374	11 Sep. 1889	Unsigned	'I will cach him for you.'
375	n.d.	To Desford Industrial School, near Leicester	A 'Dear Boss' letter.
376	n.d.	Unsigned	"Think nothing of . . .' above letter.
377	6 Oct. 1888	Unsigned	Asks if the London Hospital has been searched.
378	"	"	Part of above letter.
379	Nov. 1888	No signature. London postmark	The man seen in Mitre Court with black bag corresponds with description of Parnell.
380	4 Oct. 1888	Unsigned	'Dr Chambers . . . mania for experiments'
381	3 Oct. 1888	Jack the Ripper, London	'Might do more of my business in the West part of London . . .'
382	4 Feb. 1889	Jack the Ripper	'Dear Boss' letter, is going to visit Mile End.
383	n.d.		Description of suspect 'from jail'.
384	21 Sep.		Envelope.
385	30 Jul. 1889		Printed message 'The Lord is in This House'.
386	6 Feb. 1889		London, OHMS returned unpaid letter.
387	6 Dec. 1889		London, envelope addressed, Commissioner of Detectives City of London Great Britain.
388	2 Oct. 1888	Mrs S. Fraser, 118 Guildhall Street, Folkestone, Kent	Religious tone, critical of government.
389	8 Oct. 1888	R. Hull, 4 Bloomfield Road, Bow, E	Ex-butcher, thinks the murderer is a dexterous slaughterman, describes methods.
390	16 Oct. 1888	Maj R.D.O. Stephenson, c/o London Hospital, E	Theory re the 'Juwes' message, thinks the murderer is French.

No.	Date	Sender/Address	Content/Remarks
391	12 Oct. 1888	Maj Gen E.R.C. Wilcox, 27 Ashburnham Road, Bedford	Suspects that Thomas Conway, an army pensioner, is the murderer.
392	7 May 1889	Chas. Wilkinson, Stoke-on-Trent, Staffordshire	Sent plan, the women should wear steel collars, includes drawing.
393	12 Oct. 1888	'An Observer', London postmark	Suspects two young men, 'the Conway brothers', one, Tom, is from the East End.
394	n.d.	Jack the Ripper	A 'Dear Boss' letter, 'The police will not Get me.' Signed 'Jack the Ripper'.
395	n.d.	Jack the Ripper	'I come from Boston. . . . You will hear of another murder.'
396	Oct. 1888	Ripper, London E	'I shall be in Buck's Row.' Sent to *Daily News* office, with covering letters.

Notes

2. Policing the Metropolis

1. 4 Whitehall Place and its neighbour no. 5 were two highly respectable, three-storeyed buildings, formerly private houses, that were utilised by the police as offices.
2. After Robert Peel, although in the authors' experience a century later this had switched to 'John' after the John Peel of the 'Do you ken John Peel?' hunting song.
3. David Ascoli, *The Queen's Peace. The Origin and Development of the Metropolitan Police 1829–1879*, London, Hamish Hamilton, 1979, p. 273.
4. Browne, *The Rise of Scotland Yard*, 1956, p. 177.
5. This is a brief summary of his Masonic career as given by his grandson Watkin W. Williams in his biography *The Life of General Sir Charles Warren*. Warren was initiated in the Friendship Lodge, no. 278 (formerly no. 345) at Gibraltar in 1858, he was then 19 years old, and installed as master of the Lodge in 1863. He became a joining member of the Inhabitants Lodge, Gibraltar, no. 153 (formerly no. 178) in 1860, and was senior warden of that Lodge in 1862. His further progress in Masonry was as follows: Royal Arch, October 1861; mark master in the Gibraltar Lodge, no. 43, October 1861; Rose Croix, Europa Chapter, Gibraltar, November 1861; Knight Templar, 1863; Grand Elected Knight, K.H., 1879. He attained the rank of a grand lodge officer as a past grand deacon in 1887, and also became past grand sojourner in the Supreme Grand Chapter in the same year. He was district grand master of the Eastern Archipelago under the English Constitution from 1891 to 1895. The Charles Warren Lodge, no. 1832, was founded in his honour at Kimberley in 1879.
6. Warren, *Underground Jerusalem*, 1876, p. 168.

3. King Stork Takes Command

1. The title was thought appropriate as the new officers' areas were larger than many towns and cities.
2. Margaret Harkness writing as 'John Law', *In Darkest London: Captain Lobo, Salvation Army*, London, 1889.
3. London, *The People of the Abyss*, 1903, p. 64.
4. From that time nos 4 and 5 Whitehall Place were left to the chief commissioner and his two assistants, Colonel Pearson, who was in charge of force discipline and Alexander Carmichael Bruce, who was in charge of civil business and matters connected with land, buildings, stores and provisions, and the Receiver, Mr Pennefather.
5. Porter, *The Origins of the Vigilant State*, 1987.

4. First Blood

1. The title of local inspector was given to divisional detective inspectors, while that of divisional inspector was applied to uniformed inspectors.

5. Ghastly Crimes Committed by a Maniac

1. The job of 'knocker-up' earned the police small perquisites. It involved the night beat officers in rousing workers who required an early call. Those who wanted an early 'alarm call' would visit the local police station and their names, addresses and the time for the call would be written down on a slate. The tips earned by doing this were very useful for the police but the practice was frowned upon by some senior officers who did not like the idea of their officers accepting money or performing 'menial tasks'. The job was eventually taken over by enterprising gentlemen and looked upon as a 'profession'.
2. Both authors were issued with capes and long overcoats when they joined the police force, and even then it was common for officers out on patrol to leave a heavy cape, or overcoat, with a nightwatchman or some other custodian if it was not needed.
3. Godley, then aged 30, was to remain on the Whitechapel murders inquiries and worked closely with Detective Inspector Abberline.
4. Now in a private collection.

6. Horror upon Horror

1. The cat's meat shop was run by Mrs Harriet Hardiman who slept on the premises with her 16-year-old son.
2. *East London Observer*, 15 September 1888.
3. At this time Chandler had fifteen years' police service behind him. He was to retire ten years later.
4. At this time Swanson was aged 40 and had twenty years' police service.
5. Mrs Long was also called Darrell in the newspapers which has caused confusion in various books over the years. The police file index entry HO 144/221/A49301C, f. 136 shows her as 'Long Mrs. alias Durrell'.
6. Phillips was actually called at 6.20 and saw the body at 6.30.
7. 4.30 a.m.: Dr Phillips actually said 'two or three hours earlier' according to the same report.
8. For which see Geberth, *Practical Homicide Investigation: Tactics, Procedures, and Forensic Techniques*, 1996, pp. 215–17.
9. *The Times*, 14 September 1888.
10. *Daily Telegraph*, 14 September 1888.
11. *The Times*, 27 September 1888.
12. HO 144/221/A49301C, ff. 20–1.
13. In a report Warren sent to the Home Office on 19 September 1888, HO 144/221/A49301C, ff. 90–2.
14. See *Daily Telegraph*, 13 November 1888 and Police Orders, 3 November 1888.
15. The original document was in the hands of the Swanson family but is now believed lost.
16. In a conversation with Stewart Evans.

7. The London Terror

1. Presumably as a result of her surname, i.e. 'Long Stride'.
2. Evidence that Stride stated she had had a quarrel with Kidney was given at the inquest by Catherine Lane, a fellow lodger at Flower and Dean Street.
3. The printing office was at the back of the club and was occupied at the time of the murder by the editor of *Der Arbeiter Fraint* (*The Worker's Friend*), Philip Kranz, who heard nothing. Another inquest witness was William Wess, the overseer at the printing office. He left the yard at about 12.15 a.m. and had also seen nothing.
4. This would not be surprising because many marches and demonstrations started from the club. Interestingly, in March 1889, when Monro was commissioner, there was a fight outside the club involving between 200 and 300 people, one of whom was Diemschutz, who had found Stride's body. According to one report, the police forced their way into the club, 'broke windows, tore down pictures and posters and fell with their fists and batons upon a few of the comrades who happened to be there'. Diemschutz's wife was thrown down 'and kicked, others they beat until the blood streamed, three were dragged to the station, again beaten and then charged with assaulting the police'. The houses were searched twice and a loft door broken open.
5. *Daily News*, 1 October 1888.
6. Schwartz probably did not appear at the inquest because he spoke hardly any English and required an interpreter. The coroner had the authority to accept written statements in lieu of a witness actually appearing.
7. Some newspapers stated he was a Dane.
8. He was 38 according to the police record, but 35 according to *The Times*.
9. In 1888 Smith was only 26 years old and had 5 years' service in the force.
10. The docket was the first paper given to a detective in any inquiry. It contained the bare facts and was 'marked out' to an inspector to allocate. As the papers relating to that inquiry built up, the initial docket remained with them and was tied up, labelled, catalogued, indexed and classified. In the case of an unsolved crime, the bundle of papers with the docket was stored for later retrieval if necessary.

8. A Thirst for Blood

1. *Lloyd's Weekly Newspaper*, 7 October 1888.
2. 'Casual wards' at local workhouses opened at 6 p.m. when a queue of destitute men and women would already be waiting to enter. As temporary residents of the workhouse they were asked if they had anywhere to sleep and when they replied in the negative they were allowed in. Men and women were separated, and men searched to see if they possessed more money than was allowed, usually 4*d*, or if they were concealing pipes, tobacco or matches on their person. After passing this check they had a compulsory bath and were then given a supper of a pint of gruel and bread. They were provided with a bed for the night. The next morning they received breakfast (the same fare as supper) and were then set to work, the women cleaning and washing, the men cleaning and oakum picking. They were required to work all day with only a break for a dinner of bread and cheese. In the evening they received another supper and were allocated a bed again. On the following morning, after a total of about 36 hours inside the workhouse, they were turned out on to the streets.
3. The severing of the nose may have been the murderer's way of marking her as possibly

syphilitic and a prostitute. Tertiary syphilis eats away the nose bone, leaving a hole in the face. Artificial noses could be bought in Whitechapel where prostitution was rife.

4. The difference between animal and human blood could not be distinguished until 1901. Blood grouping was unknown until 1905.

5. The inquest, presided over by the City Coroner Samuel Frederick Langham, was held at the City Mortuary in Golden Lane on 4 and 11 October.

6. Much has been made of the fact that Levy acted as a referee for Martin Kosminski (aged 43 and a furrier in 1888) in his application for British naturalisation in 1877; the implication being that Levy must have known the later-named suspect 'Kosminski'. However, no family or other connection has ever been found between Martin Kosminski and Aaron Kosminski, who was incarcerated in an asylum in 1891.

7. The exact location of the message is uncertain. Warren indicated that it was on the entrance jamb, while other reports say it was on the black fascia inside the entrance. Arnold's report indicated that it was written at shoulder height.

8. PC Long, who had only 4 years' service in 1888, was dismissed from the force for being drunk on duty in July 1889. No doubt his brief on the night of the murder was to check all doorways as he patrolled but it is very likely that he failed to do so properly. Neglect of duty was a serious offence and he certainly would have said that he checked the doorway even if he hadn't. Halse, when he rushed through Goulston Street looking for suspects, would have been taking little notice of debris on the ground or tiny chalkings on walls.

9. In the Littlechild letter to George R. Sims of 23 September 1913, now in the collection of Stewart Evans.

10. National Archives, Commissioner's Letters File, MEPO 1/48.

11. Kate Webster was a notorious Victorian murderess. In 1879 she murdered her employer, Mrs Thomas, at Richmond and then impersonated her. She dismembered the body and partly boiled it before disposal. She was hanged on 29 July 1879.

9. Sleuth-hounds and Conspiracies

1. HO 144/221/A49301C, ff. 163–70.
2. HO 144/221/A49301C f. 171.

10. The Letter Writers

1. *Daily Telegraph*, 2 October 1888.
2. *Daily Telegraph*, 3 October 1888.
3. *Daily Telegraph*, 4 September 1888.
4. Mansfield was born in Germany on 24 May 1854 of an English father and Russian mother. He moved to America with his mother (his father had died while Richard was still young) in the 1870s.
5. They were Le Grand and Batchelor of the Strand – see chapter 7.
6. Eliza Armstrong was the name of the young girl rescued from prostitution by W.T. Stead in 1885. This resulted in the 'Modern Babylon' scandal and the prosecution of Stead, who subsequently served a prison sentence.
7. See the *Star*, 19 October 1888.
8. This was stated in a letter from Lusk's grandson, Leonard Archer, dated 16 April 1966, to the editor of the *London Hospital Gazette*.

11. Whitechapel is Panic Stricken

1. The lodging house opposite the entrance to Miller's Court was known as Commercial Street Chambers and was kept by the same Crossingham who owned the one at 35 Dorset Street, where Chapman had lodged. See the *Sunday Times*, 10 November 1888. The man seen by Sarah Lewis may well have been another witness, George Hutchinson.
2. This was the Britannia public house run by Mrs Ringer and situated at the north corner of Dorset Street at its junction with Commercial Street.
3. It was not until the Kelly murder that the police thought it advisable to take photographs of the scene and the body before it was moved, thus preserving a permanent record of the crime scene as it was discovered.
4. Because of Coroner Macdonald's abrupt closure of the inquest, Dr Bagster Phillips had not been recalled to give evidence of all the wounds on Kelly's body.
5. Australian researcher S. Gouriet Ryan has noted that this report appears to be in the hand of Bond's assistant, Charles Hebbert. This indicates that Bond probably dictated at the scene while Hebbert made the notes.
6. Which is typically caused by bruising.
7. Old 'tin' kettles had the spout fixed on with solder, which had presumably melted resulting in the spout dropping off.
8. Hebbert was also curator of the Westminster Hospital Museum.
9. Richard von Krafft-Ebing, author of *Psychopathia Sexualis*, a medico-forensic study of sexual perversion first published in 1887.
10. An uncontrollable or excessive sexual desire in a man.
11. The guide for coroners, *Crowner's 'quest Law*, required that the nature of *all* wounds and the description of the weapon used, as well as the circumstances in which the injuries were inflicted, all be recorded. Macdonald's action, apparently with the agreement of the police, was definitely incorrect and resulted in the lack of detail in the information on the Kelly murder that reached the public domain.
12. While the police were engaged in their formalities, securing the crime scene and investigating the use of the bloodhounds (which were not available), the local residents were allowed to be interviewed, and confused, by the press. Thus many of the statements appeared in the newspapers before witnesses were seen by detectives.

12. Uneasy Aftermath

1. Dew, *I Caught Crippen*, 1938, p. 87.
2. Early in 1889 Abberline, a first-class inspector, moved on from heading the Whitechapel investigation and was replaced by his junior colleague, Inspector Henry Moore, who was not advanced to inspector first-class until December 1890. Both men retired in the rank of chief inspector, Abberline in 1892 and Moore in 1899.
3. It is interesting to note that during the Parnell Commission in March 1889 a query was raised as to whether Inspector Andrews, who had recently been in America, had seen the informant Le Caron before the Special Commission. He had not, but it does underline the possibility that Andrews' North American trip was a three-fold 'money saver' for the Metropolitan Police (the Canadians paid his travelling expenses of £120), combining the return of the prisoner Barnett, an attempt to seek out Tumblety and inquiries relating to the Parnell/Fenian connections. See *The Times*, 22 March 1889.
4. HO 144/221/A49301C ff. 4–6.

13. The Ripper Again?

1. The presence of these doctors is another indicator that this was initially perceived as a possible Ripper murder.
2. Police Orders show that George Frederick Farr of Slade House, 175 Kennington Road, had replaced Bond in this position as of 14 November 1888.
3. See also chapters 14 and 15.
4. All dismembered body cases.
5. *New York Herald* (London edition), 11 September 1889.
6. Tom Merry was the pen-name of British artist, cartoonist, caricaturist and performer William Mecham (1853–1902) whose main work was the large centre-spread political cartoons in *St Stephen's Review*. He also gave 'Lightning Cartoon' presentations on the music hall stage and was filmed during four separate performances. He died suddenly at Benfleet Station, Essex, on 21 August 1902 aged 49 years.

14. The End of the Whitechapel Murders

1. Lushington was permanent under-secretary at the Home Office.
2. MEPO 3/140, ff. 97–108.
3. *Daily Telegraph*, 18 February 1891.
4. *Morning Advertiser*, Monday 16 February 1891.
5. Richardson, *From the City to Fleet Street*, 1927, pp. 277–9.

15. Was there a Police Solution?

1. HO 144/221/A49301C, f. 117.
2. HO 144/221/A49301C, f. 167.
3. *Pall Mall Gazette*, 4 November 1889, article by American journalist R. Harding Davis.
4. *Cassell's Saturday Journal*, 28 May 1892.
5. *Cassell's Saturday Journal*, 11 June 1892.
6. Catherine Eddowes gave her name to the police as Mary Ann Kelly so we must assume that Arnold does not mean Mary Jane Kelly, the Dorset Street victim.
7. *Eastern Post and City Chronicle*, 3 February 1893.
8. This is interesting as, of the three suspects then named by Macnaghten, the first comment applies to M.J. Druitt and the second to Kosminski, two suspects given as better alternatives to the asylum detainee, suggested by the press. Macnaghten actually preferred the Druitt theory, while Anderson, apparently, preferred the Kosminski theory. But as Macnaghten observes, 'no shadow of proof could be thrown on any one'.
9. Thomas Hayne Cutbush was a 29-year-old asylum detainee who was claimed to be Jack the Ripper in a series of articles in the *Sun* newspaper in February 1894.
10. Although Montague John Druitt's father was a surgeon, he himself was a barrister and teacher, aged 31, who committed suicide by drowning in the Thames. The nature of Macnaghten's 'private inf.' is not known and it is solely on Macnaghten's word that his status as a suspect rests.
11. MEPO 3/140 ff. 177–83.
12. *Windsor Magazine*, vol. VI, Jan.–Jun. 1895, Griffiths writing under the pen-name 'Alfred Aylmer'.

13.   *Pall Mall Gazette*, 7 May 1895. It seems that most other reports referred to Grainger as William Grant.

14.   Griffiths, *Mysteries of Police and Crime*, 1898, pp. 28–9.

15.   *The Nineteenth Century*, February 1901.

16.   *Pall Mall Gazette*, 24 March 1903.

17.   The asylum inmate Aaron Kosminski was found by author Martin Fido during pioneering asylum records research for his 1987 book *The Crimes, Detection & Death of Jack the Ripper*.

18.   *Thomson's Weekly News*, 1 December 1906.

19.   *Daily Chronicle*, 1 September 1908, front page.

20.   *Blackwood's Edinburgh Magazine*, March 1910.

21.   *Globe*, 7 March 1910.

22.   *Morning Advertiser*, 23 April 1910.

23.   Indeed, the first suggestion of Anderson's theory was in Griffiths' piece in the *Windsor Magazine* in 1895.

24.   *People*, 9 June 1912.

25.   Adam, *The Police Encyclopaedia*, 1912, vol. i, pp. xi–xii.

26.   *Daily Mail*, 2 June 1913.

27.   The Littlechild letter of 23 September 1913 to George R. Sims (private collection).

28.   Writer Douglas G. Browne's works included short stories, novels and non-fiction. The original author of *The Rise of Scotland Yard*, Ralph Straus, was a friend of Browne's but he died in the early stages of writing the book. Straus had reached the year 1850 and the work was continued by Browne. Both he and Straus received the generous help of the Metropolitan Police authorities in researching the book and were granted access to certain closed police records.

16. Did Anderson Know?

1.   Sugden, *The Complete History of Jack the Ripper*, 2002, pp. 421–3.

2.   Begg, Fido and Skinner, *The Jack the Ripper A–Z*, 1996, p. 23.

3.   Adam, *C.I.D.: Behind the Scenes at Scotland Yard*, 1931, pp. 9–10.

4.   Adam, *C.I.D.: Behind the Scenes at Scotland Yard*, 1931, pp. 12–13.

5.   Anderson, *The Lighter Side of My Official Life*, 1910, p. 144.

6.   Adam, *Woman and Crime*, 1914.

7.   Adam, *C.I.D.: Behind the Scenes at Scotland Yard*, 1931, p. 14.

8.   *Blackwood's Edinburgh Magazine*, March 1910, p. 358.

9.   Anderson, *The Lighter Side of My Official Life*, 1910, p. 138.

10.   Swanson's use of the words 'where he had been sent by us' appears to indicate that he was not at the identification (assuming that it occurred as described), otherwise he would surely have written 'where we had taken him'.

11.   Aaron Kosminski died in Leavesden Asylum on 24 March 1919 of gangrene of the left leg.

12.   It was still generally referred to as 'the Seaside Home' when the present authors joined the police service in the 1960s.

13.   See reports in the *People*, Sunday 1 March 1891.

14.   However, recent research by author Alan Sharp has revealed that Anderson's father Matthew, former Crown Solicitor for Dublin, died aged 85 years at his residence, Knapton House, Kingstown, Ireland, on 11 October 1888. Anderson travelled to Ireland on 13 October and

attended the funeral. He then returned to London on the 17th. The house-to-house search was conducted between the 9th and the 18th.

15. MEPO 3/140 ff. 177–83.
16. *Guardian,* 7 October 1972.
17. Over the years many writers have erroneously referred to Mitre Square as Mitre Court. There were Mitre Courts off Fleet Street (City), Hatton Garden (Holborn) and Milk Street (Cheapside), so the mistake is, perhaps, understandable.
18. Anderson, *The Lighter Side of My Official Life,* p. 146.

17. Popular Ripper Myths

1. For example, Begg, Fido and Skinner, *The Jack the Ripper A–Z,* 1996, p. 300.
2. It has been argued that Mrs Long could not have identified Chapman from a brief look and that Chapman's appearance would have altered in death. However, the sighting was in near daylight and as we can see from the photograph of Chapman at about the time of her marriage she has distinctive features and is easily recognisable as the woman portrayed in the mortuary shot.
3. HO 144/221/A49301C ff. 162–70.

Authors' Epilogues

1. The Maybrick case was a great *cause célèbre* of 1889. It immediately followed the recognised 1888 Ripper murders and actually overlapped with the killing of Alice McKenzie in July 1889 when both crimes appeared in the press. Thus, over the years, these two cases have often been mentioned side by side in crime books which may have contributed to the idea that James Maybrick was 'Jack the Ripper'.
2. This was first brought into prominence in late 1988 in a US television programme, *The Secret Identity of Jack the Ripper* (Cosgrove-Muerer Productions, Los Angeles) which, oddly enough, was not broadcast in Britain although it was later available as a commercial video recording. It was hosted by Peter Ustinov and featured a panel of experts that included FBI profilers Roy Hazelwood and John Douglas.
3. Larkins was well known to the police for his 'Portuguese cattle-men' Ripper theory and especially annoyed Anderson who referred to him as 'a troublesome busybody'. His complex and unlikely theory was self-published as an impressively bound red-cloth, gilt-titled quarto book, a copy of which is preserved in the Royal London Hospital Museum archives.
4. More probably Bellsmith.
5. The original 'From hell' letter is now missing but there is a Victorian photograph of it preserved in the collection of Ripper-related material held at the Royal London Hospital Museum archives.

Bibliography

Adam, Hargrave Lee, *The Police Encyclopaedia*, 8 volumes, London, Blackfriars Publishing Company, n.d. [1912]

——, *Woman and Crime*, London, T. Werner Laurie, n.d. [1914]

——, *The Trial of George Chapman*, Edinburgh & London, William Hodge, 1930 (Notable British Trials series).

——, *C.I.D.: Behind the Scenes at Scotland Yard*, London, Sampson Low, Marston & Co., n.d. [1931]

Anderson, Sir Robert, KCB, *The Lighter Side of My Official Life*, London, Hodder & Stoughton, 1910

Andrews, Richard, *Blood on the Mountain*, London, Weidenfeld & Nicolson, 1999

Begg, Paul, *Jack the Ripper: The Facts*, London, Robson Books, 2004

——, Martin Fido and Keith Skinner, *The Jack the Ripper A–Z*, London, Headline, 1996 (revised paperback). Soon to be published in a new revised edition by Sutton.

Browne, Douglas G., *The Rise of Scotland Yard: A History of the Metropolitan Police*, London, Harrap, 1956

Campbell, Christy, *Fenian Fire*, London, HarperCollins, 2002

Clarkson, C.T., and J.H. Richardson, *Police!*, London, Simpkin, Marshall, 1889

Cobb, Belton, *Critical Years at the Yard: The Career of Frederick Williamson of the Detective Department and the C.I.D.*, London, Faber & Faber, 1956.

Cullen, Tom, *Autumn of Terror: Jack the Ripper, his Crimes & Times*, London, Bodley Head, 1965

Curtis, L. Perry, *Jack the Ripper and the London Press*, New Haven and London, Yale University Press, 2001

Dew, ex-Chief Inspector Walter, *I Caught Crippen*, London, Blackie & Sons, 1938

Dickens, Charles, *Dickens's Dictionary of London 1888*, Moretonhampstead, Old House Books (reprint), n.d.

Evans, Stewart P. and Keith Skinner, *The Ultimate Jack the Ripper Sourcebook*, London, Constable & Robinson, 2000

——, *Jack the Ripper: Letters from Hell*, Stroud, Sutton, 2001

Fido, Martin, *The Crimes, Detection & Death of Jack the Ripper*, London, Weidenfeld & Nicolson, 1987

——, *The Official Encyclopedia of Scotland Yard*, London, Virgin, 2000

Fishman, William J., *East End Jewish Radicals 1875–1914*, London, Gerald Duckworth, 1975

——, *East End 1888*, London, Gerald Duckworth, 1988

Gaute, J.H.H., and Robin Odell, *The New Murderers' Who's Who*, London, Harrap, 1989

Geberth, Vernon J., *Practical Homicide Investigation: Tactics, Procedures and Forensic Techniques*, Boca Raton, CRC Press LLC, 1996

Griffiths, Major Arthur, *Mysteries of Police and Crime*, 2 volumes, London, Cassell, 1898

Knight, Stephen, *Jack the Ripper: The Final Solution*, London, Harrap, 1976

Koven, Seth, *Slumming*, Princeton CA, Princeton University Press, 2004

Lansdowne, Andrew, *A Life's Reminiscences of Scotland Yard*, London, Leadenhall Press, n.d. [1890]

Leslie, Shane, compiler, *Sir Evelyn Ruggles-Brise: A Memoir of the Founder of Borstal*, London, John Murray, 1938

London, Jack, *The People of the Abyss*, London, Sir Isaac Pitman, 1903

McCormick, Donald, *The Identity of Jack the Ripper*, London, Jarrolds, 1959 and revised edition, 1970

Macnaghten, Sir Melville, *Days of My Years*, London, Edward Arnold, 1914

Moore-Anderson, A.P., *Sir Robert Anderson K.C.B., L.L.D. and Lady Agnes Anderson*, London, Marshall, Morgan & Scott, 1947

Odell, Robin, *Jack the Ripper in Fact and Fiction*, London, Harrap, 1965

Pellew, Jill, *The Home Office, 1848–1914: from Clerks to Bureaucrats*, London, Heinemann Educational Books, 1982

Porter, Bernard, *The Origins of the Vigilant State: The London Metropolitan Police Special Branch before the First World War*, London, Weidenfeld & Nicolson, 1987

Prothero, Margaret, *The History of the Criminal Investigation Department at Scotland Yard*, London, Herbert Jenkins, 1931

Richardson, J. Hall, *From the City to Fleet Street*, London, Stanley Paul, 1927

Rumbelow, Donald, *The Complete Jack the Ripper*, London, Penguin (revised paperback), 2004

Short, K.R.M., *The Dynamite War: Irish-American Bombers in Victorian Britain*, Dublin, Gill & Macmillan, 1979

Sims, George R., *Living London*, 3 volumes, London, Cassell & Co., 1901

Smith, Lieutenant-Colonel Sir Henry, *From Constable to Commissioner*, London, Chatto & Windus, 1910

Sugden, Philip, *The Complete History of Jack the Ripper*, London, Robinson (revised paperback), 2002

Sweeney, John, (ed. by Francis Richards), *At Scotland Yard: Being the experiences during twenty-seven years service of John Sweeney Late Detective Inspector, Criminal Investigation Department, New Scotland Yard*, London, Grant Richards, 1904

Warren, Captain [Charles], Captain the Corps of Royal Engineers, *Underground Jerusalem*, London, R. Bentley & Son, 1876

White, Jerry, *Rothschild Buildings: Life in an East End Tenement Block 1887–1920*, London, Routledge & Kegan Paul, 1980

Williams, Watkin W., *The Life of General Sir Charles Warren*, Oxford, Basil Blackwell, 1941

Newspapers, Journals and Internet Site

Blackwood's Edinburgh Magazine

Casebook: Jack the Ripper (internet site): www.casebook.org

Cassell's Saturday Journal

Daily Chronicle

Daily News

Daily Telegraph

East Anglian Daily Times

East London Advertiser

East London Observer

Eastern Post and City Chronicle

Evening News

Evening Post

Funny Faces

Illustrated Police News

Lloyd's Weekly News

Nineteenth Century, The

Pall Mall Gazette

Penny Illustrated Paper

People, The

Pictorial News

Punch

Ripper Notes

Ripperana

Ripperologist

Star

Star of the East

Sunday Chronicle

Times, The

Index

Page numbers in italic refer to illustrations.